ADVANCES IN

EXPERIMENTAL
SOCIAL PSYCHOLOGY

VOLUME 3

CONTRIBUTORS TO VOLUME 3

ROBERT P. ABELSON

MICHAEL ARGYLE

N. T. FEATHER

IRVING L. JANIS

ADAM KENDON

SERGE MOSCOVICI

PERCY H. TANNENBAUM

ADVANCES IN

Experimental
Social Psychology

EDITED BY

Leonard Berkowitz
DEPARTMENT OF PSYCHOLOGY
UNIVERSITY OF WISCONSIN
MADISON, WISCONSIN

VOLUME 3

 ACADEMIC PRESS   New York and London   1967

ACADEMIC PRESS, INC.
111 Fifth Avenue, New York, New York 10003

United Kingdom Edition published by
ACADEMIC PRESS, INC. (LONDON) LTD.
Berkeley Square House, London W.1

LIBRARY OF CONGRESS CATALOG CARD NUMBER: 64–23452

Second Printing, 1969

PRINTED IN THE UNITED STATES OF AMERICA

CONTRIBUTORS

Numbers in parentheses indicate the pages on which the authors' contributions begin.

ROBERT P. ABELSON, *Department of Psychology, Yale University, New Haven, Connecticut* (1)

MICHAEL ARGYLE, *Institute of Experimental Psychology, Oxford University, Oxford, England* (55)

N. T. FEATHER, *Department of Psychology, University of New England, New South Wales, Australia* (99)

IRVING L. JANIS, *Department of Psychology, Yale University, New Haven, Connecticut* (166)

ADAM KENDON,[1] *Institute of Experimental Psychology, Oxford University, Oxford, England* (55)

SERGE MOSCOVICI, *École Pratique des Hautes Études, Université de Paris, Paris, France* (225)

PERCY H. TANNENBAUM, *Mass Communications Research Center, University of Wisconsin, Madison, Wisconsin* (271)

[1] *Present address*: Department of Psychology, Morrill Hall, Cornell University, Ithaca, New York.

v

PREFACE

This volume will report much that is new, and perhaps even surprising, to many of its readers. For one thing, although social psychology is often regarded as an exclusively American science, especially by Americans, four of the six chapters were written by citizens of other nations: Argyle and Kendon, Feather, Moscovici, and Tannenbaum (although both Feather and Tannenbaum received their doctorates in this country and Tannenbaum, fortunately for us, has remained in the United States). American social psychologists typically confine their professional reading to American journals to the neglect of the important non-American publications in their field. This book, hopefully, will contribute to a greater, and multi-directional, exchange of social-psychological information across national boundaries.

Then too, if we are to judge from the problems receiving the greatest attention we might think social psychology dealt primarily with cognitively mediated defensive or autistic processes. The chapters by Argyle and Kendon and by Moscovici can help us to broaden our professional outlook. Analyzing focused social interactions in terms of the performance of social skills, Argyle and Kendon show how the individual's actions toward other people are regulated by a wide variety of determinants, including such factors as the physical distance between the people, the reason they have come together and the setting they are in, and the speech characteristics of the other persons. Moscovici's paper concentrates on the communicative aspects of social interaction. Demonstrating a truly impressive cross-national scholarship (as do Argyle and Kendon), Moscovici calls on social psychologists to give greater attention to the interplay between social relationships and language behavior. His chapter introduces a relatively new (for many of our readers) and rapidly developing field of study and, more than this, reports a number of important investigations conducted both in Moscovici's own laboratory and elsewhere.

To say there is more to social psychology than self-defense and cognitive consistency, however, is not to deny the role of cognitive and defensive processes in human behavior. Three papers in this volume are concerned with such processes, and testify to the continuing interest in them. Like the Argyle and Kendon and Moscovici chapters, they deal with communications, but this time are addressed to the person's reactions to information received from other people. Feather presents a general model derived from balance-theory considerations for analyzing these communication effects.

In addition to summarizing his own research, he provides us with a very comprehensive survey of the relevant literature in this area. Tannenbaum's chapter is focused on the problem of inculcating resistance to persuasive communications. Developing his ideas from the congruity version of the cognitive consistency formulations, he reports the results of an extensive research program and also points out the connection between his findings and those obtained by McGuire (as given in his chapter in Volume 1 of this serial publication). Janis also discusses resistance to persuasion attempts: the resistance sometimes created by fear arousal. As many of our readers know, Janis and Feshbach had found, in one of the best-known studies conducted by the Yale Attitude Change Project, that fear-arousing communications can produce a "defensive-avoidance" of the communicator's arguments. Later investigations, however, have not always yielded the same results, and Janis advances a theoretical model designed to reconcile these apparent contradictions.

Now that I have referred several times to general theoretical schemes, let me repeat a comment I made in the Preface to Volume 1. The papers in this serial publication will typically try to provide a theoretical integration of findings in a particular research area rather than an exhaustive literature survey. These theoretical generalizations give meaning to the facts accumulated by investigators. Equally important, they can also stimulate the further research endeavors which will lead, inevitably, to their demise and replacement by better formulations. Most of the theoretical models with which we are familiar in social psychology consist entirely of verbal statements. As our science matures, however, theoretical generalizations will increasingly be couched in mathematical terms. Abelson's chapter in this volume discusses the present status of mathematical models in social psychology and can serve as a very helpful introduction to subsequent developments along these lines.

LEONARD BERKOWITZ

September, 1967

CONTENTS

Mathematical Models in Social Psychology

Robert P. Abelson

The Experimental Analysis of Social Performance

Michael Argyle and Adam Kendon

A Structural Balance Approach to the Analysis of Communication Effects

N. T. Feather

Effects of Fear Arousal on Attitude Change: Recent Developments in Theory and Experimental Research

Irving L. Janis

Communication Processes and the Properties of Language

Serge Moscovici

The Congruity Principle Revisited: Studies in the Reduction, Induction, and Generalization of Persuasion

Percy H. Tannenbaum

CONTENTS OF OTHER VOLUMES

xi

MATHEMATICAL MODELS IN SOCIAL PSYCHOLOGY[1]

Robert P. Abelson

DEPARTMENT OF PSYCHOLOGY
YALE UNIVERSITY
NEW HAVEN, CONNECTICUT

I. The Nature and Role of Mathematical Models

The phrase "mathematical model" strongly connotes the ultimate in precise scientific analysis. It has sometimes been argued that social psychology has not sufficiently advanced theoretically to reap the benefits of precise mathematical analysis, yet at the same time it is widely granted that theoretical progress is critically dependent on the organizing power that mathematical models can provide. This chapter is intended as a contribution to the continuing bootstrap operation by which the level of mathematization of social psychology is gradually being raised.

[1] This chapter was written while the author was a beneficiary of the atmosphere and facilities of the Center for Advanced Study in the Behavioral Sciences.

A.   INTRODUCTORY CONSIDERATIONS

Mathematical models are used in the physical sciences as a technique for forming abstractions from reality, manipulating the abstractions, and applying the results again to reality to encompass other consequences. It is necessary for the abstracting principle to be precisely specified and to be coordinated with essential features of the reality under consideration. The power of the technique depends on the flexibility with which the abstraction can be manipulated in concert with other relevant abstractions.

Newton's law of gravitation provides a simple (if overworked) example. The property of mass is the essential feature of physical bodies appropriate to gravitational force. Newton's law specified the size of the gravitational force between two bodies solely in terms of their masses and the distance between them. Together with the mathematical tools of the differential calculus and another abstract law relating force to acceleration, a complete mathematical model is formed enabling the calculation of the orbits of natural and artificial bodies. For present purposes, one thing is especially noteworthy about this example.

A great many properties of physical bodies (such as color, volume, hardness, and temperature) do not appear in the mathematical model. The property of mass is an "abstraction" in the sense not only of being mathematically symbolizable but also by virtue of all the other properties of the real objects that are ignored. It is sometimes supposed that mathematical models cannot usefully be constructed in the social sciences because human behavior is too complex to be represented mathematically. This argument seriously underestimates the very high level of abstraction necessary to the construction of mathematical models, even in the physical sciences. One never tries to represent the objects of study literally, only very limited aspects of them. Of course, the difficulty lies in the selection of essential aspects. Newton would not have got very far with a gravitational law dependent on the color rather than the mass of physical bodies.

There are two quite distinct reasons for the potential scientific superiority of mathematical over purely verbal descriptions: the greater *precision* of mathematical descriptions, and their greater *manipulability*. Precision is clearly a crucial feature of models applied to physical situations as, for example, in the calculation of orbits. In applications to social situations, however, precision is less important whenever present difficulties in measurement and in the control of extraneous variables render imprecise the empirical testing of models. But even if models are used only in the service of generating very approximate data fits, the greater manipulability of mathematical models is a very powerful advantage. Sometimes this advantage is difficult to achieve because mathematical derivations run into complications, but in that case recourse may often be had to computer-aided numerical methods or to the technique of computer simulation.

Computer simulation models represent an interesting alternative to mathematical models. They also involve rigorous mathematical specifications of processes, but in place of analytic derivation of the consequences of these specifications, the model is "set in motion" on the computer, supplying a symbolic imitation of the processes being modeled. This alternative has the advantage of broadening the range of mathematical and empirical possibilities that can be handled; on the other hand, it requires considerable effort and the outcomes do not have the neat, compact generality of analytic mathematical solutions. Computer simulation models in social psychology are reviewed in great detail by Abelson (1967).

B. THE MEASUREMENT PROBLEM

It is a difficult task to abstract essential theoretical variables for explaining given aspects of human behavior, but the problem of measuring these variables often seems even more forbidding. There are two broad classes of potential measures, based on *counting* and *scaling*, respectively, and the problems associated with the two are quite different.

The operation of counting whether and when particular qualitative responses have occurred offers no problems of philosophical principle. In practice, however, counting often leads to probability models that are tricky to analyze mathematically and test empirically. Common examples of qualitative responses in social psychological models are sociometric choices, occurrences of communicative acts, and choices of alternative responses in two-person games. Coleman (1964a), in his excellent treatment of mathematical models in sociology, recommends more extensive use and development of models based on counting, especially in view of the increasing availability of data gathered from large survey samples.

If the mathematical modeler wishes to use quantitative quasi-continuous measures appropriate for sensitive mathematical treatment, such as by differential equations, he must be prepared to deal with the issue of the nature of measurement in the social sciences. The question usually raised (cf. Stevens, 1951) concerns the justification for applying the properties of the real-number system to the numbers associated with "arbitrary" empirical procedures, such as the assignment of scores on an attitude scale.

One constructive stance on this question is pragmatic: the appropriateness of any given assignment procedure is judged in terms of the neatness and usefulness of its theoretical and empirical consequences rather than by a priori considerations. Fortunately, there is recent mathematical evidence (Abelson and Tukey, 1963; Shepard and Carroll, 1966; Guttman, 1967) that a number of seemingly arbitrary scaling procedures are much more robust in practice than might have been supposed when Stevens and others originally advanced their warnings.

What measurement procedures in the social sciences have lacked has been a notion of fundamentality as powerful as N. R. Campbell's (1928) concept of "fundamental measurement" in the physical sciences. A recent breakthrough has occurred however, foreshadowed by suggestions of Adams and Fagot (1959) and culminating in the publication of the Luce and Tukey (1964) paper on "conjoint measurement." Those who are not satisfied with the rough-and-ready pragmatic approach to measurement problems will now find available much firmer axiomatic foundations on which to build. Space does not permit an extended treatment of the matter here but, in brief, the basic ideas are as follows.

The axiomatic system for Campbellian measurement rests on the operation of "concatenation" of properties of distinct objects, as when two sticks are placed end to end and the length of the concatenate is found to equal the sum of the lengths of the individual sticks. It has been extraordinarily difficult to imagine how one might concatenate psychological properties, however. What Luce and Tukey propose is an alternative operation intrinsic to a different, but no less fundamental, axiomatic system: the operation of "conjoining" the levels of two separate independent variables. To conjoin level i of variable A with level j of variable B requires the application of these variable levels simultaneously to an experimental unit on which some effect X_{ij} is assessed. This is exactly the operation typically employed in two-way factorial design. Conjoint measurement on X (and on A and B) is achieved if it turns out that additivity of the independent variables obtains; that is, if over all levels i and j there are no interaction effects of A and B on X. The detailed relationship of this conceptual system to specific empirical cases has not been worked through, but there has been a burst of recent work on several aspects of conjoint measurement (Luce, 1966; Tversky and Zivian, 1966; Krantz, 1964; Roskies, 1965; Tversky, 1967; Goode, 1964; Kruskal, 1965). Against this background of axiomatic ferment the practical man, of course, continues to construct his models, even as in the physical sciences the mathematical applications ran far ahead of Campbell's attempt to rationalize the measurement process.

C.   HISTORICAL BACKGROUND

The early applications of mathematical models to psychology were individual pioneering efforts (in this country primarily associated with the name of L. L. Thurstone) that did not meet with ready acceptance by the discipline at large. Miller (1964) has provided a good summary of some of these early attempts, which fell mainly in the areas of psychophysics and mental test theory. In the 1950's mathematical learning theory was launched by Estes (1950) and Bush and Mosteller (1955) after Clark Hull had aroused interest in rigorous learning models. The great burst of sophisticated mathematical interest in probabilistic learning models that was then sparked has grown steadily and diffused into related psychological areas. By the mid-1960's the field of mathematical psychology was a booming specialty, with the center of gravity of its content very squarely in the tradition of laboratory experimental psychology. This emphasis is reflected in the topics included in the *Handbook of Mathematical Psychology* (Luce *et al.*, 1963) and in the recently established *Journal of Mathematical Psychology*.

As far as social psychology is concerned, there has not been a strong mathematical tradition. Applications have been widely scattered, with frequent borrowing from other disciplines. The review "Mathematical models of social interaction" by Rapoport (1963), who was originally a mathematical biologist, contains only 25 references to social psychological literature out of 93 bibliographic citations. Available material has recently increased in quantity somewhat, but at the time of writing of this chapter no single clear identity of the potential discipline of mathematical social psychology has yet emerged. Mathematics is a tool, not a school for social psychologists.

D. APPLICATIONS IN SOCIAL PSYCHOLOGY

The present lack of a dominant organizing theme in mathematical social psychology by no means indicates that mathematical models cannot be applied to social behavior. Indeed, there is a rich variety of applications, but they fall into widely separated categories. In the present section we try to establish certain useful categorical distinctions.

A very important dichotomy can be drawn between social structure and social process, or statics versus dynamics. In the analysis of social structure, concern centers on the characterization of communication and influence networks, of social cliques and social cleavage, of centrality and status. The modeler analyzing social dynamics attempts to account for changes over time in opinions, friendship, conformity, hostility, and other properties within and between social groups, or to trace the social diffusion of rumors, fads, and innovations. Considerations of structure and process sometimes intermingle, as when structures are distinguished from one another according to their differing potentials under hypothesized dynamic situations, or when what is changing dynamically over time happens to be the social structure itself. Typically, however, the two areas have been treated quite distinctly, and we will retain a sharp separation in this chapter.

Crosscutting this distinction is the question of the social scope of a model or the number of individuals encompassed by it. At one extreme there are models that deal only with single individuals, as in the analysis of the cognitive structure of attitudes. [We will not treat such models here, as this would lead us too far afield; the reader is referred to the recent review by Rosenberg (1967).] There are models treating social structures or inter-actions within small groups, and models dealing with very large social aggre-gates. Methods of approach are quite different in the two cases. When the group is small, structure can be analyzed in terms of particular literal details and process can often be handled by means of mathematical characterization of the behaviors of the particular individuals involved. With structure or process in a large aggregate, however, we can no longer particularize indi-vidual by individual, and it is necessary to move toward statistical character-izations. The separation between these two types of models is not complete, but we find the distinction pertinent. In this chapter, attention will be confined largely to small-group cases. Among the variegated interesting large-group models that we must pass over are those concerned with social diffusion, discussed by Coleman (1964a) among others; mass culture (McPhee, 1963, 1966); international hostility (Richardson, 1960; Abelson, 1963); and the logic of kinship systems (White, 1963). There is another type of model that has a large-group style but may apply to small groups: a statis-tical characterization is established for the group as a whole, and the indi-viduals in the group play no separate roles. This approach might be called *social mechanics*. It is well exemplified by models attempting to explain the observed distribution of sizes of "free-forming" groups (Coleman and James, 1961; White, 1962).

A third basis for distinction, particularly among process models, con-cerns the stage of development of the modeled social situation. Sometimes social *learning* is of interest, and sometimes social *performance* of behaviors already acquired. Models correspondingly focus upon changes or "tran-sients" versus asymptotic or equilibrium conditions.

Models also vary considerably in the types of characterizations of the variables, and thus in the style of mathematical analysis. Major distinctions include: deterministic versus stochastic; continuous-time versus discrete-time; continuous-variable versus qualitative state. We will not attempt anything so ambitious as a full listing of all the typological combi-nations; in fact, we will stay pretty close to the mathematical treatments already available at the possible expense of neglected improvements. For example, the mathematics of Markov chains is commonly, but not always appropriately, used in the approach to stochastic discrete-time qualitative-state situations that occur in certain models of conformity, leadership, friendship, and others. We will review these models at length. In general, our mathematical discussions will be reasonably elementary, and will be woven into the text rather than artificially segregated into separate sections. Full comprehension of the text requires a little background in undergraduate mathematics, but reading "between the equations" should prove adequate for those lacking this background.

Certain topics sometimes included within the broad rubric of mathematical social psychology will be omitted here in the interests of compactness of presentation. In particular, we will not give a systematic treatment of game theory, decision theory, and other topics concerned with individual strategies in choice situations. [Many of these have been reviewed under the heading of utility theory by Luce and Suppes (1965) and "psychoeconomics" by Rapoport (1963).] Another notable omission is the general area of statistical methods applied to social psychological data. It would have been worthwhile to have grappled with certain special topics on the boundary between statistical analysis and mathematical models. Models can sometimes be extremely neat and pleasing in the abstract, but untestable in practice, because appropriate statistical techniques are lacking. This is especially true, for example, in the case of simultaneous differential equation models such as those devised by Simon (1957, Chapters 6 and 7). Despite some possibly promising suggestions recently advanced by Coleman (1967), however, such attempts have not progressed enough to warrant coverage.

This chapter is one of four presently available reviews of mathematical models in social psychology. The others are by Coleman (1959), Rapoport (1963), and Rosenberg (1967). Models are so diverse and scattered that, as it turns out, there is not much redundancy among the four available treatments, and the serious student of the field may profit from exposure to the varied points of view of the four authors. The present review is perhaps more selective than the others, concentrating heavily on topics that struck the author's fancy at the time of writing. We stop short of a completely subjective statement, however, in order to provide the reader with some orientation toward the total field.

II. Mathematical Models of Social Structure

A. DESCRIPTION OF PROPERTIES OF SOCIOGRAMS

Social structures involving small numbers of individuals are ordinarily represented by sociograms. A sociogram is a function (usually two-valued) on all ordered pairs of individuals in the group under consideration. The function is coordinated with some kind of social relationship between individuals, such as friendship choice or influence potential, and the representation of the function can be in either of two modes: a matrix or a "directed graph" (Harary et al., 1965). In the matrix form the element a_{ij} is given the value 1 if individual i stands in the required relationship (for example, is friendly) with individual j, and the value 0 otherwise. In the directed-graph form, a "line" is established from the point representing individual i to the point representing individual *j* if they stand in the required relationship, and no line otherwise. Mathematical analysis of social structure then consists of an attempt at incisive characterization via study of the properties of these forms. Such analysis always begins and usually ends with purely descriptive statements, thus representing a taxonomic style of approach to social configurations. In this section we review an assortment of descriptive indices of key aspects of small social structures.

1. Clique Identification

For groups numbering approximately 25 to 100 individuals, it is easy to collect but difficult to cognize the data for a sociogram. There are too many entries a_{ij} in the choice or "adjacency" matrix A for compact summary comprehension without some kind of manipulation that sharpens the most important features. One set of features is the number, size, and individual memberships of *cliques*, social configurations within but not between which there is a high degree of social cohesion.

Various attempts to further specify the sense of such definitions of cliques have led to different matrix manipulations. One very basic notion concerns *indirect paths* in the social network. If *i* chooses *j* and *j* chooses *k*, there is a "sequence of length 2" from *i* to *k*. Further, there are sequences of length 3 from *i* to all the individuals in turn chosen by *k*, and so on. Between any pair of individuals within a clique, there presumably exists either direct choice (a sequence of length 1) or several indirect sequences of short length (for instance, no more than 3).

In practice it is laborious to trace sequences from a diagram of the network. Matrix procedures are more efficient. The simple expedient of multiplying the matrix **A** by itself supplies information on sequences of length 2. The ordinary definition of matrix multiplication in fact guarantees that the element in row *i* and column *j* of $\mathbf{A}^2$ gives the total number of sequences of length 2 between *i* and *j*. (For this result to be absolutely precise, it is necessary that a convention be established concerning the diagonal entries a_{ii}. Typically it is assumed that individual *i* does not stand in sociometric relation with himself, that is, that all $a_{ii} = 0$. Thus sequences that include null steps, such as *i* to *i* to *j*, are not counted.) By extension, the element in row *i* and column *j* of $\mathbf{A}^3$ gives the total number of sequences of length 3 between *i* and *j*. Luce and Perry (1949) and Festinger (1949) originally suggested that entries in matrix powers of **A** would provide a sensitive indication of clique structure. Entries in, for instance, $\mathbf{A}^3$ could tend to run very high for individuals with many shared contacts, and clique identification would thus be a matter of gathering clusters of individuals with mutually high entries in $\mathbf{A}^3$.

Although this plausible procedure has been used with profit in actual cases (cf. Festinger *et al.*, 1950), it is marred because the counting procedure includes redundant sequences (i to j to k to j), and because there is no compelling reason why a given sequence length (such as 3) should be more revealing than any other. Recently, two new approaches that overcome the redundancy problem have appeared (Spilerman, 1966; Cartwright and Gleason, 1966). Meanwhile, discontent with the definition of cliques in terms of an "arbitrary" sequence length has spurred other types of analyses.

Hubbell (1965), drawing upon an idea presented by Katz (1953), discusses the diminution of social influence as it travels through successively more remote social links. To set the stage, note that if person p chooses person q as a friend, then q is likely to be able to influence p. Consider, therefore, the transpose of the choice matrix as a candidate for an "influence matrix." Hubbell suggests weighted values w_{ij} between 0 and 1 in his influence matrix **W**, rather than simple all-or-none values. The entry w_{ij} may be interpreted as the relative strength of influence of i upon j. Indirect influence may be exercised through "chains of command," with j influenced by i and thence k by j. Again, matrix powers capture this representation: W^2 for two-step chains; W^3 for three-step chains; and so on. With strong constraints on the absolute sizes of the original elements, entries in successive powers tend to become smaller and smaller (reflecting attenuation of influence) and it is mathematically feasible to consider the infinite sum of all possible powers of **W**. Denote this matrix sum as

$$Y = I + W + W^2 + W^3 + \cdots. \tag{1}$$

Each element y_{ij} represents the total influence of i upon j, considering all degress of indirection. The identity matrix **I** is included in the sum for strictly mathematical reasons, and contributes nothing to the sum for $i \neq j$. Equation (1) may be rewritten with the aid of a standard algebraic identity, enabling easy computation of **Y** by computer, given **W**.

$$Y = (I - W)^{-1} \tag{2}$$

As with the Luce-Perry procedure, cliques are identified by gathering clusters of individuals with mutually high entries, this time in the matrix **Y**. For further details the reader is referred to Hubbell (1965).

A related model is that of Abelson (1964). He considers not raw social influence itself, but quantities upon which influence may act, namely the attitude positions $\{X_i\}$ of the members of the group on some issue of mutual concern. The assumption is made that every time j communicates with i concerning the attitude issue, the position X_i of the listener moves toward the position X_j of the communicator by an amount proportional to the difference $(X_j - X_i)$. If each constant of proportionality is multiplied by the rate at which j communicates to i, new constants of proportionality a_{ij} representing *influence rates* (for j upon i) are obtained.

Abelson considers the dynamic situation in which all the individuals are attempting attitude influence on a single issue according to the matrix of influence rates. (Where sociometric connections are lacking, the influence rates are, of course, zero.) The major focus of the model concerns the fate over time of the distribution of attitude positions $\{X_i\}$ within a group of n individuals. In Section III, A, 2 these time dynamics are considered further, but for present purposes we merely sketch the method of clique identification.

The method depends on the matrix $\mathbf{A}^*$ of the a_{ij}, modified by the insertion of negative row sums in the diagonal cells a_{ii}. Unlike the two clique-assembling procedures reviewed earlier, however, Abelson's method does not seek somehow to pull clusters out of the body of the matrix, but depends instead on a procedure for *factoring* the matrix.

The $n \times n$ matrix $\mathbf{A}^*$ is factored according to

$$\mathbf{A}^* = \xi \, \Delta \, \xi^{-1}, \tag{3}$$

where the columns of the $n \times n$ matrix ξ are the right-hand characteristic vectors of $\mathbf{A}^*$, the rows of the $n \times n$ matrix ξ^{-1} are the left-hand vectors (equivalent to the right-hand vectors only if $\mathbf{A}^*$ is symmetrical), and Δ is the diagonal matrix of characteristic roots.

Each of the rows of ξ^{-1} will have some positive and some negative entries and will specify a (bipolar) factor diagnostic of potential attitude *cleavage* that tends to vanish as mutual influence in the group proceeds. It is a consequence of the hypothetical assumptions of the dynamic model that attitude positions of individuals with positive vector entries will tend to remain distant from those with negative vector entries for a length of time inversely related to the absolute size of the corresponding characteristic root. For a group with n individuals, the analysis yields $(n - 1)$ such cleavage factors. (The nth factor has all entries equal and does not represent a cleavage.) The "cleavage structure" of a group is in some sense the obverse of the clique structure and can provide an approximately equivalent description. To say, for example, that cleavages exist by sex, by age among boys, and by race among girls, is like saying that there are four cliques: older boys, younger boys, white girls, and non-white girls.

Abelson (1964) applied the method to a matrix of empirically determined contact frequencies among a group of office workers with more or less plausible results. In principle something more subtle than sheer contact rate could be used to measure influence rates to enter in $\mathbf{A}^*$. In practice, however, the Abelson method like the Hubbell method suffers from the lack of an accompanying procedure for assessing the "strength of influence" of one individual upon another.

An alternative factor method for clique identification is based on a rationale given by McRae (1960), who proposed that individuals with similar profiles of choice of or by other group members should be considered as belonging together in cliques. This definition is not conceptually identical with a mutual choice or influence criterion for clique membership, since several individuals might possibly produce similar sociometric choice patterns without necessarily mutually choosing each other or even sharing the same reasons for their choices of others. Nevertheless the definition is not unreasonable and leads immediately to a convenient technique.

The pattern similarity notion requires self-similarity; thus it is appropriate to place unities in the diagonals a_{ii} of the sociometric choice matrix. Denoting the resulting modified matrix by $A\dagger$, McRae specified that $A\dagger$ be factored according to:

$$A\dagger = U \Lambda V',\qquad(4)$$

where the (orthogonal) columns of U give loadings of individuals on "chooser factors," the (orthogonal) rows of V' give loadings of individuals on "chosen factors," and Λ is a diagonal matrix of roots specifying the sums of squares accounted for by successive pairs of factors. Although this procedure is quite similar to Abelson's factorization, it has the following differences: the initial matrix $A\dagger$ differs from Abelson's initial A^*, especially in the treatment of the diagonals; the factorization in Eq. (4) need not be complete, and in fact would ordinarily be terminated with far fewer than n factors; the matrices U and V need not contain characteristic vectors, as McRae recommends rotation to simple structure; in any case, both matrices are interpretable, rather than just the single matrix ξ^{-1} in Eq. (3). Finally, interpretations are made in terms of perceived subgroupings of individuals relevant to friendship choice, rather than in terms of attitude cleavages.

McRae (1960) applied his direct factor method to a 67-man sociogram, extracting 11 factors each for choices received and given. Hubbell (1965) reanalyzed the same initial data and claimed clearer discrimination of cliques with his method than with McRae's. None of the four existing methods, however, can be well judged on the basis of illustrative demonstration. For an ideal comparison, it would be necessary for clique structure to be conceptualized in relation to other social variables and for the techniques to be pitted against one another for a broad range of cases to see how well each is able to bring out such postulated relationships.

2. Reachability and Connectivity

Many of the crucial mathematical properties of directed graphs (Harary *et al.*, 1965) revolve around questions of "reachability." Point *j* is said to be reachable from point *i* if there is at least one path from the latter to the former. The element r_{ij} of the *reachability matrix* takes on the value 1 if *j* is reachable from *i* and 0 otherwise. If the reachability matrix consists entirely of unities, the graph is called *strongly connected*.

Connectedness properties have several potential empirical consequences. For example, in a strongly connected communication network every individual is able eventually to receive information transmitted through the network regardless of where it originates. A less obvious example is the following. If and only if at least one row of the reachability matrix consists entirely of unities, the condition for what Abelson (1964) calls a *compact* network, then under certain strong assumptions about the nature of mutual opinion influence there must result ultimate homogeneity of opinion in the group. [This mathematical result has been derived from different points of view by Abelson (1964) and Harary (1959a).]

Coleman (1964a) takes as a measure of the "connectivity" of a group the proportion of all entries in the reachability matrix (except for the trivial diagonal entries) that equal unity. He regards connectivity as the reverse of cliquishness because focusing of choices within tightly knit subgroups can create disconnectedness ("unreachability") between subgroups.

For large groups it is convenient to have some systematic procedure for generating **R**, the reachability matrix. Coleman uses a computer program for his analysis, and Harary *et al.* (1965) give a very simple matrix formula (for which a computer program could easily be written):

$$\mathbf{R} = (\mathbf{I} + \mathbf{A})^{n-1} \sharp, \tag{5}$$

where **A** is the sociometric adjacency matrix, **I** the identity matrix, *n* the number of individuals, and the notation $\sharp$ indicates that all entries ≥ 1 in the final matrix are to be replaced by 1.

It should be noted that, although intuitively of importance, indices based on reachability (such as Coleman's connectivity index) are apt to be statistically unstable in empirical applications. The addition or subtraction of a single line to a network can make a huge difference in the reachability properties. This matter bears investigation.

3. Other Indices

Among the many other structural properties that have been the target of index construction attempts, the one that has received the most attention is the concept of relative "status" of individual members in a network. Two closely related attempts in this area, those of Katz (1953) and Hubbell (1965), are mathematical cousins of Kendall's (1955) scheme for determining a rational ranking of tournament players incompletely connected in a dominance network. Hubbell's status indices are convenient in that they derive directly as row sums of the influence matrix $\mathbf{Y}$ in Eq. (2). Another line of approach to the status index problem has been pursued by Harary (1959b). Essentially it consists of a count of the number of sub-ordinates each individual possesses, weighted by the number of levels "down" they are.

Other properties of sociograms that have received some slight attention are: "hierarchization," based on the nature of the distribution of number of choices received per individual (Coleman, 1964a); the tendency toward reciprocation of choice (Katz and Powell, 1955); the characterization of "liaison members" and other types whose presence "strengthens" or "weakens" the connectedness of a graph (Ross and Harary, 1959); indices of "centralization" of a graph (Sabidussi, 1966); the interpretation of different kinds of lines in a social network (Luce, *et al.*, 1955); and so on. Some of these properties and others have been reviewed by Glanzer and Glaser (1959, 1961), Flament (1963), and Shaw (1964).

Structural characterizations can sometimes be based upon data in forms differing from that of the sociogram. One recent and quite interesting possibility, described by Campbell, *et al.* (1966), is an index of "aggregation" (that is, of racial or other group clustering) based on observed seating patterns in classrooms. Other indices and analyses addressed to problems in the topical area of racial mixing have been and will be devised. With these, as with all the indices discussed earlier, the extent to which they prove useful as mathematical models depends on how extensively they can be used in connection with models of ongoing social process or can otherwise be embedded in larger general contexts.

B. THE BALANCE PRINCIPLE

One (perhaps to date the only) truly powerful organizing theme in the mathematical study of social structure is the balance principle and its variants. This principle pertains to sociograms for which both positive and negative relations (for example, liking and disliking) are admissible.

In the well-known original statement by Heider (1946), balance was viewed as a potential property of social *perceptions*, that is, of relationships as seen by a single observer. The structure of the triad involving the person p, another person o, and an object x was said to be balanced or imbalanced according as the number of perceived negative relations among p to o, p to x, and o to x was even or odd. Heider postulated a perceptual preference for balanced over imbalanced triads, so that individuals in certain circumstances would tend to misperceive relations in order to achieve balance. As applied to intra-individual percepts, the principle has been generalized to "attitude structures" involving more than three objects by Abelson and Rosenberg (1958) and others.

We will not pursue the attitudinal context here, but rather the socio-metric or interpersonal context. With a social triad, one may inquire whether there is a tendency toward balance in the manifest sociometric relations of the three individuals. Are there significant tendencies for two friends of a person to be friendly with each other, a friend and an enemy antagonistic, and two enemies friendly, as the balance principle would require? More generally, what could be said about the structure of interpersonal senti-ments in a larger social group if some sort of generalized balance principle were to hold? We now turn to questions of mathematical statement beyond the simple triad.

1. Structural Balance: The Generalization by Cartwright and Harary

Paraphrasing Harary *et al.* (1965), a *signed directed graph* (s-digraph) is a directed graph in which each line may be designated as either positive or negative. A *semicycle* is a traversal through two or more distinct points of the graph (ignoring the directedness of individual lines) starting and ending at the same point. (The term semicycle is perhaps poorly chosen, since the traversal comes "all the way around.") A semi-cycle is said to be positive if the number of its negative lines is even. (Zero is, of course, an even number.) Then, finally, an s-digraph is defined as *balanced if all of its semicycles are positive*.

This definition was designed by Cartwright and Harary (1965) to be consistent with the Heiderian definition for a triad (a semicycle with three points), and to go beyond it for larger configurations. A strong con-sequence of the Cartwright-Harary balance definition is the *structure theorem* originally proved by Harary (1954): The set of points of a balanced s-digraph can be partitioned into two subsets (one of which may be empty) such that each positive line joins two points of the same subset and each negative line joins two points of different subsets.

The sociometric interpretation of this partitioning condition is that in a balanced group the individuals will be divided into two camps such that all lines of friendship lie within camps and all lines of antagonism, between camps. Figure 1 depicts a balanced s-digraph for which individuals a, d, e, f, and h are in one camp, and b, c, and g are in the other. The reader may verify that all closed traversals through the digraph include an even number of negative lines. Clearly this is not a situation that we can often expect to find empirically in perfect, pure form. It might, how-

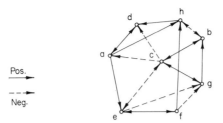

FIG. 1. A balanced signed directed graph.

ever, be a reasonable hypothesis that tendencies toward such an ultimately bipolar structure do exist in social groups. In order to test the hypothesis of dynamic sociometric tendency toward structural balance, it is necessary to employ some index of the relative degree of balance so that we are able to assert that a structure is becoming more or less balanced over time. Such indices are reviewed following further conceptual material.

2. "Clusterability": Davis's Extension

Davis (1967a) has recently questioned the sociometric applicability of the balance principle because the empirical implication that groups tend to polarize into exactly two antagonistic cliques seems too strong. He notes that sociometric studies often suggest that groups may split into three, four, or more cliques, and states an alternative principle giving an intuitively more realistic account. An s-digraph is said by Davis to be *clusterable if none of its semicycles contains one negative line.* All balanced digraphs are clusterable, but not all clusterable digraphs are balanced; in particular, when a digraph has one or more semicycles with *three* (or any higher odd number of) negative lines, it necessarily violates the conditions for balance, but not for clusterability. Thus clusterability is definitionally a less stringent structural specification. The theorem comparable to the previously stated structure theorem is: The set of points of a *clusterable* s-digraph can be partitioned into two *or more* subsets such that each positive line joins two points of the same subset and each negative line joins two points of different subsets.

In this weaker form of clique specification than the strict bipolarization demanded by the balance principle, there may be three, four, or any number of cliques all the way up to the most extreme case, *n* antagonistic cliques of one individual each. Figure 2 displays a hypothetical case of perfect clusterability with seven individuals and three cliques.

The social triangle with three negative relations (such as individuals a, c, e in Fig. 2) is the essential configuration allowed by the clusterability principle but forbidden by the balance principle. Strict balance requires that an enemy of *p*'s enemy is *p*'s friend; thus, that negative triangles

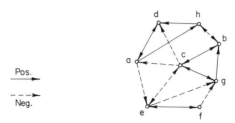

FIG. 2. A clusterable signed directed graph.

should not occur. However, Heider (1958, p. 206) suggests some uncertainty about the all-negative triad, and Davis (1967a) contends that its existence merely indicates the failure of coalition formation processes. A clusterable structure will tend toward balance if cliques sharing mutual enemies form coalitions; the ultimate in coalition formation is, of course, two antagonistic supercliques, that is, a balanced structure. Although strong pressures toward large coalitions may often characterize international relations (cf. Harary, 1961), in run-of-the-mill sociometric situations it seems unlikely that the sharing of enemies is often a compellingly cohesive force in producing permanent friendships. With empirical clusterability as with empirical balance, some index of relative degree is, of course, a necessary descriptive tool. Some possibilities are discussed in the following sections.

3. Indices of the Degree of Balance

Cartwright and Harary (1956) originally suggested as an index of the degree of balance the ratio of the number of balanced semicycles to the total number of semicycles in the graph. This ratio being extremely tedious to compute, they also suggested that the two counts might be limited only to triangles, ignoring longer semicycles. Meanwhile, Abelson and Rosenberg (1958) suggested counting simply the number of lines necessitating change of sign in order to achieve balance, a suggestion also broached by Harary (1959c) and named the "line index" of balance. The chief difficulty with this index is that its base-line chance value and other numerical properties are quite obscure.

A new and different line of approach will now be suggested. In a *complete* s-graph, there are positive or negative lines between all pairs of points; there are no "missing" lines. Consider the matrix form in which positive lines are represented by $+1$'s and negative lines by -1's. For a *balanced* complete s-graph, the points may be divided into two disjoint subsets with positive lines within subsets and negative lines between; thus the matrix representation will permit a partition of rows and columns into two corresponding blocks such that the entries within each block are

filled with + 1's and the "cross-block" entries with − 1's. If the diagonal entries representing self-relations are filled with + 1's and the matrix is factored according to McRae's procedure, Eq. (4), a single bipolar factor will be found to provide a perfect reconstruction of the matrix. The "loadings" on this single factor will be positive or negative, depending on the camp to which each member belongs.

This simple factor property of balanced complete s-graphs has apparently not previously been remarked although Mitra (1962) has implied a similar notion. In any case, the property suggests a possible index when there is less than complete balance. Suppose that for any given s-digraph, +1's and −1's are entered in the matrix as before, and 0's for all absent directed lines. The matrix need not be symmetric if different relations hold in the two directions between pairs of points. Now the matrix is factored according to Eq. (4), and the *balance index is the proportion of the total sum of squares explained by the first factor.* Numerically, this is calculable as the highest entry in the root matrix Λ divided by the number of individuals n (which equals the total "sum of squares"). With perfect balance, the index equals 1.00.

The statistical properties of such a *factor index of balance* are not, to be sure, well understood. Nevertheless, anyone with experience with factor analysis will have a good intuitive feel for the strength of the first factor in terms of the relative size of its root. And with the ready availability of computer programs, the computation is easily carried out. As with many other sociometric indices, empirical experience is sorely needed.

4. Indices of the Degree of Clusterability

Since clusterability is a recently developed notion, there has not been much work devoted to index construction. Davis (1967b) has made a beginning in this direction, however; first, he considers complete symmetric signed graphs. That is, between every pair of points there is either a positive or negative relation with direction immaterial. One interesting empirical interpretation of a complete s-graph is as an *acquaintance network*, with "knowing" as the (symmetric) positive relation between individuals and "not knowing" as the (symmetric) negative relation. (This is, of course, a special interpretation. An ordinary graph is converted into a signed graph by regarding "no relation" as the negative relation in order to apply the clusterability principle.) For what Davis calls his "Coefficient A", the unit of analysis is the social triad. The four possible configurations are characterized by three, two, one, or no positive lines. The numbers N_3, N_2, N_1, N_0 of these four respective types are tallied, using all possible triads. The strict clusterability hypothesis requires that $N_2 = 0$; that is, that there be no triangles with two positives (one negative).

Davis (1967b) gives the following formula.

$$\text{Coefficient } A \ = \ \frac{3N_1 N_3 - N_2^{\ 2}}{3N_1 N_3 + N_2^{\ 2}} \tag{6}$$

This coefficient has the conceptual property that if positive and negative lines occur at random, (that is, independently of the character of other lines in the triangle), then by expectation $A = 0$, whereas if the graph is perfectly clusterable, $A = 1$, and if there is "anticlusterability," then $0 > A \geq -1$. Davis's coefficient is not the only coefficient with these numerical properties, but can easily be shown to be the simplest involving the quantities N_1, N_2, N_3.

As Davis points out, a defect of his Coefficient A is that it uses the available data redundantly: there are only $n(n-1)/2$ lines in a complete graph, but the enumeration of triangles generates $(n-2)/3$ triangles per line. One solution for a large group is to take a sparse random sample of triangles. Another solution is to base a coefficient upon some appropriate tally using lines as the unit of analysis. Davis (1967b) has done this, suggesting two other possibly quite useful coefficients of clusterability. We will not pursue these here. In passing we note that "factor indices" do not seem to work well for assessing clusterability, though the goodness of fit of "simple structure" following rotation can with juggling be regarded as the relevant property of McRae's procedure.

Some of the uncertainties regarding the statistical properties of clusterability (and balance) indices might be resolved if Tukey's new "jackknife" procedure (Mosteller and Tukey, 1967) for setting confidence limits were tried empirically. Essentially the procedure would involve repeated calculations on the same data, each time leaving a different few individuals out of the network.

It should be noted that the finding that a social group has a high degree of clusterability (or balance) does not necessarily indicate that in the group there are dynamic forces toward clusterability (or balance) as such. It may be the case that circumstances have imposed clusterability, as for example when physical arrangements are strongly conducive to clumping of initial acquaintances. To show a dynamic tendency toward clusterability, it is necessary at a minimum to study changes in clusterability over time. This has not as yet been done in systematic fashion, though it is easy to point to isolated instances in which clusterability increases. [For example, with the first of Newcomb's (1961) carefully studied closed groups of initially unacquainted students, Coefficient A increases from .536 to .903 over a period of three months.]

Quite conceivably it will turn out that for certain kinds of superficial sociometric relations, clusterability tends to be low or to decrease if not initially low. A case in point might be the relation "tells old jokes to." Such tellings probably creep along otherwise little-used pathways tending to minimize overlap and maximize reachability in the target population. Of course, high reachability ordinarily implies low clusterability. Contrariwise, for intense social transactions wherein negative relationships are really negative rather than merely absent, the hypothesis of a dynamic tendency toward clusterability and especially toward balance is probably quite plausible. The prototypic example concerns friendship and antagonism during bitter social controversies (Coleman, 1957).

In any case, it is surely naive to expect a single generalization about social structural properties to hold for all interpretations of social structure. DeSoto *et al.* (1967) have shown that the tendency to *remember* social structures depends on clusterability differentially for acquaintance versus sentiment networks. In all likelihood the actual tendencies toward clusterability differ for these two types of relations as well.

C. LARGE SOCIAL STRUCTURES

When a social collectivity is large, it becomes impractical to describe its structural properties via a complete sociogrammatic representation. Instead, concise summarizations of a statistical nature are required. Because of mathematical difficulties, strong assumptions are necessary in order to develop tractable models, and a certain tolerance for rough-and-ready approximations may prove necessary in empirical applications. These applications, incidentally, are likely to lie on the sociological side of the boundary between sociology and social psychology, apparently quite remote from *experimental* social psychology, since large collectivities are at best observed rather than manipulated. Nevertheless this topic is included here because of recent attempts to bridge the conceptual gap between observational and experimental techniques (Campbell and Stanley, 1963) and to synthesize predictions of observed behavior "in the large" from postulates developed "in the small" (cf. Abelson and Bernstein, 1963; Coleman, 1964a, pp. 41 ff.).

1. Random versus Biased Nets

It is useful in conceptualizing the properties of large social networks to take as a point of departure the concept of a "random net" (cf. Rapoport, 1963). Among n individuals, $n(n-1)$ directed lines are possible, but only some fraction of these will actually occur. A random net is a structure determined by choosing the locations of actual lines entirely by chance; it may be said that for any arbitrary pair of points (i, j) in a random net there is a constant probability that a directed line will exist between them, independent of whatever other lines may issue from or terminate on either of them.

A random net may sometimes be defined in a more constrained way than has just been done. For example, the total number of lines may be fixed so that lines are "sampled without replacement," and a slight negative correlation between different line occurrences will thus be introduced. When the number of points and lines is large, this effect can usually be ignored. A stronger constraint occurs when the number of lines issuing from each point is constant, although their termini occur at random. [This is the form of random net discussed by Rapoport (1963), using the term "axone density" to denote the number of lines from each point.] Context will usually make clear the degree of constraint placed on the randomness of a net.

Distinct from simple constraints on randomness are a number of effects or *biases* that sharply alter from random base-lines the probabilities of occurrence of certain structural configurations. There are at least four important effects that have been invoked to account for the fact that sociometric networks usually depart very considerably from randomness. These are: (1) reciprocity bias; (2) transitivity bias; (3) distance bias; (4) popularity bias. Reciprocity bias concerns the typically strong tendency toward mutuality of choice. Transitivity bias concerns the increased probability that i chooses k given that i chooses j and j chooses k; that is, the tendency for a friend's friend to be a friend. Distance bias has to do with the clustering of choices introduced because of a physical neighborhood influence, that is, by the well-known factor of propinquity. Depending on how it is formulated, it is perhaps possible for distance bias to produce the same or similar structural effects as transitivity bias. Conceptually it is different because it explicitly takes physical distance into account. Popularity bias concerns the tendency for certain individuals to attract more than their random share of choices and for other individuals to attract less. This bias can be superimposed upon the other biases, since it is "individual" rather than "relational."

That the actual distribution of choices received in a large group can deviate markedly from a chance distribution was shown, among others, by Rapoport and Horvath (1961), who found several actual distributions that conformed to the so-called Greenwood-Yule type, rather than the Poisson, that would obtain for a random net. A subsequent study by Foster *et al.* (1963) gave empirical estimates for reciprocity and transitivity biases. Distance bias has been studied quantitatively chiefly by quantitative geographers following Hägerstrand (1965), who found a roughly exponential drop-off of intimate social contacts by geographical distance in a rural environment.

2. Rapoport's Tracing Procedure

The listed biases are localized effects. How can the consequences of these factors for large-scale structural properties be investigated? One intriguing possibility is the "tracing" procedure described by Rapoport (1963).

A small fraction p_0 of "starting" points in the network is randomly selected. From these points issue lines, some of which terminate on starting points, and others on newly contacted points. The newly contacted fraction of the population is denoted p_1. The process is continued; the newly contacted fractions are denoted $p_2, p_3, \ldots, p_t, \ldots$. The points of the tth set are those for which the shortest path from any of the starting points is exactly of length t. A tracing ends when no new points are contacted.

The quantities p_t characterize the rate of spread of sociometric contacts through successive "removes," or generations. If tangible information were being passed along the network at a constant unit rate, the cumulative quantities $x_t = \sum_{j=0}^{t} p_j$ would represent the cumulative fractions of the population informed by time t, thus generating a kind of diffusion curve. Of course, these quantities are affected by the random choice of starting points, and for stable average values the tracing procedure must be conceptualized as extensively repeated. The diffusion metaphor is to be understood as strictly dependent on *the presumption* that diffusion proceeds precisely along the paths of the specified network.

Given a particular network, repeated empirical tracings can be carried out easily with the aid of a computer program. Meanwhile (and this is the point), mathematical models incorporating local bias effects can be constructed to generate *predicted tracings*. If predicted and empirical tracings agree, the local bias effects are sufficient to account for large-scale structural phenomena. If not, new or "higher-order" biases may need to be invoked.

For a random net, an elementary derivation (Rapoport, 1951) readily establishes the following recursive equation for a theoretical tracing in an arbitrarily large group:

$$p_{t+1} = (1 - x_t)[1 - \exp(-ap_t)], \qquad (7)$$

where a is the average number of network lines per point. The cumulative curve of x_t generated by successive applications of Eq. (7) has a theoretical asymptote, γ (or x_∞) given by the implicit equation

$$\gamma = 1 - (1 - p_0)\exp(-a\gamma). \qquad (8)$$

The fraction γ represents the theoretical proportion of the population ever contacted through a predetermined random network with line density a and starting proportion p_0. This notion is intimately related to reachability. In fact, when $p_0 = 1/n$, the constant γ gives the theoretical value for a random network of Coleman's *connectivity index* (see Section II, A, 2). When $a = 2$, γ is roughly .8, a rather high value. Of course, to the extent that the network departs from randomness in the direction of greater cliquishness, connectivity will be lower.

It is much more difficult to develop a theoretical equation for a tracing of any kind of biased network, but Foster *et al.* (1963) made such an attempt. They considered: (1) reciprocity or *"parent" bias*, indexed by π, the probability that i chooses j given that j chooses i; (2) transitivity or *"sibling" bias*, indexed by σ, the probability that i chooses j given some individual k who chooses both i and j. By a combination of mathematical conjectures and empirical trials, they concluded that popularity bias probably has a very small effect on the tracing procedure in comparison with the foregoing biases. Distance bias was not considered.

Via an admittedly tortured derivation involving several rough-and-ready approximations, the authors derived the following recursive formula:

$$p_{t+1} = (1 - x_t)\left(1 - \exp\left\{-ap_t\left[1 - \frac{\pi' + \sigma'}{a(1 - x_t)}\right]\right\}\right), \qquad (9)$$

where

$$\pi' = \pi[1 + (a - 1)(p_t + p_{t-1})],$$

and

$$\sigma' = \sigma[1 + (a^2 + a - 1)x_t].$$

Although Eq. (9) looks messy, it is a straightforward matter given π, σ, a, and p_0, to generate p_1 (and x_1) and thence p_2 (and x_2), p_3 (and x_3), and so on. The parameters π, σ, and a can be estimated directly from any actual sociometric data at hand, and p_0 picked conveniently small, for example, $p_0 = .01$.

The crux of the Foster *et al.* (1963) paper was a comparison of the results of Eq. (9) with the averages of a series of empirical tracings through a sociometric network of 860 junior high school students. The empirical tracings were carried out with the aid of a computer program operating on the stored sociometric choice data. The visual fit between theoretical and "observed" tracings was quite good, suggesting that the local parameters π, σ, and a sufficed to account for large-scale structural properties.

Further work along these lines would be desirable. In particular, it would be nice to see an example in which the social networks were defined according to actual social transactions ("Whom did you talk to about this?"), so that the analysis would have more direct relevance to the study of the dynamics of diffusion.

3. Clusterability Revisited

The methods by which network biases were characterized in the last two sections raise an interesting question about Davis's clusterability principle (Sections II, B, 2 and 4) applied to triads in acquaintance networks. Consider the numbers N_1, N_2, N_3 of triangles with one, two, or three lines. Davis states his principle in terms of social preference for increased N_3 and N_1 at the expense of N_2, a presumably unstable type. Seemingly there are two network biases involved: the tendencies for two-sided triangles (a) to "fill up" to three-sidedness, and (b) to "drop down" to one-sidedness. But as far as triangles are concerned, Rapoport contemplates only the first of these possibilities: the sibling bias that tends to complete two-sided triangles. What about the second possibility? Shouldn't we expect, given some individual k who knows j but not i, that i will tend not to know j? In other words, doesn't the clusterability principle require, in addition to a positive sibling bias, a negative "out-of-the-family" bias?

To answer this question, let us try to construct a model with both kinds of biases. We start by assuming a very large network in which the probability is P that a pair of points selected at random are connected by a line. We interpret lines as the relation of "knowing." We simplify the analysis by considering knowing to be bidirectional; that is, we set "parent bias" $\pi = 1$ and do not further consider direction of lines. Next we must decide the "pairwise" question: whether the probability of a line at a point is or is not to be considered independent of the presence of another line at the point. For greatest generality, we allow for a pairwise (in effect, popularity) bias. Denote by Δ the probability that i knows k, given that a randomly selected j knows k. Also, denote by Δ_0 the probability that i knows k, given that a randomly selected j does *not* know k. (The latter is an excess parameter that will later be eliminated.)

Denote by σ (the sibling bias) the probability that i knows j, given that a randomly selected k knows both i and j. Denote by σ_1 (the out-of-family bias) the probability that i knows j, given that a randomly selected k knows i but *not* j (or j but not i). Presumably the clusterability principle would imply $\sigma > P$ and $\sigma_1 < P$. Finally, denote by σ_0 the probability that i knows j, given that a randomly selected k knows neither i nor j.

Suppose three points i, j, k, to be randomly chosen. What is the probability π_3 that all three know each other? This may be calculated as the probability P that j knows k times the probability Δ that i knows k given that j knows k, times the probability σ that i knows j given that k knows both. By similar reasoning we obtain equations for the probabilities π_2, π_1, π_0 that two, one, or no sides of the (i, j, k) triangle are filled.

$$\pi_3 = P\Delta\sigma; \tag{10}$$

$$\pi_2 = P\Delta(1 - \sigma) + P(1 - \Delta)\sigma_1 + (1 - P)\Delta_0\sigma_1; \tag{11}$$

$$\pi_1 = P(1 - \Delta)(1 - \sigma_1) + (1 - P)\Delta_0(1 - \sigma_1) + (1 - P)(1 - \Delta_0)\sigma_0; \tag{12}$$

$$\pi_0 = (1 - P)(1 - \Delta_0)(1 - \sigma_0). \tag{13}$$

The separate terms in Eq. (11) arise by considering that line (i, k) may not be filled when (i, j) and (j, k) are both filled (probability $= P\Delta(1 - \sigma)$); or (i, k) may be filled when (j, k) is filled but (i, k) not (probability $= P(1 - \Delta)\sigma_1$); or when (j, k) is not filled but (i, k) is (probability $= (1 - P)\Delta_0\sigma_1$). However, since points $i, j,$ and k are selected at random, permutations of labeling of the points cannot yield substantive differences; therefore, the three cases just listed must be equiprobable. Thus

$$P\Delta(1 - \sigma) = P(1 - \Delta)\sigma_1 = (1 - P)\Delta_0\sigma_1. \tag{14}$$

By similar reasoning,

$$P(1 - \Delta)(1 - \sigma_1) = (1 - P)\Delta_0(1 - \sigma_1) = (1 - P)(1 - \Delta_0)\sigma_0. \tag{15}$$

The four equalities in Eqs. (14)–(15) reduce to three and permit the elimination of the three extraneous parameters Δ_0, σ_1, and σ_0. Equations (10)–(13) can be rewritten entirely in terms of σ, Δ, and P.

$$\pi_3 = P\Delta\sigma; \tag{16}$$

$$\pi_2 = 3P\Delta(1 - \sigma); \tag{17}$$

$$\pi_1 = 3P(1 - \Delta) - 3P\Delta(1 - \sigma); \tag{18}$$

$$\pi_0 = 1 - 3P(1 - \Delta) - P\Delta\sigma. \tag{19}$$

The resolution, then, of our question is that sibling bias completely implies out-of-family bias when line density and pairwise popularity bias are held constant. Inspection of Eqs. (16)–(19) discloses that excess over the unbiased value P^3 for the probability π_3 of complete triangles can produce "ripples" down the line of the other probabilities; π_2 will be less, π_1 greater, and π_0 less than their values for a random net. At the level of triangles, clusterability in acquaintance networks thus essentially only involves a social preference toward completion of the "third side," and a sibling bias parameter (in concert with a pairwise parameter Δ and the line density P) suffices to account for its triangle effects.

Davis's (1967b) Coefficient A, incidentally, can be rewritten in terms of

σ, Δ, and P. Dividing numerator and denominator of Eq. (6) by T^2 where T is the total number of possible triangles, we obtain an equation in terms of the proportions of triangles of different types. Substituting Eqs. (16)–(18) with probabilities π_3, π_2, π_1, for these proportions, we obtain finally

$$A' = \frac{(\sigma - \Delta)}{(\sigma - \Delta) + 2\Delta(1 - \sigma)^2} \, . \tag{20}$$

This function depends essentially on the degree to which the triples bias σ exceeds the pairwise bias Δ, and it is entirely independent of P.

III. Mathematical Models of Social Behavior

All mathematical models of social behavior specify: an *interactive setting* involving two or more individuals; socially relevant *responses*, such as friendship choices or statements of opinion or judgment; and *configurations of conditions tending to change these responses* over time. These conditions may be either *intrinsic*, that is, implied directly by the responses, or *extrinsic*, that is, determined (perhaps somewhat arbitrarily) by an outside agent, such as an experimenter. The most tangible term signifying "conditions tending to change responses" is of course *reinforcement*; many models explicitly invoke this concept (or an equivalent, such as pay off), especially those oriented toward the *learning* of certain social responses. There are, however, a variety of other ways of conceptualizing conditions inducing response change.

We shall emphasize in this section an "aggregative" style of model construction which involves: (1) mathematical specification of the setting, responses, and change conditions from the point of view of each single individual; and (2) generation of the consequences of these individual specifications for the joint behavior of two or more individuals in social interaction. This is not the only style of model construction for social behavior: it is possible to try to characterize group behaviors globally without detailing individuals, and at the other extreme to use the social group solely as a convenient context for the study of single individuals only. Coleman (1959), Berger *et al.* (1962), and others have discussed the differences among these various types of models. Here recommending the aforementioned aggregative style as temperamentally congenial for social psychologists, we simply plow ahead.

A. SOCIAL MODIFICATION OF OPINIONS

Consider an interactive situation in which individuals express opinions on a common topic to one another. A variety of special cases are possible, depending on the number of individuals, whether the opinions are qualitative or quantitative, and what variables are taken as mediators of opinion change. We consider a nonexhaustive set of these cases.

1. The Simple Two-Person Case

The simplest case involves but two people, denoted i and j, and two possible opinion positions, denoted Pro and Con. The mathematical variables are the respective probabilities p_i and p_j for the two individuals that their expressed opinions are on the Pro side. We imagine the situation in which opinions are repeatedly elicited over an extended time period and the probabilities p_i and p_j are repeatedly subject to change.

The mathematically most rigorous way to treat this situation is in the discrete-trial style of stochastic learning theories, exemplified for quasi-social situations by Suppes and Atkinson's (1960) "Markov learning models" and Burke's (1959) application of a standard "linear operator model." However, it is easier to contemplate the consequences of alternative substantive assumptions if the social interaction is considered to occur continuously in time and differential equations are used to smooth out the probabilistic vicissitudes of response occurrences.

Consider, as in Table I, the four possible configurations of expressed opinions by the two individuals and the pressures toward change of p_i exerted by each. (Later by symmetry we consider pressure toward change of p_j.) At least two distinct intrinsic mechanisms, persuasion and reinforcement, may operate: individual j may pull i directly toward j's stated opinion or, alternatively, i may be affected by j's opinion through a positive or negative social reinforcement mechanism. The difference between these two mechanisms lies in the parameterizations to which they lead: to focus on direct persuasion is to concern oneself with the relative strength of the two sides of the opinion question and with the relative persuasiveness (or

TABLE I
MODIFICATION OF OPINIONS IN TWO-PERSON INTERACTION[a]

Probability of event	Event i	Event j	Rates of change in p_i
p_ip_j	Pro	Pro	$(\theta_P + \theta_A)(1 - p_j)$
$p_i(1 - p_j)$	Pro	Con	$-(\theta_C + \theta_D)p_i$
$(1 - p_i)p_j$	Con	Pro	$(\theta_P + \theta_D)(1 - p_i)$
$(1 - p_i)(1 - p_j)$	Con	Con	$-(\theta_C + \theta_A)p_i$

[a] Definition of Parameters: θ_P, persuasive effect of Pro position (in strengthening Pro position); θ_C, persuasive effect of Con position (in weakening Pro position); θ_A, reinforcing effect of social agreement (in strengthening expressed position); θ_D, reinforcing effect of social disagreement (in weakening expressed position). All parameters using θ refer to person i; comparable parameters for person j use φ (see text).

persuasibility) of the two debaters; a focus on reinforcement invokes a comparison of the strengthening effect of social agreement with the weakening effect of social disagreement, and possibly a comparison of the relative sensitivities of the two individuals to reinforcement. Nothing says that the two types of mechanisms cannot both be operative,[2] and in the present treatment we consider the two of them simultaneously, supposing their separate effects to be additive.

The configurations tending to increase p_i arise when person j endorses the Pro position. The direct persuasion effect toward the Pro side we characterize by the parameter θ_P. The instantaneous rate of increase dp_i/dt of p_i is taken to be proportional to the gap $(1 - p_i)$ between p_i and its maximum possible value, 1, with θ_P as the constant of proportionality. The reinforcement effects depend on the response of person i. If he has made the Pro response, then j's agreement is considered to increase p_i at the rate θ_A $(1 - p_i)$ where θ_A is the social agreement parameter. If person i has made the Con response, then j's *disagreement* would *weaken* the Con tendency, that is, would strengthen the Pro side at the rate $\theta_D (1 - p_i)$ where θ_D is the social disagreement parameter.

The foregoing statements pertain to the cases in which person j urges the Pro position. If instead he gives the Con response, there is a tendency for p_i to weaken proportionately via the persuasion mechanism (with a parameter θ_C for the Con side), as well as by reinforcement (with parameter θ_D or θ_A, depending on whether i gives the Pro response or the Con response). All of these rate of change effects are summarized in the right-hand column of Table I.

A differential equation including all of these effects may be written by noting that the net rate of change of p_i is a sum of the rates of change for the four configurations weighted by the instantaneous probabilities of occurrence given in the first column of Table I. This equation, after algebraic simplification, becomes

$$dp_i/dt = (\theta_P + \theta_D)p_j(1 - p_i) - (\theta_A + \theta_C)p_i(1 - p_j)$$
$$+ (\theta_A - \theta_D)p_i[(p_i + p_j) - 2p_ip_j]. \quad (21)$$

A completely analogous derivation for individual j, defining the four parameters φ_P, φ_C, φ_A, and φ_D parallel in meaning to the θ's, leads to the companion equation

[2] Suppes and Schlag-Rey (1962) conducted an experiment showing much stronger conditioning effects of a social stimulus occurring before rather than after a response. In present terms, their experiment might be interpreted to mean that persuasion or social pressure is a more compelling mechanism than social reinforcement. However, such a strong generalization from a single rather specialized experiment would be excessive.

$$dp_j/dt = (\varphi_P + \varphi_D)p_i(1 - p_j) - (\varphi_A + \varphi_C)p_j(1 - p_i)$$
$$+ (\varphi_A - \varphi_D)p_j[(p_i + p_j) - 2p_ip_j]. \quad (22)$$

If the system of Eqs. (21)–(22) were solvable, it would yield families of curves for p_i and p_j as functions of time, each family determined by different configurations of the θ's and φ's, with member curves of any family distinguished according to different initial values of p_i and p_j. Although such a solution is conceivable, the nonlinear character of the equations renders them mathematically formidable. We content ourselves here with the illustrative analysis of two special cases that arise when certain simple assumptions are made about the parameters: (1) no differential reinforcement effects, that is, $\theta_A = \theta_D$ and $\varphi_A = \varphi_D$, but all other parameters free to vary; (2) no differential issue-position effects, that is, $\theta_P = \theta_C$ and $\varphi_P = \varphi_C$, but all other parameters free to vary.

Each such analysis will be confined to an examination of the "phase diagram" of p_i and p_j rather than to the full analytic solution. Phase diagrams [as discussed, for example, by Kemeny and Snell (1962), Coleman (1959, pp. 42 ff.), and Richardson (1960)] can often be used to advantage whether or not analytic solutions are possible. In particular, we will be interested in the following conceivable asymptotic outcomes of the continuous two-person opinion interaction: *position-dominated* consensus, in which both parties end up in complete agreement with the "stronger" of the two issue positions; *person-dominated* consensus, in which both parties end up in complete agreement with the position initially preferred by the "stronger" of the two individuals; *partial accommodation*, in which both parties end with intermediate positions not identical to each other but more nearly alike than at the outset; and *complete accommodation*, in which both parties end with identical intermediate positions. In the phase diagram, outcomes for the pair of values (p_i, p_j) are depicted as a function of the initial situation by means of paths or "trajectories" drawn in the (p_i, p_j) plane. One may imagine a point "traveling" in this plane, starting with some initial values of p_i and p_j and continuously assuming new paired values of p_i and p_j characterizing each subsequent momentary opinion situation. (The *rate* at which the point "travels" is not given in the phase diagram.) In general, different initial values generate different trajectories, so that a family of paths must be drawn to characterize the full range of possibilities. Of special importance are the final destinations of the trajectories, as these specify the asymptotic values of p_i and p_j. Our earlier verbal definitions refer readily to the diagrams. Consensus is characterized by a family of trajectories heading toward (1, 1) or (0, 0), and accommodation by families of trajectories with negative slopes, aiming for and terminating on target points in the interior of the diagram.

The first case, no differential reinforcement effects, is depicted in two variants in Figs. 3a and 3b. Figure 3a shows the typical pattern of outcomes when the Pro side of the issue is more compelling than the Con side for both individuals (that is, $\theta_P > \theta_C$ and $\varphi_P > \varphi_C$). For convenient simplification of Eqs. (21)–(22), it is appropriate to reparametrize by incorporating the value of the common reinforcement effect $\theta_A = \theta_D = \theta_O$ in the new constants $\theta_P' = \theta_P + \theta_O$ and $\theta_C' = \theta_C + \theta_O$ (and similarly $\varphi_P' = \varphi_P + \varphi_O$ and $\varphi_C' = \varphi_C + \varphi_O$). We may note that it does not affect the relative values of θ_P and θ_C, for example, to replace them by θ_P' and θ_C', although the relative values across individuals (for example, θ_P' versus φ_P') in the reparametrization are affected by differential individual sensitivity to reinforcement.

In Fig. 3a, the specific but not unusual values $\theta_P' = .3$, $\theta_C' = .1$, $\varphi_P' = .2$, and $\varphi_C' = .1$ were chosen for convenience. We note that no matter what the initial probabilities of respective expression of the Pro side (as long as they are not both zero), ultimately both parties come to a full Pro consensus. This issue-dominated consensus holds despite some tendency for the parties to move initially toward accommodation rather than consensus. (Note the trajectories where p_i, or p_j, first decreases and then increases again.) The "prevailing wind" carries the opinion mixtures inexorably toward the stronger side, in this figure, the Pro side. Of course, if the Con parameters are stronger for both individuals, the direction of influence reverses and the trajectories head toward the lower-left instead of the upper-right corner.

An interesting variant occurs when one individual is more susceptible to the Pro side ($\theta_P' > \theta_C'$) but the other individual to the Con side ($\varphi_P' < \varphi_C'$). This might be apt, for example, if one individual were predisposed to accept liberal appeals, the other conservative appeals, and the issue under discussion tapped the liberal-conservative dimension. Perhaps surprisingly, this variant yields a similar outcome to that pictured in Fig. 3a, requiring only that $\theta_P' \varphi_P' > \theta_C' \varphi_C'$. If the product of the two Pro parameters is only slightly greater than the product of the two Con parameters, a partial accommodation is almost reached, but all trajectories nevertheless head for the point (1, 1) eventually. If $\theta_P' \varphi_P' < \theta_C' \varphi_C'$, trajectories all target on the point (0, 0).

The delicate intermediate situation with $\theta_P' \varphi_P' = \theta_C' \varphi_C'$ is depicted in Fig. 3b. (All numerical parameters are the same as in Fig. 3a except that $\varphi'_C = .6$ instead of .1.) Here partial accommodations do indeed occur. The trajectories, all parallel straight lines, terminate in the interior of the diagram somewhere along an "equilibrium curve." The equation of this curve is

$$p_j = p_i/[K + (1 - K)p_i], \tag{23}$$

where $K = \theta_P'/\theta_C' = \varphi_C'/\varphi_P' = 3$ in Fig. 3b. If the value of K is greater than

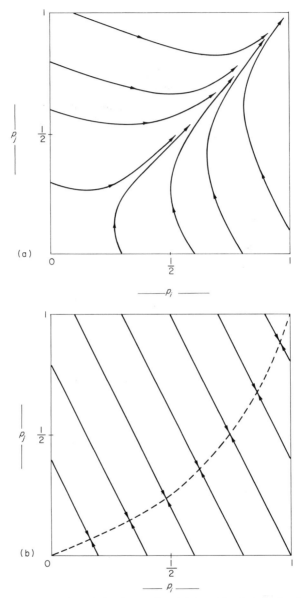

FIG. 3. Phase diagrams for opinion interaction. (a) Pro side of issue dominant; (b) competing issue effects.

unity, then the curve bends toward the (1, 0) corner, as in Fig. 3b. That is, if person i is relatively more susceptible to the Pro side and person j relatively more susceptible to the Con side, the final accommodation necessarily finds person i somewhat more Pro than person j. (If K is less than unity, the complementary assertion holds.) The degree of difference between the two final positions depends on the two initial positions and on the common slope of the trajectories given by $-\varphi'_C/\theta'_P$. This quantity in this case represents the relative persuasibility of individual j and determines his relative rate of yielding as the pair slides toward accommodation.

A special situation obtains when we assume $\theta'_P = \theta'_C = \theta'$ and $\varphi'_P = \varphi'_C = \varphi'$. Then the equilibrium curve bends toward neither corner but becomes the straight line $p_i = p_j$. That is, the equilibrium becomes a complete accommodation of the two individuals to the same shared final p; call it p^*. The model employed by Cervin and Henderson (1961) makes precisely these special assumptions, attempting to predict the asymptotic joint level p^* solely from parameters characterizing the two individuals. The appropriate equation is

$$p^* = \frac{\theta' p_{j0} + \varphi' p_{i0}}{\theta' + \varphi'} \tag{24}$$

where p_{j0} and p_{i0} are the initial p's and θ' and φ' are the persuasibilities of i and j, respectively. In this simple case Eqs. (21)–(22) are readily solved for the time trends of the p's toward asymptote, which turn out to be exponential decay curves.

Cervin and Henderson (1961) tried to fit data from actual two-person discussions to such curves, operationalizing the probabilities of expression of each of the two sides of an issue by the proportions of time each individual spent voicing arguments favorable to each side. Such a measure is troublesome in practice. The obtained curves were extremely ragged and did not fit the predicted exponentials well. Furthermore, many social pairs did not reach accommodation and it is not clear that the simplified model was appropriate. The two sides of the issue may have differed in strength and there may have been differential reinforcement effects. Our mathematical analysis thus far seems to suggest that complete accommodation is an outcome requiring unusual parametric conditions.

We turn now to the case in which differential reinforcement effects, rather than differential issue position effects, are contemplated. Figure 4a and b depicts two major variants. (In what follows, we employ the reparametrizations defined by $\theta_P = \theta_C = \theta^*$, $\theta'_A = \theta_A + \theta^*$, $\theta'_D = \theta_D + \theta^*$; $\varphi_P = \varphi_C = \varphi^*$, $\varphi'_A = \varphi_A + \varphi^*$, and $\varphi'_D = \varphi_D + \varphi^*$.)

Figure 4a shows what happens when agreement effects dominate disagreement effects for both participants, that is, $\theta'_A > \theta'_D$ and $\varphi'_A > \varphi'_D$. The concrete values $\theta'_A = .4$, $\theta'_D = .2$, $\varphi'_A = .2$, and $\varphi'_A = .1$ are used for the diagram.

There is nothing special in these values, except that both θ'_A and θ'_D are made bigger than φ'_A and φ'_D to show what happens when one individual is consistently more susceptible to reinforcement than the other. We note that

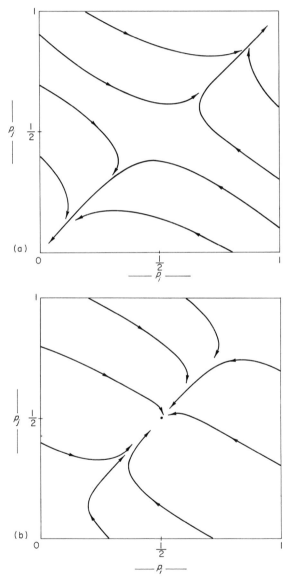

FIG. 4. Phase diagrams for opinion interaction. (a) Agreement effects dominant; (b) disagreement effects dominant.

some trajectories head toward $(1, 1)$ and others toward $(0, 0)$. Consensus is inexorable, but it may occur on either side of the issue. Looking more closely at what determines the side of the final consensus, we see in Fig. 4a that when $p_j > \frac{1}{2}$, the consensus tends most often to be on the Pro side, and when $p_j < \frac{1}{2}$, the consensus most often tends to be on the Con side. That is, person j tends to dominate the consensus. (There is a tendency for the outcome to depend also on the initial position of i, but this effect is limited.) Of course, j's domination is the result of the arbitrary assignment of greater lability (larger parameters) to i. A reverse assignment would reverse the dominance. Equal labilities would still result in consensus, but with neither party usually dominant. In any event, person-dominated consensus is a predictable outcome of the model in which the strengthening effect of social agreement is more powerful than the weakening effect of social disagreement.

The converse variant, in which disagreement is the more powerful effect, is achieved by setting $\theta'_D > \theta'_A$ and $\varphi'_D > \varphi'_A$. In Fig. 4b, the illustrative values $\theta'_D = .4$, $\theta'_A = .2$, $\varphi'_D = .2$, $\varphi'_A = .1$ are used. The mathematical result is very striking. All trajectories head for the point $(\frac{1}{2}, \frac{1}{2})$. Not only does this represent complete accommodation, it is an accommodation with both parties arguing equally often on both sides of the issue, a wishy-washy accommodation indeed. Intuitively, this phenomenon occurs because each participant is a Milquetoast strongly impelled by social disagreement to accommodate to the other. The mathematical fact of ultimate compromise at the 50–50 point is not, incidentally, affected by whether one individual is more of a Milquetoast than the other, so long as they both are (and so long as the issue parameters are respectively equal for both individuals, as required for the present case).

Thus we see mathematically that the reinforcing effects of social agreement and social disagreement produce quite different social outcomes. If social agreement effects predominate, then the less persuasible (or more persuasive) individual tends to dominate, finally leading the pair to agree totally on his preferred side of the issue; if disagreement effects predominate, then both individuals regress toward total indecision between the two sides of the issue.

Some laboratory evidence is available on the relative sizes of these two effects. Rainio (1962), with a mathematical model extremely similar to the present special case in mind, elicited repeated opinion expressions from pairs of Finnish university students. He estimated that the weakening effect of social disagreement was essentially nil and that the strengthening effect of agreement approximated $\theta_A = .2$. Doubtless the relative effects differ by type of subject, type of issue, and especially according to experimental instructions (for example, the experimenter can enjoin the subjects

to resolve their disagreements if at all possible, thus heightening the disagreement effect parameters), but it seems a reasonable general guess that
the disagreement parameter will usually be less than the agreement parameter. After all, social disagreement as a "punishment" effect suffers
from the general disadvantages of punishment as a technique for inducing
learning. McPhee (1961), in an interesting public opinion model invoking
both social agreement and disagreement, postulates that agreement fixes
opinions but disagreement does not destroy them. Rather, it sends the
individual back to the mass media to "take a new sample of opinion stimuli."
This postulated neutral effect of disagreement is in concordance with
Rainio's isolated finding and with our present speculation. A sustained investigation of the matter would be desirable.

Other cases of the general model given by Eqs. (21)–(22) would be
interesting to pursue, but we will not do so here. The presentation has
served the purpose of outlining a number of qualitative possibilities in
the two-person opinion exchange case, focusing on the formal causal
factors that might be involved.

The present model is unfortunately not immediately transferable to
laboratory or field situations because there seems no practical way in which
the "opinion mixes" represented by p_i and p_j can be continuously elicited,
expressed, and measured. [Such difficulties of experimental realization
indeed beset much of mathematical social psychology, as Bush (1962) has
aptly pointed out.]

A possibly practical type of mathematizable opinion experiment arises
when the participants express quantitative, not qualitative, "opinions."
The variables of the model then become continuous quantities, such
as X_i and X_j rather than probabilities p_i and p_j. The X dimension presumably
represents some sort of opinion or attitude continuum. Cervin and Henderson (1961) had somewhat more success in fitting a simple differential
equations model to X's than to p's after altering the situation from one of
opinion exchange to a monetary bidding game. Price provides a very well-
quantified scale, thus buyer versus seller situations have a certain appeal
as experimental settings (cf. Siegel and Fouraker, 1960; Fouraker and
Siegel, 1963).

It seems intuitively clear, however, that bargaining over a selling
price is not quite the same sort of social transaction as contention over an
opinion issue. In the former case, the two parties are much more apt to
perceive grudging compromise as a legitimate and useful "part of the game,"
with the final compromise selling price as a clear formal goal toward which
the whole interaction orients. With opinions or attitudes, on the other hand,
there is usually no such shared understanding of fair exchange toward a
structured goal. One or the other opinion will seem more correct to each

participant for reasons lying outside the interaction. Thus, specific *arguments* are much more apt to be employed in contention ("My opinion is right because . . . .") than in bargaining, and the acceptance or rejection of these arguments may influence the outcome in a manner different from the acceptance or rejection of monetary bids. Presumably the role of arguments can be reflected mathematically in the differential issue-position parameters as well as in the differential reinforcement parameters. If the foregoing distinction between opinion and bargaining situations strikes the reader as vague, he may perhaps better satisfy himself by inspecting Figs. 3a and 4a and b and asking whether the depicted trajectories could reasonably represent bargaining sequences (interpreting p_i and p_j as X_i and X_j, price asked and price offered). A sequence with positive slope ("My price is $10" . . . . "I'll give you $6" . . . . "Sorry, it will cost you $15" . . . . . . "Well, then I'll pay $12" . . . . "It just went up to $20" . . . . "All right, I'll offer $18".) seems more appropriate for a Marx brothers movie than a realistic bargaining interaction.

Unfortunately, it is not altogether clear how to write a mathematical model for dyadic opinion change along a continuum, analogous to Eqs. (21)–(22). Possibly the general class of linear models suggested by Anderson (1964) could be adapted to this problem, although these models have heretofore been employed almost entirely in situations in which the experimenter extrinsically defines correct responses for the social participants, unlike either the opinion or bargaining situations (cf. Rosenberg, 1962, 1963; Rosenberg and Schoeffler (1965)). We pursue a limited aspect of this matter further in the next section.

2. Multi-Person Cases

As part of a more abstract "stochastic theory of social contacts," Rainio (1965, 1966) expressed in stochastic learning form the common propositions that dyadic social agreement tends to increase the probability of future social contact, and dyadic social disagreement to decrease the contact probability. These two propositions were combined with two others we have previously discussed, the tendency for social agreement to strengthen an opinion and social disagreement to weaken an opinion. As previously noted, Rainio considered the disagreement parameter to be small or negligible in comparison to the agreement parameter. Thus in the terminology of the previous section, we would expect Rainio's model to generate person-dominated consensus in continued two-person interaction. The two other stochastic operators, however, modify this expectation. In the face of social disagreement, individuals in the model tend to reduce their mutual contact, biasing their future contacts toward the other individuals in the surrounding social group. In the long run, then, consensus will tend to occur as much by selective locomotion as by dyadic domination. To specify mathematically in any degree of detail what will happen to opinion and contact probabilities in a group as a function of the large number of individual parameters and initial conditions is clearly a very complicated matter, even for a group as small as three individuals. Rainio (1965, 1966) therefore abandons mathematical derivations in favor of the technique of computer simulation.

Other computer simulations involving similar variables are those of Coleman (1965), who reports a study of changes in a qualitative behavior (smoking) as conditioned by friendship patterns in a high school cohort, and Abelson and Bernstein (1963), who propose a very complex model involving the mutual dynamic interplay of attitude issue positions, social contact probabilities, and "arguments" accepted about the issue. The latter variable presumes to represent the details of opinion exchange more realistically and also allows the introduction of external attitude sources (the mass media) that present arguments to the social group. McPhee's (1961) simulation model also invokes the effects of the mass media.

These simulation models have not, as a group, been effectively validated. It is too early in the development of models of this kind to know whether the introduction of much naturalistic complexity can be a profitable modeling strategy. One of the difficulties has been that it is not easy to summarize aptly the properties of multivariable outcomes among many individuals.

One method that seemingly bypasses the summarization problem is to define the conceptual variables originally at the group rather than the individual level. This is what Simon and Guetzkow (1955) did in a differential equations model of opinion and friendship change in a social group. The essential variables were "group cohesiveness" and "opinion discrepancy" within the group. Analysis proceeded with the aid of a phase diagram depicting appropriate trajectories in these two variables, and in the most interesting of several cases, the broad qualitative prediction of the model was that groups would tend toward one or the other of two stable equilibria: high cohesiveness with low opinion deviance, or low cohesiveness with high opinion deviance. A modest empirical test of the model was reported, using data from nine groups, but unfortunately data were only available at a single time point. Operationalization of the variables presented an instructive problem. "Group cohesiveness" was approximated by the average individual rating of attractiveness of the group, and "opinion discrepancy" by the standard deviation of opinions on a topic crucial to the group. But since the mathematical model was formulated directly at the group level rather than by aggregation of models for individuals, there was nothing in the model determining the ideal way to put individual measures together. Thus the summarization problem is still present, but in a different form.

"Opinion discrepancy" is undoubtedly a useful summary concept in any case, since it suggests an intriguing question. Under what assumptions from an aggregative model will opinion discrepancy tend toward (or away from) zero in a group discussing an opinion issue? This question is the mathematical social psychologist's way of asking, "What forces eliminate (or maintain) opinion cleavage in a social group?"

Abelson (1964) approached the question by considering the postulate that the attitude positions of two discussants always move toward each other as the result of discussion. Denoting the change in X_i after discussion with person j as $\Delta_j X_i$, we may write

$$\Delta_j X_i = g(X_i, X_j) \cdot (X_j - X_i), \tag{25}$$

where $g(X_i, X_j)$ is any function such that $0 < g(X_i, X_j) \leq 1$ for all X_i and X_j. [The function g is sometimes simply replaced by a constant, as in Anderson and Hovland's (1957) model.] Equation (25) is seemingly innocuous, specifying only that person i moves his attitude X_i some fraction (perhaps very small) of the way toward the attitude X_j of his communication partner. This is a more or less standard result in laboratory studies of attitude change. Subsequent analysis shows, however, that strong consequences for group discussion are implicit in this innocent formulation.

If the change in X_i due to j's influence is multiplied by the rate a_{ij} at which j contacts i and a summation is then taken over all j, the net rate of change in X_i (smoothed over continuous time) is

$$\frac{dX_i}{dt} = \sum_{j=1}^{n} a_{ij} g(X_i, X_j) \cdot (X_j - X_i). \tag{26}$$

A similar equation obtains for each of the n individuals in the group under study; thus Eq. (26) is in effect a system of n differential equations in the variables X_1 through X_n. One may imagine an n-dimensional phase diagram, with trajectories tending toward one or more equilibrium points. The question at hand concerns the possible existence of a stable equilibrium point with all X_i equal, that is, an outcome situation with zero opinion discrepancy. The answer derived by Abelson (1964) depends on the social network properties implied by the patterns of zeros in the matrix of contact rates a_{ij}.

Networks in which there is *at least one individual who can contact everyone*, directly or *indirectly*, constitute the crucial class. (Formally, this class can be identified from the appropriate reachability matrix.)

Abelson calls such networks *compact*. In a compact network, the (only possible) equilibrium outcome of the system of Eq. (26) is a state of zero opinion discrepancy; that is, complete accommodation of all individuals in the group to a (unique) single attitude position. Noncompact networks involve two or more isolated camps, and the equilibrium outcome for such networks would in general involve a different accommodated attitude position within each camp.

If a more complicated model is postulated, allowing changes in contact rates (as in Rainio's model) in addition to changes in attitudes, the equilibrium outcome is again complete attitude accommodation if the "equilibrium network" is compact. If sufficient social cleavage comes about to destroy compactness, however, opinion deviance will be possible.

The mathematical outcome of "complete accommodation" for compact networks strikes one intuitively as being rather too strong to be realistic, in view of the many opinion issues on which social cleavage is commonly maintained. What changes in the conception of the model would be necessary to avert the completely accommodative prediction for compact networks? There are at least three possibilities: (1) Two discussants might antagonistically change their opinions *away* from each other following interaction, the so-called boomerang effect; (2) Two persons on the same side of the issue might mutually reinforce each other so that both moved toward greater extremity instead of toward a compromise of their positions; (3) Different individuals might be differentially sensitive to different sides of the issue, tending to pull clusters of individuals apart.

The first effect is perhaps not very common, although Abelson and Miller (1967) have demonstrated that a "boomerang" can be produced via personal insults during naturalistic persuasive discussions. The second and third effects we have already encountered, in the previous section, under the rubrics of reinforcement and issue-position effects leading to person-dominated or issue-dominated consensus. Thus a model based on p's, as in Eqs. (21)–(22), would presumably be able to predict nonzero asymptotic opinion discrepancy in the multiperson case, even in compact networks. This is merely a conjecture, since the mathematical analysis has not been carried out, but it is a most plausible expectation (and it is supported by simulation results as well). Two-person consensus, unlike two-person accommodation, preserves opinion extremity, and one would expect that different portions of a social network could support opposed consensuses in the face of tendencies toward accommodation induced by the social bridges between the portions.

A model using X's should be developed which does not use the form of Eq. (25). The burden of the present discussion is that Eq. (25), by invoking the difference $(X_j - X_i)$, produces a model where opinions are too socially relative and too prone to inexorable accommodation. General linear stochastic models (Anderson, 1964) employing a weighted average concept along a continuous response scale presumably suffer from the same difficulty, although the dilemma might be solved by dropping the weighted average restriction.

B.   Social Influence on Decisions, Choices, or Actions

There is a great variety of models dealing with repeated actions in a structured social context. Most of these use the mathematics of Markov chains. Certain response "states" are specified, along with presumably stable conditional probabilities that after one time unit each state will follow each of the others. If the state of the system depends probabilistically only on the preceding state, and not on the more remote history, then the chain of response states is said to be Markovian, and all the probabilistic properties of the system are mathematically specifiable (cf. Kemeny and Snell, 1960). Much flexibility is available in the definition of response states. We give several examples, each treated briefly, in the sections to follow.

1. A Voting Model

A French mathematician (Kreweras, 1963, 1965) has developed the following hypothetical but suggestive model of indirect social influence in repetitive voting situations. Suppose that each of v voters must choose to vote for one out of w candidates. There are two classes of voters: r people who are *resolute* and s people who are *floating* (with $r + s = v$). The resolute voters divide their preferences among candidates 1 through w according to the vote division $(r_1, r_2, \ldots, r_w)$, and no matter how many ballots occur, these tallies for the respective candidates remain firm (as in many presidential nominating conventions). The floating voters, on the other hand, are impressionable and without loyalty, each independently basing his vote only on certain characteristics of the result of the preceding ballot. (Prior to the first ballot, we may imagine a prediction of the vote division serving as the influence stimulus for the floating voters.) Suppose the total tallies for the respective candidates on a given ballot were given by the vector $\mathbf{J} = (v_1, v_2, \ldots, v_w)$. Each floating voter examines this result and determines his choice for the new ballot probabilistically in accordance with the manifest popularity of the candidates; that is, he chooses candidate i with probability v_i/v.

All floating voters are thus equivalent probability mechanisms, and the distribution of the frequencies of their actual votes among the candidates follows a multinomial form. Denote with the vector of random variables $(s_1', s_2', \ldots, s_w')$ the numbers of floating votes for each candidate on the new ballot and with the vector $\mathbf{K} = (v'_1, v'_2, \ldots, v'_w)$ the *total* numbers of votes for the candidates on the new ballot. (The primes are used to signify new ballot quantities as distinct from the previous ballot quantities.) By definition, each $v'_i = s'_i + r_i$, and the probabilistic dependence of the new vote vector $\mathbf{K}$ on the previous vector $\mathbf{J}$ is entirely specified by the multinomial behavior of the floating voters. It is straightforward to show that the probability of vote configuration $\mathbf{K}$ conditional on prior vote configuration $\mathbf{J}$ is

$$P\{\mathbf{K} \mid \mathbf{J}\} = \frac{s!}{v^s} \cdot \prod_{i=1}^{w} \frac{v_i^{(v'_i - r_i)}}{(v'_i - r_i)!} \, . \tag{27}$$

Since s, v, and the numbers $(r_1, r_2, \ldots, r_w)$ of resolute partisans for each candidate are fixed quantities, the probabilities $P\{\mathbf{K} \mid \mathbf{J}\}$ depend only on the vectors $\mathbf{J} = (v_1, v_2, \ldots, v_w)$ and $\mathbf{K} = (v_1', v_2', \ldots, v_w')$. If the *states of the system* are defined by vectors of vote configurations, then each $P\{\mathbf{K} \mid \mathbf{J}\}$ represents a transition probability from one particular state to another. All such quantities being specified [by Eq. (27)], the system is a Markov chain, and all relevant (probabilistic) questions about it can (in principle) be answered.

In particular, we might want to derive the average number of ballots it would take for some candidate to obtain, for example, a two-thirds majority, or the probability that the candidate with the fewest resolute voters would eventually win.

Among the several results worked out by Kreweras (1963), the most interesting is a theorem that at equilibrium (that is, in the very long run) the expected proportion of votes received by each candidate will equal the relative proportion of resolute voters he controls. This result obtains even if the number of resolute voters is a very small fraction of the whole, although in that case the equilibrium distribution would be approached relatively slowly. In the context of our discussion of the previous section, this result is an interesting exemplification of stable opinion discrepancy. Again, a model based on individual response *probability* is capable of generating a group accommodation that does not dissolve into total unanimity.

Whether there exist real voting data approximately explained by the Kreweras model has not systematically been investigated. For a Markovian model of changes in individual voting *intentions* rather than in group voting behavior, the reader is referred to a classic paper by Anderson (1954). The data analyzed therein suggest that for the mass public vis-à-vis the major parties, there are different degrees of "floatingness" associated with different population strata.

2. A Leadership Preference Model

A model that brings small-group voting patterns under strict experimental control is the leadership preference model of Binder *et al.* (1965). On each experimental trial, each of three individuals votes for a leader to make a decision on behalf of the group. Each decision entails the prediction of event A versus event B, the sequence of A's and B's being under the control of the experimenter.

Unbeknown to the participants, the experimenter deliberately reinforces the decisions of the three members differentially to study the effects on subsequent voting patterns. In an especially sharp variation, which Binder *et al.* (1965, 1966) denote the 951 condition, one member (determined randomly) is declared correct on a random .9 of the decisions he (Mr. 9) makes when leader, another member (Mr. 5) on .5 of *his* decisions, and the third (Mr. 1) on a mere .1. Presumably the group interprets these success differentials as indicative of meaningful differences in individual skill or intuition in the prediction task. Since they are presumably motivated to maximize group success, the members alter their leadership choices accordingly.

The mathematical model consists of a specification of a reasonably simple pattern of vote alterations. (The model is couched in terms of "conditioning of stimulus elements," as in learning theory models, but it need not have been. We paraphrase without this terminology.) There are two event configurations that suggest a change in an individual's choice: (1) when a leader for whom he voted makes an incorrect decision, and (2) when a leader for whom he failed to vote makes a correct decision. Some probability c of vote change is assumed to characterize these two cases for all individuals. The contrasting event configurations are assumed to induce no tendency toward vote alteration. Additionally, when the individual himself has been the leader it is assumed that his vote tendency (for one of the other two individuals, self-votes being forbidden) remains unaltered. Group voting shifts from trial to trial can then be analyzed as a Markov chain, with a single parameter c to be estimated from the data.

Since each member could vote for either of the other two members, the number of possible vote patterns is 2^3. Each pattern is treated as a "state." The 8×8 matrix of transition probabilities between states can readily be written down from the assumptions of the model, as exemplified in Table II for the 951 condition. (The general case with probabilities π_1, π_2, π_3 of respective reinforcement can, of course, also be written.) In the table, the respective group members are identified by integers denoting their reinforcement probabilities, and the pattern of votes by a listing of the votes of Mr. 9, Mr. 5 and Mr. 1 in that order. Thus the state denoted

599 signifies that Mr. 9 voted for Mr. 5 and the other two members for Mr. 9. This is one of the two patterns resulting in the election of Mr. 9. (The tie votes resulting from states 519 and 195 were procedurally resolved by a random choice of leader on those particular trials.)

TABLE II
TRANSITION PROBABILITIES BETWEEN STATES OF A LEADERSHIP PREFERENCE MODEL[a]

To From	599	199	595	515	119	115	519	195
599	$.9 + .1t$	0	$.1s$	$.1r$	0	0	$.1s$	0
199	0	$.9 + .1t$	0	0	$.1s$	$.1r$	0	$.1s$
595	$.5s$	$.5r$	$.5 + .5t$	0	0	0	0	$.5s$
515	0	0	0	$.5 + .5t$	$.5r$	$.5s$	$.5s$	0
119	$.9r$	$.9s$	0	0	$.1 + .9t$	0	$.9s$	0
115	0	0	$.9r$	$.9s$	0	$.1 + .9t$	0	$.9s$
519	$.6c$	0	0	$.2c$	$.2c$	0	$(1 - c)$	0
195	0	$.6c$	$.2c$	0	0	$.2c$	0	$(1 - c)$

[a]For compactness, the following abbreviations are used: $r = c^2$; $s = c(1 - c)$; $t = (1 - c)^2$.

We sketch the reasoning for the transition probability between state 599 and state 595. Other entries in Table II are derived similarly. In state 599, Mr. 9 was elected leader. With probability .1, his task decision was incorrect. With probability $(1 - c)$, Mr. 5 does not change his preference and votes for Mr. 9 again anyway. Independently, Mr. 1 with probability c changes his preference and votes for Mr. 5 (the only other available candidate, since he cannot vote for himself). Meanwhile, Mr. 9's vote (for Mr. 5) by assumption must remain unaltered. Multiplying the three independent probabilities, the net probability that the new state 595 will appear is $.1(1 - c)c$.

Obviously the assumptions of the model are quite simple, seemingly oversimple. Yet Binder et al. (1965) proceeded optimistically to try to predict the data from many three-man groups, each run for 600 trials, with these Markov chains. The asymptotic proportions of leadership trials for each member were predicted rather well by the model. For example, in the 951 condition, the predicted proportions of times elected were .762, .153, and .085 for the three respective members, while the corresponding experimental results, averaged over 80 trials and 5 groups, were .702, .220, and .078. (The mathematical procedure for generating the asymptotic prediction in brief is as follows. First, the parameter c is estimated from the data, this example having yielded $\hat{c} = .405$. Then the first eigenvector of the matrix of Table II is calculated, giving the equilibrium probabilities of finding the system in each of the eight states. The probabilities of election are then found by appropriate grouping of these probabilities.)

In other respects, however, the model did not fit the data especially well. The chief discrepancy concerned the experimental subjects' common tendency to change votes when there was no "reason" to do so according to the model. There were, as a consequence, more frequent switches of leadership and slower approaches to asymptotic preference levels than the Markov model predicted. The authors comment (Binder *et al.*, 1966, p. 135), "Although the zero assumption [for certain transition probabilities] seems to be a reasonable first approximation, it obviously ignores such factors as gambler's fallacy, the operation of strategies, a personal desire to be leader, and idiosyncratic reactions to frustration."

Detailed analyses of deviations from a deliberately simple mathematical model can often be revealing, the model playing the role of a baseline hypothesis. In this particular case, the base-line model postulates simple reinforcement as the sole explicator of leadership preferences, but it is clear that further explanatory principles are necessary. Incidentally, it seems to be a characteristic of stochastic learning models that they generally make good predictions of *asymptotic proportions* of repetitive human guesses or choices, but that they fail to reproduce *sequential patterns* very well. Human subjects placed in repetitive problem-solving situations are prone to formulate and test elaborate hypotheses concerning the sequential properties of the extrinsic solution (cf. Feldman, 1963). Learning models do not provide for such "hypothesis-testing," and it is extraordinarily difficult to formulate a reasonably simple mathematical model that would do so.

In the Suppes and Atkinson (1960) "game-learning" models, two participants undertake a series of interactive trials in which rewards are contingent upon their joint responses according to a probabilistic reinforcement schedule. Here, as with the Binder *et al.* situation, the models yield a mixture of predictive success and failure. It would appear that the experimental device of using an extended series of trials for purposes of obtaining statistically stable data suffers from the defect that subjects are apt to respond to unintended strategic or even superstitious aspects of the repetition per se. This is always a source of confusion, even in explicit "games of social strategy," such as the "Prisoners' Dilemma" (cf. Rapoport and Chammah, 1965).

3. Conformity in the Asch Situation

The well-known Asch situation (Asch, 1956) invokes the social pressure of group consensus on false perceptual judgments. Here, repeated trials are feasible without entailing gamelike strategic considerations, since the experimental instructions ordinarily dwell entirely on the perceptual aspect of the task.

Cohen (1963) attempted to devise a Markov chain model for successive responses in a modified Asch situation. On each trial, the same physical set of three comparison lines (made to seem new by positioning and labeling differences) was presented alongside a standard line, and the subject was to pick the comparison line matching the standard. A group of confederates, supposedly under the same instructions as the subject, successively and unanimously announced in favor of an incorrect answer prior to the subject's turn on each trial.

The two relevant response possibilities are the conforming response and the correct response. A Markov model with two states corresponding to these two responses turns out to be inadequate to describe experimental sequences of responses, however. Instead, Cohen (1963) postulated a Markov model with four *latent* states, defined as follows: S_1 ("rejection of the group"), wherein the subject responds correctly on the given trial and on every subsequent trial; S_2 ("leaning away from the group"), where he responds correctly on the given trial and may or may not respond correctly on subsequent trials; S_3 ("leaning toward the group"), wherein he responds incorrectly on the given trial and may or may not respond incorrectly on subsequent trials; S_4 ("complete acceptance of the group"), wherein he responds incorrectly on the given trial and all subsequent trials. States S_1 and S_4 are "absorbing states" (that is, once entered they are never left), whereas states S_2 and S_3 represent "transient states." A subject may spend a greater or lesser number of trials "in conflict" (that is, in either of the two transient states) before finally becoming committed either to complete rejection or complete acceptance of the group. The model is similar to Bower's (1959) model of "vicarious trial and error" at the choice point of a T-maze, and to Audley's (1960) model of decision making. All three models postulate psychological states that prepare or orient toward a final commitment or choice, but allow for vacillation between orienting states. Many variants of this type of model are possible.

Figure 5 displays the four states of Cohen's model with the general transition probabilities he postulated between them. His most general case involves four parameters: α, the probability that an individual leaning away from the group will on the next trial completely reject the group; β, the pro-

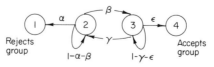

FIG. 5. States and parameters for Cohen's (1963) model.

bability that he will change his leanings toward the group; γ, the probability that an individual leaning toward the group will on the next trial lean away from the group; ε, the probability that he will completely accept the group. These parameters were assumed to apply to all individuals and to remain constant from trial to trial. All individuals were assumed to start in state S_2, leaning toward the correct judgment (away from the group).

Cohen ran 30 experimental subjects in an "extreme discrepancy" condition, with the group consensus extremely at variance with the available perceptual cues, and 36 subjects in a "moderate discrepancy" condition, in which the false consensus was slightly less perceptually remarkable. Data for the two conditions were analyzed independently. The four-parameter model embodies considerable estimation difficulties and Cohen tried a combination of special assumptions and trial-and-error procedures. (In Markov models with directly observable states, the estimation of transition probabilities is quite straightforward. With latent-state models this is, in general, not the case.) A one-parameter model with $\alpha = \beta = \gamma = \varepsilon$ enabled satisfactory estimation, but did not fit the observed data very well. Nor did a two-parameter model. However, a three-parameter model was strikingly successful. Using the values $\alpha = .130, \beta = \gamma = .390,$ and $\varepsilon = .015,$ the following characteristics of the extreme condition data were well reproduced: the curve of mean number of "errors" per trial; the proportion of subjects giving their last error response prior to trials 10, 20, or 30; the frequency distribution of total number of errors per subject; the mean number of alternations per subject between conforming and nonconforming sequences; and the frequency distribution of run lengths of same-response sequences. For the moderate condition, the three-parameter model with the apparently best values $\alpha = .050, \beta = \gamma = .117,$ and $\varepsilon = .032$ yielded an adequate reconstruction of quantities involving summary error counts, but ran into difficulties with the sequential properties of the data (a common complaint, as we have seen). Cohen accounted for at least some of these difficulties in terms of experimental artifacts coming into play whenever the orientation of the comparison stimuli was shifted.

In a very impressive retrospective analysis, Cohen (1963, Chapter 8) applied the best parameter values for moderate and extreme conditions from his own data to the data that had earlier been gathered by Asch using different subjects and a slightly different procedure, including interspersed moderate and extreme trials. Simulated data were generated via appropriate random number selections (the so-called Monte Carlo method) and compared with the actual data, with fits on a number of characteristics that were very good.

It would be desirable for Cohen-type models to be applied in other related situations, so that we might develop more of a feeling for the applicability of the model and the psychological meaning of the parameters.

4. A Model of "Speaker Switching"

The most ubiquitous form of human social interaction, conversation, is one of the most difficult phenomena to characterize in terms amenable to quantitative treatment. It might be supposed that Bales' well-known scheme (Bales, 1951) of classification of utterances into twelve qualitative categories would have spawned some mathematical model characterizing the occurrence of particular sequences of categories. This has, to the writer's knowledge, never been done. However, if the classification of utterance is carried to the crudest level, simple presence or absence, then several mathematical treatments are available. Even though these treatments omit the heart of conversation, they are not entirely without psychological interest.

A single speaker may be characterized as either silent or speaking (as detected by a voice-operated relay) within any given small time interval. These two states may be provisionally identified with the states of a Markov chain, and we may inquire whether the transition probabilities among states are essentially constant over time and unconditional upon the preceding states of the system. Jaffe *et al.* (1964) performed such an analysis and reached the conclusion that such a Markov chain adequately fit their speech sample.

For this analysis, 200 observations a minute were used. The rate is, of course, arbitrary, and it is instructive to inquire what mathematical consequences ensue when Markovian properties hold with an infinitesimally small observation interval. (Note that in the three Markov models reviewed earlier, observations were paced systematically by discrete trials and the question of dividing the observation interval did not arise.) This limiting case is referred to as a continuous-time Markov model. Such models, with transition *rates* between states replacing transition probabilities, form the novel core of Coleman's (1964a) suggestions for mathematical sociology. Apparently there are a number of potential applications of these models that have not yet been sufficiently explored by psychologists. In the utterance example, the continuous-time Markov model would lead to the prediction that the probability distributions of lengths of utterances and lengths of silences would both assume the form of exponential decay functions, as indeed has been found by Matarazzo *et al.* (1962) and several others. [The important mathematical topic of latency distributions in psychology has been thoroughly reviewed by McGill (1963). For an interesting application of latency distributions to the area of group problem solving, see Restle and Davis (1962).]

If the on–off characteristics of monologue are Markovian, what about the characteristics of dialogue? This is the problem addressed by Jaffe *et al.* (1966). The dominating fact of a dialogue is, of course, that the two individuals do not ordinarily speak simultaneously. Thus the utterance states of a pair of speakers cannot be reproduced by conjoining two parallel two-state Markov chains. Instead, Jaffe *et al.* postulated a Markov chain with four dyadic states: both parties silent; one vocalizing; the other vocalizing; or both vocalizing. The observation rate was again 200 per minute, and a 4×4 matrix of transition probabilities was established for each of several speaker pairs. These matrices give quantitative estimates of the transience of the socially unstable "simultaneous" state, as well as of the relative domin-ance of the two speakers in seizing the available conversational time. The authors also used the second-order transition probabilities [that is, the pro-babilities of entering given states at time t, given the states at times $(t - 1)$ and $(t - 2)$] in the statistical test, devised by Anderson and Goodman (1957), of the adequacy of the simple first-order Markovian description. They con-cluded that the departures from the simple model, although consistently significant in large-sample tests, were not large enough to render the model substantially inaccurate.

This very simple model must undergo further substantive development in order to gain greater relevance to the general study of social interaction. Mathematically speaking, the model is probably better converted to con-tinuous time than left in its present discrete form. Conversational dominance is nevertheless an interesting phenomenon. Perhaps mathematical and empirical bridges could be constructed between the Jaffe *et al.* models and the speculations of Horvath (1965). The latter attempted to explain the observed geometric law of relative rates of participation in group discussion (Stephan, 1952; Stephan and Mishler, 1952) by an elaborate stochastic deference mechanism said to operate during moments of group silence.

An entirely different aspect of the quantitative study of human com-munication concerns "referential processes"—the choice of an appropriate word by a speaker to convey a reference, and the identification by the listener of the intended referent. Both speaker and listener are fallible, and it is a challenging problem to account for the probability of error as a function of the nature of the specific communication task. Rosenberg and Cohen (1964, 1966) have provided extensive data and a detailed model in this area.

5. A Sociometric Choice Model

The sociometric choice model of Katz and Proctor (1959) is also con-cerned with dyadic social states that are essentially continuous in time but that may be characterized at discrete intervals for convenience. A social pair is classified into one of three alternative sociometric states at any given time: mutual choice; asymmetric choice; or mutual indifference. At a later time, the same dyad may again be so classified. With a large number of dyads, the proportions may be tabulated of pairs remaining in the same state or changing to another state over the time interval. The 3×3 matrix of proportions may provisionally be treated as an estimate of the matrix of transition probabilities for a three-state Markov chain. (We may note that the present model develops only three states from dyadic responses, rather than four states, as in the utterance model, because direction is ignored in the asymmetric choice state. There seems to be no intrinsic reason why one form should be preferred to the other, except that in the four-state model it is necessary to distinguish the two individuals in some uniform way if it is desired to pool over different individuals.)

Katz and Proctor (1959) analyzed the transitions between these three states for 105 junior high school dyads over two 4-month intervals. (Actually only 15 individuals were involved, but the pairs among them were analyzed as though independent of each other. The extent to which the empirical lack of independence perturbs the mathematical analysis is not known, but the effect is probably slight.) The Anderson and Goodman (1957) tests were applied to determine whether the transition probabilities over the second 4-month interval could be regarded as independent of the earlier history of dyadic states and as equal to the transition probabilities over the first 4-month interval. These Markovian assumptions were statistically acceptable. Table III displays the final pooled estimates of transition probabilities between states for this one sample.

TABLE III

TRANSITION PROBABILITIES BETWEEN STATES OF A SOCIOMETRIC CHOICE MODEL

To From	Mutual	Asymmetric	Indifferent
Mutual	.414	.345	.241
Asymmetric	.130	.337	.533
Indifferent	.013	.102	.885

The implications of this Markovian model for sociometric choice are somewhat surprising if the model is taken literally. Independence from remote history, for example, implies that the distribution of latencies with which broken friendships are remade is the same as the distribution of latencies with which new friendships are formed from initially indifferent partners. Perhaps an even more startling thought is that, according to the model, *every* dyad will eventually go through all states: indifference, asymmetric, and mutual choice, although it may take considerable time for this to occur. Using the parameters in Table III, for example, it can be shown that on the average it would take thirty 4-month intervals, or over 10 years, for an asymmetric choice to become mutual. Perhaps the literal model is not so surprising after all, applied over short time intervals.

The Katz and Proctor study was intended to be primarily illustrative and any serious future effort along these lines would want to use shorter time intervals and perhaps a continuous-time model. Additionally, such a model would gain psychological interest if the transition rates between states could be rationalized in terms of the rates of molecular probabilistic events, such as positive or negative interactive experiences; cf. Rainio's (1966) model, discussed in Section III, A, 2. In any serious study of this kind, attention would have to be paid to any slight unreliability in the socio-metric measurements. The potential confusion between "real transitions" and "apparent transitions" between states resulting from errors of measurement is a serious problem for a number of stochastic models, especially those involving field data. Coleman (1964b) has devoted a great deal of attention to this matter.

An extension of the Katz and Proctor type of model to sociometric *triads* would be quite interesting, since it would have direct relevance to Davis's clusterability principle (Section II, B, 2). According to that principle, triads with three positive links or with one positive link are socially preferred to those with two positive links. In dynamic terms, this presumably means that there are high transition probabilities out of the two-link state to the three-link and one-link states, but low transition probabilities into the two-link state. A full matrix of such probabilities could be estimated from long-itudinal data. (The problem of nonindependence of observations would, however, be sticky, since each sociometric link enters in many triangles.) The Markovian properties of the system could be tested and, if satisfactory, would lead to a rigorous characterization of the equilibrium degree of clusterability. If, furthermore, the larger-scale properties of networks were often predictable from triangle properties, as speculated in Section II, C, 3, a Markovian characterization of triangle properties might prove very powerful indeed. Copious data are, of course, necessary for testing these notions. Indeed, the general progress of mathematical models in social psychology is very much dependent upon the persistent and careful pursuit of interesting empirical results.

REFERENCES

Abelson, R. P. (1963). A 'derivation' of Richardson's equations. *J. Conflict Resolut*. **7**, 13–15.
Abelson, R. P. (1964). Mathematical models of the distribution of attitudes under controversy. In N. Frederiksen and H. Gulliksen (Eds.), *Contributions to mathematical psychology*. New York: Holt, Rinehart & Winston, pp. 141–160.
Abelson, R. P. (1967). Simulation of social behavior. In G. Lindzey and E. Aronson (Eds.), *Handbook of social psychology*. Cambridge, Massachusetts: Addison-Wesley, in press.

Abelson, R. P., and Bernstein, A. (1963). A computer simulation model of community referendum controversies. *Publ. Opin. Quart.* **27**, 93–122.

Abelson, R. P., and Miller, J. C. (1967). Negative persuasion via personal insult. *J. exp. soc. Psychol.*, in press.

Abelson, R. P., and Rosenberg, M. J. (1958). Symbolic psycho-logic: a model of attitudinal cognition. *Behav. Sci.* **3**, 1–13.

Abelson, R. P., and Tukey, J. W. (1963). Efficient utilization of non-numerical information in quantitative analysis: general theory and the case of simple order. *Ann. Math. Statist.* **34**, 1347–1369.

Adams, E. W., and Fagot, R. F. (1959). A model of riskless choice. *Behav. Sci.* **4**, 1–10.

Anderson, N. H. (1964). Linear models for responses measured on a continuous scale. *J. math. Psychol.* **1**, 121–142.

Anderson, N. H., and Hovland, C. I. (1957). The representation of order effects in communication research. In C. I. Hovland (Ed.), *The order of presentation in persuasion*. New Haven, Connecticut: Yale Univ. Press, pp. 158–169.

Anderson, T. W. (1954). Probability models for analyzing time changes in attitudes. In P. Lazarsfeld (Ed.), *Mathematical thinking in the social sciences*. New York: Macmillan (Free Press), pp. 17–66.

Anderson, T. W., and Goodman, L. A. (1957). Statistical inference about Markov chains. *Ann. Math. Statist.* **28**, 89–100.

Asch, S. E. (1956). Studies of independence and submission to group pressure: I. A minority of one against a unanimous majority. *Psychol. Monogr.* **70**.

Audley, R. J. (1960). A stochastic model for individual choice behavior. *Psychol. Rev.* **67**, 1–15.

Bales, R. F. (1951). *Interaction process analysis*. Cambridge, Massachusetts: Addison-Wesley.

Berger, J., Cohen, B. P., Snell, J. L., and Zelditch, M., Jr. (1962). *Types of formalization in small group research*. Boston: Houghton Mifflin.

Binder, A., Wolin, B. R., and Terebinski, S. J. (1965). Leadership in small groups: a mathematical approach. *J. exp. Psychol.* **69**, 126–134.

Binder, A., Wolin, B. R., and Terebinski, S. J. (1966). Learning and extinction of leadership preferences in small groups. *J. math. Psychol.* **3**, 129–139.

Bower, G. H. (1959). Choice-point behavior. In R. R. Bush and W. K. Estes (Eds.), *Studies in mathematical learning theory*. Stanford, California: Stanford Univ. Press, pp. 109–124.

Burke, C. J. (1959). Applications of a linear model to two-person interactions. In R. R. Bush and W. K. Estes (Eds.), *Studies in mathematical learning theory*. Stanford, California: Stanford Univ. Press, pp. 180–203.

Bush, R. R. (1962). The application of learning models to interactive behavior. In J. Criswell, H. Solomon, and P. Suppes (Eds.), *Mathematical methods in small group processes*. Stanford, California: Stanford Univ. Press, pp. 69–73.

Bush, R. R., and Mosteller, F. (1955). *Stochastic models for learning*. New York: Wiley.

Campbell, D. T., and Stanley, J. C. (1963). Experimental and quasi-experimental designs for research on teaching. In N. L. Gage (Ed.), *Handbook of research on teaching*. Chicago: Rand McNally, pp. 171–246.

Campbell, D. T., Kruskal, W. H., and Wallace, W. P. (1966). Seating aggregation as an index of attitude. *Sociometry* **29**, 1–15.

Campbell, N. R. (1928). *Measurement and calculation*. New York: Longmans, Green.

Cartwright, D., and Gleason, T. C. (1966). The number of paths and cycles in a digraph. *Psychometrika* **31**, 179–199.

Cartwright, D., and Harary, F. (1956). Structural balance: a generalization of Heider's theory. *Psychol. Rev.* **62**, 277–293.

Cervin, V. B., and Henderson, G. P. (1961). Statistical theory of persuasion. *Psychol. Rev.* **68**, 157–166.

Cohen, B. P. (1963). *Conflict and conformity.* Cambridge, Massachusetts: M.I.T. Press.

Coleman, J. S. (1957). *Community conflict.* New York: Macmillan (Free Press).

Coleman, J. S. (1959). The mathematical study of small groups. In H. Solomon (Ed.), *Mathematical thinking in the measurement of behavior.* New York: Macmillan (Free Press), pp. 1–149.

Coleman, J. S. (1964a). *Introduction to mathematical sociology.* New York: Macmillan (Free Press).

Coleman, J. S. (1964b). *Models of change and response uncertainty.* Englewood Cliffs, New Jersey: Prentice-Hall.

Coleman, J. S. (1965). The use of electronic computers in the study of social organizations. *European J. Sociol.* **6,** 89–107.

Coleman, J. S. (1967). The mathematical study of change. (Unpublished manuscript.)

Coleman, J. S., and James, J. (1961). The equilibrium size distribution of freely-forming groups. *Sociometry* **24,** 1–12.

Davis, J. A. (1967a). Clustering and structural balance in graphs. *Hum. Relat.,* in press.

Davis, J. A. (1967b). Coefficients to describe the degree of clusterability in a graph. (Unpublished manuscript.)

DeSoto, C. B., Henley, N. M., and London, M. (1967). Balance and the grouping schema. *J. Pers. soc. Psychol.,* in press.

Estes, W. K. (1950). Toward a statistical theory of learning. *Psychol. Rev.* **57,** 94–107.

Feldman, J. (1963). Simulation of behavior in the binary choice experiment. In E. Feigenbaum and J. Feldman (Eds.), *Computers and thought.* New York: McGraw-Hill, pp. 329–346.

Festinger, L. (1949). The analysis of sociograms using matrix algebra. *Hum. Relat.* **2,** 153–158.

Festinger, L., Schachter, S., and Back, K. W. (1950). *Social pressures in informal groups.* New York: Harper and Row.

Flament, C. (1963). *Applications of graph theory to group structure.* Englewood Cliffs, New Jersey: Prentice-Hall.

Foster, C. C., Rapoport, A., and Orwant, C. J. (1963). A study of a large sociogram II. Elimination of free parameters. *Behav. Sci.* **8,** 56–65.

Fouraker, L. E., and Siegel, S. (1963). *Bargaining behavior.* New York: McGraw-Hill.

Glanzer, M., and Glaser, R. (1959). Techniques for the study of group structure and behavior I: Analysis of structure. *Psychol. Bull.* **56,** 317–332.

Glanzer, M., and Glaser, R. (1961). Techniques for the study of group structure and behavior II. Empirical studies of the effects of structure in small groups. *Psychol. Bull.* **58,** 1–27.

Goode, F. M. (1964). An algorithm for the additive conjoint measurement of finite data matrices. *Amer. Psychol.* **19,** 579.

Guttman, L. (1967). A general nonmetric technique for finding the smallest Euclidean space for a configuration of points. *Psychometrika,* in press.

Hägerstrand, T. (1965). On Monte Carlo simulation of diffusion. *European J. Sociol.* **6,** 43–67.

Harary, F. (1954). On the notion of balance of a signed graph. *Michigan Math. J.* **2,** 143–146.

Harary, F. (1959a). A criterion for unanimity in French's theory of social power. In D. Cartwright (Ed.), *Studies in social power.* Ann Arbor, Michigan: Inst. soc. Res., pp. 168–182.

Harary, F. (1959b). Status and contrastatus. *Sociometry* **22,** 23–43.

Harary, F. (1959c). On the measurement of structural balance. *Behav. Sci.* **4,** 316–323.

Harary, F. (1961). A structural analysis of the situation in the Middle East in 1956. *J. Conflict Resolut.* **5,** 167–178.

Harary, F., Norman, R. Z., and Cartwright, D. (1965). *Structural models: an introduction to the theory of directed graphs.* New York: Wiley.

Heider, F. (1946). Attitudes and cognitive organization. *J. Psychol.* **21,** 107–112.

Heider, F. (1958). *The psychology of interpersonal relations.* New York: Wiley.

Horvath, W. J. (1965). A mathematical model of participation in small group discussions. *Behav. Sci.* **10,** 164–166.

Hubbell, C. H. (1965). An input-output approach to clique identification. *Sociometry* **28**, 377–399.

Jaffe, J., Cassotta, L., and Feldstein, S. (1964). Markovian model of time patterns of speech. *Science* **144**, 884–886.

Jaffe, J., Feldstein, S., and Cassotta, L. (1966). A stochastic model of speaker switching in natural dialogue. (Unpublished manuscript.)

Katz, L. (1953). A new status index derived from sociometric analysis. *Psychometrika* **18**, 39–43.

Katz, L., and Powell, J. H. (1955). Measurement of the tendency toward reciprocation of choice. *Sociometry* **18**, 659–665.

Katz, L., and Proctor, C. H. (1959). The concept of configuration of interpersonal relations in a group as a time-dependent stochastic process. *Psychometrika* **24**, 317–327.

Kemeny, J. G., and Snell, J. L. (1960). *Finite Markov chains*. Princeton, New Jersey: Van Nostrand.

Kemeny, J. G., and Snell, J. L. (1962). *Mathematical models in the social sciences*. Boston: Ginn.

Kendall, M. G. (1955). Further contributions to the theory of paired comparisons. *Biometrics* **2**, 43–62.

Krantz, D. H. (1964). Conjoint measurement: the Luce-Tukey axiomatization and some extensions. *J. math. Psychol.* **1**, 248–277.

Kreweras, G. (1963). Un modèle d'évolution de l'opinion exprimées par les votes successifs. *Publ. Inst. Statist. Univ. Paris* **12**.

Kreweras, G. (1965). Model to weight individual authority in a group. In S. Sternberg *et al.* (Eds.), *Mathematics and social sciences*. The Hague: Mouton, pp. 111–120.

Kruskal, J. B. (1965). Analysis of factorial experiments by estimating transformations of the data. *J. roy. Statist. Soc. Ser. B.* **27**, 251–263.

Luce, R. D. (1966). Two extensions of conjoint measurement. *J. math. Psychol.* **3**, 348–370.

Luce, R. D., and Perry, A. D. (1949). A method of matrix analysis of group structure. *Psychometrika* **14**, 95–116.

Luce, R. D., and Suppes, P. (1965). Preference, utility and subjective probability. In R. D. Luce, R. R. Bush, and E. Galanter (Eds.), *Handbook of mathematical psychology*. New York: Wiley, Vol. 3, pp. 249–410

Luce, R. D., and Tukey, J. W. (1964). Simultaneous conjoint measurement: a new type of fundamental measurement, *J. math. Psychol.* **1**, 1–27.

Luce, R. D., Macy, J., and Tagiuri, R. (1955). A statistical model for relational analysis. *Psychometrika* **20**, 319–327.

Luce, R. D., Bush, R. R., and Galanter, E. (Eds.) (1963). *Handbook of mathematical psychology*. New York: Wiley. 3 vols.

McGill, W. J. (1963). Stochastic latency mechanisms. In R. D. Luce, R. R. Bush, and E. Galanter (Eds.), *Handbook of mathematical psychology*. New York: Wiley, Vol. 1, pp. 309–360.

McPhee, W. N. (1961). Note on a campaign simulator. *Publ. Opin. Quart.* **25**, 184–193.

McPhee, W. N. (1963). *Formal theories of mass behavior*. New York: Macmillan (Free Press).

McPhee, W. N. (1966). When culture becomes a business. In J. Berger, M. Zelditch, Jr., and B. Anderson (Eds.), *Sociological theories in progress*. Boston: Houghton Mifflin, pp. 227–243.

McRae, D., Jr. (1960). Direct factor analysis of sociometric data. *Sociometry* **23**, 360–371.

Matarazzo, J. D., Hess, H., and Saslow, G. (1962). Frequency and duration characteristics of speech and silence behavior during interviews. *J. clin. Psychol.* **18**, 416–428.

Miller, G. A. (1964). *Mathematics and psychology*. New York: Wiley.

Mitra, S. (1962). Letter to the Editors. *Behav. Sci.* **7**, 107.

Mosteller, F., and Tukey, J. W. (1967). Data analysis, including statistics. In G. Lindzey and E. Aronson (Eds.), *Handbook of social psychology*. Cambridge, Massachusetts: Addison-Wesley, in press.

Newcomb, T. M. (1961). *The acquaintance process.* New York: Holt, Rinehart & Winston.

Rainio, K. (1962). *A stochastic theory of social contacts: a laboratory study and an application to sociometry* (*Trans. Westermarck Soc.* **8**). Copenhagen: Munksgaard.

Rainio, K. (1965). Social interaction as a stochastic learning process. *European J. Sociol.* **6**, 68–88.

Rainio, K. (1966). A study on sociometric group structure: an application of a stochastic theory of social interaction. In J. Berger, M. Zelditch, Jr., and B. Anderson (Eds.), *Sociological theories in progress.* Boston: Houghton Mifflin, pp. 102–123.

Rapoport, A. (1951). Nets with distance bias. *Bull. math. Biophysics* **13**, 85–91.

Rapoport, A. (1963). Mathematical models of social interaction. In R. D. Luce, R. R. Bush, and E. Galanter (Eds.), *Handbook of mathematical psychology.* New York: Wiley, Vol. 2, pp. 493–580.

Rapoport, A., and Chammah, A. (1965). *Prisoners' dilemma.* Ann Arbor, Michigan: Univ. of Michigan Press.

Rapoport, A., and Horvath, W. J. (1961). A study of a large sociogram. *Behav. Sci.* **6**, 279–291.

Restle, F., and Davis, J. H. (1962). Success and speed of problem solving by individuals and groups. *Psychol. Rev.* **69**, 520–536.

Richardson, L. F. (1960). *Arms and insecurity.* Pittsburgh: Boxwood Press.

Rosenberg, S. (1962). Two-person interactions in a continuous-response task. In J. Criswell, H. Solomon, and P. Suppes (Eds.), *Mathematical methods in small group processes.* Stanford, California: Stanford Univ. Press, pp. 282–304.

Rosenberg, S. (1963). Influence and reward in structured two-person interactions. *J. abnorm. soc. Psychol.* **67**, 379–387.

Rosenberg, S. (1967). Mathematical models of social behavior. In G. Lindzey and E. Aronson (Eds.), *Handbook of social psychology.* Cambridge, Massachusetts: Addison-Wesley, in press.

Rosenberg, S., and Cohen, B. D. (1964). Speakers' and listeners' processes in a word-communication task. *Science* **145**, 1201–1203.

Rosenberg, S., and Cohen, B. D. (1966). Referential processes of speakers and listeners. *Psychol. Rev.* **73**, 208–231.

Rosenberg, S., and Schoeffler, M. S. (1965). Stochastic learning models for social competition. *J. math. Psychol.* **2**, 219–241.

Roskies, R. (1965). A measurement axiomatization for an essentially multiplicative representation of two factors. *J. math. Psychol.* **2**, 266–276.

Ross, I. C., and Harary, F. (1959). A description of strengthening and weakening members of a group. *Sociometry* **22**, 139–147.

Sabidussi, G. (1966). The centrality index of a graph. *Psychometrika* **4**, 581–604.

Shaw, M. E. (1964). Communication networks. *Advanc. exp. soc. Psychol.* **1**, 111–147.

Shepard, R. N., and Carroll, J. D. (1966). Parametric representation of nonlinear data structures. In P. R. Krishnaiah (Ed.), *Symposium on multivariate analysis.* New York: Academic Press, pp. 561–592.

Siegel, S., and Fouraker, L. E. (1960). *Bargaining and group decision making.* New York: McGraw-Hill.

Simon, H. A. (1957). *Models of man.* New York: Wiley.

Simon, H. A., and Guetzkow, H. (1955). A model of short- and long-run mechanisms involved in pressures toward uniformity in groups. *Psychol. Rev.* **62**, 56–58.

Spilerman, S. (1966). Structural analysis and the generation of sociograms. *Behav. Sci.* **11**, 312–318.

Stephan, F. (1952). The relative rate of communication between members of small groups. *Amer. sociol. Rev.* **17**, 482–486.

Stephan, F., and Mishler, E. G. (1952). The distribution of participation in small groups: an exponential approximation. *Amer. sociol. Rev.* **17**, 598–608.

Stevens, S. S. (1951). Mathematics, measurement, and psychophysics. In S. S. Stevens, (Ed.), *Handbook of experimental psychology*. New York: Wiley, pp. 1–49.

Suppes, P., and Atkinson, R. C. (1960). *Markov learning models for multiperson interactions*. Stanford, California: Stanford Univ. Press.

Suppes, P., and Schlag-Rey, M. (1962). Analysis of social conformity in terms of generalized conditioning models. In J. Criswell, H. Solomon, and P. Suppes (Eds.), *Mathematical methods in small group processes*. Stanford, California: Stanford Univ. Press, pp. 334–361.

Tversky, A. (1967). A general theory of polynomial conjoint measurement. *J. math. Psychol.* **4**, 1–20.

Tversky, A., and Zivian, A. (1966). An IBM 7090 program for additivity analysis. *Behav. Sci.* **11**, 78–79.

White, H. (1962). Chance models of systems of causal groups. *Sociometry* **25**, 153–171.

White, H. (1963). *An anatomy of kinship: mathematical models for structures of cumulative roles*. Englewood Cliffs, New Jersey: Prentice-Hall.

THE EXPERIMENTAL ANALYSIS
OF SOCIAL PERFORMANCE[1]

Michael Argyle and Adam Kendon[2]

INSTITUTE OF EXPERIMENTAL PSYCHOLOGY
OXFORD UNIVERSITY
OXFORD, ENGLAND

I. Introduction

This article deals with what people do when they openly cooperate in one another's presence to sustain some joint form of activity. Such occasions, termed by Goffman (1963) *focused interaction*, are exemplified by card games, musical performances, fist fights, cooperative tasks such as sawing down a large tree, dancing, and by conversation, interviews, lectures, and other social occasions when people talk together. Occasions of talk have, of course, been the main concern of those interested in this field, and are our main concern also.

[1]We are greatly indebted to the Department of Scientific and Industrial Research, and later to the Social Science Research Council, for giving financial support to the Oxford Social Skills Project, and to Professor Ralph Exline and Mr. Nicholas Johnson for their comments on this paper.

[2]*Present address*: Department of Psychology, Morrill Hall, Cornell University, Ithaca, New York.

We shall here suggest that it is fruitful to look upon the behavior of people engaged in focused interaction as an organized, skilled performance, analogous to skills such as car driving. First, an outline will be presented of the model that has been developed in the last fifteen years for the analysis of sensorimotor skills, but with specific reference to the interaction situation. Studies of the patterns of activity involved in interaction will then be reviewed; here we shall consider all aspects of a person's behavior that have been found to affect the other in interaction, including physical proximity, posture, orientation, language and speech, patterns of looking at the other, bodily movements, and facial expression. Where possible, we shall indicate the way these different aspects of behavior are interrelated. The final section will be concerned with the presentation of the self-image, the breakdown of the social performance, and the question of training in specific social skills.

II. Theoretical Framework

A. The Sensorimotor Skill Model and Interaction

A skill may be defined as an organized, coordinated activity, in relation to an object or a situation, that involves a chain of sensory, central, and motor mechanisms. One of its main characteristics is that the performance, or stream of action, is continuously under the control of the sensory input. This input derives in part from the object or situation at which the performance may be said to be directed, and it controls the performance in the sense that the outcomes of actions are continuously matched against some criterion of achievement or degree of approach to a goal, according to which the performance is corrected. Thus skilled performance is performance that is nicely adapted to its occasion (Bartlett, 1958; Welford, 1958).

We suggest that an individual engaged in interaction is engaged in a more or less skilled performance. His behavior here, as when he is driving a car, is directed, adaptive, and far from automatic, though it may be seen to be built of elements that are automatized. Here, too, we have an individual carrying out a series of actions that are related to consequences that he has in mind to bring about; in order to do this, he has to match his output with the input available to him and must correct his output in the light of this matching process. Thus he may be discussing current affairs with an acquaintance, and be concerned perhaps merely to sustain a pleasant flow of talk. He must be on the watch, then, for signs of emotional disturbance in his acquaintance, which might signal that he had said something that might provoke an argument. At another level, he must be on the lookout for signals that his acquaintance is ready for him to talk or for him to listen. He must make sure his tone of voice and choice of words, his gestures, and the level of involvement in what he is saying, are appropriate for the kind of occasion of the encounter (cf. Goffman, 1957).

In the treatment of human performance as developed by such workers as Welford (1958) and Crossman (1964) distinctions are drawn between the perceptual input, the central translation processes by which this input is integrated into a plan of action that is governed by the goal the individual has set for himself, and the motor output, or performance. These three stages of the process are interrelated as shown in Fig. 1.

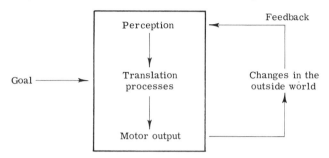

Fig. 1. The sensorimotor skill model.

1. Perception

Students of perceptual processes in human performance have stressed its selective nature, and that the aspects of the input that are selected are determined by the aim of the performer (Welford, 1958; Broadbent, 1958). It is, indeed, a mark of a highly skilled performer that he has learned what input he can ignore (Annett and Kay, 1956). Similar considerations probably apply in social interaction. Thus, as Jones and Thibaut (1958) suggested, an interactor's main requirement is for information relative to the adequate maintenance of a particular performance. They suggested that the type of cues an individual will be on the lookout for in interaction and the use he makes of these cues will vary according to his aim in the situation. A few studies that lend support to this idea have been reported: Lundy (1956) showed that a subject's conception of the person with whom he has interacted differs according to whether the subject was attending mostly to the other person or to himself; Rosenbaum (1959) demonstrated that the perception of others varies according to whether the interaction with them is co-operative or competitive; and Steiner (1955) has reviewed a number of studies which show that effectiveness in social performance is related to the accurate perception of relevant features of the situation rather than to the accuracy of perception of others in general. There is room for much more work here, however, especially on the information selected and made use of within the ongoing activity of interaction.

2. Translation Processes

When the input has been selected and interpreted, it must be put to use. Welford (1958) distinguished as *translation processes* the way in which items perceived are acted upon; *translation* is the term used to refer to the rule by which a particular signal is interpreted as requiring a particular action. A great deal of what occurs while a skill is built up consists in the development of translations which, once established, are "ready to hand," so that action taken in regard to incoming signals is usually immediate. Where a new translation has to be set up, a great deal of hesitancy and halting can be observed in the subject's performance.

Little in current studies on the social performance is concerned with the acquisition and development of translations. Yet it is clear that anyone who can interact competently must have a large repertoire of translations with which he deals with input that distinguishes one kind of encounter from another and that enables him to adapt his style of handling another person as an encounter progresses. There are also the whole set of translations that are involved in processing language and other communicative systems. A great deal of training in specific social skills consists of training people to deal with particular kinds of persons or interaction situations. Much that is involved in the acquisition of these skills consists in building up new translations or in developing already existing ones.

3. Effector Processes

Effector processes are the actions the person takes, or the performance itself. Welford (1958) noted that the effector processes are to be seen as organized on a number of levels, hierarchically arranged. He suggested that it is useful to distinguish a general orientation, or plan, which determines in broad outline what is to be done. This plan may be seen as composed of a number of general methods, or subplans, that are in turn composed of "particular knacks and dexterities which in turn bring into play detailed muscular movements" (Welford, 1958, p. 26). Thus, we may describe an activity, such as typing, at the level of general orientation, which will include how the typist will sit before her typewriter and sustain a particular posture. At the level of general methods, we divide the task as a whole into several subtasks, such as changing the sheets of paper and typing. The activity of typing may itself be further subdivided into producing a line of words and moving the carriage back at the end of each line. At the level of knacks and dexterities, we describe how the finger movements are grouped into complex units by which the phrases, words, and letter combinations within the words are put onto the paper.

The social performance can probably be analyzed in a similar way. Thus we distinguish at the level of *general orientation* how individuals may adopt a distinctive pattern of activities appropriate for, say, an interview, a cocktail party, or a stroll on the beach with a friend. At the level of *general method*, or subplans, we note that, for instance, an interview may have several phases: an opening "greeting" phase; a phase in which rapport is established; one in which the main business of the interview may be accomplished; and a terminating phase. At the level of *knacks and dexterities*, we deal with such things as sequencing of acts of communication. Below this level, we must analyze the actual muscular movements—the motor structure of utterance and movement patterns, for instance. In Section III of this article an attempt will be made to suggest how some studies of patterns of activity in interaction might be fitted into a scheme of this sort.

In considering a performance in this way, we note how it may be said to be made up of a combination of elements, though what we refer to as an element will depend on the level in the hierarchy we are discussing. Elements may often be recombined in a fairly flexible way, and this makes a skill very adaptive. On the other hand, once a particular combination of elements achieves, for the performer, an acceptable level of success, and provided the sequence of sensory input is stable when the skill is used on subsequent occasions, it is found that many sequences of actions in the performance become "automatized," that is, freed from continuous sensory control. Though we shall not give it much consideration here, it seems likely that a similar phenomenon of automatization occurs with social skills. Lecturers and interviewers, for instance, who use a fairly standard social technique on repeated occasions, may be able to run off long sequences of actions automatically. Museum guides offer a notorious example of automatization that has gone too far. Lecturers have occasionally reported on this process in themselves. Thus Lashley (1951) mentioned a colleague who reported to him that "he had reached a stage where he could arise before an audience, turn his mouth loose, and go to sleep" (p. 184).

B. The Interrelating of Performances

In any consideration of the social performance we cannot ignore the fact that it takes place within an encounter, and is thus interrelated with the performance of another individual who can take initiatives of his own and is not, like the machine, entirely dependent on the operator. Indeed, the existence of an encounter presupposes that the participants can interrelate their performances. They must do this in several ways at once. They must be able to agree as to what the encounter is about, who is dominant, who submissive; they must agree upon the level of intimacy; and there must be coordination in terms of emotionality and the patterning of actions in time. All these are aspects of what Goffman (1959) called the *working consensus* of an encounter. The following are some of the conditions that bring it about.

In some encounters, where the form is highly structured and the participants all know their "parts" in advance, the working consensus is, as it were, ready-made. This is often the case in the early stages of many encounters where stereotyped patterns of interaction are adopted. If, however, there is no ready-made formula to provide the working consensus, the participants have to work out some accomodation between themselves. Usually they proceed by edging rather cautiously forward from stereotyped patterns of response, trying out different social techniques to see how the other responds.

An important factor that sets limits upon people's ability to work out such an accomodation is the character of the individual's style of handling encounters. This factor has been investigated at several different levels. Chapple, for example, whose work is discussed later, showed how individuals differ in their styles of interaction, assessed in terms of the patterning of actions in time. For many years he has stressed that successful, stabilized relations between people will depend on their ability to bring their action patterns into an appropriate relation with one another (Chapple, 1940a,b, 1962; Chapple and Coon, 1942). At other levels of description, there are studies such as those summarized by Tharp (1963), which stress the importance of compatibility of role expectation for marital relations. Related to this is the notion of "interpersonal orientation" as developed by Schutz (1958). No studies have been made of the behavioral styles or social performance strategies manifested by people with different interpersonal orientations, but Schutz (1955) was able to show that groups vary, in their productiveness and in the degree of satisfaction they afford members, in relation to the kinds of interpersonal orientation the group members have as determined from his FIRO questionnaire, which assesses desires for affection, inclusion, and control on the part of self and others.

Breer (1960) showed that by combining measures of the personality and social characteristics of individuals in a group, a better prediction could be made of a given individual's dominance in subsequent interaction than if these characteristics of the individual were taken on their own. Carment *et al.* (1965) similarly were able to predict who in a dyad would speak more, and dominate, from a consideration of the relative extraversion and intelligence of the interactants. Studies of friendship pairs or groupings in relation to the characteristics of the individuals involved are also relevant here. Work such as that of Jennings (1950) and Northway and Wigdor (1947) has emphasized importance of compatibility in interaction; studies such as those of Triandis (1960) illustrated the limiting effect of differences in cognitive style; and Newcomb's (1961) work illustrated the importance of compatibility of values. This area has been fully reviewed by Lott and Lott (1965).

The characteristics of interaction in pairs or groups of people who have stable relationships have been described by several workers, and some studies have traced the way the patterns of interaction change with time toward a stable state (for example, Heinicke and Bales, 1953; Lennard and Bernstein, 1960). This stable state has been described by some investigators as an equilibrium. Chapple and Coon (1942) made explicit use of the idea that the pattern of interaction in a group was a stable equilibrium in the sense that anything tending to change the pattern would produce compensating changes. This idea has been taken up by Homans (1950), Simon (1952), and in a rather different form by Bales (1953). An equilibrium model has also been used by Goffman (1955). Explicit evidence for the appropriateness of this notion is, however, rather scant; Lennard and Bernstein (1960), in their longitudinal study of psychotherapeutic dyads, provided the most relevant data. They found that after 2 months of daily sessions the proportion of time occupied in speech by the therapist had become highly stable, not deviating by more that 6.5% from his average. But in comparing one session with the next it was found that if the therapist had spoken rather less than usual on one occasion, he would make up for it by talking more on the next.

An attempt at a detailed theoretical analysis of this problem was put forward by Thibaut and Kelley (1959) in terms of games theory. They posited that each interactor, A and B, has a repertoire of alternative social responses. For each combination of responses there will be rewards or costs for each interactor. A stable relationship will be formed if each gains rewards that are better than those obtainable in alternative situations or relationships that are available to him. At initial meetings the interactor will explore the situation to see if this is likely to be the case. It is generally supposed that people will select styles of behavior that offer the maximum rewards, or the minimum costs, or some combination of these.

It should be noted that during unstable periods of interaction there can be the very reverse of equilibrium, that is positive feedback cycles. If A is very nice to B, this elicits similar behavior from B, and so on. Such increasing intimacy develops until it is halted by anxiety about excessive intimacy, increased difficulties of meshing, and other demands on time: the result is an equilibrium point. Such an equilibrium point can also be looked at as the result of a balance between approach and avoidance forces, as described by Miller (1944). This idea has been explicitly developed in a study of the role of distance and eye-contact in interaction by Argyle and Dean (1965).

III. Structure of the Social Performance

In this section we shall review a selection of studies dealing with the analysis of patterns of activity in focused encounters. That is, we shall concentrate on the performance itself. Some attempt will be made to follow the descriptive model proposed by Welford (1958). Thus certain components of the performance can be distinguished, such as posture, distance, and orientation, which change little throughout a given encounter; these can perhaps be seen as functioning at the level of general orientation. They are called the *standing features* of the performance. There are, on the other hand, *dynamic features*—the utterances, movements, and patterns of looking that each participant in any focused interaction is likely to engage in. The latter activities may be ordered into a hierarchical set of units, much as was indicated earlier for typing. Where possible we shall show how this might be done.

A. STANDING FEATURES

In focused interaction participants tend to group themselves into huddles in which they make each other available to mutual visual inspection (Goffman, 1963). This positioning in space and orientation appears to be a distinctive behavioral mark of focused interaction, setting it off from other kinds of activity. Focused interactions themselves are varied in type, however, and within a given culture or subculture only a certain range of types will be found. For instance, dons at Oxford many encounter students in about five ways—at a tutorial, seminar, lecture, private consultation, or sherry. The rules of behavior differ in each of these occasions, and one way to classify them might be in terms of the different sets of rules prevailing. One dimension of a rule classification is that of formality, for example, the amount of variation of behavior permitted—compare taking Communion with a party. An example of an attempt at encounter classification from this point of view may be found in Barker and Wright (1955).

Encounters can also be classified by the motivation of those taking part. Thus we can show how people seek different sorts of satisfaction in social interaction, and that encounters may differ in type according to the satisfactions they may more readily or typically give rise to. Besides this, in encounters such as psychotherapy sessions or tutorials, the therapist or tutor may be aiming at a particular goal that is defined by his job. Watson and Potter (1962) and Jones and Thibaut (1958), in rather different ways, provided examples of classifications from this functional point of view. In each case the motivation can be looked at as a need for certain types of response on the part of others or for the establishment of certain kinds of relationship.

Such differences are partly marked by their settings and by the type of equipment present and how it is used. However, there are also differences in postures, spacings, and orientations, and in styles of behavior that vary systematically with the type of interaction and that may also indicate the type of encounter each participant takes it to be. This section presents some of the static features of the performance, which appear to function in this way.

The static aspects of the social performance have been systematically treated by Hall (1963). He distinguished seven such components: posture, orientation, the physical distance between interactants, the presence or absence of physical contact, the form physical contact takes, whether (and if so, how) the interactants are looking at one another, and whether thermal and olfactory sensory channels could be operative in the encounter. He pointed out how each of these components may form different combinations, and that different participants may employ different combinations so that the system may be highly flexible. More recently Hall (1964) attempted to show how these components may be coordinated into a system to define four different "distance sets," which he termed (following Joos, 1962) *Intimate, Casual-Personal, Social-Consultative,* and *Public*, after the type of interaction with which each is associated. Each of these distance sets is distinguishable from the others partly, at least, in terms of the different sets of senses that can operate. For example, at the Intimate distance, physical contact, olfaction, and the thermal senses all play a part, but vision plays a rather minor role. Compared with this, at the limit of the Casual-Personal distance, where interactants are about 5 feet apart, only vision and hearing are employed.

From this analysis of what the senses are capable of at different distances, we would expect, as Hall suggested, systematic differences in their use, and this would have consequences for the type of interaction that is possible. Variations in posture and orientation at different distances might also be expected. A number of interesting questions are generated by this framework, but few have been investigated yet. For instance, how invariable are the interrelations Hall has described? If there are variations, what are their consequences? Some studies dealing with some of these components follow.

1. Distance

Sommer (1959) pioneered in the experimental study of the use of distance in interaction; he found that for conversation subjects tend to choose a nose-to-nose distance of roughly 5 feet. Little (1965) approached this question perceptually. His subjects positioned either cardboard cutout silhouettes or actual people for different types of interaction in different settings. He found that Americans tend to think of friends as standing closer to one another than acquaintances or strangers, and he also found that distances tend to be less when the setting was impersonal, such as a public street, than when it was an intimate setting, such as a living room. Congruent with this, Sommer (1965) noted that chairs are placed at much greater distances in living rooms than they are when people gather together in a larger room. Presumably, merely to be present in a living room is to be in a social gathering, so proximity is not necessary to indicate that such is the case; in a public street, however, it is only through spatial positioning that people can signal, to each other and to others, the boundaries of a gathering.

Argyle and Dean (1965) investigated how visual orientation may vary with the distance separating interactors; they found that when subjects were placed only 2 feet from one another, they looked into the other's line of regard very much less than they did when they were 6 or 10 feet apart. They proposed, as does Hall, that both closer distances and increased amounts of looking at the other mark higher degrees of intimacy. Here the level of intimacy between the subjects was constant and the changes in amount of looking were seen as compensating for the changes in distance.

As will be noted later, changes of distance during an encounter have definite significance and may function to signal changes in the relationship. The movements of A when he enters B's office vary considerably with the intimacy and relative status of the two people; observers of silent films of such an occurrence had no difficulty in deducing the relations between them (Burns, 1964).

It should be borne in mind that all these studies were carried out in Anglo-American cultures. As Hall (1959, 1963) has emphasized, physical distance, as well as the other components to be dealt with, is used in rather different ways in other cultures.

Distance is also of significance among animals. Thus, in several primate species, social relationships may be indicated by distance; for instance, the position of the male langur in the dominance hierarchy in his group is reflected in the distance others in the group sit from him (Jay, 1965). Hediger (1955) showed that animals adopt distances between one another that are characteristic of their species; they also seek to maintain a certain population density, and instinctive biological mechanisms have evolved for doing this (Wynne-Edwards, 1962). Hutt and Vaizey (1966) found a similar process operating in children in an experiment in which they varied the density of children in a playroom. Whereas normal and brain-damaged children became more aggressive as the density increased, this was not the case with autistic children.

2. Orientation

Besides the distances interactors place between one another, the manner of their orientation to one another may also be important. Hall (1963) classified orientation by angle, ranging from face-to-face to back-to-back, and noted that positions from face-to-face to side-to-side are used for various kinds of interaction. Spiegel (summarized in Machotka, 1965) proposed a similar scheme. Sommer (1959) found that people who are sitting at a table for conversation frequently sit diagonally across the corner from one another rather than directly opposite or side by side. In another study Sommer (1965) found that different seating patterns are adopted by pairs of people according to the type of interaction they are engaged in. Where this interaction is unfocused, as when two students are studying together at the same table, a distance seating pattern is chosen: the interactors sit so that they are distant but not facing one another. Where the pair is cooperating on some task, such as going through a problem together, they choose the "corner" arrangement or they sit side by side (though this is much rarer). In competitive dyads Sommer found an overwhelming tendency for the people to sit directly opposite one another. To account for these findings he suggested that a major determinant of seating pattern is the way in which it facilitates or inhibits visual contact between people.

In groups larger than two there is some evidence that people tend to position themselves opposite those in the group with whom they talk most; where the seating arrangements limit the freedom of movement of the group members, this determines to some extent the communication structure of the group. Thus Steinzor (1950) observed that in a discussion group of ten, most interaction took place between those who were sitting opposite each other, and not between neighbors; similar observations were reported by Bass and Klubeck (1952). Hare and Bales (1963) found that where a group of five is arranged around three sides of a long rectangular table, those occupying the two end positions and the person in the middle of the long side interacted with each other more than they did with those at the corners of the table.

Where there are differences in role or status between the group members, this is often expressed in the pattern of positions the members take up in space. A chairman or a lecturer usually faces as many of the others as he can (Sommer, 1961). Furniture is arranged accordingly; Hazard (1962) noted, for instance, how the arrangement of furniture in a courtroom reflects the role relationships of the various functionaries. Blood and Livant (1957) observed how, within a cabin at a boys' summer camp, the beds were arranged in a way that was related to who was friends with whom, and also to who was trying to protect himself from whom.

3. Posture

Hall (1963) distinguished three types of posture: standing, sitting, and lying; but there are clearly many more possibilities. Scheflen (1964), for instance, drew attention to the way participants in focused gatherings may vary the way in which they are sitting or standing to be congruent with or noncongruent with others present—for example, by having their legs crossed or arms folded. Goffman (1961a) noted how, at the staff meetings of a psychiatric hospital, those with high status, such as the psychiatrists, would sit in relaxed postures, putting their feet on the table, whereas those junior to them would assume more formal ways of sitting. Few other authors have reported on this topic. Hewes (1955) examined the variety of typical postures in different societies, but his work has only marginal relevance to social interaction. Sarbin and Hardyck (1955) asked subjects to make judgments of stick figure drawings in various postures; they found considerable consistency in judgment, and suggested that this be used as a test of social perceptiveness. The work of Machotka and Spiegel (Machotka, 1965), in which drawings of groups of people in various positions were judged by subjects, showed that posture and orientation are compelling indicators of social relationships. It is clear that posture is an important feature of the social performance, but a great deal more needs to be done before we can say much about how it functions.

4. Physical Contact

Physical contact is a static component where, for instance, walking arm-in-arm or holding hands occurs. This kind of physical contact usually signals extreme intimacy. Mention may also be made of the way physical contact may play its part, in a more momentary fashion, in the communicative system. Thus, shaking hands, kissing, steering by the elbow, and patting on the back all have particular significance and a particular place within the interaction sequence. Physical contact as a communicative system has received systematic treatment by Frank (1957). Jourard (1966) also reported a study in which he asked subjects to report where they had been touched and by whom. He found students were touched most by their mothers and by friends of the opposite sex; for many of them, their fathers touched no more than their hands. This study illustrated how amount and type of physical contact may be one of the defining features of a relationship. Physical contact is far more widely used in some cultures than in others. Mediterranean peoples, for instance, use touch considerably, whereas it is used relatively little in northwest Europe and the United States.

Besides the components we have discussed, Hall (1963, 1964) distinguished amount and type of visual contact, loudness of voice, and linguistic style. We shall deal with these components as part of the set of dynamic features of the performance. So far as thermal and olfactory sensory channels are concerned, Hall (1963) gives a few examples of their use, but no systematic studies of them have been reported.

B. DYNAMIC FEATURES

Posture, orientation, and distance may be said to form the backdrop for a particular flow of events, just as sitting in a particular posture at the typewriter may be said to form a backdrop to the actions in typing. We have suggested that these static aspects of the performance function partly as continuous indications of how and with whom a particular individual is "in play." We must now look at the things a person is doing while he is in play. This includes movements of the body, changes in facial expression, changes in the direction of gaze, and bursts of speech. This flow of events has structure, but in spite of the considerable work that has been done on interaction, our understanding of this structure is remarkably sketchy.

An attempt to describe this structure was initiated by Scheflen (1964, 1965a, b), who analyzed in detail sound film records of psychotherapy encounters. He aimed at a full analysis of the elements of the social performance, and he attempted to show how changes in posture, smaller bodily movements, utterances, and so on, are integrated into units of communication, which are organized into a hierarchy quite analogous to the hierarchical models of behavior proposed by Lashley (1951), Welford (1958), and Miller *et al.* (1960), and employed also for the description of language structure (Gleason, 1961). He proposed that the total performance of an individual in a given encounter be termed a *presentation*; that this unit be seen as being composed of one or more *positions*; and that these positions in turn be seen as comprising one or more *points*. For instance, at a seminar, an individual's presentation can be seen as made up of a series of positions— that of listener, arguer, challenger, questioner, and so on. Each of these units is then said to be composed of one or more points; for instance, when a question is asked, there may be several parts to it or it may be iterated several times.

Scheflen showed how each of these units of communication is marked by changes in posture, visual orientation, the semantic and syntactic features of the language employed, and the stress patterns, intonation patterns, and patterns of pausing in the units of speech. Reference will be made to Scheflen's work again in the discussion of bodily movement and patterns of looking, since he put forward several suggestions in regard to their functions. However, his analytic framework will not be used in the review that follows, since it is as yet insufficiently developed. Instead, some of the different components of the performance that have been studied will each be dealt with in turn.

1. The Patterning of Action in Time

A participant in focused interaction may be observed to alternate between periods when he is actively sending messages to the other—usually by speech and gesture—and periods when he is not. These periods may be called *actions* and *silences*, respectively. Measurement of their occurrence, length, patterning in time, and interrelation with those of the others in the encounter, was first developed by Chapple (1940a), and has since been taken up by a number of others. Chapple suggested that the patterning of action in time and the interrelation of actions are dimensions of social interaction of major significance, and that the degree and manner of coordination of actions in an encounter may have important consequences for its outcome. He compared (1940b) frequency distributions by length of actions and silences for several individuals in several conversations, and found that these frequency distributions and the way they change from one conversation to the next are characteristic of the individuals concerned. This finding has since been confirmed by Goldman-Eisler (1951), among others. Subsequently Chapple (1953) developed a "standard interview" in which the length and timing of the interviewer's actions and silences are governed by fixed rules. In this way direct comparisons between the interaction patterns of different individuals are possible. Using this interview, Chapple (1949) and Matarazzo and his colleagues (Saslow and Matarazzo, 1959) have shown that on a number of indices of the temporal patterning of action and silences people are highly stable. Some attention has been paid to the relationship between differences in interaction pattern and other measures of personality; in particular, it has been shown that this technique of analysis can discriminate between categories of psychiatric patient (Chapple and Lindeman, 1942; Matarazzo and Saslow, 1961). Chronic schizophrenics, for instance, in comparison to normals, have highly irregular action lengths, and they do not coordinate their actions with those of the interviewer (Chapple *et al.*, 1960). Chapple and Donald (1947) have shown that an analysis of individual interaction patterns is useful in personnel selection, at least where the jobs to be done, as in selling, involve interaction.

Here our interest is in how the performance of one individual is affected by that of his interlocuter. A few studies pertinent to this question will be reviewed. A number of investigators have compared the performance of individuals in several different encounters. Borgatta and Bales (1953) measured the act-rates (that is, number of acts per unit of time) of individuals as they took part in several different three-person discussion groups. They found that the lower the act-rates of the other participants, the higher the individual's act-rate. However, each individual appeared to have a maximum act-rate, which was characteristic of him. Thus it was possible to predict a given individual's act-rate in a group provided his own maximum and that of the other participants was known. Similar findings were reported by Leik (1965).

Goldman-Eisler (1952) compared the performance of three psychiatrists, each of whom interviewed five depressed and five active patients. She measured act-rate, amount of action, and patterns of silence. She found that over the ten interviews each psychiatrist remained relatively stable and characteristic in his rate of action, but the amount he spoke varied inversely with the amount the patient spoke. However, the psychiatrists always retained the same rank order in amount of action relative to one another. The patients, on the other hand, always spoke the same amount, regardless of which psychiatrist interviewed them, but the occasions on which they spoke, and hence their rate of action, depended on the psychiatrist. Similar findings were reported by Saslow et al. (1956). They illustrate how different aspects of an individual's performance are differently affected, according to his position in the role system of the encounter.

Kendon (1963) reported a study of twenty-two individuals who each took part in three to five conversations with different partners. He measured act-rate, lengths of actions and silences, the total amount of action, and the amount of time the interactors spent in waiting before replying or in simultaneous action. He confirmed that individuals were characteristic in their patterning of action from one conversation to the next and that their behavior in the conversations was related to their behavior in Chapple's Standard Interview. He found that the mean length of an individual's actions was strongly and positively related to the mean length of his partner's silences, but was inversely related to his partner's action lengths. His rate of action changed relatively less from conversation to conversation, however. It seemed that the subjects varied the total amount of time spent in action by altering the length of their actions and silences rather than by altering their rate of action. It was also found that subjects were highly characteristic in their tendency to pause before replying and in their tendency to interrupt, though each individual would interrupt the other more in proportion to the amount that he was interrupted.

Kendon, as just mentioned, found that the lengths of a subject's actions were inversely related to the lengths of those of his partners. Here the partners were initially unacquainted, and were merely instructed to get to know one another. Where partners are closely acquainted, however, the relationship between lengths of actions appears to be positive. This was found by Chapple (1940a) for a pair of close friends, by B.W. Lundy (1955) in a psychotherapy pair, and by Kendon (1963) for twelve pairs of spouses. A similarly positive relationship has been found in situations where, presumably, there is no competition for available time. Thus the relationship between the action lengths of astronauts and their ground communicators has been found to be positive (Matarazzo *et al.*, 1964b); in interviews where the interviewer systematically lengthens and shortens his actions in different periods, the interviewee shows concomitant variations (Matarazzo, *et al.*, 1963; Matarazzo *et al.*, 1965).

Variations in the timing of actions of one person have been found to have dramatic effects on the lengths of the actions of the other. This has been studied in the Chapple Standard Interview, where the lengths of the interviewer's actions are held constant at 5 seconds throughout, but in which, according to the period of the interview, he either inserts his actions immediately after those of the interviewee, inserts an action only if the interviewee has been silent for 15 seconds, or persistently interrupts the interviewee. Where the interviewer does not pause before replying, the interviewee tends to become stable in the lengths of his actions, though there are marked individual differences in their actual values (Guze and Mensch, 1959; Tuason *et al.*, 1961; Matarazzo *et al.*, 1965). Where the interviewer fails to respond, however, there is a dramatic drop in the subject's action length and a tendency for his rate to increase. Usually the subject will stop acting altogether after a while, and will sit and wait until the interviewer speaks again. When he does so, the subject's reply tends to be of greatly increased length. There are, however, very large individual differences in the subject's response to the "silence" behavior of the interviewer, and general statements are difficult. Interruption by the interviewer more often produces marked shortening of utterances, and it induces the subject to interrupt the interviewer. The foregoing findings were reported by Kendon (1963), who made a detailed study of the patterning of action in Chapple's Standard Interview of thirty-nine professional and student employees at a large New York psychiatric hospital. Data on the behavior of schizophrenics, neurotics, and various normal groups in this interview have also been reported, though in less detail, by Matarazzo and his colleagues (Saslow and Matarazzo, 1959; Matarazzo and Saslow, 1961; Matarazzo, 1962).

A few studies have investigated changes in behavior over a series of encounters between the same pair of individuals. Lennard and Bernstein (1960), in a longitudinal study of eight psychotherapeutic dyads, found that after two months the psychotherapists' utterances had decreased in frequency but increased in length, as had the utterances of the patient. Further, the utterance lengths of both patient and therapist tended to approach a stable value, the particular value depending on the dyad. Similarly, Jaffe (1964) reported that, over a series of psychotherapy sessions, variations in the length of sentences became positively correlated between interviewer and interviewee. A positive correlation also developed between the frequency ratio of "I" to "you" for patient and therapist, and there was an increase in similarity of vocabulary.

Some studies have varied other aspects of an interviewer's behavior. Kanfer *et al.* (1960) found that, during a period in an interview when the interviewer changed from open-ended to interpretive utterances, the lengths of subjects' actions were much reduced. Likewise, Pope and Siegman (1962, 1965) reported several studies of the effects of the specificity of the interviewer's utterances. It was found that both decreasing the specificity of the question and increasing the anxiety-provoking potential of the topic were associated with more talk from the subjects, but that these effects were independent of one another. An analysis of certain features of utterance structure showed that where the topic was anxiety-arousing the subjects showed more speech disturbances, and that where the questions were less specific the subjects showed greater hesitancy in their speech (Pope and Siegman, 1965; Siegman and Pope, 1965).

Matarazzo *et al.* (1964a) reported a study in which the interview included a 15-minute period during which the interviewer supplied "head-nods." This led to an increase in the lengths of the subjects' action. A similar result was obtained by Matarazzo and Wiens (1965) with "Um-hums."

By way of conclusion to this section, it may be said that although sufficient work along these lines has been done to show that interesting results can be gathered by this method of analysis, a properly developed theoretical framework is still much needed. In particular, a definition of Chapple's units is needed which specifies their relationship to other possible units of behavior into which the social performance may be analyzed.

2. Language and Speech

It will be clear from our review of the work of Kanfer *et al.* (1960), Pope and Siegman (1962, 1965), and Matarazzo *et al.* (1964a), that what is said may often have important consequences for the structuring of the performance. However, there is as yet little systematic understanding of the functioning of language in social interaction. Anthropologists such as Sapir (1921) and Malinowski (1928), and linguists such as Bloomfield (1933) and, more recently, Pike (1954) have recognized the importance of this question, yet it is only quite recently that any relevant studies have been reported. No systematic treatment of the results of these studies seems possible at this time, and here we shall merely cite a few examples.

Soskin and John (1963) have made one of the most direct attacks on this question. By means of portable radio transmitters, they recorded all the verbal output of two married couples over a period of two weeks, and their results clearly illustrate the diversity of functions language has for people. Other studies have been concerned with more limited questions. Ferguson (1964) has studied baby talk in a variety of languages, and he has discussed its appearance in situations where the role relationships of the interactants are that of an adult and small child, either actually, symbolically, or playfully. Joos (1962) has pointed out that for different types of encounters a different linguistic style is adopted. He distinguished Intimate, Casual-Personal, Social-Consultative, Formal and Frozen styles, and he provided some description of their differences. For instance, Casual style contrasts with Consultative style in that ellipses in grammatical construction and jargon or slang are common, and no attempt is made, as in Consultative style, to supply background information on what is being talked of. Both of these differ from intimate style, where there is no reference to public information at all, but where speakers only use language as a means of regulating their relationship. A related idea has been developed by Bernstein (1964), who drew a distinction between "elaborated" and "restricted" linguistic codes. He suggested that a restricted code, in which the range of grammatical forms is small and the actual words are restricted in number and highly predictable, may be used to regulate more or less formalized or conventionalized encounters, whereas an elaborated code is made use of in situations where new material is being dealt with or new relationships are being developed.

Moscovici and Plon (1966) have shown experimentally how the physical arrangement of interactants may affect the style of language that is used. They compared the linguistic styles used by pairs of subjects seated face-to-face; facing, but screened; side-by-side; and back-to-back. They found that in the first two conditions, the subjects spoke more, used more verbs and more redundancy, and the conversation was less abstract; in the other two conditions, regarded as more formal, the speech was more like writing.

Also relevant to this line of inquiry are those studies that have been concerned with the use of different languages in different social situations. Ferguson (1959) examined a number of communities in which two languages are in common use, and has shown how their use is systematically related to the social situation. A similar type of study has been reported by Herman (1961). Ervin-Tripp (1964) made an experimental study of the circumstances in which Japanese-speaking Japanese Americans make use of English and Japanese, and what sort of consequences this may have for the social relationships involved and the sort of things talked about.

So far as the study of speech is concerned, some attempts have been made to analyze the communicative functions of variations in tones of voice, speed of utterance, patterns of intonation, and so forth. Many such studies adopted a method analogous to the one most widely used in the study of facial expression, in which subjects are presented with samples of speech varied in a number of ways. It has been found that people are able to judge what emotion is being expressed through variations of this sort. This work was recently reviewed by Kramer (1963), and a representative and illuminating set of studies was presented by Davitz (1964). There has been little research on these variations as they actually occur in interaction, however, and much useful work would be possible. Thus, many observers have noted that there are appropriate voice levels, tones of voice, speeds of communication, and so on, which particularly suit either funerals, wedding receptions, or formal interviews. Although descriptive systems for dealing with these aspects of speech have now been developed (Trager, 1958; Crystal and Quirk, 1964), very little appears to have been done with them. Pittinger *et al.* (1960; Pittinger, 1958; Pittinger and Smith, 1957); Dittman and Wynne (1961), and Eldred and Price (1958) have applied Trager's descriptive system to interaction sequences in psychotherapeutic sessions, but their work is only suggestive of the sort of findings this may yield.

A more fully developed line of research into speech has been the analysis of patterns of hesitations and of disturbances in the production of words or sequences of words. The focus of interest here, however, has been on the light these phenomena may throw upon the processes of linguistic encoding (Maclay and Osgood, 1959; Goldman-Eisler, 1958), or on the possibility that such variations in speech performance are associated with variations in the speaker's emotional state (see, for example, Mahl, 1963). It seems fairly clear that there are more hesitation pauses and a faster rate of speech when subjects are anxious. This whole area of research was very fully reviewed by Mahl and Schulze (1964), who reported that they found no studies in which the place of these phenomena in interaction had been considered.

3. Visual Orientation

It is widely acknowledged that where a person is looking or where he is likely to look is a matter of considerable social significance. Recent studies, such as those of Goffman (1963) and Sommer (1965) have, as we have seen, drawn attention to the way interactants tend to arrange themselves so that they may readily look at one another. Gibson and Pick (1963) have shown that people are able to discriminate when another is looking at them with a high degree of efficiency. A study to be reported by Exline, in which a Mackworth eye-marker camera was used, suggests however that the efficiency of these judgments is much affected by the subject's response set, and by where in his face the other is looking. A survey by Tomkins (1963) testified to the very ancient social traditions concerning the significance of the look. In this section we shall survey recent experimental studies that throw light on this.

We may distinguish three ways in which visual orientation functions in interactions: (1) to look at another is a social act in itself; (2) to meet the gaze of another is a significant event, and may often be an important part of the goal sought in interaction; (3) in seeing another, much important information about him may be gathered, in addition to his direction of gaze.

First, we consider the act of looking, and how it is interpreted. Focused interaction is often started by a period of eye-contact, which seems to signal that each is ready to interact with the other (Goffman, 1963). Once under way, each person looks at the other in the region of the eyes intermittently, in glances of varying length, usually between 1 and 7 seconds. The proportion of time each person looks at the other may vary from 0% to 100%. The proportion of time spent in eye-contact is, however, always much less than the proportion of time spent looking by either subject. The person listening gives longer glances than the one talking, and tends to look considerably more, at least in dyads (Nielsen, 1962; Kendon, 1967; Exline and Winters, 1965). Use is also made of peripheral vision, and waiters and chairmen are able to avoid having their eye caught in this way.

There are a few studies that throw light on how being looked at is interpreted. Weisbrod (1965) studied looking patterns in a seven-member seminar and found that who looked at whom during the discussion was most strongly related to the power coalitions that were formed in the group. Thus, those individuals in the group who looked most at a speaker were rated by the speaker as instrumental to his goals and as valuing him more. Further, the more looks an individual received while he was speaking, the more powerful he felt himself to be. Those individuals who were looked at most by speakers in the group saw themselves, and were seen by other group members, as being more powerful in the group than those who were looked at less. Weisbrod concluded that to look at someone while he is speaking is to signal a request to be included by him in discussion, and that to receive looks back from the speaker is seen as a signal from the speaker that he is including the other.

Another study on the perception of being looked at is that of Mehrabian (Winer and Mehrabian, no date), where the experimenter interviewed two subjects simultaneously, but spent more time looking at one subject than at the other. The subjects were then asked to rate the attitude of the interviewer toward them, and it was found that the subject who received the most looking judged the experimenter to be more positive toward her than the subject who was looked at less. Kendon (1966*) found that subjects thought that an interviewer who did not look at them for part of the interview had lost interest in what they were saying. Exline and Kendon, in an unpublished study, found that individuals are judged as more "potent" where they do not look while the subject is speaking, as compared to a condition in which they do look while he is speaking. Exline and Eldridge, also in an unpublished study, showed that subjects judge a speaker as more sincere if he looks at them when he speaks than if does not.

Studies complementary to these have investigated some of the factors

*Unpublished data.

associated with how much an individual looks at another. Exline and Winters (1965) had subjects interviewed simultaneously by two interviewers, both of whom looked at the subject continuously throughout the interview. It was found that subjects showed a clear tendency to look more at the interviewer they preferred. In another experiment reported in the same paper, participants were subjected to either positive or negative treatment by an interviewer: this produced feelings of dislike in the negatively treated subjects, and these subjects looked less at the interviewer than did those in the positive condition.

Other studies reported by Exline and his colleagues (Exline, 1963; Exline *et al.*, 1965) lend further support to the notion that the general level of looking is related to the subject's orientation to the others. They showed that, in noncompetitive discussion and in an interview, people who score high on a measure of "affiliativeness" (measured by French's sentence-completion test and by Schutz's FIRO) look more than do those who score lower on this dimension. Where the discussion is competitive, however, people who are low on affiliativeness look more and high "affiliates" look less.

There is some evidence that the recognition of the look in another is instinctive, and that to see a pair of eyes looking at one acts as a releaser for specifically social action. Thus Ambrose (1963) argued that the eyes of another may be the first figural entity consistently perceived by the infant. Furthermore, as Ahrens has shown (cited by Ambrose, 1963), the pair of eyes is the first visual stimulus to elicit a smiling response. Ambrose suggested that this may be likened to the following response in birds. The infant's smile and his fixation of the eyes of the person looking at him may be seen as component instinctual responses of the infant, which themselves may elicit further approach and caring behavior in the mother (Bowlby, 1958; Wolff, 1963). This may be one of the bases for the affiliative function of eye contact that was suggested by some of the studies by Exline already cited.

The look also plays a part in sexual behavior, though the systematic evidence here is less direct. Tomkins (1963) showed that taboos on mutual looking are very widespread and are associated with the sexually arousing properties of eye-contact, which he also discusses. Finally, the widespread belief in the evil eye (Elworthy, 1895) and the use of the look as a gesture of threat both in man and in monkeys and apes (see DeVore, 1965, for example), suggests a further motivational function, that of arousing fight-flight reactions.

Variations in the look associated with the elicitation of affiliative, sexual, or fight-flight reaction is little understood, though recent work of Hess (1965) suggested that enlarged pupil size in a woman is sexually arousing to a man, and the narrowed pupils of the aggressive look are proverbial. The associated facial expression is doubtless of great importance as well.

Taken together, these considerations suggest that in the mutual look the participants express their involvement with one another. The longer the periods of eye-contact, the greater the level of this mutual involvement, other things being equal. But in any situation there is a limit to the amount of mutual involvement that may be tolerated, and too much mutual looking may arouse anxiety. Argyle and Dean (1965) put forward the theory that there is an approach-avoidance balance, following the N. E. Miller (1944) model, resulting in an equilibrium level of both eye contact, physical proximity, and other components of intimacy. It was suggested that a shift along one dimension would lead to compensating shifts along the others. This received some support in the experiment described earlier where it was found that eye-contact fell off rapidly with physical proximity.

Some work has been done on factors associated with the avoidance of eye-contact, though more is needed. Exline and his colleagues (1965) showed that subjects look away when they are asked personally embarrassing questions and, with the exception of those who score high on Christie's Machiavellianism scale, when they are lying. These authors suggested that this may be a result of either an attempt at self-concealment or an attempt to avoid the unwelcome responses of the other person. It could also reflect an attempt to escape the relationship with the other. A further possibility is that it is more difficult to answer personal questions or to lie during mutual gaze. In addition, the turning away of the gaze is probably an attempt to reduce the intake of information. In another study Exline and Winters (1965) showed that when subjects have to talk about cognitively more difficult material they look less at the other. Kendon (1967) reported that during passages of hesitant speech subjects look away, but during fluent speech they look back. These findings suggest that it is during the formulation of thought, when subjects might want to reduce information intake, that they look away. They look back as they speak only when their sentence is fully formed.

Emotional processes undoubtedly contribute to the aversion of the gaze. Laing (1960) reported on a series of adult patients who characteristically averted their gaze: they were "overwhelmed by a feeling of rejection" and did not wish to be seen. Riemer (1955) described a number of different types of abnormal gaze, all of which, according to him, serve to "wall off" the individual from the world, and arise as a result of unexpressed hostility. Hutt and Ounsted (1966) reported extreme aversion of gaze in autistic children, which may reflect an extreme fear of being rejected by others. These authors also suggested that autistic children are chronically overaroused, and their averted gaze is interpreted as a device whereby the arousal is kept at manageable levels.

Finally, as we mentioned, when A looks at B he can pick up information about him. He can see whether or not B is looking at him; he can also observe B's facial expression, posture, movements, and so on. The face is, of course, a peculiarly expressive instrument, and the eyes may be its most expressive part. The mere fact that it is an area of such high information value may be sufficient to explain why people look there, more than at other parts of their co-interactants. Argyle *et al.* (1967), in a study to be reported, found that as B was progressively concealed from A (by dark glasses, mask, no vision), A found interaction increasingly uncomfortable, though it is noteworthy that they found a greater increase in difficulty when the face, rather than just the eyes, was concealed.

4. *Bodily Movement, Facial Expression, and Looking Patterns*

Studies in which the functioning of posture and bodily movement has been examined in interaction have only recently appeared. Scheflen (1964, 1965a) has begun to report the results of his detailed analyses of psychotherapy encounters; while here he aims at a full analysis of the elements of the social performance, his main work so far has been concerned with the functions of postural change.

He found that each of the units of communication into which he suggests that social performance may be analyzed are marked by changes in posture and patterns of movement. He suggested that the presentation is marked by gross changes in space. At the end of a conversation the participants may leave the room, for instance, or perhaps, at a party, they may turn to talk with other people. As we have seen, any given presentation may be seen to be signaled by a particular general orientation and position in space. The *positions* that occur within a given presentation are marked by particular postures, their boundaries being indicated by changes in posture. In Scheflen's (1965a) analysis of the performance of a psychotherapist, for instance, the latter was found to lean forward toward the patient when he was engaged in "active interpretation," and he would then lean back in his chair when the patient was "free associating."

The *points* of which positions may be composed are marked, Scheflen suggested, by shifts in head position and in visual orientation. He reported (1964) that interactants in psychotherapy show three to five head positions which occur repeatedly and which appear in contrasting sequences as the successive points appear. He gave an example of two head positions a therapist was observed to use repeatedly during an interpreting position. While listening to the patient, the therapist's head was slightly lowered and cocked to the right, so that her eyes were averted from the patient. With the onset of making an interpretative remark, she would raise her head, hold it erect, look directly at the patient, and then speak. At the end, she would turn her head to the right, away from the patient, and then resume the listening head position. Studies by Kendon (1967) of visual orientation in fourteen subjects filmed in conversation showed associated patterns of looking, with the individual looking directly at his interlocutor at the ends of grammatically complete phrases. These patterns are clearly similar to those reported by Scheflen.

There is as yet no clear evidence of the functions of these changes in posture, head position, and visual orientation, though it seems probable that they have a regulatory function for the recipients. The distinctive postures of the different positions, for instance, may serve as continuous signals to the other and assist in keeping him in step. Scheflen (1965a,b) suggested that encounters follow characteristic programs that may be described in terms of the sequences of positions, and if positions are marked by distinctive postures, this may help to keep people together as the program proceeds. Scheflen (1965a) described the progression of positions of two closely collaborating psychotherapists as they attempted to establish a particular pattern of relationships with the patient, and he indicated how each therapist waited for the postural signal from the other before shifting into the next position in the sequence.

Rather similar considerations may apply to the changes in head position and visual orientation, which are closely associated with this and which appear to mark the succession of points. Thus Kendon (1967) reported that the ends of utterances where there is a change of speaker are often marked by a sustained gaze at the other combined with a characteristic head position. Where such kinesic accompaniments to utterance endings did not appear, as was the case in several instances, the response of the other person was less immediate. This suggested that the look and the associated head position functioned in part as change-over signals and assisted in the smooth progression of the interaction. Kendon also reported that the speaker looks up at his interlocuter intermittently while he is speaking, and that this occurs at the ends of sentences or completed phrases, and it is here that the listener most often supplies his attention signals. During hesitations, on the other hand, the speaker characteristically turns his head away, and Kendon suggested that this may partly function as an inhibitory signal to the other. Certainly during periods of hesitation associated with averted head and gaze, responses of the listener were found to be very rare.

Besides these shifts in posture and head and eye positions, an individual may be observed to make a variety of other complex movements as he is talking. He may move his hands, nod his head up and down, move his eye-brows, and vary the positions of his eyelids. Some of these movements do not appear to be integrated into the total flow of behavior. Such extraneous movements were studied recently by Dittman (1962) and were found to be associated with hesitation pauses. Birdwhistell (1964) recently reported some of his observations on the close relation between speech and body movement. He described how nods or sweeps of the head, eye blinks or brow movements, and movements of the hands or fingers appear in association with points of linguistic stress. He also reported observations of units of movement, variable in the actual body part involved, that appear to be associated with particular kinds of utterance. In references to the self, he noted a consistent tendency for the speaker to make a proximal movement, whereas in references to others the movement is distal. When the pronoun is plural, the movement normally associated with it is modified with a slight sweep. *Area markers* refer to movements made with prepositions or prepositional phrases and include, for instance, a backward jerk of the head over "behind," as in "Put that behind the stove," or a forward jerk of the head over "to" as in "I am going to London." *Manner markers* are movements that mark adverbs and adverbial phrases, such as "roughly," "quickly," and so on (Birdwhistell, 1966).

These observations have yet to be fully reported, and again we can only speculate as to what the functions of these movements might be. From the point of view of the recipient, however, they may serve to reduce the ambiguity of what the speaker is saying, and in dividing up the discourse into relatively small chunks, they may keep his attention. It is fairly easy to observe that when a person is speaking loudly and with emphasis the kinesic accompaniments to his speech become much more pronounced. One or two studies have been reported which show that comprehension of speech is better if the speaker can be seen (Sumby and Pollack, 1954), and it is possible that the speech-related movements Birdwhistell described play a part in this. On the other hand, these movements may have some functional significance for the speaker rather than the listener. Recent work (Condon and Ogston, 1966) has indicated that people in interaction closely coordinate one another's movement. In a study to be reported by Argyle *et al.* (1967), interaction took place with one subject progressively concealed from the other; the one who was not concealed found the encounter increasingly uncomfortable, but only if he could still be seen by the other person. Perhaps it is of particular value for A to be able to see B only when B can also see A, because in these circumstances A must co-ordinate his movements with those of B, which he need not do if B cannot see him.

The work just described has been primarily concerned with the functions of postural changes, bodily movements, and changes in visual orientation as regulators of the interaction process. Besides this there is a considerable body of work concerned with the function of movement, particularly of facial expressions as expressive of emotion. Schlosberg

(1954) and Osgood (1966), among others, studied the dimensions along which people distribute their judgments of facial expressions, and they showed that there is considerable consistency in this. Sarbin and Hardyck (1955), Ekman (1965), and Machotka (1965) have begun to make analogous explorations with posture. Ekman suggested, for instance, that whereas affective information of various kinds is conveyed by the face, posture is judged predominantly along a dimension of tension-relaxation. None of the work in this tradition has, however, concerned itself with the question of the functions of, for example, facial expression within an interaction sequence. Although we may now place a photograph of a smiling face fairly precisely on Schlosberg's Oval, thus placing it within a set of "dimensions of emotional expression," even a cursory consideration of where smiles actually occur in interaction sequences should be enough to show that their meaning is not to be exclusively defined in terms of their position on these judgmental dimensions. For instance, smiles may be used to reassure another or to appease him: they are an integral part of greetings, and they may be used as a device for establishing the range of expressiveness that is to be permitted within a given encounter. It does not seem particularly helpful to say, in each of these cases, that a particular emotion is being expressed. It seems far more likely that smiles are, so often as not, employed as part of a more or less ritualized code that serves to handle particular aspects of the interaction process. A large field of research awaits cultivation here.

IV. Self-Presentation and Competence

We turn now from the study of the behavioral details of the social performance to certain higher order features of it. In all encounters, since each person's performance is built upon his conception of the kind of other he is dealing with, so one of the main functions of the social performance must be to convey this conception. This is the problem of self-presentation, which we shall discuss first. Second, in many encounters, those taking part are aiming at fairly specific outcomes, the achievement of which depends on the participants' success in keeping the encounter going and steering it in appropriate directions. Some people are better at this than others; we say they have greater social competence, or better social skills. We shall outline some studies that deal with this question and with methods of training people in social skills. Next we will comment on research into specific social skills, and finally, we will briefly consider mental illness and will indicate how much of it may be seen as a failure of social skill or competence.

A. THE PRESENTATION OF SELF IN SOCIAL ENCOUNTERS

One of the special features of social interaction is that interactors are open to observation by the others present and are concerned about the perceptions and attitudes that the others have of them. This can be regarded as a special case of the processes that have already been described—the goal here is to bring about certain perceptions and attitudes on the part of the others, and a repertoire of social techniques is used for doing so; the equilibrium includes certain stabilized appraisals of one another by the participants. This is a very important aspect of interaction, however, as it is intimately bound up with the establishment of social relationships and with their breakdown. Information about this aspect of social behavior has been derived mainly from observational studies (Goffman, 1955, 1956, 1961a) and clinical studies (Erikson, 1956), though there have also been a few experimental studies. This field has been reviewed by D.R. Miller (1963) and Stagner (1961).

1. The Motivation for Self-Presentation

Perhaps the most basic motivation for self-presentation by A is that interaction is impossible for B unless he knows enough about A to know how to respond to him appropriately. Similarly A wants B to react to him appropriately. There are at least two further sources of motivation for self-presentation:

1. People who are unsure of their self-image need continual confirmation that they really are what they half-believe themselves to be and would like to be. Similarly, they may need confirmation of their uncertain self-esteem. Maslow *et al.* (1945) called this condition *insecurity*, and showed how people in the various combinations of high and low security and high and low self-esteem characteristically behave. Adolescents are particularly insecure; they have not crystallized a stable self-image, so that reactions from others may have a more disturbing effect on them than on older people. Hysterics are another insecure group and are constantly trying to project their self-image on others: this reaches an extreme in imposters and people in fugue states.

2. Others may want to project a self-image primarily for professional reasons. Teachers, psychotherapists, and other social skill performers are more successful if they can project an image of professional competence and thereby, win the confidence of their clients. Goffman (1956) has described some of the professional techniques that are used to do this.

The self-image is the descriptive part of the self, including such things as body image, age, sex, occupation, and social class, and it can be assessed by the Semantic Differential or a Q sort. Self-esteem is evaluative and can be assessed by attitude scales, as was done by Rosenberg (1965). Both seem to be associated with motivational forces in the personality. Clinical writers are widely agreed that there are "pressures toward consistency," toward the establishment of a unitary ego-identity (D.R. Miller, 1963, pp. 696 f.).

According to Erikson, 1956), these pressures become heightened during late adolescence in Western society. There are also pressures to maximize self-esteem, though this may be due to an effort to obtain self-reactions and other reactions that are consistent with earlier reactions to the self of parents (Secord and Backman, 1964). This drive is constantly in conflict with evidence from current performance and reactions of others in the present; if reality loses, a state of paranoia ensues. Self-image and self-esteem probably have three main origins: (1) introjection of the reactions of others (Argyle, 1964); (2) comparision of self with siblings and other peers; and (3) the playing of roles. The individual has to select which of these items to emphasize and which to de-emphasize in order to construct a prestigeful and unitary identity.

2. *The Social Techniques Used for Self-Presentation*

To create perceptions of and attitudes toward the self on the part of others present is a subtle social skill, though one that is usually practiced quite unconsciously. How is it done? A can simply tell B about himself, but this is not socially acceptable, except in the most modest and indirect form. The same is true of hints, name-dropping, and the various techniques of one-upmanship described by Stephen Potter (1952). Another method of projecting an identity is by means of clothes and general appearance, which are in fact excellent clues to a person's self-image. Third, a person's style of behavior can indicate, by gesture, manner of speech, and general demeanor, the kind of person he thinks he is and the way he is used to being treated. Finally, the most effective way is by aspects of behavior that are relevant to the self-image; these can prove, as words cannot, that a person really is what he claims to be. Generally speaking, people present a somewhat idealized, or at least edited, version of themselves for public inspection. Thus they conceal a great deal about themselves; they reveal most to those whom they can trust not to reject them, and reveal least about topics such as sex and money (Jourard, 1964).

What happens when a self-image is presented but is not accepted by the others present? As will be shown later, this is one of the main sources of embarrassment. If a person is able to retain his poise, various strategies are open to him. He may adopt alternative techniques for establishing the same image, though these often involve more overt claims and may make the speaker look ridiculous. He may have to alter the image he is presenting, perhaps temporarily accepting the group's evaluation of him. Finally, he may engage in defensive behavior, categorizing the others negatively and preserving his self-image, as salesgirls do for customers who won't buy (Lombard, 1955); or simply failing to perceive the responses of others accurately.

3. Embarrassment and Stage Fright

Both embarrassment and stage fright are conditions in which the social performance is disrupted because of anxiety about the reactions of others toward the self.

When a person becomes embarrassed, he blushes, sweats, stutters, and in extreme cases flees from the situation or commits suicide. He loses control of his social behavior and is temporarily incapable of interacting; his state is liable to spread to the others present. Gross and Stone (1964) collected 1000 descriptions of instances of embarrassment from students and others. They classified the causes into three main types: (1) failure to be able to confirm the self-image that was presented; (2) loss of poise through failing to control self or physical objects in the situation; (3) disturbance of assumptions about other people or about the situation. Goffman (1955) emphasized the first of these causes—the inability to sustain an identity. He also mentioned (Goffman, 1957) some other sources of embarrassment—when one person is underinvolved in the encounter; when he is overinvolved; and when he talks about this interaction itself. The common element behind most of these causes is the sudden breakdown of the smooth course of interaction for one or another reason. Garfinkel (1963) experimented with various ways of disturbing interaction: (1) treating the other in an inappropriate role, such as treating a customer in a shop as a salesman; (2) behaving in an inappropriate role, such as a student behaving like a lodger in his own family; (3) breaking the rules of a game, such as moving the opponent's pieces. All of these kinds of behavior created embarrassment and in some cases anger. It follows from the first process mentioned that some people—those who are presenting a false front or concealing large areas of their true selves (Jourard, 1964)—will be more easily embarrassed than others. When a person has become embarrassed he needs time to recover his poise, and may need to be helped back into the pattern of interaction. Goffman (1955) described how the others present may help: they may try to avoid its happening by being "tactful;" they may pretend that nothing has happened; they may make excuses for A's lapse of behavior; and they may help to provide him with a new image and thus to rehabilitate him in the group.

While self-presentation can be looked at as an example of social skill, embarrassment can best be seen as a failure to establish or maintain equilibrium. The social system includes patterns of interaction with the other, and perceptions and attitudes toward him; the two parts are intimately bound up together. If the perceptions are suddenly changed, a breakdown of interaction follows, and a new one must be established if a relationship is to be resumed.

Audience anxiety may be experienced in some degree whenever a person can be perceived by another, because the former is concerned about how the latter will react. Experiments comparing performance with an audience, without an audience, and with audiences of different sizes, showed that speech errors increase (Levin *et al.*, 1960), and that there are more mistakes and greater rigidity at tasks when an audience is present. Probably the Yerkes-Dodson principle operates, so that performance at first improves, but deteriorates with larger and more critical or important audiences. Paivio *et al.* (1961) found that readiness to volunteer to speak was positively correlated with a questionnaire measure of exhibitionism and negatively with self-consciousness. Levin *et al.* suggested that an approach-avoidance conflict is produced by these opposing forces; this is confirmed by their finding that speech errors were highest for subjects high in both exhibitionism and self-consciousness. Subjects both seek positive responses and fear negative ones from those who can see them; the strength of these two expectations presumably depends on past experience.

Argyle *et al.* (1967) varied the conditions of vision between a speaker and his audience. Subjective ratings of discomfort and speech errors were lowest when the speaker was behind the audience; next lowest was when he was in front but some distance away, and greatest when he was wearing dark glasses. It looks as if cutting down feedback from the audience, or perhaps simply reducing eye contact, reduces audience anxiety. Unfortunately this also reduces useful aspects of the feedback, so that the performance is likely to be worse under these conditions. It is commonly found that adolescents suffer from this kind of anxiety—they do not like being looked at, and are very concerned about their personal appearance. This is probably because their ego-identity is not yet stabilized, so that the reactions of others are very important to them.

B. Social Competence; Training in Social Skills

a. Measures of competence. Competence in the performance of nonsocial motor skills can be measured by the speed and quality of performance; competence in social skills is more difficult to assess. In the case of professional social skills, competence clearly involves the successful attainment of some combination of goals. The good salesman, for example, both sells a lot of goods *and* satisfies the customer, so that the latter is likely to go to that shop again. In the case of nonprofessional social skills the criteria are less clear, though they might include such things as establishing and maintaining friendly relationships, being cooperative and helpful in everyday encounters, being able to communicate clearly and to persuade other people to do things. Negatively, many mental patients are deficient in social skills: they cannot sustain friendly, cooperative behavior with others, and they annoy people. Attempts have been made to assess "social intelligence" and competence at particular skills, such as foremanship, by means of questionnaires. There appears to be a high correlation between such measures and IQ (Thorndike and Stein, 1937), although their relation to actual behavior is less certain. Somewhat better results have recently been obtained with the Chapin Social Insight Test (Gough, 1965). It is not known how far there is a general factor of social skill. People vary in their capacity to perform different social tasks, such as teaching, psychotherapy and interviewing, mainly as a result of special training and experience. Although special social techniques must be mastered for each of these skills, there may be a number of common elements as well, such as perceptual sensitivity, warmth, flexibility, energy, and a large repertoire of social techniques.

b. Learning by repetition. Whereas manual workers are often given carefully designed training courses, those who have to deal with people are often given none at all, and have to pick it up as they go along. Experiments with small groups by Mohanna and Argyle (1960) and Crossman and Everstine (1965) showed that groups can increase in their speed and efficiency of communicating and solving problems: time fell to one-sixth and errors to one-third in the former experiment, and new methods of coding messages were observed to be evolved in the latter. Other studies have been concerned with one subject dealing with a succession of "clients." Experiments by Argyle, Lalljee, and Lydall (cf. Argyle, 1967) showed that sheer repetition of teaching another the slide rule or how to play Scrabble produced fewer speech errors, more fluency, and longer speeches. The performance also became more stereotyped. Studies of salesgirls by the same investigators found an over-all average increase of 60% — 100% over 12 months in different shops, but some individuals did not improve at all, while some actually got worse.

Whether sheer repetition will lead to improvement probably depends on the amount of feedback and the motivation of the learners.

c. Role-playing with feedback. In this method of training, the trainees role-play a series of typical situations encountered in interviewing, selling, and similar situations. They are then given feedback, which may be verbal commentary from the trainer, the other trainees, a tape recording, or a video tape recording, or by earphones during the actual performance. It seems probable that the immediate playback of a video tape recording is one of the most effective methods of feedback. Haines and Eachus (1965) found that there was better learning of the behavior appropriate in an imaginary other country when a video tape was used in addition to verbal commentary.

A number of studies have found that role-playing with verbal feedback is effective in training for supervision. The feedback is not enjoyed, but is essential for learning, (cf. Argyle *et al.*, 1962, for a review of these studies), and several sets of suitable situations for role-playing have been prepared (Corsini *et al.*, 1961; Maier *et al.*, 1957). Several variations on this theme can be used; for example, the same trainee confronts a variety of programmed others, or roles are reversed in a second session. The main practical difficulty with role-playing is in giving the feedback in a way that is not disturbing and is acceptable. It is also essential to have a good set of situations.

d. T-group training. This method has gained rapidly in popularity since it was first developed at Bethel, Maine, in 1947. The procedure is for a trainer to meet with about 12 trainees for a series of 2-hour sessions, during which the only task of the group is to study itself. The trainer does not direct the group's activities, but may intervene to interpret what is happening, or to show how to give feedback on a member's behavior. There have now been a number of fairly well-controlled follow-up studies, using before and after measure and control groups (cf. Stock, 1964). The most satisfactory is that by Bunker (1965) of 200 people who attended the Bethel laboratories. The conclusion of these studies is that $60\% - 75\%$ benefit whereas a small percentage become emotionally disturbed and some have nervous breakdowns. The benefits are mainly greater sensitivity to interpersonal phenomena and clearer self-perception.

Various criticism can be made of T-group methods: (1) They are emotionally disturbing for a minority of participants. This could be avoided by reducing the emotional violence of feedback, but it is recognized that this might reduce the positive effects—"It depends on what you are prepared to pay for psychically," as one trainer put it. Another alternative would be to screen out those who are likely to be upset by these procedures. (2) T-group methods increase sensitivity and insight, but may not improve job *performance*. Furthermore, each job has its own special problems and social techniques that must be dealt with; T-group courses usually include some relevant role-playing in addition to the T-group sessions. An earlier report by Lippitt (1949) showed that good follow-up results were obtained from a laboratory course that included role-playing and some of the other ingredients, but no actual T-groups: it would be interesting to know which part of the T-group procedures is responsible for the positive effects. (3) T-groups are unlike any real groups, since the latter have real jobs to do, and contain leaders wielding real power, often undemocratically. In other words, the social techniques learned in T-groups could be used in other T-groups but may be ineffective in many real-life situations.

e. Other methods of training. Sensitivity can be increased by other methods than T-groups. For example, Jecker *et al.* (1964) succeeded in training teachers to perceive more accurately whether pupils had understood what they were being taught. The measure consisted of a series of 1-minute films of a child; the training consisted in studying films and drawing attention to the cues for comprehension.

The imitation of models, for example of experts observed through one-way screen or filmed, can be useful. This is valuable when rather unfamiliar social skills are being taught, and can be used to draw attention to the variety of social techniques needed to deal with particular problems.

Lectures, discussion, reading, and case studies are all used regularly for human relations training. There is evidence from follow-up studies that the combination of lectures and group methods can be successful here (Sorenson, 1958). On the other hand, cognitive methods alone, such as lectures and reading, probably do not have much effect on social performance (Argyle *et al.*, 1962).

C. RESEARCH INTO SPECIFIC SOCIAL SKILLS

There has been a considerable amount of research into specific social skills, such as the survey, assessment, and personnel interview, psychotherapy, teaching and lecturing, the supervision of groups, and so on. Research has been concerned with which techniques are most effective under particular conditions and what happens during the encounters. One kind of research consists in the comparison of good and bad performers where this can be assessed in some fairly objective way. There have been a number of such studies comparing supervisors of high- and low-output work groups that were similar in other respects (for example, Argyle *et al.*, 1958). Such studies have not usually analyzed behavior in terms of the kind of variables that we have been considering in this chapter, and research of this kind could be greatly extended by so doing. One of the most interesting questions in this field could be solved in this way: Fiedler (1953) and others have shown that effective psychotherapists establish a similar kind of relationship with their patients: they are warm, permissive, interested in the patient and able to empathize with him, and they treat him as a co-worker on a common problem; but they do not share any therapeutic techniques. To this it has been replied, however, that this common element must consist of certain shared social (or therapeutic) techniques (Gardner, 1964).

Nor do these comparative studies allow for the possibility of superior methods of skill performance not used by anybody—yet manual skills are commonly improved by method study. An example of such a suggested set of superior social techniques was put forward by McGregor (1960) for supervision. He suggested that supervisors should lead subordinates to set their own goals and assess their own progress, and that they try to align the needs of individuals and the aims of the organization by showing individuals how to meet their needs in an acceptable manner. A social skill that is urgently in need of new techniques at present is the handling of adolescent children by parents. McPhail (1966) found some of the things that are ineffective— emotional tirades, unreasonable restriction, and pointless punishments— but which techniques *are* effective must still be discovered.

The social techniques that are evolved by experienced performers are often very complex and may involve a carefully planned sequence of moves, or a "strategy." The personnel interview, for instance, may include the following steps: (1) The supervisor (S) obtains background information about the worker (W); (2) S meets W and establishes rapport; (3) S explains objectively that there is a problem; (4) S sympathetically invites W to give his side of the story; (5) S and W engage in joint problem-solving. (6) If W is uncooperative, S uses persuasion, appealing to relevant needs in W. (7) If W is still uncooperative, the possibility of stronger sanctions is mentioned. (8) S reviews what has been decided, when they shall meet again, and so on (Sidney and Brown, 1961; Maier, 1952).

It may be necessary to vary the social techniques used with the personality of the other or with the situation. Although democratic supervisors usually get better results with their work groups, this is not the case if the group members are themselves authoritarian (Haythorn, 1956), if the task must be carried out with meticulous accuracy and timing (Fiedler, 1953), or in times of crisis (Hamblin, 1958).

Further discussion of research into problems connected with specific social skills is given in Argyle (1967).

D. MENTAL DISORDERS AS FAILURES OF SOCIAL SKILL

If social interaction is regarded as a social skill, it should be instructive to examine the ways in which failures of skill may occur—the equivalents of breakdowns of motor skill under stress or fatigue, including accidents. Some of the most interesting kinds of failure in social performance occur in mental disorders; study of such failures may, therefore, throw light on social interaction and may be important for the study of mental disorders. There are two main ways in which failure of social performance may be causally related to other aspects of disorder. (1) Social failure may be primary, leading to social rejection and failure to cope, which lead to anxiety and other symptoms. (2) Social failure may be a secondary result of other personality disturbances, but may lead to social rejection and incompetence and hence to an exacerbation of stress.

It is not necessary to repeat the more familiar aspects of the social incompetence of mental patients; the general features of the social behavior of schizophrenics, hysterics, and psychopaths, etc., are described in textbooks of psychiatry. What can be added to such descriptions are the results of using special test situations or special measuring instruments. A brief list of some examples of these studies follows.

a. Voice quality. Ostwald (1965) made frequency analyses of the speech of different kinds of patients, showing that, for example, the speech of depressives is flat, low-pitched, and monotonous, whereas that of manics has a robust, resonant quality.

b. Timing of speech. Chapple's Standard Interview (1953) has been used in a number of studies of patients: Matarazzo and Saslow (1961), for example, found that schizophrenics had longer silences than normals before replying, often failed to respond at all, and at other times interrupted; their meshing is poor.

c. Person perception. This factor was studied in patients by laboratory tests for accuracy of recognizing emotion from characteristics such as speech and facial expression. Davitz (1964) found that schizophrenics were poor at recognizing emotions from speech quality. McDavid and Schroder (1957) found that delinquents were poor at discriminating approval and disapproval as presented in a series of situational descriptions.

d. Gaze direction. Hutt and Ounsted (1966) found that autistic children suffered from avoidance of gaze; furthermore, in a test room they took no interest in masks of human faces, but were interested in animal faces and the furniture. The present authors observed a series of schizophrenics interacting with a continuously staring confederate: the patients showed almost no eye contact and their glances were extremely short.

e. Physical appearance. A person's clothes and posture are an important clue to his concern with projecting a self-image. The drab, ill-kept appearance of many mental patients suggests that they do not care; this is far from true, however, of manics, hysterics, and paranoids. Manics wear smart, striking, but loud, clothes: hysterics are greatly concerned with their appearance; paranoids dress to fit their fantasies.

We will now consider the different ways in which the social performance of mental patients may fail. It is possible to classify these failures in terms of the model for social skill presented earlier.

a. Failures of perception. All kinds of patients who have been studied showed failures of perception. In schizophrenia, failures seem to result from a deliberate misattention to social stimuli, though schizophrenics are least aware of emotional elements—they can, for example, follow instructions quite well. Paranoids fail to receive messages that contain any criticism of themselves. Manics and depressives fail to perceive *themselves* realistically.

b. Disturbances of motivation. There may be general overarousal or underarousal, as in the affective psychoses. There may be undue strength of particular drives, such as aggression. Schizophrenics appear to be lacking in affiliative motivation, but there is recent evidence that in childhood schizophrenia there is physiological *over*arousal producing frozen inactivity (Hutt *et al.*, 1964); this does not, however, explain why there should be social inactivity in particular. Psychopaths also appear to have low affiliative needs, but they continue to seek out social situations in order to disrupt them.

c. Disturbances of translation, social techniques, and meshing. Schizophrenics cannot interact at all because of an inability to mesh and establish any kind of interaction system. Delinquents and many other adolescents can interact within the peer group, but not with anyone else. Most mental patients apart from schizophrenics can interact, but cannot form social relationships because they are so unrewarding to be with. This could be due to a failure to correct social techniques in the light of feedback, or failure of perception, or lack of alternative social techniques. Berne (1966) described the games used by his neurotic patients. These games are destructive and aggressive social strategies motivated by the desire to humiliate others or by complex dynamic processes, much as avoiding the recognition of personal inadequacies.

d. Disturbance of self-image. Such failures occur in most disorders. Hysterics are much concerned with getting confirmation of their self-image; this is particularly true of imposters and pretenders who half-believe the parts they are playing (Deutsch, 1955). Paranoids, on the other hand, have no doubt about their self-image, but are upset because no one else will accept it. Another type of failure occurs in adolescents and schizophrenics—a failure to integrate the elements of self-perception into a stable ego-identity (ego diffusion).

V. Summary and Conclusion

In this article it has been suggested that the model developed by Welford (1958) and Broadbent (1958) for the analysis of sensorimotor performance may be usefully applied in the analysis of the behavior of people engaged in social interaction. Since we deal with *interaction*, however, the interrelationship of performances cannot be ignored, and the notion of equilibrium was put forward as a useful one for dealing with this.

A wide variety of studies have been reviewed, in an attempt to show how the social performance may be analyzed into a number of components, each differing in function. Thus a distinction was drawn between features of the performance that remain relatively constant throughout the interaction, such as relative spatial position and orientation, and posture, and aspects of the performance that are more dynamic. The constant or standing features of the performance appear to function to "set the stage" of a given encounter. The dynamic features, which include speech, and patterns of movement, have a variety of functions according to the kind of encounter considered. It was noted, for instance, how movement may serve to clarify or emphasize aspects of messages transmitted through speech; how patterns of looking and movement may serve to regulate the pacing of action in the encounter; and how the emotional relationships between the participants may be regulated, particularly through facial expression and levels of eye-contact. This analysis remains sketchy. Much yet remains to be learned. The structure and function of movements significant for interaction is only beginning to be understood. The place of facial and other kinds of expression awaits systematic formulation. And, perhaps surprisingly, remarkably little is known about the role of language and speech.

There is no doubt of the value of studies such as these. As we have tried to make clear in the discussion of self-presentation and competence in social skill, the more we know about how the social performance is organized, what its components are, the better we shall be able to understand the nature of interpersonal processes. We have stressed the idea that there are a number of different social skills, each specific in function, and a detailed understanding of their organization opens up the possibility of social skills training, analogous to training in industrial skills which has followed so fruitfully upon the analysis of sensorimotor performance. This may have an important application in dealing with mental illness, insofar as these may be seen as breakdowns in social skill.

REFERENCES

Ambrose, J. A. (1963). The concept of a critical period for the development of social responsiveness in early human infancy. In B. M. Foss (Ed.), *Determinants of infant behaviour.* Vol. II. London: Methuen, pp. 201–225.

Annett, J., and Kay, H. (1956). Skilled performance. *Occup. Psychol.* **30**, 112–117.

Argyle, M. (1964). Introjection: a form of social learning. *Brit. J. Psychol.* **55**, 391–402.

Argyle, M. (1967). *The psychology of interpersonal behaviour.* London: Penguin.

Argyle, M., and Dean, J. (1965). Eye-contact, distance and affiliation. *Sociometry* **28**, 289–304.

Argyle, M., Gardner, G., and Cioffi, F. (1958). Supervisory methods related to productivity, absenteeism and labour turnover. *Hum. Relat.* **11**, 23–45.

Argyle, M., Smith, T., and Kirton, M. (1962). *Training managers.* London: Acton Society Trust.

Argyle, M., Lalljee, M., Cook, M., and Latané, J. (1967). Effects of the visibility of the other in social interactions. Unpublished paper.

Bales, R. F. (1953). The equilibrium problem in small groups. In T. Parsons, R. F. Bales, and C. A. Shils (Eds.), *Working papers in the theory of action.* New York: Free Press, pp. 111–161.

Barker, R. G., and Wright, H. (1955). *Midwest and its children.* New York: Harper & Row.

Bartlett, F. C. (1958). *Thinking: an experimental and social study.* New York: Basic Books.

Bass B. M., and Klubeck, S. (1952). Effects of seating arrangements in leaderless group discussions. *J. abnorm. soc. Psychol.* **47**, 724–727.

Berne, E. (1966). *Games people play.* New York: Grove Press.

Bernstein, B. (1964). Elaborated and restricted codes: their social origin and some consequences. *Amer. Anthrop.* **66**, Pt. 2, 55–69.

Birdwhistell, R. L. (1964). Communication without words. To appear in Paul Alexandre (Ed.), *L'aventure humaine.*

Birdwhistell, R. L. (1966). Some relations between kinesics and spoken American English. In A. G. Smith (Ed.), *Communication and culture: readings in the codes of human interaction.* New York: Holt, Rinehart & Winston, pp. 182–189.

Bloomfield, L. (1933). *Language.* New York: Henry Holt.

Blood, R. O., and Livant, W. P. (1957). The use of space within the cabin group. *J. soc. Issues.* **13**, 47–53.

Borgatta, E. F., and Bales, R. F. (1953). Interaction of individuals in reconstituted groups. *Sociometry* **16**, 302–320.

Bowlby, J. (1958). The nature of the child's tie to his mother. *Internat. J. Psychoanal.* **39**, 350–373.

Breer, P. E. (1960). Predicting interpersonal behavior from personality and role. Unpublished doctoral dissertation, Harvard.

Broadbent, D. E. (1958). *Perception and communication.* New York: Macmillan (Pergamon).

Bunker, D. (1965). The effect of laboratory education on individual behaviour. In E. H. Schein and W. G. Bennis (Eds.), *Personal and organizational change through group methods.* New York: Wiley.

Burns, T. (1964). Non-verbal communication. *Discovery* **25** (10), 30–37.

Carment, D. W., Miles, C. G., and Cervin, V. B. (1965). Persuasiveness and persuasibility as related to intelligence and extraversion. *Brit. J. soc. clin. Psychol.* **4**, 1–7.

Chapple, E. D. (1940a). Measuring human relations. *Genetic Psychol. Monogr.* **22**, 3–147.

Chapple, E. D. (1940b). "Personality" differences as described by invariant properties of individuals in interaction. *Proc. Nat. Acad. Sci.* **26**, 10–16.

Chapple, E. D. (1949). The interaction chronograph: its evolution and present application. *Personnel* **25**, 295–307.

Chapple, E. D. (1953). The standard interview as used in interaction chronograph investigations *Hum. Organization* **12**(2), 23–32.

Chapple, E. D. (1962). Quantitative analysis of complex organizational systems. *Hum. Organization* **21**, 67–80.

Chapple, E. D., and Coon, C. S. (1942). *Principles of anthropology.* New York: Holt, Rinehart & Winston.

Chapple, E. D., and Donald, G., Jr. (1947). An evaluation of department store sales people by the interaction chronograph. *J. Marketing* **12**, 173–185.

Chapple, E. D., and Lindemann, E. (1942). Clinical implications of measurements on interaction rates in psychiatric interviews. *Appl. Anthrop.* **1**, 1–11.

Chapple, E. D., Chapple, Martha F., Wood, Lucie A., Miklowitz, Amy, Kline, N. S., and Saunders, J. C. (1960). Interaction chronograph method for analysis of differences between schizophrenics and controls. *A M A Arch. gen. Psychiat.* **3**, 160–167.

Condon, W., and Ogston, W. D. (1966). Sound film analysis of normal and pathological behavior patterns *J. nerv. ment. Dis.* **143**, 338–347.

Corsini, R. J., Shaw, M. C., and Blake, R. R. (1961). *Role playing in business and industry.* New York: Free Press.

Crossman, E. R. F. W. (1964). Information processes in human skill. *Brit. med. Bull.* **20**, 32–37.

Crossman, E. R. F. W., and Everstine, L. (1965). Information transfer, feedback, and the coding of communications within task-oriented groups. Unpublished paper.

Crystal, D., and Quirk, R. (1964). Systems of prosodic and paralinguistic features in English. *Janua linguarum* (Ser. Minor), No. XXXIX. The Hague: Mouton.

Davitz, J. R. (1964). *The communication of emotional meaning.* New York: McGraw-Hill.

Deutsch, H. (1955). The imposter: contribution to ego psychology of a type of psychopath. *Psychoanal. Quart.* **24**, 483–505.

DeVore, I. (Ed.) (1965). *Primate behavior: field studies of monkeys and apes.* New York: Holt, Rinehart & Winston.

Dittman, A. T. (1962). The relationship between body movements and moods in interviews. *J. consult. Psychol.* **26**, 480.

Dittman, A. T., and Wynne, L. C. (1961). Linguistic techniques and the analysis of emotionality in interviews. *J. abnorm. soc. Psychol.* **63**, 201–204.

Ekman, P. (1965). Communication through nonverbal behavior: a source of information about an interpersonal relationship. In S. S. Tomkins and C. E. Izzard (Eds.), *Affect, cognition and personality.* New York: Springer, pp. 390–442.

Eldred, S. H., and Price, D. B. (1958). A linguistic evaluation of feeling states in psychotherapy. *Psychiatry* **21**, 115–121.

Elworthy, F. T. (1895). *The evil eye: the origins and practices of superstition.* London: John Murray.

Erikson, E. H. (1956). The problem of ego identity. *J. Amer. Psychoanal. Assoc.* **4**, 56–111.

Ervin-Tripp, Susan (1964). An analysis of the interaction of language, topic and listener. *Amer. Anthrop.* **66** (6), Pt. 2, 86–102.

Exline, R. V. (1963). Explorations in the process of person perception: visual interaction in relation to competition, sex and need for affiliation. *J. Pers.* **31**, 1–20.

Exline, R. V., and Winters, L. C. (1965). Affective relations and mutual glances in dyads. In S. Tomkins and C. Izzard (Eds.), *Affect, cognition and personality.* New York: Springer, pp. 319–351.

Exline, R. V., Thibaut, J., Brannon, C., and Gumpert, P. (1961). Visual interaction in relation to Machiavellianism and an unethical act. *Amer. Psychol.* **16**, 396.

Exline, R. V., Gray, D., and Schuette, D. (1965). Visual behaviour in a dyad as affected by interview content, and sex of respondent. *J. Pers. soc. Psychol.* **1**, 201–209.

Ferguson, C. (1959). Diglossia. *Word* **15**, 325–340.

Ferguson, C. (1964). Baby talk in six languages. *Amer. Anthrop.* **66** (6), Pt. 2, 103–114.

Fiedler, F. E. (1953). Quantitative studies on the role of therapists' feelings towards their patients. In O. H. Mowrer (Ed.), *Psychotherapy, theory and research.* New York: Ronald.

Fiedler, F. E. (1964). A contingency model of leadership effectiveness. Advanc. exp. soc. Psychol. **1**, 150–190.

Frank, L. K. (1957). Tactile communication. *Genet. psychol. Monogr.* **56**, 209–225.

Fries, C. C. (1952). *The structure of english.* New York: Harcourt, Brace, and World.

Gardner, Gail (1964). The psychotherapeutic relationship. *Psychol. Bull.* **61**, 426–437.

Garfinkel, H. (1963). Trust and stable actions. In O. J. Harvey (Ed.), *Motivation and social interaction.* New York: Ronald Press.

Gibson, J. J., and Pick, Anne D. (1963). Perception of another person's looking behavior. *Amer. J. Psychol.* **76**, 386–394.

Gleason, H. A., Jr. (1961). *An introduction to descriptive linguistics.* 2nd ed. New York: Holt, Rinehart & Winston.

Goffman, E. (1955). On face-work: an analysis of ritual elements in social interaction. *Psychiatry* **18**, 213–231.

Goffman, E. (1956). Embarrassment and social organization. *Amer. J. Sociol.* **62**, 264–271.

Goffman, E. (1957). Alienation from interaction. *Hum. Relat.* **10**, 47–60.

Goffman, E. (1959). *Presentation of self in everyday life.* New York: Doubleday.

Goffman, E. (1961a). *Asylums.* Chicago: Aldine.

Goffman, E. (1961b). *Encounters.* Indianapolis: Bobbs-Merrill.

Goffman, E. (1963). *Behavior in public places.* New York: Free Press.

Goldman-Eisler, Frieda (1951). The measurement of time sequences in conversational behavior. *Brit. J. Psychol.* **42**, 355–362.

Goldman-Eisler, Frieda (1952). Individual differences between interviewers and their effect on interviewees' conversational behavior. *J. ment. Sci.* **98**, 660–671.

Goldman-Eisler, Frieda (1958). Speech analysis and mental processes. *Lang. Speech* **1**, 59–75.

Gough, H. G. (1965). A validational study of the Chapin Social Insight Test. *Psychol. Rep.* **17**, 355–368.

Gross, E., and Stone, C. P. (1964). Embarrassment and the analysis of role requirements. *Amer. J. Sociol.* **70**, 1–15.

Guze, S. B., and Mensch, I. N. (1959). An analysis of some features of the interview with the interaction chronograph. *J. abnorm. soc. Psychol.* **58**, 269–271.

Haines, D. B., and Eachus, H. T. (1965). A preliminary study of acquiring cross-cultural interaction skills through self-confrontation. Ohio: Aerospace Med. Res. Lab., Wright-Patterson Air Force Base.

Hall, E. T. (1959). *The silent language.* New York: Doubleday.

Hall, E. T. (1963). A system for the notation of proxemic behavior. *Amer. Anthrop.* **65**, 1003–1026.

Hall, E. T. (1964). Silent assumptions in social communication. *Res. Publ. Assoc. nerv. ment. Dis.* **42**, 41–55.

Hamblin, R. L. (1958). Leadership and crises. *Sociometry* **21**, 322–335.

Hare, A. P., and Bales, R. F. (1963). Seating position and small group interaction. *Sociometry* **26**, 480–486.

Haythorn, W. (1956). The effects of varying combinations of authoritarian and equalitarian leaders and followers. *J. abnorm. soc. Psychol.* **52**, 210–219.

Hazard, J. (1962). Furniture arrangement and judicial roles. *Etc.* **19**, 181–188.

Hediger, H. (1955). *Studies of the psychology and behaviour of captive animals in zoos and circuses.* London and Washington, D. C.: Butterworth.

Heinicke, C., and Bales, R. F. (1953). Developmental trends in the structure of small groups. *Sociometry* **16**, 7–38.

Herman, S. N. (1961). Explorations in the social psychology of language choice. *Human Relat.* **14**, 149–164.

Hess, E. H. (1965). Attitude and pupil size. *Sci. Amer.* **212**(4), 46–54.

Hewes, G. W. (1955). World distribution of certain postural habits. *Amer. Anthrop.* **57**, 231–244.

Homans, G. C. (1950). *The human group.* New York: Harcourt, Brace, and World.

Hutt, C., and Ounsted, C. (1966). The biological significance of gaze aversion: with special reference to childhood autism. *Behav. Sci.* **11**, 346–356.

Hutt, C., and Vaizy, M. J. (1966). Differential effects of group density on social behaviour. *Nature* **209**, 1371–1372.

Hutt, C., Hutt, S. J., Lee, D., and Ounsted, C. (1964). Arousal and childhood autism. *Nature* **204**, 908.

Jaffe, J. (1964). Verbal behavior analysis in psychiatric interviews with the aid of digital computers. *Res. Publ. Assoc. nerv. ment. Dis.* **42**, 389–399.

Jay, Phyllis (1965). The common langur of North India. In I. DeVore (Ed.), *Primate behavior: field studies of monkeys and apes.* New York: Holt, Rinehart & Winston, pp. 197–249.

Jecker, J. D., Maccoby, H., Breitrose, H. S., and Rose, E. D. (1964). Teacher accuracy in assessing cognitive visual feedback. *J. appl. Psychol.* **48**, 393–397.

Jennings, H. S. (1950). *Leadership and isolation.* 2nd ed. New York: McKay.

Jones, E. E., and Thibaut, J. W. (1958). Interaction goals as bases of inference in interpersonal perception. In R. Tagiuri and L. Petrullo (Eds.), *Person perception and interpersonal behavior.* Stanford, California: Stanford Univ. Press, pp. 151–178.

Joos, M. (1962). The five clocks. *Internat. J. Amer. Linguistics* **28**(2), Pt.V.

Jourard, S. M. (1964). *The transparent self.* Princeton, New Jersey: Van Nostrand.

Jourard, S. M. (1966). An exploratory study of body-accessibility. *Brit. J. clin. soc. Psychol.* in press.

Kanfer, F. H., Phillips, Jeanne S., Matarazzo, J. D., and Saslow, G. (1960). The experimental modification of interviewer content in standardized interviews. *J. consult. Psychol.* **24**, 528–536.

Kendon, A. (1963). *Temporal aspects of the social performance in two-person encounters.* Unpublished doctoral thesis, Oxford.

Kendon, A. (1967). Some functions of gaze direction in social interaction. *Acta Psychol.* **26**, 22–63.

Kramer, E. (1963). Judgment of personal characteristics and emotions from non-verbal properties of speech. *Psychol. Bull.* **60**, 408–420.

Laing, R. (1960). *The divided self.* Chicago: Quadrangle.

Lashley, K. S. (1951). The problem of serial order in behavior. In L. A. Jeffress (Ed.), *Cerebral mechanisms in behavior.* New York: Wiley, pp. 112–136.

Lennard, H. L., and Bernstein, A. (1960). *The anatomy of psychotherapy.* New York: Columbia Univ. Press.

Leik, R. K. (1965). Type of group and probability of initiating acts. *Sociometry* **28**, 57–65.

Levin, H., Baldwin, A. L., Gallwey, M., and Paivio, A. (1960). Audience stress, personality and speech. *J. abnorm. soc. Psychol.* **61**, 469–473.

Lippitt, R. (1949). *Training in community relations.* New York: Harper & Row.

Little, K. B. (1965). Personal space. *J. exp. soc. Psychol.* **1**, 237–247.

Lombard, G. G. F. (1955). *Behaviour in a selling group.* Cambridge, Massachusetts: Harvard Univ. Press.

Lott, A. J., and Lott, Bernice E. (1965). Group cohesiveness as interpersonal attraction: a review of relationships with antecedent and consequent variables. *Psychol. Bull.* **64**, 259–309.

Lundy, B. W. (1955). *Temporal factors of interaction in psychotherapy.* Unpublished doctoral thesis, Univ. of Chicago.

Lundy, R. M. (1956). Assimilative projection and accuracy of prediction in interpersonal perceptions. *J. abnorm. soc. Psychol.* **52**, 33–38.

McDavid, J., Jr., and Schroder, H. M: (1957). The interpretation of approval and disapproval by delinquent and non-delinquent adolescents. *J. Pers.* **25**, 539–549.

McGregor, D. (1960). *The human side of enterprise.* New York: McGraw-Hill.

Machotka, P. (1965). Body movement as communication. *Dialogue: behavioral science research.* Boulder, Colorado: Western Interstate Commission for Higher Education.

Maclay, H., and Osgood, C. E. (1959). Hesitation phenomena in English. *Word* **15**, 19–44.

McPhail, P. (1966). Adolescent problems of adjustment. In G. N. P. Howat (Ed.), *Essays to a young teacher.* New York: Macmillan (Pergamon).

Mahl, G. F. (1963). The lexical and linguistic levels in the expression of the emotions. In H. Knapp (Ed.), *Expressions of emotion in man.* New York: Internat. Univ. Press.

Mahl, G. F., and Schulze, G. (1964). Psychological research in the extralinguistic area. In T. A. Sebeok, A. S. Hayes, and Mary C. Bateson (Eds.), *Approaches to semiotics.* The Hague: Mouton, pp. 51–124.

Maier, N. R. F. (1952). *Principles of human relations.* New York: Wiley.

Maier, N. R. F., Solem, A. R., and Maier, A. A. (1957). *Supervising and executive development.* New York: Wiley.

Malinowski, B. (1928). The problem of meaning in primitive languages. Supplement I to C. K. Ogden and I. A. Richards, *The meaning of meaning.* Rev. ed., 1966. New York: Harcourt, Brace, and World.

Maslow, A. H., Hirsh, Elisa, Stein, Marcella, and Honigmann, Irma (1945). A clinically derived test for measuring psychological security-insecurity. *J. gen. Psychol.* **33**, 24–41.

Matarazzo, J. D. (1962). Prescribed behavior therapy. Suggestions from noncontent interview research. In A. Bachrach (Ed.), *Experimental foundations of clinical psychology*. New York: Basic Books.

Matarazzo, J. D., and Saslow, G. (1961). Difference in interview interaction behaviour among normal and deviant groups. In I. A. Berg and B. M. Bass (Eds.), *Conformity and deviation*. New York: Harper and Row.

Matarazzo, J. D., and Wiens, A. N. (1965). Studies of interview speech behavior. In L. Krasner and L. P. Ullman (Eds.), *Research in behavior modification: new developments and their clinical implications*. New York: Holt, Rinehart & Winston, 179–210.

Matarazzo, J. D., Weitman, M., Saslow, G., and Wiens, A. N. (1963). Interviewer influence on duration of interviewee speech. *J. verb. Learning verb. Behav.* **1**, 451–458.

Matarazzo, J. D., Saslow, G., Wiens, A. N., Weitman, M., and Allen, B. V. (1964a). Interviewer headnodding and interviewee speech durations. *Psychother. Theor. res. Practise* **1**, 54–63.

Matarazzo, J. D., Wiens, A. N., Saslow, G. , Dunham, R. M., and Voas, R. B. (1964b). Speech duration of astronaut and ground communicator. *Science* **143**, 148–150.

Matarazzo, J. D., Wiens, A. N., and Saslow, G. (1965). Studies of interview speech behavior. In L. Krasner and L. P. Ullman (Eds.), *Research in behavior modification: new developments and their clinical implications*. New York: Holt, Rinehart and Winston.

Miller, D. R. (1963). The study of social relationships: situation, identity, and social interaction. *Psychology: A study of a science*. **5**, 639–737.

Miller, G. A., Galanter, E., and Pribram, K. H. (1960). *Plans and the structure of behavior*. New York: Holt, Rinehart & Winston.

Miller, N. E. (1944). Experimental studies of conflict. In J. McV. Hunt, (Ed.), *Personality and the behaviour disorders*. New York: Ronald Press.

Mohanna, A. I., and Argyle, M. (1960). A cross-cultural study of structured groups with unpopular central members. *J. abnorm. soc. Psychol.* **60**, 139–140.

Moscovici, S., and Plon, M. (1966). Les situations collogues: observations théoriques et expérimentales. *Bull Psychol.* **247**, 702–22.

Newcomb, T. M. (1961). *The acquaintance process*. New York: Holt, Rinehart & Winston.

Nielsen, G. (1962). *Studies in self confrontation*. Copenhagen: Munksgaard.

Northway, M. L., and Wigdor, B. T. (1947). Rorschach patterns as related to the sociometric status of school children. *Sociometry* **10**, 186–199.

Osgood, C. E. (1966). Dimensionality of the semantic space for communication via facial expressions. *Scand. J. Psychol.* **7**, 1–30.

Ostwald, P. F. (1965). Acoustic methods in psychiatry. *Sci. Amer.* **212**(3), 82–91.

Paivio, A., Baldwin, A. L., and Berger, S. M. (1961). Measurement of children's sensitivity to audiences. *Child Developm.* **32**, 721–730.

Pike, K. L. (1954). *Language in relation to a unified theory of the structure of human behavior*. Glendale, California: Summer Institute of Linguistics, Vol. I.

Pittinger, R. E. (1958). Linguistic analysis of tone of voice in communication of affect. *Psychiat. Res. Rep.* **8**, 41–54.

Pittinger, R. E., and Smith, H. L. (1957). A basis for some contributions of linguistics to psychiatry. *Psychiatry* **20**, 61–78.

Pittinger, R. E., Hockett, C. F., and Danchy, J. J. (1960). *The first five minutes: a sample of microscopic interview analysis*. New York: Martineau.

Pope, B., and Siegman, A. W. (1962). The effect of therapist activity level and specificity on patient productivity and speech disturbances in the initial interview. *J. consult. Psychol.* **26**, 489.

Pope, B., and Siegman, A. W. (1965). Interviewer specificity and topical focus in relation to interviewee productivity. *J. verb. Learning verb. Behav.* **4**, 188–192.

Potter, S. (1952). *One-upmanship*. London: Hart-Davis.

Riemer, M. D. (1955). Abnormalities of the gaze—a classification. *Psychiat. Quart.* **29**, 659–672.

Rosenbaum, M. E. (1959). Social perception and the motivational structure of interpersonal relations. *J. abnorm. soc. Psychol.* **59**, 130–133.

Rosenberg, M. (1965). *Society and the adolescent self-image*. Princeton, New Jersey: Princeton Univ. Press.

Sapir, E. (1921). *Language: an introduction to the study of speech*. New York: Harcourt, Brace.

Sarbin, T. R., and Hardyck, C. R. (1955). Conformance in role perception as a personality variable. *J. consult. Psychol.* **19**, 109–111.

Saslow, G., and Matarazzo, J. D. (1959). A technique for studying changes in interview behavior. In E. A. Rubinstein and M. B. Parloff (Eds.), *Research in psychotherapy*. Washington, D. C.: Amer. Psychol. Assoc.

Saslow, G., Goodrich, D. W., and Stein, M. (1956). Study of therapist behavior in diagnostic interviews by means of the interaction chronograph. *J. clin. Psychol.* **12**, 133–139.

Scheflen, A. E. (1964). The significance of posture in communication systems. *Psychiatry* **27**, 316–321.

Scheflen, A. E. (1965a). *Stream and structure of communicational behavior*. Commonwealth of Pennsylvania: Eastern Pennsylvania Psychiat. Inst.

Scheflen, A. E. (1965b). Natural history method in psychotherapy: communicational research. In L. Gottschalk and A. H. Auerbach (Eds.), *Methods of research in psychotherapy*. New York: Appleton-Century-Crofts, pp. 263–289.

Schlosberg, H. (1954). Three dimensions of emotion. *Psychol. Rev.* **61**, 81–88.

Schutz, W. C. (1955). What makes groups productive? *Hum. Relat.* **8**, 429–465.

Schutz, W. C. (1958). *FIRO: a three dimensional theory of interpersonal behavior*. New York: Holt, Rinehart & Winston.

Secord, P. F., and Backman, C. W. (1964). *Social psychology*. New York: McGraw-Hill.

Sidney, C., and Brown, M. (1961). *The skills of interviewing*. London: Tavistock.

Siegman, A. W., and Pope, B. (1962). An empirical scale for the measurement of therapist specificity in the initial psychiatric interview. *Psychol. Rep.* **11**, 515–520.

Siegman, A. W., and Pope, B. (1965). Effects of question specificity and anxiety producing messages on verbal fluency in the initial interview. *J. Pers. soc. Psychol.* **2**, 522–530.

Simon, H. A. (1952). A formal theory of interaction in social groups. *Amer. sociol. Rev.* **17**, 202–211.

Sommer, R. (1959). Studies in personal space. *Sociometry* **22**, 247–260.

Sommer, R. (1961). Leadership and group geography. *Sociometry* **24**, 99–109.

Sommer, R. (1962). The distance for comfortable conversation. *Sociometry* **25**, 111–116.

Sommer, R. (1965). Further studies of small group ecology. *Sociometry* **28**, 337–348.

Sorensen, O. (1958). *The observed changes enquiry*. New York: General Electric Company.

Soskin, W. F., and John, Vera P. (1963). The study of spontaneous talk. In R. G. Barker (Ed.), *The stream of behavior: exploration of its structure and content*. New York: Appleton-Century-Croft, pp. 228–281.

Stagner, R. (1961). *Psychology of personality*. New York: McGraw-Hill.

Steiner, I. D. (1955). Interpersonal behaviour as influenced by accuracy of social perception. *Psychol. Rev.* **62**, 268–274.

Steinzor, B. (1950). The spatial factor in face to face discussion groups. *J. abnorm. soc. Psychol.* **45**, 552–555.

Stock, D. (1964). A survey of research on T-group. In L. P. Bradford, J. R. Gibb, and K. D. Benns (Eds.), *T-Group theory and laboratory method*. New York: Wiley.

Sumby, W. H., and Pollack, I. (1954). Visual contribution to speech intelligibility in noise. *J. Acoust. Soc. Amer.* **26**, 212–215.

Tharp, R. G. (1963). Psychological patterning in marriage. *Psychol. Bull.* **60**, 97–117.

Thibaut, J. W., and Kelley, H. H. (1959). *The social psychology of groups.* New York: Wiley.

Thorndike, R. L., and Stein, S. (1937). An evaluation of the attempts to measure social intelligence. *Psychol. Bull.* **34**, 275–285.

Tomkins, S. S. (1963). *Affect, imagery, consciousness.* Vol. II. *The negative effects.* New York: Springer.

Trager, G. L. (1958). Paralanguage: a first approximation. *Studies Linguistics* **13**, 1–12.

Triandis, H. C. (1960). Cognitive similarity and communication in a dyad. *Hum. Relat.* **13**, 175–183.

Tuason, V. B., Guze, S. B., McClure, J., and Begnelin, J. (1961). A further study of some features of the interview with the interaction chronograph. *Amer. J. Psychiat.* **118**, 438–446.

Watson, Jeanne and Potter, R. J. (1962). An analytic unit for the study of interaction. *Hum. Relat.* **15**, 245–263.

Weisbrod, Rita M. (1965). Looking behavior in a discussion group. Term paper submitted for Psychology 546, under the direction of Prof. Longabaugh, Cornell Univ., Ithaca, New York.

Welford, A. T. (1958). *Ageing and human skill.* London and New York: Oxford Univ. Press.

Winer, M., and Mehrabian, A. *Beyond meaning: a communication channel in verbal behavior.* Unpublished manuscript.

Wolff, P. H. (1963). Observations on the early development of smiling. In B.M. Foss (Ed.), *Determinants of infant behaviour.* Vol. II. London: Methuen.

Wynn-Edwards, V. C. (1962). *Animal dispersion in relation to social behavior.* New York: Harcourt, Brace, and World.

A STRUCTURAL BALANCE APPROACH TO THE ANALYSIS OF COMMUNICATION EFFECTS

N. T. Feather

DEPARTMENT OF PSYCHOLOGY
UNIVERSITY OF NEW ENGLAND
NEW SOUTH WALES, AUSTRALIA

I. Introduction

The main aim of this paper is to present a model that was developed to further understanding of the way in which people react in communication situations. This model does not deal with the factors that influence the initiation of communications between people, nor does it consider different communication networks that might exist within groups. Rather, the model focuses upon the consequences that follow the presentation of a communication or message by a source to a receiver. It is especially concerned with the cognitive adjustments that may ensue. The model enables theoretical analysis of questions such as the following: Under what conditions will a communication be accepted or rejected by the receiver? When might one expect attitude change to occur as a result of a communication? What are the characteristics of the source of a communication which influence the fate of his communication? How might a source react to attitude-discrepant communication?

These kinds of question are not new in the literature of communication. Many of them have been investigated in the important set of studies that were conducted at Yale by Hovland and his associates. What is distinctive in the present approach is the attempt to represent the way a person perceives and structures a communication situation in terms of the mathematical theory of linear graphs (Cartwright and Harary, 1956; Harary, 1959: Harary *et al.*, 1965). This cognitive structure is considered as an interdependent system involving a set of relations that tend to follow a principle of consistency or balance; that is, we expect cognitive adjustments to occur in the direction of a consistent or balanced set of relations.

The general principle that man prefers a state of affairs in which his cognitions are organized in a balanced or consistent manner is one that has occupied a central place in a number of models developed in recent years. There is no space in the present paper to discuss these models in detail. In any case, excellent reviews are already available in the literature (see Brown, 1962; Osgood, 1960; Zajonc, 1960b). Instead, we intend to focus upon Heider's (1946, 1958) principle of balance since it is a seminal contribution that is quite basic to the present analysis of communication effects. This paper is therefore developed in the following way: Heider's principle of balance is first discussed, together with relevant experimental evidence and theoretical extensions. The structural balance model of communication effects is then presented and some recent studies explicitly based upon this model are described, after which other experimental studies relevant to the model are reviewed. The paper concludes with an examination of a number of issues that appear important, perhaps critical, and whose solution may demand further refinements of the basic model. The focus of the review is on *recent* theory and research.

II. Balance Theory

Heider's principle of balance was first published some twenty years ago (Heider, 1946) in a paper dealing with attitudes and cognitive organization. Its more recent statement is contained in *The Psychology of Interpersonal Relations* (Heider, 1958), a book that is avowedly cognitive in approach and rich in insights whose scientific testing could occupy psychologists for many years to come. Heider argues that scientific psychology has much to learn from common-sense psychology, particularly in regard to the analysis of interpersonal relations. His principle of balance is presented in the context of a discussion of sentiment that refers to the way a person p feels about or evaluates another person o or an impersonal entity x. A positive *sentiment relation* is written as L, a negative sentiment relation as DL. Thus p L o means that p likes, values, or admires o; p DL o means that p dislikes, disapproves of, or rejects o. The second major type of relation presented by Heider is the *unit relation*. This is introduced in the context of a discussion of unit formation and cognitive organization, a discussion that, in particular, draws attention to the Gestalt principles of formal organization in perception as principles specifying some of the conditions under which unit formation occurs. Heider (1958) suggests that:

. . . separate entities comprise a unit when they are perceived as belonging together . . . Persons and objects are the units that first come to mind; the parts of such units are perceived as belonging together in a specially close way. But also two (or more) separate entities can form a unit. The two entities may be related through similarity, causality, ownership or other unit-forming characteristics . . . (p. 176; pp. 200–201).

A cognitive unit between two entities is denoted by U; not U is taken to imply that the two entities are segregated. Thus p U x can mean that p owns x, p made x, p causes x; and p not U x can mean that p does not own x, is not associated with x, and so on.

Heider assumes that there is a tendency for the relations among the entities p, o, and x to fit together harmoniously. In particular, sentiment relations and unit relations are assumed to be interdependent and to tend toward a balanced state. The conditions for balance are defined as follows:

A dyad is balanced if the relations between the two entities are all positive (L and U) or all negative (DL and not U). Disharmony results when relations of different sign character exist.

A triad is balanced when all three of the relations are positive or when two of the relations are negative and one is positive. Imbalance occurs when two of the relations are positive and one is negative. The case of three negative relations is somewhat ambiguous . . . (Heider, 1958, pp. 202–203).

The following are some examples of balanced sets of relations between entities using the principle just described: p likes something he made (p L x, p U x); p likes what his friend likes (p L o, o L x, p L x); p's son likes what p likes (p U o, p L x, o L x); p dislikes what his enemy likes (p DL x, p DL o, o L x). Some examples of unbalanced sets of relations are as follows: p's friend dislikes him (p L o, o DL p); p likes what his friend dislikes (p L x, p L o, o DL x).

Heider's basic hypothesis therefore asserts that sentiment and unit relations between entities tend toward a balanced state. He suggests that these states of balance are preferred over disharmony; that new relations may be induced by existing relations so as to produce a balanced state; that where relations are not in balance there will be a tendency for them to change so that a balanced configuration is achieved; and that if such a change is not possible the state of imbalance will produce tension.

Heider (1958, Chapter 7) cites a number of studies whose results are generally consistent with his principle of balance. For example, Horowitz et al. (1951), in a study concerned with the induction of forces in discussion groups, found that agreement or disagreement with a person's acts was directly related to his valence. They considered not only the p-o-x unit but higher order units as well, such as the p-o-q-x unit, which represents what p thinks q would say about o's act x. Jordan (1953) required subjects to rate p-o-x triads involving positive and negative L and U relations for their pleasantness. Of the 64 triads that were rated 32 were balanced and 32 were unbalanced according to Heider's principle. Jordan found that unbalanced situations were rated as more unpleasant than balanced situations. Situations involving positive relations between p and o or p and x were rated as more pleasant than situations having negative relations; situations involving positive U relations were rated as more pleasant than those involving positive U relations; situations involving negative U relations were rated as more pleasant than those having negative L relations. Relations between p and o seemed to carry the most weight.

Kogan and Tagiuri (1958), using groups of enlisted naval personnel who had been living together on board ship for at least two months, requested subjects to indicate the three crew members with whom they would most like to go on a 72-hour liberty and to identify the three choices that would be made by the other members. It was also possible to obtain information from one group about the three persons with whom they would least like to go on liberty. Kogan and Tagiuri found that there were more balanced cognitive units in the relationships the men believed existed than would have occurred by chance, or that did exist in actuality. Burdick and Burnes (1958) reported two studies that are consistent with a balance hypothesis. In a first experiment they found that GSR deflections were associated with disagreement with a positively valent experimenter. In a second experiment they found that subjects who reported liking the source of a communication tended to change their opinions toward more agreement with him. When they were subsequently induced to dislike him, they tended to change their opinions toward greater disagreement.

More recently, Zajonc and Burnstein (1965a) found that subjects had more difficulty learning an unbalanced structure than a balanced one, but only when the issue was an important one. They also found that negative relationships were more difficult to learn than positive relationships. In addition, their experiments (Zajonc and Burnstein, 1965b) disclosed that subjects made fewer errors in learning relationships embedded in structures with a high degree of balance than in structures with a low degree of balance.

It should be noted that the conditions for structural balance specified by Heider presuppose that p has a *positive* attitude toward himself. Heider makes this quite clear in his book (Heider, 1958, p. 210). If p were to evaluate himself negatively, then the conditions for balance would be altered. In this case, for example, p might like an o who disliked him. Deutsch and Solomon (1959) reported an experiment in which it was found that subjects' evaluations of their own performances strongly influenced their reactions to evaluations received from others. If subjects received negative notes, they evaluated the note-writers very unfavorably if they thought they themselves had done well, but rather favorably if they thought they had performed poorly. Subjects who received positive notes evaluated the note-writers favorably if they thought well rather than poorly of their own performances. Deutsch and Solomon also found that when the subjects' evaluations of their own performances were held constant they responded more favorably to positive than to negative evaluations from another. They called this the "positivity effect." When this effect was held constant subjects responded more favorably to evaluations from another that were consistent with their own evaluations. Deutsch and Solomon called this the "cognitive balance effect."

In 1956 Cartwright and Harary published a generalization of Heider's principle of structural balance which involved the application of the mathematical theory of linear graphs. In this paper the authors noted certain limitations and ambiguities in Heider's statement of his principle. In particular, they argued that it would be an advantage (a) to treat asymmetric relations in the model, (b) to extend the principle of balance to units consisting of more than three entities, (c) to distinguish clearly between the complement and the opposite of a relation, (d) to consider relations of different types (not merely sentiment and unit relations), and (e) to extend the principle of balance to social systems rather than to limit it to cognitive units that involve entities and relations as perceived by the individual.

In a very recent book, Harary *et al.* (1965) stated that an important advantage of graph theory lies in its potential usefulness as "... a mathematical model of the structural properties of any empirical system consisting of relationships among pairs of elements" (p. 2). It provides the psychologist with a mathematics that enables him to represent the hitherto slippery and rather ambiguous concept of structure. A structure may be considered as involving a set of elements and a set of relations between some or all of these elements. By applying graph theory one may coordinate the elements to points of a graph and the relations to lines of a graph. Thus concepts such as social structure, personality structure, kinship structure, attitude structure, and syntactical structure would become amenable to mathematical representation, and the concepts, theorems, and methods of graph theory can then help to clarify the properties of empirical structures.

Cartwright and Harary (1956) indicated that by using graph theory it would be possible to give a mathematical representation to cognitive units that are balanced according to Heider's principle. Figure 1 presents a number of structures, half of which are balanced and half of which are unbalanced. In these structures a solid line represents a positive sentiment (or attitudinal) relation; a dashed line represents a negative sentiment (or attitudinal) relation. A solid bracket represents a positive unit relation; a dashed bracket represents a negative unit relation. The structures in Fig. 1 are called *signed digraphs* (s - digraphs) since lines in a structure

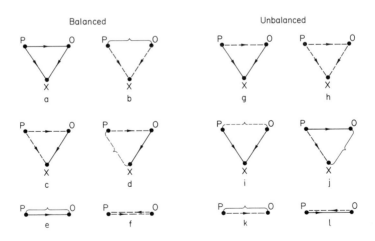

FIG. 1. Balanced and unbalanced signed digraphs involving sentiment and unit relations.

may have both *sign* (positive or negative) and *direction*. In Fig. 1 structures a, b, c, d, e, and f are balanced, and structures g, h, i, j, k, and l are unbalanced. In Fig. 1 signed digraphs a, c, f, g, h, and l involve only the one type of relation, in each case a sentiment relation. They are called signed digraphs of *type 1*. The remaining signed digraphs involve both sentiment and unit relations, that is, two types of relation, and are called signed digraphs of *type 2*. The signed digraphs in Fig. 1 can easily be translated into Heider's entities and relations. Signed digraph a, for example, represents the cognitive unit in which p L o, p L x, and o L x; signed digraph j represents the cognitive unit in which p L o, p DL x, and o U x.

Each of the signed digraphs in Fig. 1 involves a semicycle which is defined by Carwright and Harary as "... a collection of lines obtained by taking exactly one from each pair $\overrightarrow{AB}$ or $\overrightarrow{BA}$, $\overrightarrow{BC}$ or $\overrightarrow{CB}$, ..., $\overrightarrow{DE}$ or $\overrightarrow{ED}$. and $\overrightarrow{EA}$ or $\overrightarrow{AE}$" (1956, p. 283). For example, s-digraph a involves the semicycle $\overrightarrow{PO}$, $\overrightarrow{OX}$, and $\overrightarrow{XP}$. A comparison of the balanced and unbalanced s-digraphs in Fig. 1 suggests a simple principle that may be used to decide whether or not a structure is balanced. If, in each of the s-digraphs of Fig. 1, the *signs* of the lines are multiplied, it is apparent that the product is *positive* for balanced structures and *negative* for unbalanced structures, that is, in s-digraphs a, b, c, d, e, and f each semicycle is positive in sign; in s-digraphs g, h, i, j, k, and l each semicycle is negative in sign. This indicates that in the dyadic and triadic structures in Fig. 1 balanced units involve a positive semicycle, unbalanced units involve a negative semicycle. By this principle s-digraph h is unbalanced although its status is somewhat ambiguous in Heider's discussion.

Cartwright and Harary formulated the foregoing principle and extended it to structures containing any number of points, so that a more complex s-digraph would be completely balanced if all semicycles contained in the s-digraph were positive in sign. They also developed a *structure theorem* that makes it easier to identify a completely balanced s-digraph when the structure is complex. Some of the ideas presented in this early paper are developed in more detail in the recent book (Harary *et al.*, 1965, Chapter 13). There, two measures of structural balance are defined; the first, called the *degree of balance of an s-digraph*, is defined as "... the ratio of the number of positive semicycles b^+ to the total number of semicycles b in the digraph ...." (p. 346). The second measure, called the *line-index for balance*, considers the amount of balance in an s-digraph in terms of the number of lines that must be removed or whose sign must be changed in order to achieve balance (pp. 348–352). The authors also discuss *local balance* and *N-balance*. They define an s-digraph S as "... *locally balanced at v*, ... if every semicycle containing v is positive" (p. 344). The concept of local balance thus enables one to consider balance at various points of an s-digraph. The concept of N-balance is introduced to allow for the fact that, beyond a certain length, semicycles may be empirically unimportant insofar as balance is concerned. "For instance, it may make little difference in an affective structure whether rather long semicycles are negative. A signed digraph S is *N-balanced* if every semicycle of length N or less is positive" (p. 352). Harary and his colleagues also consider *cycle-balance* and *path-balance*, but these concepts will not concern us at this stage. It should be apparent, however, that these authors have generalized Heider's principle of balance considerably, so that structures which are of higher order than dyads and triads can be examined for balance, different measures of balance can be computed, and specific types of balance can be investigated.

In a study designed to evaluate some of the refinements of Heider's principle of balance proposed by Cartwright and Harary, Morrissette (1958) investigated hypothetical three-entity systems and four-entity systems in a paper and pencil setting. Subjects were required to predict sentiment relations and to rate the degree of tension they thought they would experience in the given system. Morrissette defined concepts of degree of total balance and degree of local balance at point p, and found that both of these ordered the data consistently for three-entity systems in which positive unit ($+U$) relations were assumed to exist among all pairs of entities. In four-entity systems, where $+U$ relations were again assumed to exist between all pairs of entities, an analysis in terms of local three-balance at point p ordered the data consistently with hypotheses. The tension reported by subjects decreased as the degree of balance of the given structures increased. Morrissette also attempted to induce $-U$ relations, but the results that he obtained suggest that he was unsuccessful.

In a later study, Shrader and Lewit (1962) introduced the concepts of the *plausibility* and *differentiability* of structures. Plausibility is defined as " ... the *mean degree of balance* of all completely connected structures which can be constructed, from the incompletely connected structure, by insertion of positive or negative relations where none are given" (p. 266). Differentiability is defined as " ... the *standard deviation of balances* calculated from these various completions" (p. 266). Using paper and pencil tests similar to Morrissette's, Shrader and Lewit found that as a structure became more plausible and/or more differentiable, subjects were more likely to infer such relations as to yield a completely connected structure with maximum balance, and to report lower tension and greater confidence in making completions. King (1964) recently attempted to generalize Heider's formulation of structural balance, tension, and segregation by using psychological scaling techniques. He described three distinct types of structural balance in groups. The results of his investigation indicated that his experimental group fitted one of these categories.

As we have noted, the applications of graph theory to social science center about the possibility that it will provide a means of representing the concept of structure using a mathematical language. Harary *et al.*, (1965) suggested some possible applications, although their presentation is mainly concerned with the development of the mathematical theory. Flament (1963) considered the applications of graph theory to group structure, but the presentation was again mainly concerned with the mathematical basis. Davis (1963) restated some propositions from the sociological and social-psychological literature using graph-theoretical concepts and balance theory. Oeser and Harary (1962; 1964) developed a mathematical model for structural role theory in which concepts from graph theory are employed. The main focus of the present paper is, however, on a structural balance model of communication effects (Feather, 1964a), and we now turn to a consideration of this model.

III. The Communication Model

The basic communication situation with which the model is concerned has a source (S) presenting a communication (C) about an issue (I) to a receiver (R). The communication may be presented verbally or may be written, but it does take some stand vis-à-vis the issue. As an example, the situation might be one in which a politician is presenting an argument about American intervention in South Vietnam to a member of a student group, or one in which a person watching television hears an announcer deliver a commercial about a particular product, or one where a psycho-therapist makes an evaluative statement to a patient about his progress. In each of these situations there are four elements, namely, a source or communicator (S), a receiver or communicatee (R), a communication (C), and an issue (I).

Two types of *relations* between these elements are considered, namely, attitudinal (sentiment) and unit relations. These relations may be positive or negative in sign. In the present statement of the model no allowance is made for differences in the *strength* of a relation; only the *sign* of a relation is considered. The relations dealt with are as they are understood by the source or receiver.

These four elements and relations that constitute a cognitive structuring of the communication situation are coordinated to concepts from graph theory. The elements are mapped into points of a graph; the relations are mapped into lines of a graph. Figure 2 presents the eight distinct s-digraphs which are *completely balanced* according to Heider's principle. In these s-digraphs the convention is again employed that solid lines are positive and

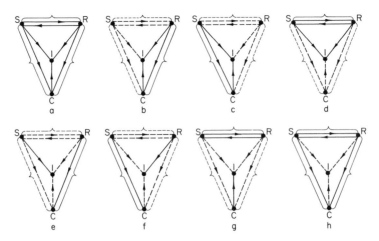

FIG. 2. Signed digraphs representing the eight communication structures in which all semicycles involving attitudinal and unit relations are completely balanced.

dashed lines are negative. A straight line represents an attitudinal relation; a bracket represents a unit relation. The arrows on the lines represent the direction of an attitudinal relation. It will be noted that some attitudinal relations are asymmetric. Source, receiver, and communication may have attitudes toward the issue, but the issue cannot have attitudes toward them. Attitudinal relations between source and receiver may, however, be symmetric.

The s-digraphs in Fig. 2 are of type 2 since two different relations (attitudinal and unit) are defined on the same set of elements. It should be obvious that each of the eight s-digraphs in Fig. 2 is completely balanced since all semicycles are positive in each s-digraph. For example, the semicycle consisting of $\overrightarrow{SI}$, $\overrightarrow{IR}$, and $\overrightarrow{RS}$ is positive in each of the eight s-digraphs, and this applies to all other semicycles irrespective of whether they involve only attitudinal relations, unit relations, or both types of relation, or whether they are of length 2, 3, or 4.

The model presented in Fig. 2 has considerable predictive power. In fact, all the relations represented in each s-digraph in Fig. 2 may be predicted using the principle of structural balance provided any *three* relations that involve the *four* elements (S, C, I, R) of the communication structure are given. A proper test of the foregoing model depends on how successfully one is able to coordinate the theoretical concepts to empirical operations. In particular, it is necessary to have precise operational specification of both attitudinal and unit relations. This problem of coordination was discussed in the original statement of the model (Feather, 1964a, pp. 298–299), where it was also indicated that use of the model involves a mapping into the cognitive structure of either the source or the receiver of the communication since it is this cognitive structure that is represented by the s-digraphs. If, for example, we are interested in how the receiver might react to a communication, we must know how relations within the communication situation are perceived from his point of view. In contrast, if we are interested in the source's reactions, it would be important to know how the source understood the relations within the communication situation. The source and the receiver may perceive relations between elements of the communication situation quite differently; their cognitive structuring of the situation may vary in important ways.

Several studies have been conducted to test various aspects of the structural balance model of communication effects. To date most of these studies have involved presenting subjects with hypothetical communication situations for which certain relations between the elements are given. Subjects are required to predict other relations, and their predictions are then examined to see whether or not they are consistent with the relations represented in the balanced structures of Fig. 2. We now turn to a consideration of these studies.

IV. Studies Based upon the Communication Model

A. EXPERIMENT I: EVALUATION AND CREDIBILITY

1. Aim

In the first experiment (Feather, 1965a) subjects were provided with information about the attitudes of source (S), receiver (R), and communication (C) toward the issue (I). When both positive and negative attitudinal relations are considered, there are eight possible sets of these relations; these are represented in the eight s-digraphs in Fig. 3. A positive unit relation between S and C is included in Fig. 3 to represent the source's ownership or responsibility for the communication.

The question we asked in this first experiment was whether subjects under role-playing conditions, given information about the attitudinal relations represented in Fig. 3, would predict the sign of the remaining attitudinal relations in accordance with the balanced structures shown in Fig. 2. It was expected that they would do so, but that their predictions based on the information represented in structures a, c, f, and h in Fig. 3 would be relatively more balanced than their predictions based on the information represented in structures b, d, e, and g in Fig. 3, since the latter structures are out of balance from the outset (the S – I – C triad is unbalanced since the sign of the semicycle is negative).

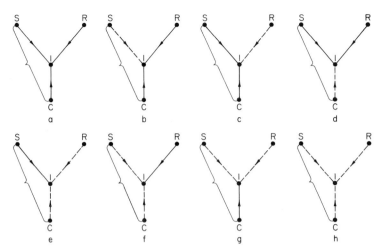

FIG. 3. Signed digraphs representing the eight possible combinations of positive and negative attitudinal relations of source (S), receiver (R), and communication (C) to issue (I), and positive unit relation of S to C (responsibility condition).

2. Procedure

Male and female undergraduate students enrolled in an introductory course in psychology at the University of New England in 1963 completed a Test of Identification. This test described a hypothetical communication situation in which a source (who was given a fictitious name) was delivering an argument about a controversial issue to a receiver (who was also given a fictitious name). The issue concerned the new visiting regulations that had been introduced by the university for students. Subjects were required to identify with either the source or the receiver of the communication. They were told the attitude (positive or negative) of source, receiver, and communication toward the issue for each of the eight communication situations corresponding to the eight s-digraphs in Fig. 3, and were required to predict the reactions of the person (source or receiver) with whom they identified. The eight communication situations were presented in random order to each subject. Male subjects identified with a male source (Form MS) or male receiver (Form MR). Female subjects identified with a female source (Form FS) or female receiver (Form FR).

All subjects had to predict whether the source and receiver would agree or disagree with the communication. These predictions were assumed to provide information about the $\overrightarrow{SC}$ and $\overrightarrow{RC}$ attitudinal relations for each communication situation. Subjects identified with the source had to predict whether the source would regard the receiver as well informed or not well informed about the issue. Subjects identified with the receiver had to predict whether the receiver would regard the source as well informed or not well informed about the issue. It was assumed that these predictions would provide information about the $\overrightarrow{SR}$ and $\overrightarrow{RS}$ attitudinal relations for each communication situation. In other words, attitudinal relations of source and receiver to the communication were assumed to be reflected in how they would *evaluate* the communication. Attitudinal relations of source and receiver toward one another were assumed to be reflected in judgments of *credibility* of source or receiver.

In this discussion, a subject's judgment of how the source would evaluate the argument is called an S-C response; his judgment of how the receiver would evaluate the argument is called an R-C response; and his judgment of the source's attitude toward the receiver (and vice versa) is called an S–R response. Responses were scored as balanced if they were consistent with the predicted attitudinal relations in Fig. 2. For example, for s-digraph d in Fig. 3 responses corresponding to a positive $\overrightarrow{SR}$ or $\overrightarrow{RS}$ attitudinal relation, a negative $\overrightarrow{RC}$ attitudinal relation, and a negative $\overrightarrow{SC}$ attitudinal relation would each be scored as balanced. Since subjects gave an S-C, an R–C, and an S–R response to each of the eight hypothetical communication situations, the total number of balanced responses possible for each subject in the Test of Identification was 24, made up of four balanced S–C responses, four balanced R-C responses, and four balanced S-R responses for the communication situations corresponding to structures a, c, f, and h in Fig. 3, and four balanced S-C responses, four balanced R-C responses, and four balanced S-R responses for the communication situations corresponding to structures b, d, e, and g in Fig. 3.

3. Results

The main results of this experiment are presented in Tables I and II. It is apparent that there is a general tendency to give balanced responses. The means are all above 2.00, the score to be expected in each cell of Tables I and II if subjects were to give equal numbers of balanced and unbalanced responses. The results also show that subjects tend to give relatively more balanced S-C and R-C responses than balanced S-R responses. Apparently, a judgment about the credibility of source or receiver is less likely to be balanced than a prediction about how the source or receiver will evaluate the communication. Finally, Tables I and II also show, as predicted, that subjects give fewer balanced responses to communication situations corresponding to s-digraphs b, d, e, and g than to communication situations corresponding to s-digraphs a, c, f, and h. The former structures represent communication situations in which the source is engaged in attitude-discrepant behavior, and are out of balance from the outset. The tendency to give balanced responses is especially low when

TABLE I

MEAN NUMBER OF BALANCED RESPONSES FOR MALE SUBJECTS,
EXPERIMENT I ($N = 20$)

| | Responses | | | | | |
| | Form MS | | | Form MR | | |
	S–C	R–C	S–R	S–C	R–C	S–R
Structures a, c, f, h	3.75	3.85	3.40	3.90	3.90	3.50
Structures b, d, e, g	3.55	3.50	3.35	3.70	3.70	2.25

| Analysis of variance | | | |
Source	df	MS	F
Between subjects	39		
Forms (A)	1	.338	< 1
Error a	38	1.692	
Within subjects	200		
Structures (B)	1	8.438	13.23[a]
A × B	1	1.837	2.88
Error b	38	.638	
Responses (C)	2	9.805	19.30[a]
A × C	2	2.712	5.34[b]
Error c	76	.508	
B × C	2	1.162	2.66
A × B × C	2	2.738	6.27[b]
Error bc	76	.437	

[a] $p < .001$.
[b] $p < .01$.

subjects identified with the receiver are required to judge whether or not
a source who is engaged in attitude-discrepant behavior is well-informed.

B.   EXPERIMENT II: RESPONSIBILITY AND COERCION

1. Aim

This experiment (Feather, 1965a) served as a partial replication of the
preceding study. As in Experiment I, subjects were presented with information about the eight sets of attitudinal relations presented in Fig. 3, and
it was expected that they would predict the signs of the remaining attitudinal
relations in accordance with the balanced structures in Fig. 2. It should be
noted that each of the s-digraphs in Fig. 3 involves a positive unit relation
between source and communication to represent the source's ownership or

TABLE II

MEAN NUMBER OF BALANCED RESPONSES FOR FEMALE SUBJECTS,
EXPERIMENT I $(N = 33)$

| | Responses | | | | | |
| | Form FS | | | Form FR | | |
	S–C	R–C	S–R	S–C	R–C	S–R
Structures a, c, f, h	3.97	3.97	3.42	3.94	3.94	3.30
Structures b, d, e, g	3.67	3.58	3.39	3.70	3.70	2.73

Analysis of variance

Source	df	MS	F
Between subjects	65		
Forms (A)	1	1.336	1.60
Error a	64	.836	
Within subjects	330		
Structures (B)	1	8.790	17.00[a]
A × B	1	.306	< 1
Error b	64	.517	
Responses (C)	2	15.579	26.23[a]
A × C	2	1.927	3.24[b]
Error c	128	.594	
B × C	2	.018	
A × B × C	2	1.184	3.45[b]
Error bc	128	.343	

[a] $p < .001$.
[b] $p < .05$.

responsibility for the communication. The main variation in the present experiment was to investigate a further condition: it was stated that the source had been *coerced* to present the argument. The assumption here was that coercion of the source could be represented by a negative unit relation between source and communication, as shown in the eight s-digraphs of Fig. 4.

Note that s-digraphs a, c, f, and h in Fig. 4 are out of balance from the outset. Hence we expected that subjects in the coercion condition would be less likely to give balanced responses to communication situations represented by these structures than to communication situations corresponding to s-digraphs b, d, e, and g. The present argument also held that the results for the responsibility condition of the experiment would replicate those of the prior study.

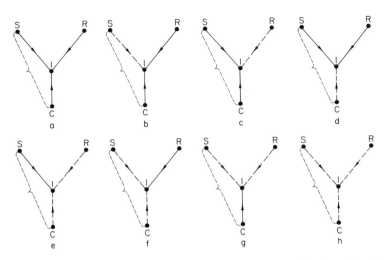

FIG. 4. Signed digraphs representing the eight possible combinations of positive and negative attitudinal relations of source (S), receiver (R), and communication (C) to issue (I), and negative unit relation of S to C (coercion condition).

2. Procedure

Male and female students attending a vacation school in introductory psychology at the University of New England in 1963 completed a Test of Identification. The procedure was exactly the same as in the previous experiment except that: (1) all subjects were required to identify with the receiver of the communication; (2) the communication concerned a different issue (state aid to independent schools); and (3) the degree to which the source was responsible for the communication was varied. In the responsibility condition subjects were told that the source was "*willingly* presenting the argument." In the coercion condition subjects were told that the source had been "*induced* by the payment of money to present an argument." The eight sets of attitudinal relations shown in either Fig. 3 or Fig. 4 were presented to subjects in random order, and subjects had to predict whether the source and receiver would agree or disagree with the argument, and whether the receiver would judge the source as well informed or not well informed.

3. Results

The main results of this experiment are given in Tables III and IV. Again it is apparent that there is a general tendency for subjects to give balanced responses, and that judgments about the credibility of the source are less balanced than are predictions about how source and receiver will evaluate the argument. Surprisingly, however, there is no difference in results between the responsibility and coercion conditions. Subjects in the coercion

TABLE III

MEAN NUMBER OF BALANCED RESPONSES FOR MALE SUBJECTS,
EXPERIMENT II ($N = 44$)

	Responses					
	Responsibility condition			Coercion condition		
	S–C	R–C	S–R	S–C	R–C	S–R
Structures a, c, f, h	3.64	3.75	3.18	3.50	3.55	3.14
Structures b, d, e, g	3.27	3.30	2.48	3.48	3.30	2.68

Analysis of variance			
Source	df	MS	F
Between subjects	87		
Conditions (A)	1	.002	< 1
Error a	86	1.528	
Within subjects	440		
Structures (B)	1	18.563	17.36[a]
A × B	1	2.320	2.17
Error b	86	1.069	
Responses (C)	2	21.280	40.23[a]
A × C	2	.394	< 1
Error c	172	.529	
B × C	2	1.659	3.80[b]
A × B × C	2	.053	< 1
Error bc	172	.437	

[a] $p < .001$.
[b] $p < .05$.

condition behave like subjects in the responsibility condition. These results therefore suggest that the communication situations for both conditions of this experiment should be mapped into the structures in Fig. 3 where a positive unit relation is assumed between source and communication. It is apparently an over-simplification to assume that coercion of a source to present an argument may be represented by a negative unit relation between S and C, as in Fig. 4.

C. EXPERIMENT III: RESPONSIBILITY AND COERCION

1. Aim

This experiment was conducted at the same time as the experiment just described, but used a different group of subjects and a different set of given relations (Feather, 1965b). These sets of relations are shown in Fig. 5 for the

TABLE IV
MEAN NUMBER OF BALANCED RESPONSES FOR FEMALE SUBJECTS,
EXPERIMENT II ($N = 16$)

	Responses					
	Responsibility condition			Coercion condition		
	S–C	R–C	S–R	S–C	R–C	S–R
Structures a, c, f, h	3.44	3.44	2.94	3.44	3.69	3.06
Structures b, d, e, g	3.56	3.25	2.69	3.13	3.44	2.56

Analysis of variance			
Source	df	MS	F
Between subjects	31		
Conditions (A)	1	0	0
Error a	30	2.116	
Within subjects	160		
Structures (B)	1	2.520	3.43^a
A × B	1	.750	1.02
Error b	30	.735	
Responses (C)	2	7.984	10.45^b
A × C	2	.766	1.00
Error c	60	.764	
B × C	2	.319	<1
A × B × C	2	.140	<1
Error bc	60	.529	

[a] $p < .05$ (one-tail).
[b] $p < .001$

responsibility condition and in Fig. 6 for the coercion condition. As in the experiment just discussed, a positive unit relation between S and C was assumed for the responsibility condition, and a negative unit relation between S and C was assumed for the coercion condition. Here we expected: (1) subjects would predict the remaining attitudinal relations in accordance with the balanced attitudinal relations in Fig. 2; (2) subjects in the responsibility .condition would give more balanced responses to communication situations corresponding to structures a, c, f, and h than to communication situations corresponding to structures b, d, e, and g, which are out of balance from the outset (Fig. 5); and (3) subjects in the coercion condition would do the reverse, giving more balanced responses to communication situations corresponding to structures b, d, e, and g than to those represented in structures a, c, f, and h, which are already out of balance (Fig. 6).

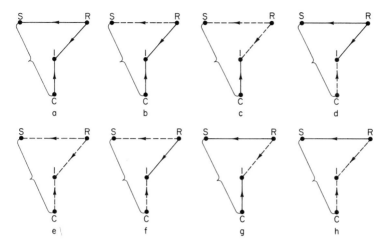

FIG. 5. Signed digraphs representing the eight possible combinations of positive and negative attitudinal relations of receiver (R) to source (S), receiver to issue (I), and communication (C) to issue, and positive unit relation of S to C (responsibility condition).

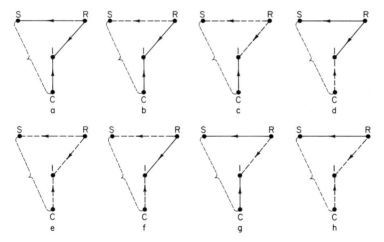

FIG. 6. Signed digraphs representing the eight possible combinations of positive and negative attitudinal relations of receiver (R) to source (S), receiver to issue (I), and communication (C) to issue, and negative unit relation of S to C (coercion condition).

2. Procedure

A Test of Identification was administered to male subjects attending a vacation school in introductory psychology at the University of New England in 1963. The procedure was exactly the same as in the preceding experiment, except that a different basic set of attitudinal relations was used.

For each communication situation subjects who identified with the receiver were told whether or not the source was well informed, whether or not the receiver agreed with the issue (state aid to independent schools), and whether or not the communication was in favor of the issue. They were required to predict how the source and receiver would evaluate the communication, and the source's attitude toward the issue. Responses were again scored as balanced if they were consistent with the predicted attitudinal relations in Fig. 2.

3. Results

The main results are summarized in Table V, where it is again evident that results do not differ significantly between the responsibility and coercion conditions of the experiment. For both conditions, subjects give fewer balanced responses to communication situations corresponding to s-digraphs b, d, e, and g than to communication situations corresponding

TABLE V

MEAN NUMBER OF BALANCED RESPONSES,
EXPERIMENT III ($N = 45$)

	Responses					
	Responsibility condition			Coercion condition		
	R–C	S–I	S–C	R–C	S–I	S–C
Structures a, c, f, h	3.56	3.62	3.38	3.69	3.47	3.24
Structures b, d, e, g	2.91	.64	.40	3.11	.58	.98

Analysis of variance			
Source	df	MS	F
Between subjects	89		
Conditions (A)	1	1.157	1.17
Error a	88	.989	
Within subjects	450		
Structures (B)	1	570.416	544.29[a]
A × B	1	2.817	2.69
Error b	88	1.048	
Responses (C)	2	98.235	175.73[a]
A × C	2	1.436	2.57
Error c	176	.559	
B × C	2	71.506	105.78[a]
A × B × C	2	1.505	2.23
Error bc	176	.676	

[a] $p < .001$.

to s-digraphs a, c, f, and h. The responses given are such as to balance the
S-I-C and the R-I-C triads in Fig. 5. For s-digraphs b, d, e, and g in Fig. 5 the
S-I and S-C responses given by subjects imply attitudinal relations that are
opposite to those that one would predict from the corresponding balanced
structures in Fig. 2 given the attitudinal relations in Fig. 5. In fact, these
results are quite consistent in indicating that, in the absence of contrary
information, a receiver tends to see a source as having the same
attitude toward the issue as the communication he presents and as agreeing
with the communication he presents. These results are obtained both
when the source is represented as willingly presenting the communication
(responsibility condition) and when he is represented as induced by money
to present the communication (ceorcion condition). Again, these results
are consistent with the assumption of a positive unit relation between
S and C in both conditions of the experiment; that is, they suggest
that the eight communication situations in both responsibility and
ceorcion conditions should be mapped into the eight structures shown
in Fig. 5. In common with the data presented in the previous section,
the present results therefore imply that even under conditions involving
ceorcion the receiver tends to see the communication as belonging
to the source. The source is linked with the communication from the
outset; he is seen as the person who is presenting the communication and
as having some ownership of it. Responsibility for the act is attributed
to him.

D.   EXPERIMENT IV: INTERPERSONAL ATTRACTION

The three studies summarized in the preceding sections required
subjects to predict the *sign* of various relations, for example, whether or not
the source and receiver would agree with the communication, whether or not
the source would be seen as well informed, whether or not the source would
be in favor of the issue. These studies were not concerned with the *strength*
of relations. In the study now to be described (Feather, 1966) the basic aim
was to obtain information about factors that might influence the strength of
a predicted relation when subjects were provided with information about
other relations. The study focused upon the attitudinal (liking) relation
between receiver (R) and source (S) and dealt only with dyadic and triadic
structures. The particular structures that were investigated are presented in
Fig. 7, 8, and 9, where the letters S and W on a line or bracket mean strong
relation and weak relation, respectively. Subjects given information about
the relations in each of these structures were required to predict the
$\overrightarrow{RS}$ attitudinal relation. The results of the study are relevant to the psychology of interpersonal attraction; in addition, they provide information concerning one of the principal unsolved problems of balance theory: How do

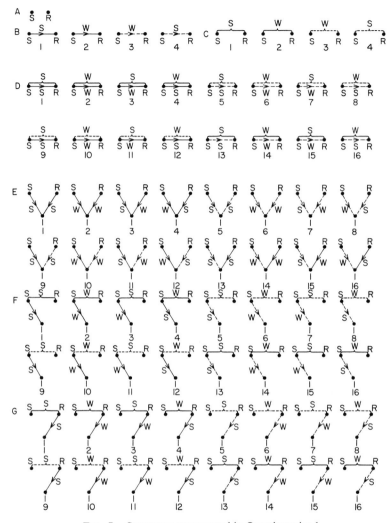

FIG. 7.   Structures represented in Questionnaire 1.

relations that differ in *strength* as well as in *sign* combine within a semicycle?
Only certain aspects of this study can be considered in the space available.

1. *Aim*

To a large extent the investigation was exploratory, although there were
certain well-formulated hypothesis in mind. It was expected that subjects
would predict an $\overrightarrow{RS}$ attitudinal relation that would determine balanced
structures where this was possible. Where only one relation (attitudinal or

FIG. 8.   Structures represented in Questionnaire 2.

unit) was given between S and R, we expected that the $\overrightarrow{RS}$ attitudinal relation predicted by subjects would mirror the given relation in strength as well as in sign. Where the attitudinal relations of S and R to I were given, various principles were considered that might underly subjects' predictions of the $\overrightarrow{RS}$ attitudinal relation. One of these, called the discrepancy principle, takes into account both the sign and strength of relations. Suppose there is an attitude continuum ranging from strong positive through neutral to strong negative. Discrepancy is measured by distance along this attitude continuum.

FIG. 9. Structures represented in Questionnaire 3.

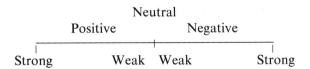

According to the discrepancy principle, when the given $\overrightarrow{SI}$ and $\overrightarrow{RI}$ attitudinal relations both have the same sign, *small* discrepancies will be associated with a strong predicted *positive* $\overrightarrow{RS}$ attitudinal relation. When the given attitudinal relations are of opposite sign, however, *large* discrepancies will be associated with a strong predicted *negative* $\overrightarrow{RS}$ attitudinal relation.

As a general assumption, it also seemed plausible that given relations would influence the predicted relation only if they were contained in a semicycle completed by the predicted relation.

In structures that already involved a semicycle a *summation principle* might operate. According to this principle, if the semicycle were already balanced, the $\overrightarrow{RS}$ attitudinal relation predicted by subjects would be stronger than if it had been predicted on the basis of the separate components of the semicycle; if the structure were already unbalanced, however, the $\overrightarrow{RS}$ attitudinal relation predicted by subjects would be some compromise between the $\overrightarrow{RS}$ attitudinal relation to be expected on the basis of the separate components of the semicycle. It was also expected that an $\overrightarrow{SR}$ attitudinal relation, where given, might prove especially salient in determining the $\overrightarrow{RS}$ attitudinal relation (see Jordan, 1953).

2. Procedure

Three questionnaires were constructed as follows: Questionnaire 1 consisted of 73 items which were coordinated to the 73 structures in Fig. 7; Questionnaire 2 consisted of 65 items which were coordinated to the 65 structures in Fig. 8; Questionnaire 3 consisted of 65 items which were co-

TABLE VI
EXAMPLES OF ITEMS FROM QUESTIONNAIRES, EXPERIMENT IV

Structure	Item
A	Jack and Joe know each other. Does Joe like Jack?
B1	Joe knows that Jack likes him a lot. Does Joe like Jack?
C3	Jack and Joe belong to different groups which are rather inclined to remain separate and to avoid much contact with each other. Does Joe like Jack?
D2	Joe knows that Jack rather likes him. Jack and Joe belong to the same loosely organized group. Does Joe like Jack?
D5	Joe knows that Jack strongly dislikes him. Jack and Joe belong to different groups which are strongly inclined to remain separate and to avoid any contact with each other. Does Joe like Jack?
E12	Joe knows that Jack is mildly in favor of the present immigration policy. Joe is strongly opposed to the present immigration policy. Does Joe like Jack?
F1	Jack and Joe belong to the same tightly knit group. Joe knows that Jack is strongly in favor of the present immigration policy. Does Joe like Jack?
G16	Jack and Joe belong to the same loosely organized group. Joe is strongly opposed to the present immigration policy. Does Joe like Jack?
H54	Joe knows that Jack rather dislikes him and that Jack is strongly in favor of the present immigration policy. Joe is mildly in favor of the present immigration policy. Does Joe like Jack?
J37	Jack and Joe belong to the same tightly knit group. Joe knows that Jack is strongly in favor of the present immigration policy. Joe is mildly opposed to the present immigration policy. Does Joe like Jack?

ordinated to the 65 structures in Fig. 9. Three forms of each questionnaire were prepared in which the items were arranged in different random orders to control for possible fatigue and sequence effects. The questionnaires were randomly distributed among male students attending a vacation school in introductory psychology at the University of New England in 1964. Examples of the items used in the three questionnaires are presented in Table VI. Subjects answered each question by choosing a number from 1 through 7 corresponding to different verbal labels as follows: 1 = Definitely No; 2 = Very Probably No; 3 = Probably No; 4 = Chances about Even; 5 = Probably Yes; 6 = Very Probably Yes; 7 = Definitely Yes. Ratings above 4 may therefore be taken as implying a *positive* attitudinal relation increasing in strength as the rating approaches 7. Ratings below 4 may be taken as implying a *negative* attitudinal relation increasing in strength as the rating approaches 1.

3. Results

The mean ratings for items in Questionnaires 1, 2, and 3 are presented

TABLE VII
MEAN ATTRACTION RESPONSES FOR QUESTIONNAIRE 1,
EXPERIMENT IV $(N = 51)^a$

Structure	A	B_1	B_2	B_3	B_4	C_1	C_2	C_3	C_4
Mean	4.10	5.49	5.04	2.75	2.39	5.43	4.55	3.10	2.69
Structure	D_1	D_2	D_3	D_4	D_5	D_6	D_7	D_8	
Mean	5.88	5.08	5.51	5.51	1.78	2.22	2.12	1.80	
Structure	D_9	D_{10}	D_{11}	D_{12}	D_{13}	D_{14}	D_{15}	D_{16}	
Mean	4.63	4.21	4.16	4.51	2.57	2.88	3.02	2.61	
Structure	E_1	E_2	E_3	E_4	E_5	E_6	E_7	E_8	
Mean	5.69	4.98	5.00	5.04	4.88	4.92	4.86	4.75	
Structure	E_9	E_{10}	E_{11}	E_{12}	E_{13}	E_{14}	E_{15}	E_{16}	
Mean	3.14	3.96	3.69	3.43	2.78	3.90	3.57	3.61	
Structure	F_1	F_2	F_3	F_4	F_5	F_6	F_7	F_8	
Mean	5.31	4.61	5.29	4.53	2.71	3.37	2.76	3.08	
Structure	F_9	F_{10}	F_{11}	F_{12}	F_{13}	F_{14}	F_{15}	F_{16}	
Mean	2.94	3.18	3.08	3.39	5.08	4.39	5.18	4.24	
Structure	G_1	G_2	G_3	G_4	G_5	G_6	G_7	G_8	
Mean	5.55	4.53	5.18	4.84	2.61	3.22	2.92	2.82	
Structure	G_9	G_{10}	G_{11}	G_{12}	G_{13}	G_{14}	G_{15}	G_{16}	
Mean	2.80	3.29	2.98	3.16	5.06	4.43	5.14	4.35	

^{a} A difference between means of .41 or greater is significant at the .01 level by two-tail *t* test; a difference of .31 or greater is significant at the .05 level by two-tail *t* test.

TABLE VIII
MEAN ATTRACTION RESPONSES FOR QUESTIONNAIRE 2,
EXPERIMENT IV $(N = 51)^a$

Structure	A	H_1	H_2	H_3	H_4	H_5	H_6	H_7	H_8
Mean	4.22	6.25	5.51	5.84	5.88	5.47	5.49	5.94	5.45

Structure	H_9	H_{10}	H_{11}	H_{12}	H_{13}	H_{14}	H_{15}	H_{16}
Mean	6.16	5.35	5.82	5.61	5.65	5.39	5.49	5.25

Structure	H_{17}	H_{18}	H_{19}	H_{20}	H_{21}	H_{22}	H_{23}	H_{24}
Mean	1.65	2.92	2.27	2.37	2.18	2.75	2.04	2.55

Structure	H_{25}	H_{26}	H_{27}	H_{28}	H_{29}	H_{30}	H_{31}	H_{32}
Mean	1.75	3.06	2.24	2.16	2.14	2.73	2.08	2.67

Structure	H_{33}	H_{34}	H_{35}	H_{36}	H_{37}	H_{38}	H_{39}	H_{40}
Mean	4.67	4.82	4.96	4.20	5.16	4.71	4.98	4.37

Structure	H_{41}	H_{42}	H_{43}	H_{44}	H_{45}	H_{46}	H_{47}	H_{48}
Mean	4.82	4.78	5.18	4.33	5.02	4.69	4.80	4.55

Structure	H_{49}	H_{50}	H_{51}	H_{52}	H_{53}	H_{54}	H_{55}	H_{56}
Mean	2.82	3.24	2.45	3.20	2.39	3.06	2.86	3.22

Structure	H_{57}	H_{58}	H_{59}	H_{60}	H_{61}	H_{62}	H_{63}	H_{64}
Mean	2.69	3.37	2.37	3.35	2.39	3.08	2.57	3.08

^{a}A difference between means of .41 or greater is significant at the .01 level by two-tail t test; a difference of .31 or greater is significant at the .05 level by two-tail t test.

in Tables VII, VIII, and IX, respectively. (These tables should be read in conjunction with Fig. 7, 8, and 9, respectively.) The results are generally consistent with hypotheses. There is convincing support for the principle of structural balance where complete balance is possible in structures. Where complete balance is not possible in structures, however, subjects evidently tend to rely on the sign of the $\overrightarrow{SR}$ attitudinal relation, where it is given, in making their predictions about attraction. Where a single relation is given, the predicted relation that completes the semicycle tends to follow the strength of the given relation. Results also suggest that both the sign and strength of a predicted relation completing a semicycle are influenced by the sign and strength of the given relations within that semicycle. Relations not contained in the completed semicycle do not appear to influence the predicted relation. There is some support for the discrepancy principle, particularly when the attitudes of S and R toward I are discrepant (opposite in sign). In structures already involving a balanced semicycle the results support a summation principle. Where a semicycle is already un-

TABLE IX
MEAN ATTRACTION RESPONSES FOR QUESTIONNAIRE 3,
EXPERIMENT IV $(N = 51)^a$

Structure	A	J_1	J_2	J_3	J_4	J_5	J_6	J_7	J_8
Mean	4.16	6.14	5.10	5.55	5.75	5.31	5.10	5.41	5.16

Structure	J_9	J_{10}	J_{11}	J_{12}	J_{13}	J_{14}	J_{15}	J_{16}
Mean	5.84	5.06	5.84	5.31	5.16	4.92	5.27	4.98

Structure	J_{17}	J_{18}	J_{19}	J_{20}	J_{21}	J_{22}	J_{23}	J_{24}
Mean	2.16	3.27	3.10	2.39	2.78	3.04	2.67	3.10

Structure	J_{25}	J_{26}	J_{27}	J_{28}	J_{29}	J_{30}	J_{31}	J_{32}
Mean	1.98	3.51	3.06	2.49	2.86	3.20	2.53	2.69

Structure	J_{33}	J_{34}	J_{35}	J_{36}	J_{37}	J_{38}	J_{39}	J_{40}
Mean	3.65	4.18	4.57	3.51	4.12	3.78	3.88	3.51

Structure	J_{41}	J_{42}	J_{43}	J_{44}	J_{45}	J_{46}	J_{47}	J_{48}
Mean	3.63	4.12	4.57	3.29	4.14	3.69	4.08	3.67

Structure	J_{49}	J_{50}	J_{51}	J_{52}	J_{53}	J_{54}	J_{55}	J_{56}
Mean	4.06	4.29	3.98	4.63	3.84	4.16	3.94	4.27

Structure	J_{57}	J_{58}	J_{59}	J_{60}	J_{61}	J_{62}	J_{63}	J_{64}
Mean	4.16	4.10	3.92	4.47	3.80	4.12	3.88	3.92

^{a} A difference between means of .47 or greater is significant at the .01 level by two-tail t test; a difference of .35 or greater is significant at the .05 level by two-tail t test.

balanced, strength of the predicted $\overrightarrow{RS}$ attitudinal relation appears to be influenced mainly by strength of the $\overrightarrow{SR}$ attitudinal relation, where it is given, and compromise responses are apparent. In fact, wherever an interpersonal attitudinal relation is given in a structure, it seems to be a dominant influence in determining the sign and strength of the predicted reciprocal attitudinal relation.

E. EXPERIMENT V: INSTITUTIONAL AFFILIATION AND ATTITUDE DISCREPANCY

1. Aim

This fifth experiment (Feather, 1967b) was designed to investigate the degree to which a person's evaluation of a communication is influenced by knowledge of the institutional affiliation of the source of a communication. As a supplementary problem, the degree to which the receiver feels friendly toward the source was also investigated for each of the communication situations involved in the experiment. The results could also throw further light upon the discrepancy principle and the summation principle mentioned in Section IV, D.

2. Procedure

Students at the University of New England live in "colleges," which are somewhat similar to American residence halls. In the present study students were presented with a set of 15 statements about the college system. These statements were either all strongly positive, all moderately positive, all moderately negative, or all strongly negative in the stand they took toward the college system. Examples of items used in the different question-naires are given in Table X. The statements were represented as coming

TABLE X

EXAMPLES OF ITEMS USED IN **DIFFERENT** FORMS OF QUESTIONNAIRE, EXPERIMENT V

Strength and sign of statement	Examples of items
Strongly positive	1. College life is very important in teaching students to live together harmoniously.
	2. The college system is of great value in promoting student self-government.
Moderately positive	1. College life is fairly important in teaching students to live together harmoniously.
	2. The college system is of moderate value in promoting student self-government.
Moderately negative	1. College life is fairly unimportant in teaching students to live together harmoniously.
	2. The college system is of little value in promoting student self-government.
Strongly negative	1. College life is quite unimportant in teaching students to live together harmoniously.
	2. The college system has failed in promoting student self-government.

either from a member of the subject's own college or from a member of the other college. For subjects in North College and South College (both male colleges) the statements were said to come from a source either in North College or South College. For subjects in East College or West College (both female colleges) the statements were represented as coming from a source either in East College or West College.

Subjects answered each statement by using a scale numbered $+3, +2, +1, -1, -2, -3$, corresponding to the following respective categories: I agree very much; I agree on the whole; I agree a little; I disagree a little; I disagree on the whole; I disagree very much. A constant of $+4$ was added to each answer and a total score for the 15 items was computed for each subject. This score could range from $+15$ to $+105$. A score above 60 would imply general agreement with the set of items; a score below 60 would imply general disagreement with the set of items. When they had responded to the 15 statements, subjects answered four questions presented in Likert-type form, two of which concerned how friendly they felt toward the source, whereas the others assessed their general attitude toward the college system as a whole.

The eight communication situations investigated in the present study may be mapped into the eight structures shown in Fig. 10. The letters S, M, and W on the lines and brackets of the s-digraphs in Fig. 10 denote strong, moderate, and weak relations, respectively. The positive unit relation

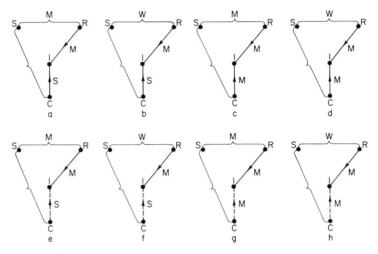

FIG. 10.   Signed digraphs representing communication situations in which source (S) is from the same college as receiver, R (s-digraphs a, c, e, g); S is from a different college than R (s-digraphs b, d, f, h); R is moderately (M) in favor of issue (I); and communication (C) is either strongly (S) or moderately in favor of I (s-digraphs a, b, c, d) or strongly or moderately opposed to I (s-digraphs e, f, g, h). Weak relations are indicated by W.

between source and receiver is assumed to be of moderate strength when S comes from the same college as R, and of weak strength when S comes from the other college. The attitude of R to I (the college system) is assumed to be moderately in favor. Thus, for example, s-digraph c in Fig. 10 would represent the communication situation in which a source from the same college as the receiver presents a set of 15 statements that are moderately in favor of the college system to the receiver, who is moderately in favor of the college system.

3. Results

The mean total evaluative responses are presented in Table XI for the different conditions of the experiment. Table XII contains the results of an analysis of variance applied to these data.

TABLE XI

MEAN TOTAL EVALUATIVE RESPONSES FROM FOUR COLLEGES IN RELATION
TO SOURCE, STRENGTH, AND SIGN OF COMMUNICATIONS (EXPERIMENT V)

Communications			Mean total evaluative responses			
			Male colleges		Female colleges	
Source	Strength	Sign	North	South	East	West
Own college	Strong	Positive	69.59	59.21	74.92	69.67
	Moderate	Positive	69.71	67.63	71.83	69.17
	Strong	Negative	50.18	56.95	45.50	54.42
	Moderate	Negative	55.65	61.47	49.92	58.58
Other college	Strong	Positive	62.18	62.05	71.67	64.17
	Moderate	Positive	71.53	65.37	75.92	72.08
	Strong	Negative	52.71	58.00	45.75	54.00
	Moderate	Negative	59.00	61.74	53.17	61.75

TABLE XII

ANALYSIS OF VARIANCE OF DATA PRESENTED IN TABLE XI

Source	df	MS	F
Source (A)	1	18.802	< 1
Strength (B)	1	2655.502	16.44^a
Sign (C)	1	18,812.552	116.44^a
College (D)	3	72.224	< 1
A × B	1	222.769	1.38
A × C	1	193.802	1.20
A × D	3	6.039	< 1
B × C	1	50.052	< 1
B × D	3	22.302	< 1
C × D	3	2187.412	13.54^a
A × B × C	1	60.919	< 1
A × B × D	3	150.311	< 1
A × C × D	3	46.806	< 1
B × C × D	3	63.611	< 1
A × B × C × D	3	65.629	< 1
Residual	448	161.561	

[a] $p < .001$.

The results show that although the affiliation of the source has no effect on subjects' evaluations, these evaluations are influenced by the sign and strength of the statements. Agreement is relatively stronger with statements that are positively worded and take a moderate stand. This result is consistent with the discrepancy principle. Friendliness ratings are higher when the source is from the subject's own college and when his statements take a positive stand. The data imply that when $\vec{RI}$ and $\vec{CI}$ attitudinal relations are of the same sign, small discrepancies will be associated with stronger agreement with the communication and stronger liking for the source. When the $\overline{RI}$ and $\overline{CI}$ attitudinal relations are of opposite sign, however, large discrepancies will be associated with stronger disagreement with the communication and stronger disliking of the source.

F. EXPERIMENT VI: BALANCING AND EXTREMITY EFFECTS

1. Aim

The sixth experiment (Feather and Jeffries, 1967) examined the above implication by testing the following general predictions: (1) When the stand taken by a communication toward an issue is in the same direction (i.e., same sign) as the receiver's attitude toward the issue, the receiver will show both stronger agreement with the communication and a more positive evaluation of the source as the communication stand comes closer to the receiver's attitude; (2) when the stand taken by the communication is in the opposite direction (i.e., different sign) to the receiver's attitude, the receiver will show both stronger disagreement with the communication and a more negative evaluation of the source as the communication stand becomes more removed from the receiver's attitude. In addition, the study investigated the receiver's judgment of the credibility, potency, and activity of the source as well as his perception of communication content.

2. Procedure

Male and female subjects enrolled at the Armidale Teachers' College in 1965 read a set of four communications which took strong positive (S +), weak positive (W +), weak negative (W −), and strong negative (S −) stands toward the same issue (creation of a new State of New England). Each subject was therefore the receiver of four communications which differed in their communication stand. These communications were presented in random order and each was described as coming from a different source who was of like sex to the receiver. Subjects had previously been classified as S + , W + , W − , or S − with respect to the strength and direction of their own attitude toward the issue, using their scores on a specially constructed attitude measure. The 4 × 4 possible combinations of communication stand and receiver attitude investigated in the experiment are represented in Fig. 11. All that a receiver knew about the source of each communication was the stand taken in the communication being presented.

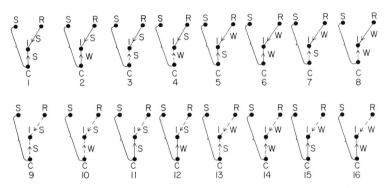

FIG. 11. Signed digraphs representing the sixteen communication structures investigated in Experiment VI.

After reading each communication, subjects used semantic differential scales (Osgood *et al.*, 1957) to rate the source of that communication with respect to evaluation, potency, activity, and credibility. An alternative evaluation measure devised by Kelman and Eagly (1965) was also employed. Subjects also judged the stand taken by each communication toward the issue and rated their degree of agreement/disagreement with each communication.

3. Results

Space does not permit detailed presentation of the results of this study but the main findings are as follows: Subjects rate the source of a more extreme communication as less valued, less credible, more potent, and more active than the source of a moderate communication. The data therefore reveal the presence of an *extremity effect* [although an alternative interpretation is possible for the evaluation data (see Feather and Jeffries, 1967)]. Balancing effects also occur, particularly in the receiver's agreement/disagreement with each communication; subjects tend to agree with communications of like sign to their own attitude and to disagree with communications of different sign from their own attitude. There is also a tendency for subjects to evaluate the source of a communication positively (a *positivity effect*), and there is some evidence of assimilation and contrast effects in judgments of communication stand by the male subjects. Finally, subjects tend to rate a source more favorably and to regard him as more credible, the more they agree with the communication he presents. The positive relationship between evaluation scores and agreement scores is consistent with the major prediction of the study.

G. EXPERIMENT VII: VARIATIONS IN SOURCE ATTITUDE, RECEIVER ATTITUDE, AND COMMUNICATION STAND

1. Aim

The most recent investigation of the communication model (Feather and Armstrong, 1967) again explored the structures in Fig. 3 with the important difference that the *strengths* as well as the signs of the given attitudes were specified. The communication situations investigated are represented in Fig. 12. An S or M on the lines in each s-digraph in Fig. 12 refers to a strong or moderate relation, respectively.

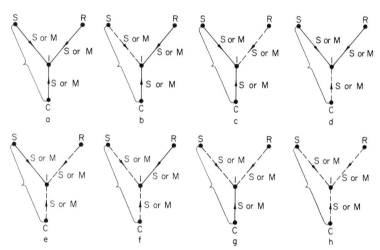

FIG. 12.   Signed digraphs representing the combinations of relations investigated in Experiment vii.

2. Procedure

Male and female undergraduate students enrolled in an introductory course in psychology at the University of New England in 1965 were required to identify with a fictitious person of like sex whose attitude toward a controversial issue (Integration of the Australian aborigines into community life) was specified in a short personality profile. There were eight such profiles and each contained information about the direction of the fictitious person's attitude (positive or negative), the strength of this attitude (strong or moderate), and whether or not the issue was important or unimportant to him. Each subject read only one of these personality profiles and identified with the receiver described therein. Thus, for each subject the sign and strength of the $\overrightarrow{RI}$ attitudinal relation was constant throughout, as it was in the preceding study (Feather and Jeffries, 1967).

Each subject was then presented with descriptions of 16 communication situations corresponding to all possible variations in the sign and strength of both the $\overrightarrow{SI}$ and $\overrightarrow{CI}$ attitudinal relations in Fig. 12. The source of the communications was always of the same sex as the receiver. Each communication situation was presented on a separate page of the test booklet and the subject answered six questions about it using the 1 to 7 probability scale described above for Experiment IV. These questions concerned whether the receiver agreed with the communication, whether he liked the source, whether he thought that the source would agree with the communication, whether he thought the source was presenting the communication against his will, whether he thought the source was well-informed, and whether he thought the source had been coerced by some pressure group to present the communication. It is evident that the first three questions were designed to map into the $\overrightarrow{RC}$, $\overrightarrow{RS}$, and $\overrightarrow{SC}$ attitudinal relations respectively. Questions 4 and 6 were designed to map into the SC unit relation. Question 5 was concerned with credibility of the source.

3. Results

The main findings may be summarized as follows: A receiver is judged as more likely to agree with a communication which is congruent with his attitude (i.e., of the same sign) the more similar its stand is to his attitude. He is more likely to disagree with a communication which is discrepant with his attitude (i.e., of opposite sign) the more dissimilar its stand is to his attitude. The source is also expected to behave in the same way. These results support the discrepancy principle. A source is also judged as more likely to be liked by a receiver when they share similar attitudes toward the issue, when the stand taken in his communication is close to the receiver's attitude, and when the source's communication is congruent with the source's attitude. A source is judged as more likely to be well-informed when his communication takes a stand close to the receiver's attitude. A source is judged as more likely to be not well-informed, as acting against his will, and as coerced by an outside pressure group when the source's communication is discrepant with his known attitude than when it is congruent with his known attitude toward the issue. There is a bias toward evaluating the source positively (a positivity effect), and also a bias toward evaluating the source more favorably and toward judging him as more responsible for his communication when this communication takes a moderate stand than when it takes an extreme stand (an extremity effect).

These results are therefore consistent with those of the previous study (Feather and Jeffries, 1967) which involved different experimental procedures. They strongly indicate the operation of cognitive biases (positivity, extremity) in addition to the balancing tendency and imply the necessity of developing principles that take account of the interdependence of relations within the complex communication structure when dealing with strength of relations. The discrepancy principle, which is concerned with triadic relations, may have to be supplemented by more complex principles that allow for structural independence (e.g., a summation principle, Experiment IV).

H. SUMMARY

The studies described in the preceding sections show that there is a pervasive tendency for subjects to predict responses that lead to balanced structures especially when the S-I-C and R-I-C triads are considered. The more recent studies, however, suggest two basic problems that at present confront the model: (1) The problem of conceptualizing the interaction of relations which differ in strength; and (2) the problem of conceptualizing forms of cognitive bias other than balance (e.g., positivity, extremity). These issues along with other critical problems will be considered later in this chapter.

We now turn to a consideration of other studies which though not specifically based upon the structural balance model of communication effects are nevertheless relevant to its validity. Each of the strands of experimentation considered in the next section is relevant to a particular relation within the communication model.

V. Other Relevant Evidence

A.   ATTITUDES BETWEEN SOURCE AND RECEIVER

A vast number of studies in social psychology have investigated factors that influence attraction between people. These studies will not be discussed in the present paper since excellent reviews of them are already available. Thus, Lott and Lott (1965) have recently presented a comprehensive review of the literature on group cohesiveness and interpersonal attraction. A review of some of the main theories of interpersonal attraction may be found in the recent text by Secord and Backman (1964). These reviews amply testify that *attitudinal similarity* is an important basis for interpersonal attraction. The results of several studies they report are consistent with the implications of the structural balance model of communication effects with respect to attitudinal relations between source (S) and receiver (R), that is, the $\overrightarrow{SR}$ and $\overrightarrow{RS}$ relations, and with the results presented in Section IV, D.

Of particular relevance is Newcomb's A-B-X model and the research that has followed from it. Newcomb (1959) postulates a system involving two people, A and B, an object X, and the orientations that exist between them. Two types of orientation are assumed. Attitudes are orientations toward any nonperson object. Attractions are orientations toward people. Orientations are assumed to have both cathectic and cognitive aspects. The fundamental postulate of Newcomb's model is that "... all of the foregoing kinds of orientations, and of judged orientations of others (assuming that all of them may be said to exist) are dynamically interdependent.... The totality of these orientations is therefore regarded as having system pro-perties, in the sense that a change in any one of them, under certain hypo-thetical conditions, induces change in one or more of the others" (Newcomb, 1959, p. 392). The "strain toward symmetry" in the system is assumed to be a function of the degree of perceived discrepancy, the sign and degree of attraction, the importance of the object, the certainty or com-mittedness of one's own orientation, and the degree to which the object has common relevance. System strain would be very high, for example, if A were strongly attracted to B, if he felt that B reciprocated this attraction, but if he perceived that their attitudes toward an important and highly relevant object X were discrepant.

It should be apparent that there are many changes that could occur within the A-B-X system that would lead to a reduction in strain. Newcomb lists the basic possible changes as follows.

... a change in A's attitude toward X, such as to reduce the perceived dis-crepancy with B; (2) a discrepancy-reducing change in his perception of B's attitude; (3) a reduction in the importance assigned by A to his attitude toward X; (4) a re-duction in the strength of A's positive attraction toward B; or (5) a reduction in the degree of perceived common relevance that A attributes to X for himself and B (Newcomb, 1961, p. 17).

These changes may occur as a result of communication so that A obtains additional information about B or X, which reduces strain (Newcomb, 1953). They may also come about in the absence of communicative behavior between A and B, as when A autistically distorts information, recalls selectively, or shows other forms of cognitive distortion.

Newcomb distinguishes between *individual* and *collective* systems of orientation where an individual system is "... a private version, on the part of a participant in a collective system, of that collective system" (1961, p. 19). The individual system therefore refers to person A *or* person B's perception of the A-B-X relations and is the more fundamental; the collective system is of a higher order and allows for treatment of groups of people, although the analysis of change is in terms of individual systems of orientations. Newcomb (1959) cites a considerable body of research that is consistent with his model and discusses some alternative formulations that are similar to his own (pp. 395–406); some of the early research generated by the A-B-X model is also described (pp. 416–419). The most important recent study of the model is reported in *The Acquaintance Process* (Newcomb, 1961). Other investigations, by Kipnis (1961), Stotland *et al.* (1960), Broxton (1963), Sampson and Insko (1964), Byrne and his associates (Byrne, 1961a, b, 1962; Byrne and Wong, 1962; Byrne and Blaylock, 1963; Byrne and McGraw, 1964; Byrne and Nelson, 1965), and Price *et al.* (1965), are also generally consistent with the model. The last-mentioned study is of particular interest since it broadened Newcomb's concept of perceived discrepancy with results that are clearly on a continuum with the prior investigations of Jordan (1953) and Morrissette (1958) and that supplement those reported in Section IV, D.

The A-B-X model with its assumption of a system involving a set of interdependent relations tending toward a state of balance is clearly similar to Heider's P-O-X model (Heider, 1958) and to the structural balance model of communication effects described in Section III. The discrepancy principle discussed in Section IV, D is also similar to Newcomb's concept of perceived discrepancy. There are, however, some points of difference between Newcomb's approach and the present model: (1) Most of Newcomb's discussion is concerned with the case where the attraction of A to B is positive. The case where B is negatively attracted to A is considered to be more complex and it appears from Newcomb's discussion (1959, p. 398) that situations could arise where the attitudes of A and B to X are similar despite the negative attraction. According to Heider's principle, these cases would be unbalanced. (2) Another point of difference is that Newcomb's model is concerned with the instigation to communicate as well as with the receipt of information. As indicated earlier in this paper, the structural balance model of communication effects is concerned with the *consequences* of communication for cognitive adjustments of either source or receiver, and factors that might determine the initiation of communications are not considered in the model. (3) Newcomb's model contains three elements: A, B, and X; whereas the present model contains four: S, C, I, and R, enabling a rather more detailed analysis of communication effects. (4) Newcomb's model considers only orientations, that is, attitudes and attractions, which are akin to Heider's sentiment relations but which have cognitive as well as cathectic properties. Unit relations are not included in the model. (5) The present model is concerned only with systems of relations as perceived by the individual. Newcomb's model is also concerned with collective systems. (6) The research following from Newcomb's model has been more concerned with changes in orientations over relatively long time intervals.

The research discussed in Section IV dealt with relatively immediate re-actions to communications.

B. REACTIONS TO COMMUNICATIONS

1. Alternative Ways of Reducing Imbalance

Hovland *et al.* (1953) have discussed the situation in which a positively regarded communicator presents a communication that would tend to be rejected on its merits. They considered various ways in which the receiver of the communication might react to such a situation. These reactions in-clude dissociating the source and the communication, reinterpreting the meaning or stand taken in the communication, and a change in the receiver's attitude toward the source. In terms of the structural balance model these possibilities correspond to changes in the SR unit relation, the $\overrightarrow{CI}$ attitudinal relation, and the $\overrightarrow{RS}$ attitudinal relation, respectively. Studies by Kelley and Woodruff (1956) and by Harvey *et al.* (1957) are also relevant to the question of what alternative ways might be used within a communication situation to reduce imbalance. In the latter study subjects were experimentally exposed to evaluations of themselves that were unfavorable to varying degrees. It was hypothesized that subjects would experience more tension and discom-fort the more informed the source and the more negative his evaluations. They presumably would tend to relieve this tension by displaying one or more of the following reactions: (a) devaluating the source; (b) distorting his evaluations; and (c) dissociating the source from his evaluations. In general, the results were consistent with this hypothesis. In the study by Kelley and Woodruff (1956) opinion change, as well as distortion and dissociation, was investigated.

The problem that arises from the results of studies such as these is that of specifying the conditions under which one or other of these reactions will occur to the relative exclusion of the others. For example, when will dis-sociation occur rather than distortion? This problem was discussed in the original statement of the model (Feather, 1964a, pp. 311–312) and will be considered again in the concluding section of the present paper.

2. Receiver's Attitude to Issue

Several studies have investigated changes in the receiver's attitude toward the issue as a function of the *discrepancy* between this attitude and the stand taken in the communication. As one would expect from the structural balance model, whether or not change occurs in the receiver's attitude toward the issue depends on such factors as the receiver's attitude toward the source and the importance of the issue. Hovland and Pritzker (1957) found that attitude change increased with increasing discrepancy when the source was represented as a respected authority and when the issues were relatively non-ego-involving (see also Weiss, 1958). But Hovland *et al.* (1957) found that under conditions where there was some doubt about the credibility of the communicator and where selected groups of subjects who felt deeply about the issue ("prohibition") were included in the experiment, there was less frequent change with greater discrepancies between the subject's initial stand on the issue and the position taken in the communication. Similar results were obtained in another study (Sherif and Hovland, 1961), which again included groups of subjects who were highly ego-involved with respect to the issue (the 1956 national presidential campaign).

Sherif and Hovland (1961) explained these results in terms of a model based upon psychophysical studies of judgment and involving the concepts of judgmental anchors and latitudes of acceptance and rejection (see also Berkowitz, 1960). When a person is highly ego-involved in an issue it is assumed that the range of positions vis-à-vis the issue that he will accept (his latitude of acceptance) is small and that the range of positions vis-à-vis the issue that he will reject (his latitude of rejection) is large. The individual's own stand on the ego-involving issue becomes the main anchor for his appraisal of communications on the issue. Sherif and Hovland (1961) hypothesized that under these conditions, "With small discrepancies between the position of communication and that of the subject, changes of opinion in the direction advocated by communication will occur. With large distances between the stands taken in communication and by the subject, opinion changes will be infrequent" (p. 157).

Where the issue is less ego-involving, as in the Hovland and Pritzker (1957) study, the range of assimilation should be more extensive. Hence attitudes toward these less ego-involving issues should be more influenced by highly discrepant communications. A detailed discussion of the social judgment-involvement approach has recently been presented by Sherif *et al.* (1965).

A contrasting approach to the question of the effects of receiver-communication discrepancy on attitude change has employed concepts from dissonance theory (Festinger, 1957). Thus, Cohen (1959) found that when the subject made some behavioral commitment toward a contrary communication a greater discrepancy led to more attitude change (see also Cohen *et al.*, 1959). Zimbardo (1960), using a dissonance theory analysis, argued that opinion change would increase with increase both in involvement and in discrepancy. In an experiment to test this hypothesis subjects first gave their opinions about a case of juvenile delinquency. They were then exposed to the alleged opinion of their friend and were asked to give their opinions a second time. Zimbardo varied "response-involvement" and found that highly involved subjects changed their opinions more than subjects not involved and that opinion change increased with increase in discrepancy. It should be noted that Zimbardo's procedure for varying involvement appealed to the subjects' "values and personality," a procedure clearly different from that used by Hovland *et al.* (1957) to vary commitment to an issue. Bergin (1962) found evidence that subjects' attitudes changed with increasing discrepancy under conditions of high credibility in contrast to little or no change under conditions of low credibility.

Aronson *et al.* (1963), also using a dissonance theory analysis, have attempted to reconcile conflicting results by suggesting that opinion change involves a complex interaction between the credibility of the communicator and the discrepancy between the stand taken in the communication and the initial attitude of the receiver. They found that greater opinion change was associated with increasing discrepancy when the source was highly credible. When the same communication was attributed to a source represented as only moderately credible, however, opinion change increased with discrepancy up to a point but thereafter decreased as the discrepancy became more extreme. They attempted a reconciliation of preceding findings by pointing out that in the studies by Hovland and Pritzker (1957) and Zimbardo (1960) one can assume that the source was highly credible, whereas in the study by Hovland *et al.* (1957) the source was unknown.

In a recent experiment involving use of a concept-formation task, Freedman (1964) found results to support his prediction that under conditions of low involvement there would be more opinion change with greater discrepancy, but with high involvement maximum change would occur at a moderate level of discrepancy. He argued that with increasing discrepancy the difficulty of employing opinion change would increase relative to the difficulty of rejecting the information. Hence the relationship of opinion change to discrepancy should be nonmonotonic for both high and low involvement; that is, a change in opinion would occur up to a certain discrepancy but not thereafter since the information would be rejected. Nonmonotonic relationships have not been found for low involvement conditions, however, because sufficiently large discrepancies have not been employed. Freedman also suggested that if one were able to eliminate all modes of resolution other than opinion change one would obtain a direct positive relationship between amount of discrepancy and opinion change. In practice, however, it is most difficult to eliminate these alternative modes. Hence the nonmonotonic relationship should generally hold.

In a recent statement, Sherif and Sherif (1965) predicted unequivocally

...that the highly committed person exposed to an extremely discrepant communication will *never* react to it by changing his attitude toward the communication. He will feel irritated, derogate the communicator, speak to his friends about it; but he will *never* resort to the alternative of changing toward communication in order to reduce his irritation, tension or dissonance (p. 15).

They suggested that many dissonance studies have involved conditions of low involvement, ambiguous communications, or highly valued sources, and have employed a limited range of discrepant communications. Clearly, the battle still rages and further carefully controlled experiments are needed.

The foregoing studies are pertinent to the structural balance model of communication effects in suggesting the different factors that might produce change in the $\overrightarrow{RI}$ attitudinal relation. We now turn to a set of closely related investigations that are concerned with how the receiver judges the stand taken by the communication toward the issue. These studies are clearly relevant to factors determining the $\overrightarrow{CI}$ attitudinal relation.

3. Perception of Communication Position

Sherif and Hovland (1961, p. 149) argue that: "When the position in communication is susceptible to alternative interpretations, displacements of the position advocated will vary as a function of its distance from the subject's stand. The greater the discrepancy between the subject's own stand and the position advocated, the greater the displacement away from the subject's position ('contrast effect'). When only a small discrepancy in positions exists, there will be a tendency for displacement toward his own stand ('assimilation effect')." The results of the study by Hovland *et al.* (1957) are consistent with this hypothesis. Subjects who had extreme positions on the issue tended to perceive a moderate communication as farther removed from their own stand than it actually was (a contrast effect). Subject with stands close to the position advocated in the moderate communication tended to perceive the communication as closer to their own stand than was actually the case (an assimilation effect).

In recent years there has been a spate of studies concerned with assimilation and contrast effects in the judgment of the position taken in a communication. As in the studies reviewed in the previous section, such factors as degree of involvement with the issue and credibility of the source seem to be important. And, as before, some interpretations of results consider the operation of motivationally neutral processes while other interpretations stress attempts to reduce dissonance or imbalance. In addition to the investigations summarized by Sherif and Hovland (1961), recent relevant studies have been conducted by Manis (1960, 1961a, b, 1965), Manis and Blake (1963), Upshaw (1962, 1965), Hinckley (1963), Berkowitz and Goranson (1964), Zavalloni and Cook (1965), Kelman and Eagly (1965), Ager and Dawes (1965), and Dillehay (1965). Sherif *et al.* (1965) have also reviewed relevant studies.

The study by Kelman and Eagly (1965) is of particular interest to the present discussion since predictions were based upon balance theory. In a first experiment involving Negro subjects and the segregation issue they found that there was a marked tendency for subjects to misperceive the content of the message of a negative communicator by displacing it away from one's own position—a contrast effect. In a second experiment this contrast effect was found to be a direct function of the strength of negative feeling toward the communicator. There was also a tendency to displace the message of a positive communicator toward one's own position—an assimilation effect. This effect was shown to be a direct function of the strength of positive feeling toward the communicator. Kelman and Eagly (1965) also found evidence (p. 61) that was generally consistent with predictions based upon an analysis they made of *direct* and *indirect* effects on attitude change. In discussion of results they made certain qualitative extensions of balance theory that will be considered in the concluding section of this paper.

The studies reported by Sherif and Hovland (1961) and by Kelman and Eagly (1965) recognized that similar factors may influence both the receiver's attitude toward the issue and his perception of communication content. Harvey and Caldwell (1959) indicated that assimilation and contrast effects may occur both in a subject's perception of a discrepant stimulus and in his own concept. They suggested that: "While assimilation and contrast may be phenotypically opposite processes, they both have the common effect of maintaining congruency between the external world and relevant internal standards" (p. 126). The structural balance model of communication effects conceives of the $\overrightarrow{RI}$ and $\overrightarrow{CI}$ attitudinal relations as part of a system of interdependent relations tending toward balance. As indicated in the original statement of the model (Feather, 1964a), an adequate interpretation of the results of the various studies reviewed in the preceding two sections must await the solution of some basic problems in balance theory. These include conceptualization of the importance of the issue, strength of relations, and specific effects of imbalance within a structure (Feather, 1964a).

4. Attitude of Receiver to Communication

In this section we will consider studies concerned with evaluation of the communication per se by the receiver. Sherif and Sherif (1965) suggest that there is ample evidence to support the conclusion that a communication is judged as fair, factual, unbiased, and pleasing to the degree to which it lies within the subject's latitude of acceptance or nearby in his latitude of noncommitment. In contrast, as the communication is perceived as moving more and more into the latitude of rejection there is an increasing tendency to consider it as propagandistic, false, and biased (see also Freedman, 1964). Data from the study by Hovland *et al.* (1957) support this conclusion, as do other results mentioned by Sherif and Hovland (1961, pp. 154–157). The evidence reported in Section IV, E, indicating that subjects agree more with statements whose position is close to their own attitude toward the issue, is also consistent with the conclusion just mentioned. Data from the study reported in Section IV, C (Feather, 1965b) show that a receiver is less likely to *agree* with a communication that is congruent with his own attitude toward the issue when the communication comes from a source who is represented to him as not well informed, and is less likely to *disagree* with a communication that is discrepant with his own attitude toward the issue when the source is represented to him as well informed (see also Hovland *et al.*, 1953). These studies are all relevant to determining those factors that influence the RC attitudinal relation.

We have seen that the matter of the extent of discrepancy between the stand taken in the communication and the receiver's attitude looms large in the discussions of Hovland and his associates. Their concept of "the extent of discrepancy" as a factor influencing reactions in communication situations is obviously similar to the discrepancy principle discussed in Section IV, D. In fact, an early attempt was made in the original statement of the structural balance model to translate the concepts of latitudes of acceptance and rejection into the language of s-digraph theory using a principle taking account of the signs of relations (see Feather, 1964a, pp. 301–303).

5. Responsibility of Source for Communication

The degree to which a person is seen as responsible for his act, or sees himself as responsible for it, is an important variable in social perception and deserves more attention than it has received in the past. Heider (1944) reviewed some of the literature on phenomenal causality. In his more recent book (Heider, 1958) he suggested that personal responsibility " ... varies with the relative contribution of environmental factors to the action outcome; in general, the more they are felt to influence the action, the less the person is held responsible" (p. 113). He distinguished between five levels in which attribution of responsibility to the person decreases as attribution of responsibility to the environment increases (see also Piaget, 1930). At the fourth level, for example, " ... only what *p* intended is perceived as having its source in him" (Heider, 1958, p. 113), and at the fifth level, " ... *p*'s own motives are not entirely ascribed to him but are seen as having their source in the environment ... responsibility for the act is at least shared by the environment" (p. 114). In a recent paper these two levels were labeled by Shaw and Sulzer (1964) as "purposive commission" and "justified commission," respectively. In a study based upon Heider's levels of attribution of responsibility, Shaw and Sulzer found that there was only a slight tendency for subjects to reduce attribution of responsibility when they judged a person's responsibility in situations where he was provoked or coerced to act. Their results complement those of the studies reported in Section IV, B and C, where little difference was found in results between the responsibility and coercion conditions of the experiments (for a fuller discussion see Feather, 1965b).

The concept of responsibility used by Heider (see also Pepitone, 1958) is similar to that of "volition" employed by Brehm and Cohen (1962) in discussing dissonance theory and research. They suggested that the magnitude of dissonance in a situation should increase as the degree of volition involved in the occurrence of the dissonant cognitions increases. They defined volition as " ... the extent to which a person feels that he controls his behavior. ... Volition implies not only initiation and selection of behavior but also responsibility for its consequences" (p. 201). A difference in high and low volition would seem to correspond to the difference in purposive and justified commission as just defined. Brehm and Cohen (1962, Chapter 11) reported studies in which the effects of volition were investigated and clearly regard it as a most important variable in dissonance experiments.

A similar type of variable was discussed by Rotter (1966). He distinguished between external and internal control of reinforcement. In external control a reinforcement " ... is perceived by the subject as following some action of his own but not being entirely contingent upon his action ... it is typically perceived as the result of luck, chance, fate, as under the control of powerful others, or as unpredictable because of the greater complexity of the forces surrounding him" (p. 1). In internal control the person perceives that " ... the event is contingent upon his own behavior or his own relatively permanent characteristics ... " (p. 1). Rotter argued that generalized expectancies develop with respect to internal versus external control of reinforcement. He discussed related concepts in the literature and reviewed studies in which this variable is manipulated. This variable appears to be a particularly important one in the study of achievement behavior (see Feather, 1959a, b; Atkinson and Feather, 1966), where a distinction is often made between situations involving skill and situations involving luck. It may also be important in the process of group decision making since diffusion of responsibility has been suggested as a factor leading to greater risk taking (Wallach et al., 1964).

These different strands of enquiry all seem to be focused upon a basic variable having to do with the degree to which a person sees himself or is seen by others as causing an event. In the structural balance model we have called this variable *responsibility*, and the responsibility of source for communication has been represented by a positive unit relation between S and C. The work just reviewed suggests that attribution of responsibility to a source for a communication would probably be less when the receiver sees the source (a) as coerced to present the argument, (b) as having little choice in the matter, or (c) as having been paid a large sum of money to present the argument, than in a situation where the source is seen as willingly presenting the argument without external inducement. Attribution of responsibility to a source by a receiver should be especially low when the source is seen as obviously engaged in attitude-discrepant behavior, that is, as presenting a communication whose stand toward the issue differs in sign from his own. This latter prediction was supported in the study by Feather and Armstrong (1967) described in Section IV, G. As indicated previously, however, it is likely that a receiver always sees the source as responsible for his communication to some degree. The situation may be rather different, however, when the source's perceptions are considered. It may be easier to create experimental situations where the source sees himself as disowning the communication (Feather, 1965b). Further research obviously is needed in this area.

6. Miscellaneous Studies

Some recent studies have been concerned with the role of forewarning in persuasive communications (Allyn and Festinger, 1961; Kiesler and Kiesler, 1964; Mills and Aronson, 1965), the effectiveness of "overheard" communications (Walster and Festinger, 1962), and the effects of distraction while listening to a communication (Festinger and Maccoby, 1964). A common factor in these studies is the extent to which the source may be perceived as wanting to influence the receiver. The *role* of a source in a communication situation may vary considerably. On some occasions he may simply present information with no strong intention of persuading the receiver; on other occasions his role may be such that he is expected to do his best to influence the receiver. It may be, as Hovland *et al.* (1953) suggested, that a "desire to influence" on the part of the communicator will make him less effective by reducing his trustworthiness. But this does not seem always to be the case: a highly competent and well-liked barrister trying to persuade a jury might be extremely effective (see Mills and Aronson, 1965). In many cases the source occupies a position in a larger organizational structure and certain actions are required of him because of his position in this structure. Under these circumstances he may feel less responsible for actions that are discrepant with his own attitudes and he may also be seen as less responsible for these actions. What he does is taken as a result of his role position rather than as expressing his own personal attitudes. Steiner and Field (1960) suggested that the tendency to interpret behavior or to expect others to construe one's behavior as indicating personal preference " . . . is greatest when no roles are assigned, less when there is self-assignment to roles, still less when assignment is by appointment or election, and least when roles are imposed from above" (p. 240). These considerations suggest the need for a detailed analysis of the role of the source in a communication situation. His role is obviously different from that of the receiver. It is possible that some combination of the structural balance model of communication effects with structural role theory (Oeser and Harary, 1962, 1964) will pay dividends.

Zajonc (1960a) has investigated the cognitive effects of the person's role in the communication process. He found that persons expecting to *transmit* information had cognitive structures that were more differentiated, complex, unified, and organized than those of persons expecting to *receive* information. When persons expected to deal with incongruent information the differences between transmitters and receivers were less pronounced than when they anticipated congruent information. Zajonc presented methods of analyzing differentiation and other techniques that should prove valuable in future studies of cognitive structures.

Triandis (1960), using the semantic differential technique, found that when two people have semantic profiles of a concept that are similar it is more likely that they will communicate effectively about the concept. Apparently cognitive similarity leads to greater communication effectiveness. Brock (1965), in a field experiment conducted in the paint department of a large retail store, found evidence to support the conclusion that " . . . the recipient changes toward the position of a communicator to the extent he perceives that he shares with the communicator an attribute pertinent to the dimension along which the change is advocated" (p. 653).

Some other recent studies of communication have been concerned with aspects of source credibility. Brehm and Lipsher (1959) investigated the relationship of the perceived trustworthiness of a source to the discrepancy between the position taken in his communication and the receiver's attitude toward the issue. In one condition of their experiment they found a tendency for perceived trustworthiness to decrease with increasing discrepancy size, but with extreme discrepancy size the receiver saw the source as trustworthy. Aronson and Golden (1962) studied the relative importance of objectively relevant and objectively irrelevant aspects of source credibility on changes in audience opinion. Both relevant and irrelevant aspects of credibility were found to be important determinants of opinion change. The concept of source credibility appears to be a complex one (Hovland et al., 1953) and a detailed conceptual analysis of the term is necessary. While source credibility is probably related to positive attitudes toward issues, such as honesty and expertness, that the receiver sees himself as sharing with the source, it also appears to be a function of the role and status of the source.

VI. Some Critical Problems

The questions raised in the concluding section of the original discussion of the structural balance model of communication effects (Feather, 1964a) still remain to be answered, although there has been some progress in research since they were asked. These questions were concerned with the representation within the model of (a) strength of relations, (b) importance of the issue, (c) specific effects of imbalance, and (d) individual differences in reactions to imbalance. We now turn to a further consideration of these questions and to a discussion of factors that might underly structural balance.

A. STRENGTH OF RELATIONS

The development of the structural balance model will require the representation of relations that differ in *strength* as well as in *sign*. At present the model deals only with relations that are either positive or negative. Whether relations are strong, moderate, or weak is not allowed for in the model.

The studies reported in Section IV, D, E, F, and G, represent initial attempts to obtain, under controlled conditions, data that might suggest answers to this question. As indicated, there is some support for a principle of reciprocal strength with respect to dyadic structures and for a discrepancy principle with respect to triadic structures. The data also suggest that summation effects occur in more complex structures and that a given attitudinal relation of source to receiver is more salient than a given unit relation in determining the sign and strength of a predicted reciprocal relation. Jordan (1953) also found that relations between p and o appeared to carry most weight in determining ratings of pleasantness.

Our strategy in attempting to discover just how relations of different strength may combine within semicycles has been to formulate different principles of combination and to devise experimental situations that might enable us to decide between these different principles on the basis of the data obtained (Feather, 1966). There are other principles apart from those already mentioned that might be considered further. For example, Morrissette (1958) assumed that the strength of a relation may vary continuously from $+1$ through 0 to -1. He defined the *strength of a cycle* as the product of the strength of its lines, and combined this idea with the Cartwright and Harary (1956) definition of the *sign of a cycle* to develop a formula for the degree of total balance of a signed graph. Presumably this approach, if applied generally, would imply that, given relations of equal strength, a long balanced semicycle would have a lower degree of balance than a short balanced semicycle.

Osgood (1960) believed that a major weakness of Heider's balance theory is that it deals only with relations between the P-O-X elements of the structure and these relations are assigned both affective and connecting properties. In his view the model would be improved if the cognitive elements themselves were assigned affective or attitudinal values. For example, a *positive* P likes a *positive* O (see Osgood, 1960, pp. 347–349). In our view, however, where the dimension of evaluation is involved, the affective "charge" or polarization of a concept summarizes a relation between some person and that concept. The type of model proposed by Osgood and Tannenbaum (1955) and by Rosenberg and Abelson (1960) can therefore be decomposed into a set of relations that can be represented by using graph theory (see Feather, 1964a, pp. 305–307). The congruity principle proposed by Osgood and Tannenbaum does, however, enable one to predict changes in the degree of polarization of both source and concept when they are connected by an assertion. The provision of a quantitative principle is an important contribution of congruity theory. It has led to interesting research (see Osgood, 1960, pp. 359–363), and to the development of alternative principles (see Triandis and Fishbein, 1963; Rokeach and Rothman, 1965; Manis *et al.*, 1966). Recent studies by Tannenbaum and Gengel (1966) and by Tannenbaum (1966) have also applied the congruity principle to predicting the generalization of attitude change. In these studies the general procedure was to set up a source-concept linkage, to modify the polarization of the concept by means of an experimental manipulation, and then to observe the effect of this manipulation on the polarization of the source. In terms of the present communication model, the results of these studies may be interpreted as indicating changes in the $\overrightarrow{RS}$ attitudinal relation that follow an induced change in the $\overrightarrow{RI}$ attitudinal relation, assuming that the $\overrightarrow{CI}$ attitudinal relation remains constant. These changes tend to be consistent with a balance formulation.

Two attempts to deal with the problem of strength of relations have appeared quite recently. In the first place, Price *et al.* (1965), working within the context of Newcomb's A-B-X model, used a concept of perceived discrepancy involving strength as well as sign of relations. They set up hypothetical situations involving three persons, A, B, and X. The attraction of A to B was always positive. Their results were generally consistent with the following hypotheses: (1) When degree of perceived discrepancy is constant, positive or negative affect varies with the degree of attraction between A and B. (2) When the positive attraction of A to B is constant, positive or negative affect varies with the degree of A's perceived discrepancy. This study is clearly on a continuum with the prior investigations of Jordan (1953) and Morrissette (1958) and supplements the results reported in Section IV, D. Second, Wiest (1965), in a quantitative extension of

Heider's theory of cognitive balance, proposed a tetrahedron model in which the relations among elements in the structures are treated as continua (such as degree of liking) rather than as simple dichotomies (such as like versus dislike). Using correlation techniques he found evidence to support the following two hypotheses: (1) " . . . the more a person p, likes someone, o (q), the more positive is the correlation between p's evaluation of a set of other persons and p's perception of o's feelings toward the same set of other persons (or p's perception of the feelings of this set of others toward q)" (p. 11); and (2) " . . . the higher a person's self-esteem, the more positive is the correlation between his feelings toward a set of others and his perception of their feelings toward him" (p. 15). Wiest examined the general implications of his model for balance theory.

Finally, in the last chapter of their recent book on directed graphs, Harary *et al.* (1965) discussed the representation of relations of different strength in terms of "networks". It is rather early to comment on the usefulness of their concepts, but it should prove valuable to employ them in future investigations of balance theory.

Whatever direction research takes in the future, however, it is apparent that an adequate representation of the strength of relations and the development of principles about how relations combine within semicycles are both important questions that need to be answered if the structural balance model of communication effects is to deal with the results of those many studies where there is variation in the strength of attitudes (for example, Sherif and Hovland, 1961; Osgood and Tannenbaum, 1955).

B.   IMPORTANCE OF THE ISSUE

The structural balance model might also be extended to take account of differences in the *importance* of the issue for source or for receiver, or for both. Dissonance theory (Festinger, 1957) allows for such a concept by including the importance of the cognitive elements involved in a dissonant relationship as a factor influencing the magnitude of dissonance. In practice, however, it seldom deals with the variable of "element importance." Newcomb (1961) defined importance as " . . . the valence, positive or negative, of the attitude object, X for A. Ideally, one would measure this variable in terms of the individual's degree of resistance to changing his attitude toward X; operationally, we have generally used as an index of importance the individual's expressed degree of favorability or unfavorability toward the attitude object" (pp. 12–13). Sherif and Hovland (1961) assumed that when an individual is personally involved in an issue his stand functions as a strong anchor influencing his judgments. He has a narrower latitude of acceptance and a wider latitude of rejection and is less likely to be influenced by discrepant persuasive communications. Zajonc and

Burnstein (1965a) suggested that it might be possible in balance theory to conceptualize importance in terms of a positive unit relation between person and issue.

It seems to us that there is less likelihood that a person will change his attitude toward an issue as it becomes more important to him, that is, importance implies resistance to change. Moreover, it would probably be an oversimplification to equate importance with a person's degree of favorability or unfavorability toward an issue, since he might feel strongly about some issues that are not particularly important to him. As we have indicated previously (Feather, 1964a, p. 311), the intensity or strength of an attitude is probably only one factor governing its resistance to change. Katz (1960) referred to the specificity or generality of the attitude, its degree of differentiation, the number and strength of its linkages to a related value system, and the centrality of the attitude as other important factors governing resistance to change. In a similar vein, Newcomb suggested that "committedness" to an existing attitude will influence resistance to change. This " . . . may be an aspect of a more or less generalized personality characteristic, or . . . may be anchored in other systems of orientations, e.g., in 'reference groups' of strong positive attraction" (Newcomb, 1959, p. 401). Pilisuk (1962) has shown in a recent study that attitudes toward attributes of one's self-concept and toward significant others tend to resist change. He argued that such attitudes provide stable anchors for evaluating new information.

In terms of the structural balance model, it should be possible to represent an important issue as one toward which the person has a strong attitude and as one that is closely bound together with other issues toward which the person also has strong attitudes of the same sign. Figure 13 represents such a situation, in which issues I, J, and K are important to receiver R, and in which a communication (C) about issue I is sent by a positive source (S). The stand taken in this communication is discrepant

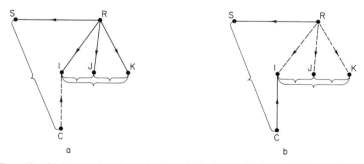

Fig. 13. Unbalanced s-digraphs in which issues I, J, and K are important to receiver R.

with R's attitude toward I in both s-digraph a and s-digraph b, and the structures are unbalanced. Balance could be restored in the S-C-I-R semi-cycle if the RI attitudinal relation were to change from positive to negative (s-digraph a) or from negative to positive (s-digraph b). But such changes would throw the semicycles involving I, J, and K out of balance and would therefore be resisted. Thus in the two cases represented, the receiver might dissociate the source from the communication, misperceive the stand taken in the communication (if there is some ambiguity), or disparage the source.

C. SPECIFIC EFFECTS OF IMBALANCE

In regard to the example just given one might ask: But which of these alternative reactions is most likely to happen? This raises what Kelman and Eagly (1965) refer to as " . . . the major unresolved question in balance theory: the question of what determines the particular mechanism that a person chooses, out of the range of possibilities available to him in a given situation, in order to restore balance or reduce dissonance" (p. 64). In accounting for the results of their study, they distinguish between *source orientation* and *content orientation*. In source orientation the receiver cannot separate the content of the communication from the source; the source's relationship to the receiver's self-definition is of prime importance. Under source orientation it is important to achieve congruity between source and message. Displacement of the stand taken in the communication (assimilation or contrast) and attitude change are alternative ways of achieving this congruity. The former is assumed to be more likely to occur when the message is ambiguous. Typically, however, both mechanisms occur since messages are usually intermediate in ambiguity. This joint occurrence makes it difficult to predict attitude change since there are both *direct* and *indirect* effects of source orientation on attitude change (Kelman and Eagly, 1965, p. 75). Content orientation occurs when the receiver is primarily concerned with the content of the communication especially in relation to goal achievement and value maximization. The receiver is able to divorce the content from the source. Under content orientation the receiver is more alert to the implications of the message and more open to change. Whether or not attitude change does occur depends on the nature of the content. Kelman and Eagly related source orientation and content orientation to the processes of identification and internalization respectively (see Kelman, 1961).

Other studies concerned with alternative ways of reducing dissonance or imbalance have been conducted by Kelley and Woodruff (1956), Harvey *et al.* (1957), Steiner (1960), Steiner and Rogers (1963), Steiner and Johnson (1964), Freedman and Steinbruner (1964), and Pervin and Yatko (1965).

Kelley and Woodruff (1956) found that in one of their experimental conditions ("members' applause") the three reactions of opinion change, distortion of message, and dissociation of source from communication tended to be mutually exclusive; if one occurred, the others tended not to occur. Steiner and Rogers (1963) investigated a situation in which subjects found their judgments contradicted by a respected associate of the same sex. They could resolve the imbalance by conforming to the associate's judgments, rejecting the associate as less competent than he had been thought to be, underrecalling the extent of disagreement, or devaluating the importance of the topics. Steiner and Rogers reported that females made less use of rejection than did males and were more inclined to tolerate the conflict. Results also indicated that the four responses were used as alternative means of reducing the dissonance or imbalance rather than as supplementary means. Steiner and Rogers (1963, p. 135) suggested that the fact that subjects emphasize the use of some means but minimize the use of others implies that their responses to imbalance or dissonance are governed by a habit-family hierarchy based on earlier experience in unbalanced situations. Freedman and Steinbruner (1964) observed that subjects who had high choice in an initial decision more strongly resisted influence by a countercommunication than subjects who had low choice. The resistance was manifested in a stronger tendency to reject the communication and the communicators than in distortion of the relevant information. Pervin and Yatko (1965) also found a tendency for subjects to use alternative methods for reducing dissonance.

How are these results to be accounted for in terms of the structural balance model of communication effects? It is reasonable to suppose that the weaker relations in a structure will be modified before the stronger relations in the direction of achieving the maximum possible degree of balance, but that such changes will be conditional upon other factors, such as the importance of the issue. To use this principle in predictive studies, it would be necessary to know in advance the precise nature of the structure, including the strengths of all relations contained in it. These strengths are clearly a function of both situational and personality factors. For example, the extent to which the source is perceived as responsible for his communication will depend to a large degree on the situational circumstances in which he presents the communication. The attitude of the receiver to the issue, however, is probably less tied to the immediate situation and is more a function of the personality. In addition to the assumption that the type of change that occurs will depend on the character of the structure, especially the strength of the relations it contains, there may also exist relatively stable individual differences in reactions to imbalance (see Steiner and Rogers, 1963). These differences would depend on learning experiences in prior unbalanced situations. Past learning might determine relatively *habitual* modes of responding so that some persons, for example, would be more likely to denigrate the source than to distort his message. These differences in habitual modes of response could be conceptualized in terms of the concept of *response availability* (see Atkinson and Feather, 1966; Feather, 1967a).

In some cases, of course, multiple changes may occur in a structure rather than single changes. In the congruity model Osgood and Tannenbaum (1955) allowed for a number of possible reactions that involve changes in the polarization of both source and concept and, in some situations, a reaction of incredulity. Some of these possible ways of dealing with incongruity have recently been investigated by Tannenbaum, MacAuley, and Norris (1966). Osgood (1960, p. 357) also suggested that " ... those cognitive modifications (changes in assertions or in element valences) will occur which require the minimum restructuring of the entire cognitive map." This principle is consistent with the assumption of Rosenberg and Abelson (1960) that balance will be restored by a minimal number of changes in a structure. They deal with cognitive units consisting of pairs of concepts linked by a relation. Imbalance in a cognitive unit may be handled by changing the sign of either of the concepts or the relation, by redefining or differentiating one of the concepts, or by stopping thinking about the imbalance (see also Abelson, 1959). The imbalance might also be tolerated.

Obviously there is a potentially fruitful field of research involving exploration of different assumptions about specific modes of balance resolution.

D   INDIVIDUAL DIFFERENCES

In the preceding section we noted the likelihood that persons might show consistent differences in the methods they use to resolve imbalance in communication situations. One might ask if these different methods are a function of personality variables. To date, the evidence on this question is rather scant. The studies by Steiner (1960) and by Steiner and Rogers (1963) included personality variables. In the former study tolerance of an A-B-X conflict was found to be associated with high Minnesota Multiphasic Personality Inventory (MMPI) profile elevations in males but with low profile elevations in females. In the latter study the results implied that the effects of anxiety upon a person's choice of dissonance-reducing response depended on sex; correlations relating conformity, underrecall, and tolerance, to scores on the Taylor Scale of Manifest Anxiety were significantly different for the two sexes.

A study by Powell (1962), based on Rokeach's (1960) distinction between open and closed belief-disbelief systems, tested the hypothesis that a person with an open belief system would be more able to distinguish between the message content and the message source and to judge each on its intrinsic merits. Powell used the Rokeach Dogmatism Scale to measure "openness" versus "closedness," and his results were generally consistent with his predictions. Earlier, Vidulich and Kaiman (1961), also using the dogmatism scale, found that "closed" groups agreed more with a high status than with a low status source. "Open" groups tended to agree more with a low than with a high status source. These investigations suggest that dogmatism as measured by the Rokeach scale might relate to source orientation as defined by Kelman and Eagly (1965). Certainly Rokeach's discussion (1960, pp. 57–59) implies a similar distinction to that made by Kelman and Eagly. The latter investigators also reported a study by Weil (1962), which used an index of source orientation versus message orientation developed by McDavid (1959), and which showed that source-oriented subjects are more likely to assimilate the content of a communication when it is ascribed to a positive reference group.

Other studies (for example, Janicki, 1964; Harvey, 1965) have been based upon the theoretical notions developed by Harvey *et al.* (1961). For example, Harvey (1965) found that opinion change was affected significantly by concreteness-abstractness, the concrete subjects changing their opinions more than the abstract subjects. Wright and Harvey (1965) suggested that authoritarianism and opinion change tend to be positively related when the source of the incongruous input is of high status and when the target concept is of low involvement, but negatively related when the source has low status and the target concept is of high involvement. There are other studies from the literature of social influence and conformity that may provide clues about personality variables that influence reactions to imbalance. Self-esteem, anxiety, intolerance of ambiguity, dogmatism, field-dependence, defense preference, and authoritarianism seem to be variables worthy of future investigation (see Hovland and Janis, 1959; Leventhal and Perloe, 1962; Dabbs, 1964; Silverman, 1964; and Vaughan, 1964).

It should be noted that there may also be personality variables influencing the magnitude of imbalance that individuals report and the extent to which individuals can tolerate states of imbalance. Brehm and Cohen (1962, pp. 171–177) indicated the difficulties in studying these problems. They reported an experiment (p. 175) the results of which imply that magnitude of dissonance may be a function of individual differences in the degree to which people feel that they control their own fate. These results suggest that in future investigations it might be valuable to include the test of internal versus external control described by Rotter (1966). Rosen (1961) found a relationship between high dissonance reduction (an extreme preference for information supporting a decision) and narrow category width (Pettigrew, 1958) in male subjects but not in females. In a recent study (Feather, 1964b) we investigated the effect of differences in attitude strength, critical ability, and intolerance of inconsistency on the tendency to evaluate logical arguments in a manner consistent with attitude. These three variables were found to influence evaluations in the predicted direction for subjects with positive attitudes toward the issue (religion). These subjects were more likely to evaluate religious arguments in a manner consistent with their religious attitude the stronger their attitude, the less critical they were, and the more they were intolerant of ambiguity. Results for subjects with negative attitudes, however, were rather inconclusive. A further study (Feather, 1967c), using groups differing in their religious affiliation and a group of atheists, also found relationships in the predicted direction between evaluation of arguments and both intolerance of ambiguity and critical ability. This time predictions were supported for both positive and negative attitude groups. More recently (Feather, 1967a) it has been found that subjects who are high in intolerance of ambiguity are more likely to seek out information consistent with their attitude than subjects low in intolerance of ambiguity. These results were interpreted in terms of an expectancy-value model of information-seeking behavior which assumes motives to approach consistency and to avoid inconsistency (Feather, 1967a). Further research in this relatively unexplored area is needed.

E. OTHER TYPES OF COGNITIVE BIAS

We have seen that the tendency toward balance is a very pervasive type of cognitive bias. There are, however, other types of cognitive bias which may impose limiting conditions upon balance theory. The positivity bias—in general, a cognitive bias toward positive rather than negative interpersonal relations (other factors being held constant)—has already been noted and there is plenty of evidence to support it (Jordan, 1953; Deutsch and Solomon, 1959; Harary, 1959; Rosenberg and Abelson, 1960; Zajonc and Burnstein, 1965a; Armstrong, 1965; Wiest, 1965). In addition to positivity, Zajonc and Burnstein (1965b) reported other forms of bias (for example, reciprocity), and suggested that the interpersonal nucleus of a structure is especially important in the learning of that structure. We have previously noted the dominance of a given interpersonal attitudinal relation when the reciprocal attitudinal interpersonal relation has to be predicted by subjects (Section IV, D). In two separate studies involving p-o-x triads and using measures of tension, Rodriques (1965; 1966) presented data suggesting that subjects tend to prefer states where p and o agree about an impersonal object x to states where they disagree about x. In addition to this agreement bias Rodriques found evidence to support cognitive biases toward balance and positivity. Ohashi (1964), in studies involving triads of persons (p-o-q triads) noted a similar tendency toward agreement. Rodriques (1966) made the important point that measures of balance/imbalance in terms of ratings of pleasantness/unpleasantness may be contaminated by extraneous factors. He investigated alternative measures of tension (in Heider's sense) based upon p's willingness to change parts of the structure. As indicated in Section IV, F, Feather and Jeffries (1967) have discovered an extremity effect—a tendency to judge an unknown source of a communication as less valued and less credible and more potent and more active when he presents a communication taking an extreme stand than when his communication takes a moderate stand. This extremity effect was also found in the study by Feather and Armstrong (1967)—see Section IV, G. Finally, Price *et al.* (1966) found that subjects' ratings of affect (that is, how pleasant or unpleasant they found a given situation) were less in accord with expectations from balance theory when, in p-o-q structures involving three persons, p strongly disliked o. They suggested that it may be necessary to consider parameters such as reciprocity, uncertainty, ambivalence, and engagement in order to account for these data.

These several studies imply that the principle of balance may not be sufficient to account for all of the observed results and that other types of cognitive bias may have to be considered if a complete explanation of findings is to be achieved. An important methodological problem involved in the investigation of the different forms of cognitive bias (such as balance, positivity, and agreement) is that of designing experiments that will enable us to determine the *separate* effects of each, independently of the others. The danger of confounding forms of bias is obvious in that the balance principle is a structural principle, whereas positivity and agreement apply to bonds within a structure.

F.   WHY BALANCE?

The structural balance model of communication effects presented in this paper specifies the conditions for balanced structures, but does not attempt to explain just why these are the conditions. There are, however, a number of suggestions in the literature concerning the basis for man's preference for consistency. We will now review some of these.

Heider's (1958) theory of balance is cast in the Gestalt mold. In fact, Heider (1960) related his balance theory more to classical Gestalt notions than to Lewinian ideas. His emphasis on balanced structures is similar to the Gestalt principle of *prägnanz* or "good form," although more clearly defined. He also saw the tendency toward balanced sentiment and unit relations as serving the organism in his striving toward greater perfection (Heider, 1958, p. 216). Osgood and Tannenbaum argued (1955,

p. 43) that "... judgmental frames of reference tend towards maximal simplicity." The congruity principle, which states that "... changes in evaluation are always in the direction of increased congruity with the existing frame of reference ... " (p. 43), is seen as a manifestation of this tendency toward maximal simplicity. Scott (1963) considered that balance consists of " ... a close correspondence between the affective attribute and whatever other attribute is used for categorizing the objects ... " (p. 68). He suggested that in simple cognitive structures these are attributes that are not well distinguished from the affective, whereas in complex structures all dimensions cannot be highly correlated with the affective attribute (p. 69). Peak (1958) developed a model of psychological structure consisting of parts and relations. She applied this model to the analysis of balanced and unbalanced structures. In a balanced structure there is " ... a high probability activation of definite reactions and prompt completion of activity within the particular structure" (p. 345). In contrast, in the unbalanced structure there is "... longer continued activation within the structure" (p. 345).

In contrast to these approaches there are some that place more emphasis on past learning. Hovland and Rosenberg (1960, pp. 223–227) examined three possible explanations of the tendency for affective, cognitive, and conative components of an attitude to be consistently interrelated. The first is the Gestalt interpretation noted earlier, the striving for organized structures and stable forms. The second and third explanations, however, relate to the past learning experiences of the individual. In the first place, Hovland and Rosenberg argued that as a result of a long history of handling conflicts and frustrations, consistency may come to have the status of a basic learned incentive. Extensive inconsistency between the affective, cognitive, and overt components of an attitude will be psychologically painful and the individual may use his learned skills to produce reorganization. Second, they suggested that it is a common part of social experience for children to be trained to be consistent. There is " ... the normative expectation that feelings, percepts, and overt acts will be integrated with one another" (Hovland and Rosenberg, 1960, p. 226).

In regard to interpersonal attraction and the A-B-X model, Newcomb (1956) suggested that attraction between two persons is related to the extent to which reciprocal rewards are involved in their interaction. Some of these rewards have to do with consensual validation occurring when a trusted or liked person is found to have attitudes similar to one's own. Newcomb (1963) stated that "It is relationships that are simultaneously rewarding to each and realistically apprehended by each that tend to be stable. Such relationships are psychologically (intrapersonally) balanced and objectively (interpersonally) balanced" (p. 385). In a similar vein, disliking may be a function of reciprocal punishments involved in the interaction (Newcomb, 1960; Byrne, 1962). This emphasis on reciprocal rewards and punishments involved in interaction has been formalized in *exchange theory* (Thibaut and Kelley, 1959; Homans, 1961), where the development of interpersonal attraction is related to profits (rewards minus costs arising from the interaction) that fall above some minimum level of expectation or comparison level (see Secord and Backman, 1964, Chapter 7).

Brehm and Cohen (1962) contended that a state of dissonance exists when the person commits himself to a behavior that will involve the frustration of important motives: "Basic to the arousal of dissonance appears to be the incompatibility introduced by the individual's commitment to behave in some way, presumably out of some strong motive, which frustrates another strong motive" (Brehm and Cohen, 1962, pp. 229–230).

Gerard and Greenbaum (1962) employed Festinger's theory of social comparison (1954) and argued that Heider's principle of liking others who agree with you " . . . may be a result of a generalized tendency for the individual to like another who is acting in a manner similar to others in the past who have reduced uncertainty by agreeing with him . . . the other person may be acting not only to reduce uncertainty, but also in a manner which prevents uncertainty from arising" (p. 492).

Finally, in a recent book Pepitone (1964) maintained that cognitive consistency models are too general: "The effects of cognitive inconsistency can usually be decomposed into the effects of social motivations, particularly status and security needs, and a cognitive motivation to form and maintain a veridical cognitive structure" (p. 49).

These different theories about the underlying determinants of the tendency to prefer consistency imply that the complete explanation will be complex. This explanation should be able to account for differences in the strength of this tendency between individuals in the same situation and for one individual across different situations (see Hovland and Rosenberg, 1960, p. 220). Our own thinking about this problem has been guided by the assumption that past experience in social situations is a major determinant of the preference for consistency. In particular, it is likely that, as a result of their own experience in communication situations and from observation of the reactions of others, people come to develop a set of expectations about what happens once a communication is presented. It is as if they develop a simplified theory about the relational structure in most communication situations. Such a theory corresponds to what De Soto (1960) and Kuethe (1962, 1964) call a *social schema*, an implicit theory that is used by the individual in situations containing social stimuli, a theory that may be applied in an all-or-none manner. The results of several studies by De Soto and by Kuethe were consistent with this concept of social schemata that may be shared by many people. Results of a recent experiment by Bem (1965) were also consistent with this line of thinking, although he discussed his results in terms of Skinner's concepts of "mands" and "tacts" (Skinner, 1957). Kuethe (1962) argued that "When many people use the same schema in organizing a social response there is the implication that comparable experiences have produced the commonality of response" (p. 31). It seems likely that the role-playing experiments discussed in Section IV, A–D, G involve a social schema held by individuals generally, a schema concerning balanced relations in communication situations and based upon common experiences in past situations in which communication occurred. The set of rules governing the schema is determined by past experience, but the precise form that the schema takes at any given time (for example, with respect to the particular pattern and strength of relations) is a function of the present communication situation. The schema does, however, tend toward a balanced state. Moreover, the evidence reviewed in this paper suggests that it can be adequately represented by using the mathematical theory of linear graphs.

VII. Concluding Remarks

We have attempted to show that the evidence from experiments involving both hypothetical and real communication situations provides fairly solid support for the structural balance model of communication effects. There is some evidence that the model cannot yet encompass completely because of its present formal simplicity. Further extensions are needed to enable conceptualization of strength of relations, importance of the issue, specific effects of imbalance, individual differences, and forms of cognitive bias other than balance. But these extensions should be possible in the future.

It is important to note that this is a mathematical model of balanced cognitive structures. It is not concerned with accounting for the *initiation* of communications, but with what happens once a communication is presented. The problem of why a communication is initiated is complex: People may have different motives for acting as source; their expectations about the success of their behavior as source may vary; and the incentives toward which their communicative behavior is directed may differ. For example, the source may be a salesman trying to persuade the receiver or client to buy his product so as to improve the volume of his sales and to increase the chances of his promotion. The behavior of the receiver can also be related to a wider goal structure. For example, he may be agreeing with the source against his privately held attitudes in the hope of obtaining the source's patronage. It may, in fact, be possible to conceptualize such instrumental behaviors in terms of an "expectancy-value" model (see

Atkinson, 1964; Atkinson and Feather, 1966), but that is a job for the future. We are not concerned with this type of analysis in the present model, although an expectancy-value approach may also be relevant to the analysis of "cognitive adjustments" just as it has proved to be of value to our understanding of achievement behavior and the seeking of information (Feather, 1967a). The present structural model has focused not upon the instrumentality of behavior but upon the individual's structuring of a communication situation, the conditions under which his cognitive structure is balanced or unbalanced, and the implications that balance or imbalance has for cognitive adjustments.

That is not to say that the present model has no relevance for instrumental behavior. It does indicate ploys that might be used to increase the likelihood that an argument will be accepted, that the source will be liked, that attitude change will occur, and so on. In this regard the model suggests a set of tactics that would be important in social influence, just as Heider's (1958) balance theory implies tactics relevant to the process of ingratiation (Jones, 1964). The set of tactics suggested by the structural balance model of communication effects could be put to good use in fields, such as education and psychotherapy, where the problem of changing attitudes through communication is of major importance.

References

Abelson, R. P. (1959). Modes of resolution of belief dilemmas. *J. Conflict Resolut.* **3**, 343–352.

Ager, J. W., and Dawes, R. M. (1965). The effect of judges' attitudes on judgment. *J. pers. soc. Psychol.* **1**, 533–538.

Allyn, Jane, and Festinger, L. (1961). The effectiveness of unanticipated persuasive communications. *J. abnorm. soc. Psychol.* **62**, 35–40.

Armstrong, D. J. (1965). A structural balance analysis of source attraction, source responsibility, and receiver's evaluation of communications: Effects of sign and strength of relations in different structures. Unpublished honors thesis, Univ. of New England.

Aronson, E., and Golden, B. W. (1962). The effect of relevant and irrelevant aspects of communicator credibility on opinion change. *J. Pers.* **30**, 135–146.

Aronson, E., Turner, Judith A., and Carlsmith, J. M. (1963). Communicator credibility and communication discrepancy as determinants of opinion change. *J. abnorm. soc. Psychol.* **67**, 31–36

Atkinson, J. W. (1964). *An introduction to motivation.* Princeton, New Jersey: Van Nostrand.

Atkinson, J. W., and Feather, N. T. (1966). *A theory of achievement motivation.* New York: Wiley.

Bem, D. J. (1965). An experimental analysis of self-persuasion. *J. exp. soc. Psychol.* **1**, 199–218.

Berkowitz, L. (1960). The judgmental process in personality functioning. *Psychol. Rev.* **67**, 130–142.

Berkowitz, L., and Goranson, R. E. (1964). Motivational and judgmental determinants of social perception. *J. abnorm. soc. Psychol.* **69**, 296–302.

Bergin, A. (1962). The effect of dissonant persuasive communications upon changes in a self-referring attitude. *J. Pers.* **30**, 423–438.

Brehm, J. W., and Lipsher, D. (1959). Communicator-communicatee discrepancy and perceived communicator trustworthiness. *J. Pers.* **27**, 352–361.

Brehm, J. W., and Cohen, A. R. (1962). *Explorations in cognitive dissonance.* New York: Wiley.

Brock, T. C. (1965). Communicator-recipient similarity and decision change. *J. pers. soc. Psychol.* **1**. 650–654.

Brown, R. W. (1962). Models of attitude change. In R. W. Brown, E. Galanter, E. H. Hess, and G. Mandler (Eds.), *New directions in psychology.* New York: Holt, Rinehart & Winston.

Broxton, June (1963). A test of interpersonal attraction derived from balance theory. *J. Abnorm. soc. Psychol.* **66**, 394–397.

Burdick, H. A., and Burnes, A. J. (1958). A test of "strain toward symmetry" theories. *J. abnorm. soc. Psychol.* **57**, 367–370.

Byrne, D. (1961a). Interpersonal attraction and attitude similarity. *J. abnorm. soc. Psychol.* **62**, 713–715.

Byrne, D. (1961b). The influence of propinquity and opportunities for interaction on classroom relationships. *Hum. Relat.* **14**, 63–69.

Byrne, D. (1962). Response to attitude similarity-dissimilarity as a function of affiliation need. *J. Pers.* **30**, 164–177.

Byrne, D., and Blaylock, Barbara (1963). Similarity and assumed similarity of attitudes between husbands and wives. *J. abnorm. soc. Psychol.* **67**, 636–640.

Byrne, D., and McGraw, C. (1964). Interpersonal attraction toward Negroes. *Hum. Relat.* **17**, 199–292.

Byrne, D., and Nelson, D. (1965). Attraction as a linear function of proportion of positive reinforcements. *J. pers. soc. Psychol.* **1**, 659–663.

Byrne, D., and Wong, T. J. (1962). Racial prejudice, interpersonal attraction, and assumed dissimilarity of attitudes. *J. abnorm. soc. Psychol.* **65**, 246–253.

Cartwright, D., and Harary, F. (1956). Structural balance: A generalization of Heider's theory. *Psychol. Rev.* **63**, 277–293.

Cohen, A. R. (1959). Communication discrepancy and attitude change: A dissonance theory approach. *J. Pers.* **27**, 386–396.

Cohen, A. R., Terry, H. I., and Jones, C. B. (1959). Attitudinal effects of choice in exposure to counterpropaganda. *J. abnorm. soc. Psychol.* **58**, 388–391.

Dabbs, J., Jr. (1964). Self-esteem, communicator characteristics, and attitude change. *J. abnorm. soc. Psychol.* **69**, 173–181.

Davis, J. A. (1963). Structural balance, mechanical solidarity, and interpersonal relations. *Amer. J. Sociol.* **68**, 444–462.

De Soto, C. B. (1960). Learning a social structure. *J. abnorm. soc. Psychol.* **60**, 417–421.

Deutsch, M., and Solomon, L. (1959). Reactions to evaluations by others as influenced by self-evaluations. *Sociometry* **22**, 93–112.

Dillehay, R. C. (1965). Judgmental processes in response to a persuasive communication. *J. pers. soc. Psychol.* **1**, 631–641.

Feather, N. T. (1959a). Subjective probability and decision under uncertainty. *Psychol. Rev.* **66**, 150–164.

Feather, N. T. (1959b). Success probability and choice behavior. *J. exp. Psychol.* **58**, 257–266.

Feather, N. T. (1964a). A structural balance model of communication effects. *Psychol. Rev.* **71**, 291–313.

Feather, N. T. (1964b). Acceptance and rejection of arguments in relation to attitude strength, critical ability, and intolerance of inconsistency. *J. abnorm. soc. Psychol.* **69**, 127–136.

Feather, N. T. (1965a). A structural balance analysis of evaluative behavior. *Hum. Relat.* **18**, 171–185.

Feather, N. T. (1965b). Reactions to communications under conditions of source responsibility and source coercion. *Australian J. Psychol.* **17**, 179–194.

Feather, N. T. (1966). The prediction of interpersonal attraction: Effects of sign and strength of relations in different structures. *Hum. Relat.* **19**, 213–237.

Feather, N. T. (1967a). An expectancy-value model of information-seeking behavior. *Psychol. Rev.* in press.

Feather, N. T. (1967b). Effects of institutional affiliation and attitude discrepancy on evaluation of communications and interpersonal attraction. *Hum. Relat.* in press.

Feather, N. T. (1967c). Evaluation of religious and neutral arguments by religious and atheist student groups. *Australian J. Psychol.* in press.

Feather, N. T., and Armstrong, D. J. (1967). Effects of variations in source attitude, receiver attitude, and communication stand on reactions to source and content of communications. *J. Pers.* in press.

Feather, N. T., and Jeffries, D. G. (1967). Balancing and extremity effects in reactions of receivers to source and content of communications. *J. Pers.* **35**, 194–213.

Festinger, L. (1954). A theory of social comparison processess. *Hum. Relat.* **7**, 117–140.

Festinger, L. (1957). *A theory of cognitive dissonance.* New York: Harper & Row.

Festinger, L., and Maccoby, N. (1964). On resistance to persuasive communications. *J. abnorm. soc. Psychol.* **68**, 359–366.

Flament, C. (1963). *Applications of graph theory to group structure.* Englewood Cliffs, New Jersey: Prentice-Hall.

Freedman, J. L. (1964). Involvement, discrepancy, and change. *J. abnorm. soc. Psychol.* **69**, 290–295.

Freedman, J. L., and Steinbruner, J. D. (1964). Perceived choice and resistance to persuasion. *J. abnorm. soc. Psychol.* **68**, 678–681.

Gerard, H. B., and Greenbaum, C. W. (1962). Attitudes toward an agent of uncertainty reduction. *J. Pers.* **30**, 485–495.

Harary, F. (1959). On the measurement of structural balance. *Behav. Sci.* **4**, 316–323.

Harary, F., Norman, R. Z., and Cartwright, D. (1965). *Structural models: An introduction to the theory of directed graphs.* New York: Wiley.

Harvey, O. J. (1965). Some situational and cognitive determinants of dissonance resolution. *J. pers. soc. Psychol.* **1**, 349–355.

Harvey, O. J., and Caldwell, D. F. (1959). Assimilation and contrast phenomena in response to environmental stimulation. *J. Pers.* **27**, 125–135.

Harvey, O. J., Kelley, H. H., and Shapiro, M. M. (1957). Reactions to unfavorable evaluations of the self made by other persons. *J. Pers.* **25**, 393–411.

Harvey, O. J., Hunt, D. E., and Schroder, H. M. (1961). *Conceptual systems and personality organization.* New York: Wiley.

Heider, F. (1944). Social perception and phenomenal causality. *Psychol. Rev.* **51**, 358–374.

Heider, F. (1946). Attitudes and cognitive organization. *J. Psychol.* **21**, 107–112.

Heider, F. (1958). *The psychology of interpersonal relations.* New York: Wiley.

Heider, F. (1960). The gestalt theory of motivation. In M. R. Jones (Ed.), *Nebraska symposium on motivation.* Lincoln, Nebraska: Univ. of Nebraska Press.

Hinckley, E. D. (1963). A follow-up study on the influence of individual opinion on the construction of an attitude scale. *J. abnorm. soc. Psychol.* **67**, 290–292.

Homans, G. C. (1961). *Social behavior: Its elementary forms.* New York: Harcourt, Brace, and World.

Horowitz, M. W., Lyons, J., and Perlmutter, H. V. (1951). Induction of forces in discussion groups. *Hum. Relat.* **41**, 57–76.

Hovland, C. I., and Janis, I. L. (Eds.). (1959). *Personality and persuasibility.* New Haven, Connecticut: Yale Univ. Press.

Hovland, C. I., and Pritzker, H. A. (1957). Extent of opinion change as a function of amount of change advocated. *J. abnorm. soc. Psychol.* **54**, 257–261.

Hovland, C. I., and Rosenberg, M. J. (Eds.). (1960). *Attitude organization and change.* New Haven, Connecticut: Yale Univ. Press.

Hovland, C. I., Janis, I. L., and Kelley, H. H. (1953). *Communication and persuasion.* New Haven, Connecticut: Yale Univ. Press.

Hovland, C. I., Harvey, O. J., and Sherif, M. (1957). Assimilation and contrast effects in reactions to communication and attitude change. *J. abnorm. soc. Psychol.* **55**, 244–252.

Janicki, W. P. (1964). Effect of disposition on resolution of incongruity. *J. abnorm. soc. Psychol.* **69**, 579–584.

Jones, E. E. (1964). *Ingratiation: a social psychological analysis.* New York: Appleton-Century-Crofts.

Jordan, N. (1953). Behavioral forces that are a function of attitudes and of cognitive organization. *Hum. Relat.* **6**, 273–287.

Katz, D. (1960). The functional approach to the study of attitudes. *Publ. Opin. Quart.* **24**, 163–204.

Kelley, H. H., and Woodruff, Christine (1956). Members' reactions to apparent group approval of a counternorm communication. *J. abnorm. soc. Psychol.* **52**, 67–74.

Kelman, H. C. (1961). Processes of opinion change. *Publ. Opin. Quart.* **25**, 57–78.

Kelman, H. C., and Eagly, Alice H. (1965). Attitude toward the communicator, perception of communication content, and attitude change. *J. pers. soc. Psychol.* **1**, 63–78.

Kiesler, C. A., and Kiesler, Sara B. (1964). Role of forewarning in persuasive communications. *J. abnorm. soc. Psychol.* **68**, 547–549.

King, M. G. (1964). Structural balance, tension, and segregation in a university group. *Hum. Relat.* **17**, 221–225.

Kipnis, Dorothy M. (1961). Changes in self concepts in relation to perceptions of others. *J. Pers.* **29**, 449–465.

Kogan, N., and Tagiuri, R. (1958). Interpersonal preference and cognitive organization. *J. abnorm. soc. Psychol.* **56**, 113–116.

Kuethe, J. L. (1962). Social schemas. *J. abnorm. soc. Psychol.* **64**, 31–38.

Kuethe, J. L. (1964). Pervasive influence of social schemata. *J. abnorm. soc. Psychol.* **68**, 248–254.

Leventhal, H., and Perloe, S. I. (1962). A relationship between self-esteem and persuasibility. *J. abnorm. soc. Psychol.* **64**, 385–388.

Lott, A. J., and Lott, Bernice E. (1965). Group cohesiveness as interpersonal attraction: A review of relationships with antecedent and consequent variables. *Psychol. Bull.* **64**, 259–309.

McDavid, J., Jr. (1959). Personality and situational determinants of conformity. *J. abnorm. soc. Psychol.* **58**, 241–246.

Manis, M. (1960). The interpretation of opinion statements as a function of recipient attitude. *J. abnorm. soc. Psychol.* **60**, 340–344.

Manis, M. (1961a). The interpretation of opinion statements as a function of message ambiguity and recipient attitude. *J. abnorm. soc. Psychol.* **63**, 76–81.

Manis, M. (1961b). The interpretation of opinion statements as a function of recipient attitude and source prestige. *J. abnorm. soc. Psychol.* **63**, 82–86.

Manis, M. (1965). Immunization, delay, and the interpretation of persuasive messages. *J. pers. soc. Psychol.* **1**, 541–550.

Manis, M., and Blake, Joan (1963). Interpretation of persuasive messages as a function of prior immunization. *J. abnorm. soc. Psychol.* **66**, 225–230.

Manis, M., Gleason, T. C., and Dawes, R. M. (1966). The evaluation of complex social stimuli. *J. pers. soc. Psychol.* **3**, 404–419.

Mills, J., and Aronson, E. (1965). Opinion change as a function of the communicator's attractiveness and desire to influence. *J. pers. soc. Psychol.* **1**, 173–177.

Morrissette, J. O. (1958). An experimental study of the theory of structural balance. *Hum. Relat.* **11**, 239–254.

Newcomb, T. M. (1953). An approach to the study of communicative acts. *Psychol. Rev.* **60**, 393–404.

Newcomb, T. M. (1956). The prediction of interpersonal attraction. *Amer. Psychologist* **11**, 575–586.

Newcomb, T. M. (1959). Individual systems of orientation. In S. Koch (Ed.), *Psychology: a study of a science.* Vol. 3. New York: McGraw-Hill, pp. 384–422.

Newcomb, T. M. (1960). Varieties of interpersonal attraction. In D. Cartwright and A. Zander (Eds.), *Group dynamics: research and theory,* 2nd ed. New York: Harper & Row, pp. 104–119.

Newcomb, T. M. (1961). *The acquaintance process.* New York: Holt, Rinehart & Winston.

Newcomb, T. M. (1963). Stabilities underlying changes in interpersonal attraction. *J. abnorm. soc. Psychol.* **66**, 376–386.

Oeser, O. A., and Harary, F. (1962). A mathematical model for structural role theory, I. *Hum. Relat.* **15**, 89–109.

Oeser, O. A., and Harary, F. (1964). A mathematical model for structural role theory, II. *Hum. Relat.* **17**, 3–17.

Ohashi, M. (1964). Sociometric choice behavior and interpersonal perception in a triad. *Japan. Psychol. Rev.* **6**, 72–87.

Osgood, C. E. (1960). Cognitive dynamics in the conduct of human affairs. *Publ. Opin. Quart.* **24**, 341–365.

Osgood, C. E., and Tannenbaum, P. H. (1955). The principle of congruity in the prediction of attitude change. *Psychol. Rev.* **62**, 42–55.

Osgood, C. E., Suci, G. J., and Tannenbaum, P. H. (1957). *The measurement of meaning.* Urbana, Illinois: Univ. Illinois Press.

Peak, Helen (1958). Psychological structure and psychological activity. *Psychol. Rev.* **65**, 325–347.

Pepitone, A. (1958). Attributions of causality, social attitudes, and cognitive matching processes. In R. Tagiuri and L. Petrullo (Eds.), *Person perception and interpersonal behavior.* Stanford, California: Stanford Univ. Press, pp. 258–276.

Pepitone, A. (1964). *Attraction and hostility.* New York: Atherton Press.

Pervin, L. A., and Yatko, R. J. (1965). Cigarette smoking and alternative methods of reducing dissonance. *J. pers. soc. Psychol.* **2**, 30–36.

Pettigrew, T. F. (1958). Measurement and correlates of category width. *J. Pers.* **26**, 532–544.

Piaget, J. (1930). *The child's conception of physical causality.* New York: Harcourt, Brace, and World.

Pilisuk, M. (1962). Cognitive balance and self-relevant attitudes. *J. abnorm. soc. Psychol.* **65**, 95–103.

Powell, F. A. (1962). Open- and closed-mindedness and the ability to differentiate source and message. *J. abnorm. soc. Psychol.* **65**, 61–64.

Price, K. O., Harburg, E., and McLeod, J. M. (1965). Positive and negative affect as a function of perceived discrepancy in ABX situations. *Hum. Relat.* **18**, 87–100.

Price. K. O., Harburg, E., and Newcomb, T. M. (1966). Psychological balance in situations of negative interpersonal attitudes. *J. pers. soc. Psychol.* **3**, 265–270.

Rodriques, A. (1965). On the differential effects of some parameters of balance. *J. Psychol.* **61**, 241–250.

Rodriques, A. (1966). The measurement of tension in experiments on balance. Unpublished paper.

Rokeach, M. (1960). *The open and closed mind.* New York: Basic Books.

Rokeach, M., and Rothman, G. (1965). The principle of belief congruence and the congruity principle as models of cognitive interaction. *Psychol. Rev.* **72**, 128–142.

Rosen, S. (1961). Post-decision affinity for incompatible information. *J. abnorm. soc. Psychol.* **63**, 188–190.

Rosenberg, M. J., and Abelson, R. P. (1960). An analysis of cognitive balancing. In C. I. Hovland and M. J. Rosenberg (Eds.), *Attitude organization and change.* New Haven, Connecticut: Yale Univ. Press, pp. 112–163.

Rotter, J. B. (1966). Generalized expectancies for internal versus external control of reinforcement. *Psychol. Monogr.* **80**(1).

Sampson, E. E., and Insko, C. A. (1964). Cognitive consistency and performance in the autokinetic situation. *J. abnorm. soc. Psychol.* **68**, 184–192.

Scott, W. A. (1963). Cognitive complexity and cognitive balance. *Sociometry* **26**, 66–74.

Secord, P. F., and Backman, C. W. (1964). *Social psychology.* New York: McGraw-Hill.

Shaw, M. E., and Sulzer, J. L. (1964). An empirical test of Heider's levels in attribution of responsibility. *J. abnorm. soc. Psychol.* **69**, 39–46.

Sherif, M., and Hovland, C. I. (Eds.). (1961). *Social judgment.* New Haven, Connecticut: Yale Univ. Press.

Sherif, M., and Sherif, Carolyn W. (1965). The social judgment-involvement approach versus the cognitive dissonance approach. Unpublished paper.

Sherif, Carolyn W., Sherif, M., and Nebergall, R. (1965). *Attitude and attitude change: The social judgment-involvement approach.* Philadelphia: Saunders.

Shrader, Elizabeth G., and Lewit, D. W. (1962). Structural factors in cognitive balancing behavior. *Hum. Relat.* **15**, 265–276.

Silverman, I. (1964). Differential effects of ego threat upon persuasibility for high and low self-esteem subjects. *J. abnorm. soc. Psychol.* **69**, 567–572.

Skinner, B. F. (1957). *Verbal behavior.* New York: Appleton-Century-Crofts.

Steiner, I. D. (1960). Sex differences in the resolution of A-B-X conflicts. *J. Pers.* **28**, 118–128.

Steiner, I. D., and Field, W. L. (1960). Role assignment and interpersonal influence. *J. abnorm. soc. Psychol.* **61**, 239–245.

Steiner, I. D., and Johnson, H. H. (1964). Relationships among dissonance reducing responses. *J. abnorm. soc. Psychol.* **68**, 38–44.

Steiner, I. D., and Rogers, E. D. (1963). Alternative responses to dissonance. *J. abnorm. soc. Psychol.* **66**, 128–136.

Stotland, E., Cottrell, N. B., and Laing, G. (1960). Group interaction and perceived similarity of members. *J. abnorm. soc. Psychol.* **61**, 335–340.

Tannenbaum, P. H. (1966). Mediated generalization of attitude change via the principle of congruity. *J. pers. soc. Psychol.* **3**, 493–499.

Tannenbaum, P. H., and Gengel, R. W. (1966). Generalization of attitude change through congruity principle relationships. *J. pers. soc. Psychol.* **3**, 299–304.

Tannenbaum, P. H., Macaulay, Jacqueline R., and Norris, Eleanor L. (1966). Principles of congruity and reduction of persuasion. *J. pers. soc. Psychol.* **3**, 233–238.

Thibaut, J. W., and Kelley, H. H. (1959). *The social psychology of groups.* New York: Wiley.

Triandis, H. C. (1960). Some determinants of interpersonal communication. *Hum. Relat.* **13**, 279–287.

Triandis, H. C., and Fishbein, M. (1963). Cognitive interaction in person perception. *J. abnorm. soc. Psychol.* **67**, 446–453.

Upshaw, H. S. (1962). Own attitude as an anchor in equal-appearing intervals. *J. abnorm. soc. Psychol.* **64**, 85–96.

Upshaw, H. S. (1965). The effect of variable perspectives on judgments of opinion statements for Thurstone scales: Equal-appearing intervals. *J. pers. soc. Psychol.* **2**, 60–69.

Vaughan, G. M. (1964). The trans-situational aspect of conforming behavior. *J. Pers.* **32**, 335–354.

Vidulich, R. N., and Kaiman, I. P. (1961). The effects of information source status and dogmatism upon conformity behavior. *J. abnorm. soc. Psychol.* **63**, 639–642.

Wallach, M. A., Kogan, N., and Bem, D. (1964). Diffusion of responsibility and level of risk taking in groups. *J. abnorm. soc. Psychol.* **68**, 263–274.

Walster, Elaine, and Festinger, L. (1962). The effectiveness of "overheard" persuasive communications. *J. abnorm. soc. Psychol.* **65**, 395–402.

Weil, G. M. (1962). Some effects of message orientation on the process of social influence. Unpublished paper, Harvard.

Weiss, W. (1958). The relationship between judgments of a communicator's position and extent of opinion change. *J. abnorm. soc. Psychol.* **56**, 380–384.

Wiest, W. M. (1965). A quantitative extension of Heider's theory of cognitive balance applied to interpersonal perception and self-esteem. *Psychol. Monogr.* **79** (4).

Wright, J. M., and Harvey, O. J. (1965). Attitude change as a function of authoritarianism and punitiveness. *J. pers. soc. Psychol.* **1**, 177–181.

Zajonc, R. (1960a). The process of cognitive tuning in communication. *J. abnorm. soc. Psychol.* **61**, 159–167.

Zajonc, R. (1960b). The concepts of balance, congruity, and dissonance. *Publ. Opin. Quart.* **24**, 280–296.

Zajonc, R., and Burnstein, E. (1965a). The learning of balanced and unbalanced social structures. *J. Pers.* **33**, 153–163.

Zajonc, R., and Burnstein, E. (1965b). Structural balance, reciprocity, and positivity as sources of cognitive bias. *J. Pers.* **44**, 570–583.

Zavalloni, Marisa, and Cook, S. W. (1965). Influence of judges' attitudes on ratings of favorableness of statements about a social group. *J. pers. soc. Psychol.* **1**, 43–54.

Zimbardo, P. (1960). Involvement and communication discrepancy as determinants of opinion conformity. *J. abnorm. soc. Psychol.* **60**, 86–94.

EFFECTS OF FEAR AROUSAL ON ATTITUDE CHANGE: RECENT DEVELOPMENTS IN THEORY AND EXPERIMENTAL RESEARCH[1]

Irving L. Janis

DEPARTMENT OF PSYCHOLOGY
YALE UNIVERSITY
NEW HAVEN, CONNECTICUT

[1]This chapter presents a condensed and somewhat modified version of the material in several chapters of a forthcoming book. *The Contours of Fear* (John Wiley & Sons, 1968). The theoretical analysis of factors that influence the acceptance of precautionary recommendations in warning communications grew out of recent experimental studies on tolerance for self-imposed deprivations and was facilitated by Grant MH-08564 from the National Institute of Mental Health, United States Public Health Service.

During the fall of 1966, when this chapter was written, the author was a visiting research fellow at the Western Behavioral Sciences Institute, La Jolla, California, and professor of psychology in residence at the University of California at San Diego (while on leave of absence from Yale University).

I. Introduction

A. KEY ISSUES

Is the average person more likely or less likely to accept a persuasive communication if it arouses a relatively high degree of fear, as compared with equivalent communications that arouse mild fear or no fear at all? This question is asked again and again in recent discussions of research on the effectiveness of fear-arousing appeals in inducing attitude change. But is it the right question to ask? Does not this question take too much for granted by assuming a simple monotonic relation between the intensity of fear arousal and communication effectiveness?

The questioning of assumptions is certainly our first task when we are confronted with the inconsistent outcomes of relevant experiments. One series of communication experiments shows a negative relation between fear arousal and attitude change (e.g., Janis and Feshbach, 1953; Haefner, 1956; Janis and Terwilliger, 1962), but another series shows a positive relation (e.g., Insko *et al.,* 1965; Leventhal *et al.,* 1965). A few other studies report no significant differences or a mixed outcome for essentially the same variables (Moltz and Thistlethwaite, 1955; Leventhal and Niles, 1965; Leventhal and Watts, 1966). As McGuire (1967) has pointed out, those psychologists whose views lead them to expect a monotonic function must acknowledge that the results from the relevant attitude-change experiments "constitute a remarkable show of impartiality on the part of Nature."

Nature's impartiality in this area of experimental social psychology, which often makes us feel that we are dealing with subtractive rather than additive research, creates a maximum of confusion when several different indicators of attitude change yield opposite outcomes within the same experiment. For example, Leventhal and Niles (1964) found that a strong fear-arousing version of an antismoking communication was less effective than milder fear-arousing versions in producing professed willingness to stop smoking, but was more effective in gaining acceptance for the belief that smoking causes cancer, and made no significant difference in verbal acceptance of the communicator's recommendation to obtain chest X rays.

A more recent experiment by Leventhal and Watts (1966) again reports a mixed outcome, but the specific findings are not the same as those from the earlier experiment. (See Section IV, A.)

Whenever we encounter such incompatible results from a series of experiments carried out by competent investigators, we must become highly skeptical about our way of conceptualizing the problem and start looking for hitherto neglected variables that might be interacting with those under investigation. Should we expect to find lawful cause-and-effect relations between emotional arousal and attitude change, or should we regard the observed positive, negative, and mixed relations as accidental outcomes that merely reflect the influence of other correlated variables? To what extent can the disparate outcomes be reconciled if we postulate a nonmonotonic relation between intensity of fear arousal and communication effectiveness? What new questions should we try to put to the test so that our experiments will yield more dependable outcomes? Are there any innovations in research strategy that might help us to obtain some additive findings about the conditions under which emotional arousal has a facilitating effect on attitude change and the conditions under which it has an interfering effect? These are the main questions on which the present chapter will be focused.

B. OUTLINE OF THE CHAPTER

In the sections that follow, a preliminary theoretical framework will be sketched, which may help to bring some order out of the apparently chaotic state of existing data on the relation between fear arousal and attitude change. The implications of the theoretical analysis will then be examined in the light of the available experimental findings. In reviewing the evidence, I shall not attempt to cover all investigations that purport to deal with the effects of fear arousal on attitude change, but will concentrate on those that appear to have met the necessary conditions for comparing the relative effectiveness of communications that induce different intensities of fear. It will soon become apparent that although some puzzling inconsistencies can be resolved by the proposed theoretical framework, others remain that cannot be accounted for in any compelling way. Nevertheless, even in its rudimentary form, the theoretical model seems to have considerable heuristic value, as will be pointed out by emphasis on some fresh leads concerning interacting variables that ought to be investigated. In discussing these leads, I shall indicate why I believe that research on the new questions posed by the theoretical model will have a fairly good chance of improving the quality and consistency of experimental results. The ultimate question I have in mind is this: How can this important area of experimental research, which is now plagued with excessive noise, start transmitting more intelligible and enlightening messages?

II. Theoretical Framework

A. FUNCTIONAL PROPERTIES OF ANTICIPATORY EMOTIONS

The arousal of vigilance and of efforts to gain reassurance have received strong emphasis in recent theoretical analyses and experiments bearing on anticipatory emotions whose rise and fall depend on the person's cognitive appraisals of the threat (cf. Janis, 1962, 1968; Janis and Leventhal, 1967; Schachter, 1964; Lazarus, 1966). For example, one of Schachter's key assumptions, supported by some of his experimental findings, is that whenever any environmental cue arouses emotional excitement, the person will become motivated to obtain information about what is happening to him. Schachter assigns a steering function to cognitive factors and this seems to fit in especially well with certain communication effects, such as the extraordinary responsiveness to authoritative information observed among the residents of a threatened city during the initial phases of a hurricane or tornado disaster, when there is considerable ambiguity about the nature of the danger. If emotional excitement is highly aroused at a time when the external threat remains ambiguous, informative announcements can make the difference between a mass flight in terror and a vigorous, stoical effort to maintain business as usual (Janis, 1962).

Lazarus (1966), in reviewing the extensive research from laboratory experiments and field studies on the effects of fear, also emphasizes the heightened motivation to obtain relevant information. He concludes that whenever fear is aroused, the person will become alert to internal and external cues related to the threat and will start thinking about the resources available for coping with it. Lazarus assumes, however, that once vigilant apprehensiveness is induced, the person may resort to defensive avoidances that ward off full awareness of the threat if he fails to gain emotional relief by developing plans for coping with it. Similar behavioral consequences, as will be seen shortly, are emphasized in my analysis of the way in which fear influences cognitive functions, particularly with respect to inducing vigilance and motivating the person to seek reassurance.

Although differing in many essential details, there is at least one common assumption about the cognitive consequences of induced fear that the recent theoretical analyses share with earlier theoretical formulations by psychoanalysts (e.g., Freud, 1936; Sullivan, 1953) and by reinforcement-learning theorists (e.g., Dollard and Miller, 1950; Mowrer, 1950; Skinner, 1938). This common assumption is that whenever fear or any other unpleasant emotion is strongly aroused—whether by a verbal warning or by a direct encounter with signs of danger—the person becomes motivated to ward off the painful emotional state and his efforts in this direction will persist until the distressing cues are avoided in one way or another. Thus, if the distressing threat cues do not rapidly disappear as a result of environmental changes, the emotionally aroused person is expected to try to escape from them, either physically or psychologically (for example, by imagining himself as taking successful protective action or distracting himself by pleasant daydreams). The characteristic shifts in content of cognitions, which the emotionally aroused person directs toward warding off external signs and internal anticipations that give rise to his distressing affective state, have been described in similar ways by the adherents of diverse psychological theories, although they use different terms—such as "defenses," "coping mechanisms," "security devices," "aversive habits," and "avoidance efforts" —to designate them.

B.   REFLECTIVE FEAR

The implications of the foregoing theoretical assumptions for attitude changes have been discussed by Janis (1962) in an analysis of the concept of reflective fear. The term "reflective" was introduced in order to emphasize two distinctive features of fear reactions in normal adults—first, that the emotional state is based to some extent on thoughtful *reflection*; and second, that as a result of being mediated by higher mental processes, the intensity of the emotion tends to increase or decrease as the signs of external threat increase or decrease, *reflecting* like a mirror the presence or absence of environmental threat cues. More specifically, a key assumption is that a person's level of reflective fear is roughly proportional both to the perceived probability of the dangerous event materializing and to the anticipated magnitude of the damage, if it does materialize, that could be inflicted on himself, his family, and other significant persons or groups with whom he is identified. The person's level of reflective fear will increase or decrease depending on the information he receives concerning his personal vulnerability to danger or deprivation, whether it involves anticipations of physical pain, career failure, social rejection, economic deprivation, or any other potential loss. In contrast to the relatively unmodifiable character of neurotic anxiety, reflective fear will tend to be low, moderate, or high, depending on whether warning messages are presented that evoke anticipations of a low, moderate, or high degree of personal vulnerability to the predicted danger. Reflective fear can sometimes be temporarily aroused to such a high level that it seems indistinguishable from a neurotic type of panic state, but it will nevertheless subside in response to authoritative reassurances that the threat is no longer present or that adequate coping resources are available.

The anticipations of personal vulnerability evoked by any warning communication are presumably determined by cultural norms, socializing experiences, and other predisposing factors that shape the person's expectations as to where, when, and how much he might be affected by whatever source of danger is being called to his attention. Many idiosyncratic factors in each person's temperament and past training may influence the way he processes informational inputs about potential dangers and thus determine the intensity of his reflective fear reactions. Despite these sources of individual differences, however, there may be a number of relatively invariant consequences of fear arousal that are shared by all human beings. Janis (1962) postulates three such behavioral consequences of reflective fear and presents a number of partially tested hypotheses concerning the conditions under which each is likely to become dominant.

1. One major consequence is that the aroused unpleasant emotional state gives rise to *heightened vigilance*, which takes the form of increased attention to threat-relevant events, scanning for new signs of danger, attending to information about the nature of threat, and thinking about alternative courses of action for dealing with emergency contingencies. The arousal of vigilance affects not only cognitive processes of perception, attention, and planning, but also actions: The individual becomes keyed up in a way that makes him more likely to execute precautionary actions in response to any cue indicating the onset of danger. More complicated forms of mental and physical activity may also result from a strong need for vigilance. During an epidemic, for example, apprehensive people not only learn about the danger signs and scan the newspaper for announcements by public health officials, but they also pay closer attention to internal stimuli from their own bodies. Sometimes they become hypervigilant, exaggerating the significance of their mild physical discomforts to the point where they become sleepless and demand prompt medical attention.

2. Another important consequence of reflective fear is that the person displays a strong need to *seek reassurances* in order to alleviate emotional tension. Again, the need for reassurance involves changes in both cognition and action. For example, some of the actions of moderately fearful surgery patients are oriented toward gaining verbal reassurances from the doctor and other staff members; on the cognitive side, such patients may focus their thoughts repeatedly on the reassuring instructions given them for dealing with postoperative pain (Janis, 1958). Other manifestations of the heightened need for reassurance include selective attention to complacent assertions that alleviate fear by minimizing the danger, and acquisition of new attitudes that alleviate fear by bolstering the person's confidence in his ability to cope with the danger. Some of the attitude changes may lead to highly adaptive behavior, such as taking precautionary measures recommended by trustworthy authorities. But an endangered person will sometimes resort to a fatalistic outlook, superstitious rituals for warding off bad luck, and other unrealistic forms of reassurance that foster anticipations of total invulnerability. The person may end up firmly believing that the danger will not

materialize ("It can't happen here!") or that if it does, he will somehow be completely unscathed ("Others may suffer, but we shall be safe"). These complacent anticipations, referred to as "blanket reassurances," may lead to a maladaptive lack of vigilance when the external danger is actually approaching.

3. A third consequence is that the arousal of reflective fear increases the chances that the person will develop new attitudes involving a compromise between vigilance and reassurance tendencies. The two tendencies may give rise to manifestations of conflict, as when a combat soldier feels at one moment that he must watch out for ever-present danger and at the next moment that he ought to relax and forget about it because he is safe from harm. Sometimes one tendency dominates the other entirely, as in the case of blanket reassurances. But when the average person is repeatedly exposed to impressive warnings, he is likely to develop a *compromise attitude*, which combines discriminative vigilance (seeking further information about the threat, remaining alert to signs of oncoming danger) with discriminative reassurances (expecting to be able to cope successfully, or to be helped by others, if the danger becomes extreme). Outstanding examples of compromise attitudes are seen among victims of heart disease who learn to live with their illness. Realizing they might be subject to another heart attack, they make specific plans for carrying out protective actions that will help them to survive if such an attack happens to materialize. For instance, after his first heart attack, a man will go about his business carrying a well-labeled bottle of digitalis in a prominent pocket and a legible note in his wallet stating the appropriate dosage to give in case he is found unconscious. Such an individual displays a mixed attitude, because he remains vigilant to possible signs of worsening of his illness and worries about being incapacitated or killed by it, and yet is able to gain some reassurance by adhering to a medical plan that could actually save his life in an emergency. Obviously, this type of attitude is likely to be much more adaptive than either blanket reassurance or indiscriminate vigilance.

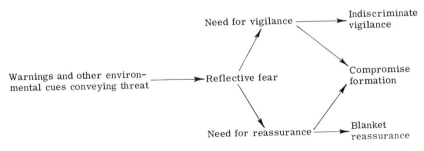

Fig. 1. Hypothetical consequences of the arousal of reflective fear (from Janis, 1962).

Figure 1 shows diagrammatically the three alternative modes of adjustment to threat that are specified in the foregoing analysis; the three different outcomes are shown in the last column. A major task for research on fear-arousing communications is to determine the conditions under which one or another of these three modes of adjustment to threat will become dominant.

One factor that is assumed to determine which of the three types of reaction will be evoked by a warning message is the magnitude of the threat. The influence of this factor is represented in Fig. 2, which shows the expected reactions of normal persons to low, moderate, and high threats. At one extreme, when the threat cues make the danger appear unlikely to

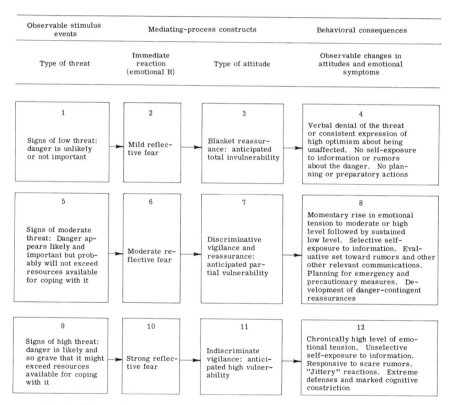

Observable stimulus events	Mediating-process constructs		Behavioral consequences
Type of threat	Immediate reaction (emotional R)	Type of attitude	Observable changes in attitudes and emotional symptoms
1 Signs of low threat: danger is unlikely or not important	**2** Mild reflective fear	**3** Blanket reassurance: anticipated total invulnerability	**4** Verbal denial of the threat or consistent expression of high optimism about being unaffected. No self-exposure to information or rumors about the danger. No planning or preparatory actions
5 Signs of moderate threat: Danger appears likely and important but probably will not exceed resources available for coping with it	**6** Moderate reflective fear	**7** Discriminative vigilance and reassurance: anticipated partial vulnerability	**8** Momentary rise in emotional tension to moderate or high level followed by sustained low level. Selective self-exposure to information. Evaluative set toward rumors and other other relevant communications. Planning for emergency and precautionary measures. Development of danger-contingent reassurances
9 Signs of high threat: danger is likely and so grave that it might exceed resources available for coping with it	**10** Strong reflective fear	**11** Indiscriminate vigilance: anticipated high vulnerability	**12** Chronically high level of emotional tension. Unselective self-exposure to information. Responsive to scare rumors. "Jittery" reactions. Extreme defenses and marked cognitive constriction

FIG. 2. Schematic summary of "normal" psychological changes evoked by warnings or signs of external danger (from Janis, 1962).

materialize or so mild as to be unimportant, the person's behavior remains essentially unchanged; an attitude of blanket reassurance is likely to be dominant. The behavioral effects of this type of complacency are described in box 4, in the upper right-hand corner of the figure. At the other extreme, when very strong warnings are given, reflective fear may mount to such a high level that indiscriminate vigilance tends to be the predominating reaction. The resulting changes in attitudes and emotional symptoms, as described in box 12 in the lower right-hand corner of the figure, are likely to be disruptive and maladaptive.

When a person is warned about an impending danger that he judges to be potentially serious but manageable, he is likely to experience a moderate degree of reflective fear, and the predominant attitude is most likely to be a combination of discriminative vigilance with reassurance. This sequence, depicted in the second row of Fig. 2, represents what happens when a person successfully carries out the "work of worrying" (cf. Janis, 1958, pp. 374–388). The compromise attitude, which develops as the person engages in the work of worrying at a relatively moderate level of arousal, is likely to be sufficiently tested by reality to help him maintain emotional control later on, if he finds himself confronted by actual danger or deprivation. Thus, the resulting changes in attitude and action described in box 8 in the figure are assumed to have a better chance of being adaptive than those resulting from either very mild or very strong arousal.

C. OTHER REFLECTIVE EMOTIONS

In a recent paper, Janis and Leventhal (1965) indicate that the distinction between a reflective emotion (which is highly modifiable by informational inputs) and an internally aroused or "neurotic" emotion (which is relatively unmodifiable by the receipt of new information) can be applied to other negative affects such as grief, guilt, and anger, as well as to fear. All reflective emotions can be regarded as sharing a number of basic functional properties, such as a fairly high degree of proportionality between perceived magnitude of the threat and the intensity of emotional arousal. The details have not yet been worked out concerning the alternative consequences of different intensities of reflective shame or reflective guilt, but we would expect them to be roughly similar to those evoked by different intensities of reflective fear, as shown in Fig. 2. For example, when reflective shame is evoked by a very mild threat of criticism from one's friends or when reflective guilt is evoked by a reminder of a minor lapse from one's ethical standards, the outcome is probably equivalent to the blanket reassurance type of attitude (shown in box 4 of Fig. 2), leading to little or no change in behavior. In contrast, a threat that evokes a moderate degree of shame or guilt would probably induce a psychological process equivalent to the "work of worrying," giving rise to a compromise attitude (similar to that described in box 8) that enables the person to cope more effectively with subsequent stresses, which might otherwise overwhelm him with extreme humiliation or with guilt of suicidal intensity. A very strong threat of social ostracism by one's friends or of unmitigated guilt for committing a crime would probably induce the equivalent of indiscriminate vigilance, resulting in disorganized maladaptive behavior (with symptoms similar to those listed in box 12).

D. FACILITATING AND INTERFERING EFFECTS OF EMOTIONAL APPEALS

In this and the next section we shall examine the theoretical implications of the foregoing analysis of reflective emotions for the relation between attitude change and the intensity of emotional arousal. Whenever a negative type of emotional appeal is introduced for the purpose of motivating people to adopt a recommended policy or to take protective action—such as stopping smoking to avoid lung disease—its success requires the development of a compromise attitude. On the one hand, the communicatee must become sufficiently vigilant to be attentive to signs of potential danger and he must continue to take the threat seriously if he is to avoid backsliding to his former attitude of complacency and inaction. On the other hand, his decision to adhere to the policy recommended by the communicator must satisfy his need for reassurance sufficiently so that he is not left in a distressing emotional state that will motivate him to seek some other (nonrecommended) means of averting or ignoring the threat.

A number of specific assumptions about the facilitating and interfering effects of emotional arousal (Janis, 1968) highlight the potential deficiencies of emotional appeals that are either very weak or very strong when a communicator is attempting to persuade the audience to adopt his recommendations for coping with a realistic threat. Three main sources of failure to produce attitude change can be singled out, one resulting from insufficient stimulation and the other two from excessive stimulation:

1. *Insufficient vigilance*: A persuasive communication may fail to achieve any facilitating effects if it evokes little or no emotional arousal. Statements about the pertinent threat, especially when presented in a bland manner without any concrete or personalized images, may pose no challenge at all to the recipients' initial beliefs about the unimportance of the predicted danger and may leave intact their anticipations of personal invulnerability. They will devote little attention or thought to the threat and will not be in the market for the proposed solution to the threat that the communicator is trying to promote. Thus, when vigilance is not stimulated, preexisting attitudes of blanket reassurance will remain dominant. (For example, an antismoking communication would be totally ineffective if it merely induced complacent thoughts in the recipient, such as "lung cancer hardly ever occurs in young people like us, so there is no reason to pay any attention to what is being said about it.")

2. *Cognitive impairment from hypervigilance*: At the opposite extreme, excessive arousal can induce a temporary state of hypervigilance that interferes with reception of the communicator's message. Members of the audience may become so preoccupied with the threat content of the communication and so disorganized in their thinking that they fail to attend to or comprehend the communicator's recommendations for averting the threat. Although the available evidence, which will be cited later on, indicates that this extremely high level of arousal is likely to be evoked only very rarely by mass communications containing strong emotional appeals, a temporary decrease in mental efficiency during exposure to a persuasive communication will interfere with attitude change insofar as it prevents the person from grasping crucial parts of the message.

3. *Unintended attitude changes resulting from residual emotional tension*: An optimal degree of emotional arousal that falls somewhere in the broad intermediate range between the extremes of insufficient vigilance and excessive vigilance is presumed to be a necessary but not a sufficient condition for acceptance of the communicator's recommendation. Emotional equanimity cannot always be restored merely by an authoritative recommendation and the audience may choose alternative means for satisfying the aroused need for reassurance. (For example, an antismoking communication that arouses fear of lung disease may lead some recipients to adopt a nonrecommended solution, such as switching to filtered cigarettes.)

The probability of selecting the particular means recommended by the communicator is a function of many independent variables that are unrelated to level of arousal—such as the degree of anticipated protection, the relative costs of adopting alternative means, and other considerations that enter into cognitive evaluation of any proposed solution to a serious problem. In addition to these independent variables, the level of arousal is assumed to be one of the determinants of degree of resistance. As the level of unpleasant emotional arousal increases, the audience will become increasingly motivated to examine the communicator's recommendation critically and to consider alternative means that might lend greater reassurance. Thus, as reflective fear, shame, or guilt mounts from a low to a moderate and then to a high level, the average person will become increasingly alert to aspects of the potential danger situation that might be overlooked by the communicator. In this more vigilant state, a person will consider more carefully than otherwise the possible loopholes in any proposed solution that purports to offer a high degree of safety. The higher the level of aroused vigilance, the greater the chances that any proposed solution will be critically evaluated to see if it offers sufficient protection, and hence the higher the probability that members of the audience will remain apprehensive about the riskiness of relying on the communicator's recommendations. Consequently, they will be motivated to seek a more reassuring solution to reduce the state of relatively high arousal that remains after they have critically evaluated the communicator's recommendation. The tendency to resist the communicator's influence and to refute his message may also be enhanced by the arousal of aggression in response to the frustration created by the unpleasant state of arousal.

Moreover, the more strongly reassurance needs are aroused by a fear-arousing appeal in a persuasive communication, the higher the likelihood that the person will try out various habitual forms of defensive avoidance that have been strongly rewarded by fear-reduction in the past. Among the effective forms of cognitive defenses that can function as powerful resistances to the communicator's message are the following: (1) doubts about the communicator's sincerity and suspicions that he may be an alarmist who is trying to manipulate the audience; (2) refutations of statements about the magnitude or personal relevance of the potential danger, which enable the person to deny that he could be affected by it; (3) selective attention to arguments and signs that the threat is not imminent, even if the potential danger is not minimized, which enables the person to set the problem aside while he passively awaits future developments before trying to work out a solution.

These cognitive defenses can operate as powerful resistances to the communicator's message during or after exposure to the communication, insofar as they succeed in enabling the person to avoid thinking about the threat. The greater the need for reassurance, the more likely the person is to make use of these and other types of defensive avoidance, such as fatalistic attitudes. Hence, the arousal of a strong need for reassurance by use of a strong emotional appeal runs the risk of inducing unintended attitude changes, since the audience becomes more inclined to dismiss the communicator as untrustworthy and to minimize the importance or imminence of the alleged threat. Later on, it will become apparent that these considerations do not lead to any simple formula for predicting the optimal level of arousal, but they do suggest some hypotheses concerning the interacting variables that will make a difference in the observable outcome. (See Section IV, B.)

E. HYPOTHETICAL CURVES DEPICTING THE OPTIMAL LEVEL OF
    AROUSAL

The implications of the foregoing analysis for the relation between level of arousal and probability of acceptance can be made more explicit if we examine the set of hypothetical curves shown in Fig. 3. In order

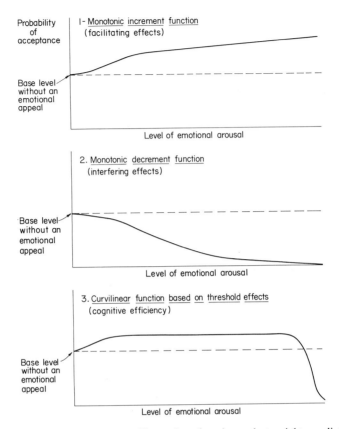

FIG. 3. Hypothetical curves illustrating functions that might mediate relation between level of emotional arousal and probability of acceptance of a communicator's recommendation (from Janis, 1968).

to concretize the types of attitude changes and decisions to which these curves might be most applicable, let us suppose that a public health campaign is instituted by respected health authorities, which urges the public to accept specific practicable means for averting the threat of certain diseases (for example, stop smoking to avoid lung cancer; go on a diet to avoid heart disease; or obtain an inoculation to avoid being stricken during a flu epidemic). Let us suppose further that the level of fear arousal can, within certain broad limits, be manipulated by the judicious selection of threat material, so that the emotional impact of the communications on the average audience could range from practically zero arousal (in cases where all discussion of the potential dangers is omitted and all allusions to the threat are accompanied by reassuring assertions about the efficacy of modern medical science) to extremely high arousal (when new and ˙unexpected information that conveys the magnitude and imminence of the danger is presented, or when dramatic films of disease victims in contexts that readily evoke empathic reactions are shown, and when emphasis is placed on incipient signs or symptoms of potential danger, such as smoker's cough, which will personalize the threat for all those members of the audience who have the prodromal symptoms). It should also be assumed that the prestige value of the communicator and the impressive non-fear-arousing arguments he presents will produce a significant amount of intended attitude change in the audience (for instance, about 15% of the audience will be favorably disposed toward the communicator's recommendation and will decide to put it into practice). Now, the questions to be answered by our theoretical analysis are: Will the percentage who accept the recommendation increase or decrease when an emotional appeal is inserted that produces a slight degree of emotional arousal? Will the percentage continue to increase or will it begin to decrease as arousal is increased to moderate, fairly high, and very high levels?

Three alternative effects of emotional arousal are represented by the hypothetical curves in Fig. 3. The first curve shows a monotonic increment function: As the level of arousal increases from slight to moderate to high, each increment yields an increase in the probability that the recipients will accept the communicator's recommendation. This is the type of curve we would expect if the main behavioral consequences of emotional arousal consisted only of facilitating effects, such as an increase in vigilant interest in the threat and a heightened need for reassurance that could be satisfied by accepting the communicator's recommendation. The second curve, which represents a monotonic decrement function, would be expected if the only behavioral consequence of arousal were the mobilization of resistances that interfere with acceptance.

The third curve is intended to represent the probable effects of emotional arousal on attention and cognitive efficiency, which indirectly influences the probability of acceptance: A message obviously cannot produce the intended attitude changes if the audience does not attend to it and comprehend it sufficiently well to understand what the communicator is recommending. At the lower end of the curve, the slight initial rise shows the expected gain in vigilant attention from inducing a mild degree of emotional arousal, which is likely to overcome initial indifference among the recipients that otherwise would incline them to "turn off" the communication either physically or psychologically. At the upper end of the curve there is a marked decrement, which represents the expected loss in attention to and comprehension of the message created by the temporary cognitive constriction accompanying hypervigilance (as described in Fig. 2, box 12). Later on (Section III, A) we shall see that the pertinent evidence concerning the effects of arousal on attention and comprehension suggests a threshold effect at each end of the curve, with a long plateau over a broad range at intermediate degrees of arousal where no detectable differences in cognitive efficiency are observed. These threshold effects seem analogous to the effects of physical illumination on acceptance of any printed persuasive message: When the lighting is so dim that the message cannot be read at all, slight increases in illumination will yield a gain in message effectiveness; but once it reaches a threshold level at the low end of the curve, where the lighting is just bright enough for the message to be read without straining one's eyes, further .increases in level of illumination will not produce any observable gain. At the upper end of the curve, a second threshold is reached where the light has become so glaringly bright that it begins to interfere with visibility, and in this region the curve will begin to descend.

If changes in cognitive efficiency were the only process that mediates the relation between emotional arousal and acceptance, we might expect a curve like the one at the bottom of Fig. 3, but the long plateau does not seem plausible when we take account of the main motivational processes that are likely to influence the average person's readiness to accept a persuasive message.

All three of the curves shown in Fig. 3 are assumed to be component functions that enter into the relation between emotional arousal and acceptance of recommendations: A monotonic increment function like the one shown at the top of Fig. 3 would be the product of the facilitating effects of certain habitual responses that are cued off in the average person by emotional arousal. These effects are not uniformly strong at all levels of arousal, but generally increase as vigilance and the need for reassurance increase. One type of facilitating effect is the heightened interest in finding a means for coping with the anticipated danger, which increases the person's receptivity to any proposed solution. Another type of facilitating effect stems from a temporary increase in dependency on authorities as a means for gaining reassurance, which tends to augment the person's readiness to accept any recommendation made by anyone in a respected leadership role.

The strength of these facilitating types of response probably depends on the degree to which the person's initial attitude of complacency is challenged. But the rate of increase, the inflection points, and the average height of the increment curve will vary, of course, as a function of such precommunication factors as degree of prior familiarity with the proposed means for coping with the threat, perceived efficacy of the means, perceived agreement or disagreement among authorities, and amount of prestige attributed to the communicator. Chronic readiness to become dependent on authority under conditions of stress and other personality predispositions that give rise to individual differences in coping styles would also affect the shape and height of the curve for each person.

A monotonic decrement function like the one shown in the middle of Fig. 3 would be the product of interfering effects from at least two other types of habitual tendencies that are also cued off by emotional arousal. One type involves the heightened receptivity to nonrecommended means for coping with the threat, resulting from the average person's greater readiness to look vigilantly for loopholes that might prevent the proposed solution from providing sufficient safety and to scan his memory for alternative solutions that might hold forth the promise of greater reassurance. Another type consists of defensive avoidance tendencies, which incline the person to minimize the threat or detach himself from it in an effort to regain his initial attitude of complacency. As in the case of the increment curve, the parameters of this decrement curve will vary as a function of specifiable situational and predispositional factors that affect the component processes. Among the major factors would be prior awareness of criticism of the recommended course of action, prior exposure to authoritative communications about the advantages of alternative recommendations concerning the same threat, and presence of cues suggesting manipulative intentions, which foster suspicions that the communicator is exaggerating or lying. There are also various chronic personality attributes that could give rise to individual differences in readiness to avoid signs of threat and to become suspicious or critical of authorities who give warnings.

The combined result of an ascending and a descending monotonic function, like the ones postulated for the facilitating and interfering effects of emotional arousal, is a nonmonotonic function that takes the form of an inverted U-shaped curve. It has been pointed out that each of the component curves will vary as a function of various observable factors, such as the person's prior exposure to information about the reasons for selecting alternative means for coping with the threat and other factors mentioned in the preceding paragraphs. Insofar as these factors affect the parameters of one or both of the component curves, they will also affect the parameters (but not the basic shape) of the combined nonmonotonic function. Consequently, the theoretical model for the relation between arousal and acceptance consists of a family of inverted U-shaped curves, as shown in Fig. 4.

The third component, representing the effects of emotional arousal on cognitive efficiency, plays only a minor role compared with the first two components in shaping the resultant family of curves. Each member of the family of curves represented in Fig. 4 starts with an initial rise

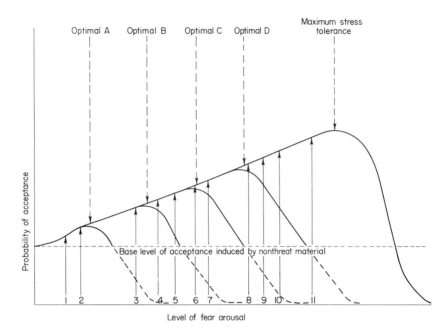

FIG. 4. Hypothetical family of nonmonotonic curves representing the relation between level of fear arousal elicited by a communication and the degree of acceptance of the attitude or decision recommended (from Janis, 1968).

at the low end of the arousal continuum, which would be partly attributable to the gain in vigilant attention postulated for the initial threshold effect shown in the curve at the bottom of Fig. 3. The other end of this cognitive efficiency curve, where the postulated threshold for hypervigilance is reached, determines the final drop-off in the resultant curve shown in Fig. 4, since this is the region where cognitive constriction begins to interfere significantly with reception of the message. In other words, the marked decrement at the high-arousal end of the cognitive efficiency curve leads us to expect that for each person there will always be a *maximum* optimal level of arousal beyond which acceptance will be adversely affected by the temporary loss of cognitive efficiency.

    If no other sources of interference were operating, the postulated nonmonotonic relation would hardly differ from the positive monotonic function shown in the first curve in Fig. 3: The resultant curve in Fig. 4 that reaches its peak at the maximal level of stress tolerance is essentially a monotonic increment curve up to the region of extremely high arousal, where the threshold for hypervigilance is assumed to be reached. But the peak of the curve is likely to fall well below this maximal level for most mass communications, except perhaps for the official emergency warnings issued at a time when people realize they are facing an imminent disaster. The relevant evidence from communication experiments, which will be reviewed shortly, indicates that mass communications rarely arouse intense fear to the point where there are observable signs of temporary cognitive impairment affecting attention, comprehension, or retention of the message. Consequently, when we examine inverted U-shaped curves obtained from studies of the effectiveness of emotional appeals in persuasive communications, we will be dealing with peaks of acceptance that are not at the maximal level of stress tolerance (for example, optimal level A, B, C, or D in Fig. 4). The drop-off portion of each of these curves starts to set in when the strength of the facilitating effects begins to be outweighed by the strength of the interfering effects arising from motivated resistances (which do not involve any temporary cognitive impairment affecting attention or comprehension).

McGuire (1967) has formulated a similar nonmonotonic theory of the relation between fear arousal and acceptance, which he has attempted to derive from well-known learning theory conceptions of the cue and drive functions of fear: As a cue, fear evokes habitual responses that are distracting and interfere with reception of the message; as a drive, fear energizes whatever responses are in progress and this is assumed to facilitate acceptance. Both the cue and drive functions are assumed to increase monotonically with level of fear, at somewhat different rates; since they operate in opposite directions, the resultant relation is nonmonotonic.

While McGuire's two-factor theory has the virtue of simplicity, it seems to me to be quite arbitrary in assuming that the only responses cued off by fear are ones that interfere with reception of the message. Would not the arousal of fear by threat statements frequently cue off certain types of facilitating, as well as interfering, responses? For example, is fear not likely to cue off the habit of relying on authoritative recommendations that offer a solution for coping with the threat, when this type of response has been rewarded in the past by reduction of fear? Similar questions can be posed concerning McGuire's assumption that the only responses energized by fear are "yielding" tendencies that facilitate attitude change. Would not the interfering responses cued off by fear be just as likely to be energized by the fear drive as the facilitating responses? For example, when the person recalls and starts thinking about the advantages of a nonrecommended solution that he had learned about earlier from an opposing communication, would not this antiyielding type of response be augmented by the fear drive? Part of the problem here is that the two learning-theory terms, "drive function" and "cue function," remain somewhat vague when they are applied to human communication processes, so that it is not clear what differential predictions, if any, follow from the use of these labels.

It should also be noted that McGuire does not deal with certain forms of motivated resistance that do not affect reception but that do interfere with yielding to influence, as specified in my second main proposition (Section II, F). Partly because these additional factors are omitted, certain of the predictions that McGuire infers from his two-factor theory are not the same as the ones inferred from the multiple-factor theoretical model proposed here.

At a very low level of arousal, the interfering effects of resistances are likely to be greatly outweighed by the facilitating effects of stimulating the recipients' vigilance and of heightening their receptivity to any recommendations that hold forth the promise of reassurance. As the level of arousal increases, however, a point is reached sooner or later for any given type of persuasive message where the interfering effects start to increase at a faster rate than the facilitating effects. This point is the *effective* optimal level for that type of message.

Thus, it is assumed that the effective optimal level of arousal is not a fixed point on the continuum, but can be shifted by variations in all those variables that determine the shape and height of the two major components, that is, the ascending curve of facilitating effects and the descending curve of interfering effects. Suppose, for example, that we were predicting the effectiveness of a persuasive message urging all chronic cigarette smokers who cannot stop smoking to avoid the danger of lung cancer by using a new type of long cigarette holder containing a chemical filter. Let us suppose further that we have prepared a series of different versions of the same basic communication, each containing a fear-arousing appeal of different intensity, ranging from the low end to the high end of the arousal continuum (as illustrated by the eleven arrows that originate along the baseline in Fig. 4). Now, we would predict a relatively low optimal level (for example, at A in Fig. 4) if the basic communication were to start off in an offensive, hard-sell manner that antagonizes many people in the audience and makes it easy for them to dismiss everything the communicator says as exaggerated propaganda intended to increase the profits of the manufacturers of the new cigarette holder. On the other hand, if the communicator starts off by giving his credentials as a medical specialist who is speaking on behalf of a respected public health institution, we would predict a much higher optimal level (for example, at B or C in Fig. 4).

We would also predict that the optimal level of arousal would be relatively higher for the women in the audience than for the men (even though on other topics sex differences might tend to be in the opposite direction).

This prediction takes account of the high probability that many men in the audience would expect to be ridiculed by their friends as being effeminate if they were to use the recommended long holder, and consequently they would regard the proposed solution as inexpedient. Their resistances would be highly mobilized as soon as they started to feel concerned about the threat and would begin to outweigh the facilitating effects of fear at a relatively low level of arousal. The effective optimal level might be raised to a much higher level for these same men, however, if the same communicator were talking about the same threat and recommended a similar, more masculine-looking holder—for example, a stubby one that resembles a cigar holder—which would be perceived as a more feasible solution.

Here we encounter a complicated implication of the family-of-curves model: Some gain in acceptance would be expected merely from offering a more attractive solution in all versions of the communication, including those that arouse little or no fear, but we would predict a disproportionately greater increase in acceptance from arousing fear up to the intensity that corresponds to the new optimal level. This type of predicted interaction effect provides a basis for testing hypotheses that specify the determinants of the optimal level of arousal (see Section V, C).

The main purpose of this example is to illustrate what is meant by the family of inverted U-shaped curves. We can see that the shape of the curve may remain constant even though there may be a shift from one curve to another as a function of specifiable variables, such as perceived efficacy of the recommendations. But this example has undoubtedly made the reader aware of some of the major weaknesses of the theory. From what has been said so far it would be quite legitimate to doubt the testability of this theory: When we think in terms of the usual communication experiment, such as those cited at the beginning of this chapter, could not any outcome whatsoever be readily explained? Although a nonmonotonic model might offer a way to account for seemingly inconsistent experimental findings, it might be so good at reconciling conflicting results that it is irrefutable and hence worthless. Nevertheless, judgment should be reserved until one looks into the interaction predictions that can be generated by the model. In the case of the family of curves shown in Fig. 4, the key interaction hypotheses pertain to the conditions under which the effective optimal level will tend to occur at relatively low, medium, and high levels of arousal. If refutable predictions can be made concerning the interacting variables, the theory can be regarded as meaningful and as a useful basis for generating original research ideas. We will return to this problem in Section IV, B, after we examine the available experimental evidence bearing on the propositions that are most central to the theory.

F. SUMMARY: MAJOR PROPOSITIONS

The following are the major propositions derived from the theoretical analysis of reflective fear, shame and guilt.

1. At very low levels of emotional arousal, the average person will remain relatively unaffected by very mild warnings that attempt to induce changes in attitude and actions as compared with warnings that arouse a moderate intensity of fear, shame, or guilt. When the warning is very mild, the average person will tend to dismiss all information about the threat as inconsequential by means of blanket reassurances, whereas when vigilance and reassurance tendencies are stimulated to a moderate degree, the chances are increased that he will develop a compromise attitude of the type required for sustained acceptance of whatever plausible safety measures are recommended by the communicator.

2. As emotional arousal increases toward the high end of the continuum, the heightened motivation to alleviate the unpleasant emotional state will generally lead to the mobilization of resistances—such as defensive detachment from the threat, minimization of the potential danger, and suspicion of the alarmist intentions of the communicator—which eventually reach a critical level where they begin to increase at a greater rate than the facilitating effects of emotional arousal; beyond this critical level, which varies as a function of stimulus variables and predispositional attributes, increases in arousal will bring diminishing returns in the degree of acceptance of the safety measures recommended by the communicator.

3. When a warning communication arouses an extremely high level of fear, shame, or guilt, the average person's state of intense emotional excitement will be characterized by hypervigilant speculations and fantasies as well involuntary constriction of cognitive processes, resulting in marked interference with attention, comprehension, and learning. Once the threshold for hypervigilant reactions is reached, the chances are reduced that the message will be correctly understood and assimilated into the person's system of beliefs and plans for action.

Since there are no established measures of emotion that form an absolute scale, these propositions are difficult to test. A very extensive experimental assessment is required in which behavioral and verbal indicators of degree of arousal and attitude change are obtained for a large series of points all along the entire arousal continuum, ranging from near-zero through a series of intermediate values up to very high emotional excitement at the upper limits of stress tolerance. No such experiments have ever been carried out. It must be acknowledged, therefore, that the evidence now at hand bears only a rough approximation to what is needed for testing the three propositions. Moreover, the propositions themselves are still in a somewhat crude state, since certain of the key terms are incompletely defined. But, as was stated earlier, it seems to me that when the conflicting experimental evidence is reexamined in the light of the analysis of reflective emotions, even though the theory is still in preliminary form, we can bring some order out of the confusing results that perplex us and pose some new questions that may reorient research on the effects of emotional arousal in a more productive direction.

III. Experimental Findings

A.   Effects of Arousal on Attention and Comprehension

A large number of experiments deal with cognitive performances of human subjects exposed to varying degrees of induced stress and many of them provide preliminary support for the notion that a nonmonotonic function might hold for the relation between cognitive efficiency and intensity of emotion arousal. Brown (1961, p. 350) points out that recent neurophysiological findings have led Hebb (1955), Malmo (1958), Schlosberg (1954), and other psychologists to consider just such a function on the presumption that the ascending reticular system may deliver insufficient stimulation to the cortex at low levels of emotional or motivational arousal and too intense bombardment of the cortex at high levels of arousal. Optimal efficiency would therefore always occur at intermediate levels, where the amount of arousal is neither too weak (as when the person remains unalert and lethargic) nor too strong (as when a person is frozen with terror). These neurophysiological considerations suggest that the relationship between emotional arousal and cognitive efficiency in attending to, comprehending, and learning the content of verbal messages might prove to be a special case of a more general relationship between the intensity of any form of motivation arousal and any type of cognitive performance (see Duffy, 1962). Nevertheless, it still remains an open question whether the inverted U-shape function does in fact accurately describe the way in which the average person's attention to and comprehension of an emotion-arousing communication will vary as a function of the intensity of his arousal.

Recent reviews of pertinent field studies and experiments (Easterbrook, 1959; Hall, 1961; Janis, 1968; Janis and Leventhal, 1967; Lazarus, 1966) indicate ·there is fairly consistent support for the proposition that arousal of very high fear, shame, or guilt will induce a significant loss in cognitive efficiency, as compared with more moderate degrees of arousal. Although most of the research does not deal with the effects of persuasive communications, the evidence nevertheless has a direct bearing on the third major proposition stated above.

Easterbrook (1959) concludes, on the basis of his extensive review of research on emotional arousal and cognitive efficiency, that the most disruptive effects of high arousal occur on the most demanding types of cognitive tasks, which require the subject to take account of large numbers of cues. He suggests that a fundamental change induced by intense fear is a narrowing of attention to central cues in the stressful situation, with a corresponding decrease in responsiveness to peripheral cues, which could improve performance on some tasks but disrupt others. Although a number of different psychological processes might be involved (see Kausler and Trapp, 1960), the evidence cited by Easterbrook as indicating a shrinkage of cue utilization under conditions of high emotional arousal can be regarded as pointing to a form of cognitive constriction that fits in with the expected consequences of hypervigilance. While scanning the environment in a keyed-up state of high alertness for signs of oncoming danger, an aroused person may become somewhat distracted from other tasks at hand and fail to notice the usual forms of perceptual feedback necessary for adequate performance. Field observations of soldiers in combat suggest that under very stressful conditions when men become highly vigilant they begin to be "trigger happy" and perform essential tasks more and more inefficiently as their attention is more and more narrowly focused on threatening sights and sounds (see Janis, 1968). The disruptive effects of intense fear on cognitive performance, as Korchin (1965) suggests, may be at least partly attributable to the constriction of the perceptual field that occurs when attention is directed almost exclusively to salient cues that appear to be relevant to the threat.

A number of experimental investigations show that when a person's fear is strongly aroused, he will tend to display marked narrowing of attention, poorer judgment, and more intellectual rigidity (Beier, 1951; Berkun *et al.*, 1962; Luchins and Luchins, 1959; Osler, 1954). In most of these experiments, plausible-sounding verbal threats were presented in the classroom or laboratory. For example, Osler (1954) arranged to have high school students told individually to report to the principal because a serious complaint had been made about their behavior, a request that aroused fear combined with some degree of shame or guilt. Then, some time after being given this distressing information but before the time of his appointment with the principal, each student was tested on various intellectual tasks. Compared with subjects in a control (nonarousal) condition, the subjects who experienced the aroused state of emotional tension showed markedly poorer test scores. This study, like a number of others that employed realistic threats, supports the conclusion that a temporary loss of perceptual and cognitive efficiency occurs when a person is exposed to communications that arouse strong anticipations of imminent danger or social punishment.

That this conclusion applies to emergency circumstances of danger is indicated by a series of extraordinarily realistic stress experiments carried out with Army recruits under field conditions that parallel those of actual disasters (Berkun et al., 1962). The investigators carefully rigged several situations in such a way that the subjects would regard themselves as seriously threatened. In one of the fear-arousing situations a group of soldiers on a routine flight suddenly felt the aircraft lurch violently, could see that one of the propellers had stopped turning, and were informed over the intercom that serious malfunctions required an emergency landing in the ocean, which everyone realized meant only a small chance for survival. At this point, a member of the crew administered a set of intellectual tests, disguised as emergency data forms that allegedly would be jettisoned before the crash landing to furnish proof to insurance companies that all emergency precautions had been properly followed. On the mental efficiency tests embedded in the emergency data forms, the stressed subjects made significantly more errors and showed markedly poorer retention of information than an equated control group on a routine flight. Thus, high fear arousal in this threatening situation produced a temporary impairment in cognitive functioning. Parallel results were obtained from another investigation in this series, which involved the arousal of intense shame and guilt, rather than fear, by making each subject feel responsible for an accident that seriously injured a fellow soldier.

From the accumulated experimental and clinical evidence on the way people react to disaster situations, it appears quite certain that at very high levels of emotional arousal, the average person's perceptual and cognitive functions become severely impaired. But it remains an open question whether at the other end of the arousal continuum a relatively mild or moderate threat will regularly produce an increase in intellectual efficiency. A few studies show such a gain at low levels of arousal, but the evidence is not very consistent on this point. A number of studies (reviewed by Janis, 1968) fail to find any difference between low and moderate or high degrees of arousal, but these comparisons may be within the intermediate range, above the threshold for cognitive facilitation and below the threshold for observable cognitive impairment.

From the research carried out so far, it seems that an inverted block-shaped U-curve, like the third curve shown in Fig. 3, might be a likely candidate for describing the relation between level of emotional arousal and cognitive efficiency. At the low end of the curve, in response to a relatively slight degree of arousal, there would be a gain in attention and comprehension; over a broad range of intermediate values of arousal the curve would remain quite level, with no additional gain or loss in cognitive efficiency from increasing arousal; but, then, at very high levels when the threshold for hypervigilant reactions is reached, there would be a decrement in cognitive performance, which can become so marked in cases of acute panic that the curve may descend well below the base level of communication effectiveness that would be attained if no emotional arousal were evoked at all.

The decrement at the upper end of the arousal continuum can be expected to occur regularly for certain limited types of extreme fear-arousing communications. Panic, stuporlike blocking, and related states of low cognitive efficiency are known to occur in response to messages issued in extreme situations such as emergency orders given during active military combat, emergency warnings issued in cities that are about to be hit by a tornado, and the urgent recommendations given by physicians to patients who require radical surgery (cf. Janis, 1958; Ley, 1966).

In experimental studies, cognitive efficiency seems to be rarely impaired by fear-arousing messages, except when severe threats of pain or punishment are given. By and large, the results from experiments on persuasive communications indicate that variations in amount of arousal via emotional appeals have little or no demonstrable effect on comprehension or retention of the essential content of the message, even though acceptance of the communicator's recommendations may be significantly influenced by these same variations. For example, in the initial experiment on fear appeals, Janis and Feshbach (1953) found that a strong fear-arousing version of a dental hygiene communication produced less attitude change among high school students than versions containing milder appeals, which evoked less worry about decayed teeth and gum disease; but the decrement in effectiveness could not be accounted for by any decrements in attention, comprehension, or learning, since the subjects exposed to the strong arousal condition attained just as high scores as the others on a comprehensive information test covering the essential content of the communication. Moreover, a higher percentage of the subjects in the strong arousal condition than in the moderate or low arousal conditions reported that it was easy to pay attention to what the speaker was saying and that they experienced little "mind-wandering" during the communication. Thus the evidence does not support an interpretation of the attitude change findings that postulates decreased attentiveness, distraction, impaired comprehension, or any temporary cognitive loss that would interfere with learning efficiency.

Similar negative results on the learning and retention of the informational content of persuasive communications have been reported in other experiments that have compared different levels of arousal evoked by emotional appeals (e.g., Berkowitz and Cottingham, 1960; Haefner, 1956; Janis and Milholland, 1954; Janis and Terwilliger, 1962). A statistically significant difference in amount of information recalled following exposure to strong versus mild fear appeals was reported by Niles (1964), but the difference was of small magnitude and was unrelated to any changes in beliefs or attitudes.

Although a null hypothesis can never be proved, the scarcity of significant differences on this point in the existing literature is consistent with the expectation stated earlier, that when sufficient data become available for plotting the entire curve for cognitive efficiency, we might find a relatively level plateau (or random fluctuations) extending over a broad range of arousal values up to a relatively high level of arousal, where the decrement from hypervigilance sets in. This expectation, however, does not preclude the possibility that the arousal of vigilance may have some selective effects on attention, without affecting over-all cognitive efficiency. This possibility is suggested by the findings from an experiment by Janis and Milholland (1954) that compared the verbatim recall of two equated groups exposed to strong and mild fear-arousing versions of a dental hygiene communication. As in the other experiments, there was no significant difference in the mean number of items of information recalled by the two groups. But there were significant differences in the types of information acquired, indicating that the high arousal condition had a selective effect on what was learned. Information about the causes of the threat (such as how food particles adhering to unbrushed teeth after each meal generate acids and dissolve the enamel coat) was better recalled by the subjects exposed to the mild arousal condition; whereas information about the unfavorable consequences of the threat (such as necessity for painful dental treatments) was better recalled by those exposed to the strong arousal condition. Janis and Milholland conclude that under conditions where relatively minor threats are depicted, elaborations of the potential dangers have the effect of focusing attention on the threatening consequences, making them more vivid and therefore better learned; but the heightened learning of the consequences detracts from attention to and learning of other material contained in the communication—in this case, material on the causes of the threat.

In this experiment, both groups recalled equally well the main recommendations made by the communication. Nevertheless, the selective recall tendency noted in the strong versus mild arousal conditions suggests that threat appeals can exert an important effect on what is learned and retained from a communication. Under certain circumstances (notably where subsequent precautionary actions are contingent upon understanding the complicated causes of a threat) this selective tendency could conceivably reduce the ultimate effectiveness of a fear-arousing communication. This lead concerning the selective attention effects of arousing vigilance has not yet been adequately explored.

B. EFFECTS OF AROUSAL ON ACCEPTANCE OF RECOMMENDATIONS

We turn next to the first two propositions derived from the analysis of reflective emotions (Section II, F). According to these propositions, the average person will be most likely to accept precautionary recommendations when his level of reflective fear is aroused to an intermediate degree, rather than when it is either very low or very high. This prediction would apply to all plausible threat-reducing recommendations in all types of warning communications—the emergency evacuation requests by local authorities when an imminent natural disaster is predicted; the advice of leaders in large business or trade union organizations urging their followers to accept new policies to counteract anticipated financial losses; the admonitions of religious leaders urging their followers to perform an act of charity or self-sacrifice to expiate their past sins; the scare propaganda by political leaders urging the public to support new policies in order to prevent a national political catastrophe; the news releases by public health authorities that call attention to the harmful effects of cigarette smoking or to any other hazards requiring adaptive changes in attitudes and action.

If the two propositions are valid, we should find in every instance that the degree to which an audience will accept the main recommendations in a warning communication will vary in nonmonotonic fashion, as depicted by the inverted U-shaped curves in Fig. 4. According to the first proposition, which refers to the positive motivating effects of arousing vigilance and reassurance needs, we should expect to find that when the level of reflective fear, shame, or guilt is increased by using increasingly more powerful emotional appeals, there will be a corresponding rise in audience acceptance of the communicator's recommendations up to a certain point. The second proposition in Section II, F, which pertains to resistances that give rise to unintended attitude changes, implies that the inflection point of the curve will generally be below the point of maximum stress tolerance. Thus, we should find that diminishing returns begin to set in somewhere in the intermediate range of fear arousal (as exemplified by optimal levels A, B, C and D in Fig. 4). In the remainder of this chapter, we shall examine the evidence from attitude change experiments that bear on the plausibility of this and other propositions pertaining to the family of curves shown in Fig. 4, which can be regarded as a tentative theoretical model of the effectiveness of emotional appeals in persuasive communications.

Unfortunately, the model can be assessed in only a very crude way. Since we lack valid quantitative measures of degree of emotional arousal, we never quite know which region of the curve is being investigated when an experiment compares so-called strong arousal conditions with milder arousal conditions. Nor can we tell whether the comparisons made in one experiment are equivalent to those made in another. Nevertheless, there is a great deal of evidence that bears at least tangentially on either the assumptions that enter into the theoretical model or the predictions that are derived from it. The most pertinent experimental findings indicate that under certain conditions a persuasive communication containing a strong threat appeal, as compared with parallel versions of the same communication containing milder appeals, can arouse psychological resistances that reduce the effectiveness of the communicator's message in the long run.

1. The Initial Experiment on Dental Hygiene Recommendations (Janis and Feshbach, 1953)

The diminishing returns from increasing the intensity of fear was first suggested in the experiment by Janis and Feshbach (1953) that compared the effectiveness of three different forms of an illustrated lecture on dental hygiene. Strong-, moderate-, and minimal-fear-arousing versions of the same persuasive message were presented to equivalent groups of high school students. As expected, immediately after the communication was over there were more signs of aroused vigilance among the subjects exposed to the strong-fear-arousing version than among those exposed to the milder versions. The former reported being more worried about the condition of their teeth, more interested in the information conveyed, and more impressed by the communication than the others. When attitude changes were assessed one week later, however, the strong-fear version proved to be less successful than the milder versions. The greatest amount of reported change in the direction of accepting the new dental hygiene practices recommended by the communicator was found in the group exposed to the mildest-fear-arousing version. Attitude changes were also assessed by observing the degree to which the subjects resisted the influence of counterpropaganda that contradicted the main theme of the original communication, and again the mildest-fear-arousing version proved to be most effective. Thus, a significantly smaller percentage of the group that had received the strong-fear-arousing version continued to accept the recommendations given by the original dental-hygiene communication. Moreover, when all subjects who rejected the counterpropaganda were asked to explain why they disagreed with it, the ones in the strong-fear group were less likely than those in the milder-fear groups to mention spontaneously any of the arguments from the illustrated talk to which they had been exposed one week earlier.

An analysis of individual differences in level of anxiety indicated that the unfavorable effects of strong-fear arousal occurred among those persons who were chronically most anxious—as manifested by high scores on a questionnaire (given a week before the communication) dealing with characteristic symptoms of anxiety (Janis and Feshbach, 1954). On the main measure of attitude change, a significant interaction effect was found ($p < .01$)

between chronic level of anxiety and intensity of fear appeals: The strong-fear-arousing version evoked markedly less attitude change than the minimal version among subjects with high scores on initial level of anxiety, but not among those with low scores.

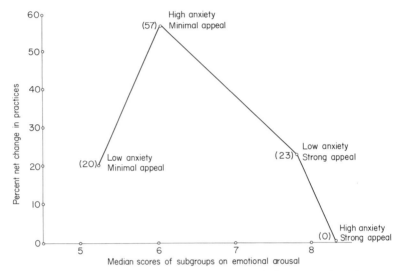

FIG. 5. Observed relationship between level of fear arousal and acceptance of the communicator's recommendations (based on data from Janis and Feshbach, 1954).

The data can be nicely fitted to an inverted U-shaped curve, as shown in Fig. 5, if we assume that the obtained level of arousal is a joint product of anxiety predisposition (as assessed by high versus low scores on the personality scale) and strength of fear appeal material presented in the communication. The lowest level of arousal would be expected in the subgroup of low predisposed subjects exposed to the mild fear appeal and the highest level of arousal in the subgroup of high predisposed subjects exposed to the strong fear appeal; intermediate degrees of arousal would be expected in the other two subgroups. This set of expectations is borne out by the data from a five-item scale dealing with feelings of worry about tooth decay and gum disease that was administered immediately after exposure to the illustrated talk. The scores on this arousal scale for the four subgroups are shown on the X axis in Fig. 5 and were used as the basis for plotting the relation between degree of fear arousal and degree of acceptance of the communicator's recommendation. The latter indicator is the net percentage of change in conformity with the recommended dental hygiene practices, as assessed by comparing each subject's description of how and when he was brushing his teeth one week after exposure to the dental hygiene communication with his answers to the same questions before exposure to the communication.

On the basis of all the various findings from their experiment, Janis and Feshbach concluded that the diminishing returns from the use of a strong-fear-arousing appeal could be explained in terms of the following "defensive avoidance" hypothesis:

> When fear is strongly aroused but is not fully relieved by the reassurances contained in a persuasive communication, the audience will become motivated to ignore, minimize, or deny the importance of the threat.

This hypothesis, which is compatible with the second proposition stated earlier concerning the resistances mobilized by residual emotional tension, has been misconstrued by some psychologists as implying a monotonic decrement function, like that shown in the second curve in Fig. 3. But the defensive avoidance hypothesis does not predict that the stronger of two fear-arousing appeals will invariably be less successful in producing attitude change; rather, it predicts that the higher the intensity of induced fear, the higher will be the degree of resistance, which will tend to reduce the amount of attitude change when this source of interference is not out-weighed by other motivating effects of arousal that facilitate attitude change. Janis and Feshbach (1953) pointed out that although the outcome of their experiment contradicts the assumption of a monotonic increment function (like that shown in the first curve in Fig. 3), it "by no means precludes the possibility that, under certain conditions, fear appeals may prove to be highly successful" (p. 87) and they suggested that their findings would be consistent with a nonmonotonic type of curvilinear relation: "Beneficial motivating effects probably occur when a relatively slight amount of fear-arousing material is inserted; but for communications of the sort used in the present experiment, the optimal dosage appears to be far below the level of the strongest fear appeals that a communicator could use if he chose to do so" (p. 88).

On the basis of the findings from this experiment, Janis called attention to the theoretical implications of the dual effects of fear arousal and formulated the following hypothesis, which specifies an inverted U-shaped relation between emotional arousal and acceptance:

> In general, the available evidence [from the Janis and Feshbach experiment] indicates that as the degree of emotional tension in the audience is increased there is *not* a corresponding increase in acceptance of the communicator's reassuring recommendations. It seems likely that for many types of persuasive communications the relationship will prove to be a curvilinear one, such that as emotional tension increases from zero to some moderate level acceptance tends to increase, but as emotional tension mounts to higher levels acceptance tends to decrease. Descending acceptance in the latter part of the curve is clearly indicated by the experimental data in [Janis and Feshbach's] Tables...; ascending

acceptance in the lower end of the curve might account for some of the findings on the superiority of "emotional" appeals cited at the beginning of this chapter . . . [Hovland *et al.*, 1953, pp. 83–84].

2. Subsequent Experiments Bearing on the Defensive-Avoidance Hypothesis

Several subsequent experiments appear to support the defensive-avoidance hypothesis and indicate that the mobilization of resistances, which accompanies increased emotional arousal, can lead to diminishing returns in acceptance of the communicator's recommendations. An extensive experiment was carried out by Haefner (1956), using communications with varying intensities of guilt-arousing appeals as well as fear-arousing appeals, to promote favorable attitudes among American college students concerning an international agreement to ban H-bomb tests. One guilt-arousing version, for example, emphasized the enormous number of people killed in the United States' A-bomb attacks on Hiroshima and Nagasaki, and the suffering unexpectedly inflicted upon Japanese fishermen exposed to radioactive fallout from the H-bomb tests in the Pacific. Haefner's results concerning the effects of the fear-arousing appeals were ambiguous (see the critique in Leventhal and Niles, 1965, p. 231), but his results were clear-cut in indicating that the high-guilt version produced more resistance and less attitude change than the low-guilt version.

The main propositions under discussion (as stated in Section II, F) pertain to the effects of arousing reflective guilt and shame, as well as fear; consequently, Haeffner's findings on guilt arousal can be regarded as relevant supporting evidence. Additional supporting data that directly bear out the predicted nonmonotonic relation were obtained by Zemach (1966). Her study was essentially a field experiment, carried out under the auspices of a civil rights organization that was trying to recruit Yale students as volunteers. The research purpose was to examine the relation between three intensities of guilt-arousing themes in the organization's persuasive pamphlets and the degree of acceptance of the recommendations for action. In response to a strong guilt-arousing version of the communication, relatively few college students volunteered to participate in the civil rights activities and relatively few expressed favorable attitudes toward the movement. A version that used a medium level of guilt-arousing material and did not personalize the blame was found to be more effective in inducing students to sign up for civil rights activities and in modifying general attitudes than either the high-guilt version or the low-guilt version.

The prediction that strong fear appeals will evoke more resistance than milder appeals is suggested by three additional experiments that used public health communications. Nunnally and Bobren (1959) investigated public willingness to expose themselves to communications concerning the treatment of mental illness. In a survey of almost 300 residents representing varied strata of an urban community, these investigators found that when the subjects were given pamphlets containing a strong fear appeal, they reported less interest in reading about the problem than when given pamphlets containing a milder appeal.

Robbins (1962) used a health education broadcast dealing with the threat of cancer and found that exposing the audience to fear-arousing material without any preliminary build-up evoked more feelings of irritation and aggression toward the communication than milder versions. No significant differences were found, however, in the subjects' answers to a question that asked if they would like to continue listening to the broadcast.

Using a public health pamphlet on the link between smoking and lung cancer, Janis and Terwilliger (1962) carried out an experiment with adult smokers and nonsmokers to test the defensive-avoidance hypothesis. They sought to obtain measures of resistance to fear-arousing material during exposure to a pamphlet containing authentic quotations from medical authorities. Each subject was given a private interview during which he was asked to express his thoughts and feelings after reading each paragraph. In order to eliminate cues that might give a distorted picture of the subject's reactions, a special device (auditory feedback suppressor) was used which enabled the subject to give his spontaneous associations aloud without hearing the sound of his own voice. The verbalizations of an experimental group exposed to a strong-threat version that played up the painful body damage and fatalities produced by lung cancer were compared with those of an equated group exposed to a milder version that merely referred to lung cancer without elaborating on the threatening consequences of the disease. The subjects in the strong-fear condition reacted differently from the subjects in the mild-fear condition in the following three ways: (1) They were somewhat less likely to express antismoking attitudes after the communication was over ($p < .10$); (2) They expressed much more emotional tension and concern about the possibility of being stricken by the disease while they were reading the communication and afterwards ($p < .05$); (3) They showed more manifestations of resistance to the main message of the communication while they were being exposed to it, making significantly more rejection statements ($p < .02$), as well as fewer favorable comments about the style and objectivity of the communication ($p < .06$) and fewer paraphrasing responses of the type that indicate implicit acceptance of what is being said ($p < .05$).

The Janis and Terwilliger experiment supplements the earlier experiments by providing more direct evidence of the interfering responses mobilized during the period when the subject is exposed to the communication. The findings indicate that the recipients of a warning communication

tend to become more strongly motivated to develop psychological resistances
to the communicator's arguments and recommendations if fear-arousing
information is added that elaborates on the dire consequences in store for
people who fail to accept the recommended precautionary measures.

3. Evidence of Facilitating Effects

Next we turn to the findings from a series of experiments that point to
the facilitating effects of emotional arousal. Most of the results fit in nicely
with the nonmonotonic model, but a few do not.

In two replicating experiments, Berkowitz and Cottingham (1960)
presented college students with illustrated talks urging the use of automobile
safety belts and compared the effectiveness of a version that played up the
risk of serious injury in an automobile accident with an equivalent one
containing the same arguments with no threat material at all. The strong-
threat version produced more reported emotional tension than the milder
version but there were no significant differences in over-all attitude change.
A breakdown of the audience into two "relevance" categories, however,
showed that the strong-threat version produced more attitude change than
the milder version among those students who infrequently rode in cars, for
whom the warning communication was of relatively low relevance.

The authors conclude that one of the determinants of the effectiveness
of a persuasive communication is its interest value, which can be augmented
when a strong threat is presented in a provocative way. This conclusion
implies that whenever a low threat version is regarded by members of the
audience as boring, uninteresting, or of low relevance to them, the inclusion
of a strong fear-arousing appeal can have a facilitating effect on attitude
change; under these circumstances, the negative effects of defensive avoidance, if any, may be offset by an increase in interest value. Those for whom
the threat was clearly relevant from the outset, however, would be less
likely to benefit from the enhanced interest-value evoked by a fear appeal
and more likely to become defensively resistant.

From the standpoint of the predicted nonmonotonic relation, the
findings from the Berkowitz and Cottingham experiments appear to support
the assumption that at the low end of the fear arousal continuum, increased
stimulation of fear will facilitate acceptance of the recommendations. The
percentage asserting that they felt uneasy when exposed to the fear-arousing
communication was comparatively low (31% of an experimental group
exposed to the strong-threat version and 5% of an equated group exposed to
the no-threat version, which contrasts markedly with the corresponding
percentages in the Janis and Feshbach experiment of 74% for the strong-
fear-appeal group, 60% for the moderate-appeal group, and 48% for the
minimal-appeal group). Although none of the percentages can be taken at

face value, these comparative findings suggest that the so-called strong-threat condition in the Berkowitz and Cottingham experiments may have aroused only a very low degree of fear, comparable to that aroused by the minimal threat appeal in the Janis and Feshbach experiment. This inference appears particularly likely for the subjects for whom the threat was of low relevance; if so, the findings would support the conclusion that when information about a potential threat arouses a slight or moderate degree of fear, in contrast to the near-zero level of fear evoked by a no-threat version, it will tend to facilitate acceptance of the communicator's recommendation. In terms of the curvilinear functions shown in Fig. 4, this interpretation would assume that we are dealing with two points near the left end of the arousal continuum, with the higher level of fear still well within the moderate range. Thus the warning communication does not appear to have aroused fear to the level where we might expect a predominance of psychological resistances that interfere with acceptance.

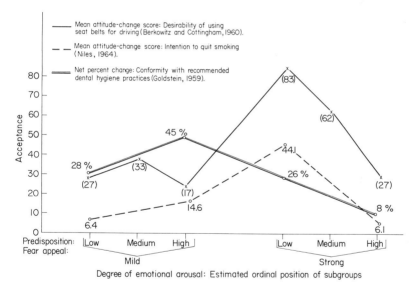

FIG. 6. Observations from three attitude-change experiments on acceptance of recommendations as a joint function of predisposition and strength of fear appeal.

In any case, it should be noted that Berkowitz and Cottingham's data actually yield a good approximation to an inverted U-shaped curve, as shown in Fig. 6, if we treat the low versus high relevant subgroups as equivalent to the low versus high predispositional groups in the Janis and Feshbach (1954) experiment. It can be seen that the peak of the acceptance curve occurs for a subgroup that is at an intermediate level of arousal (low-relevance subjects exposed to a strong-fear version); thereafter, the curve goes down sharply, since the subgroup with the highest level of arousal (high-relevance subjects exposed to the strong-fear version) shows markedly less attitude change. The data from the other two experiments included in Fig. 6, which will be discussed shortly, also show a nonmonotonic relation but the peak does not always occur at the same ordinal position on the arousal axis.

Several recent studies by Leventhal and his co-workers bear out the Berkowitz and Cottingham findings on the facilitating effects of fear arousal at the low end of the curve and indicate that this outcome can sometimes occur even among subjects for whom the threat is highly relevant. Using the same issue of automotive safety, Leventhal and Niles (1965) found that automobile drivers exposed to the greatest amount of threat material in technicolor movies focusing on the gory details of automobile accidents showed the highest arousal of fear and guilt and also the greatest amount of immediate acceptance of certain safety rules, such as "Never drive after drinking." These effects, however, tended to be dissipated by one week later.

Essentially the same facilitating type of outcome is reported by Leventhal and Singer (1966) and Singer (1965) from two experiments on the effectiveness of dental hygiene communications. But here again, just as in the Berkowitz and Cottingham (1960) experiment, there are indications suggesting that despite the efforts of the experimenters to use vivid threat material and gory film sequences to arouse strong fear, their findings nevertheless may pertain only to the low end of the arousal continuum. In other words, the findings can be plausibly interpreted as showing a slight increase in acceptance as we move from near-zero arousal to a mild degree of arousal that evokes a slight increase in vigilance and reassurance needs. In the Leventhal and Singer experiment, which was conducted with adults at a New York State Fair, the group exposed to the so-called high-fear-arousing film reported somewhat more fear than the group exposed to the so-called low-fear-arousing film, but contrary to the experimenters expectations, the low-fear group did not differ on any of the indicators of emotional arousal or concern about tooth decay and gum disease from a control group that had been exposed only to the recommendations with no references at all to threatening consequences. These findings imply that the so-called low-fear communication failed to arouse fear at all, while the so-called high-fear communication may have aroused a relatively slight degree of fear (perhaps comparable to the minimal appeal in the Janis and Feshbach experiment), which would be expected to have a predominantly facilitating effect on acceptance.

Two other experiments using dental hygiene lectures with young adults also ran into difficulties in eliciting expected differences in emotional arousal. One experiment (Moltz and Thistlethwaite, 1955) reported no significant difference in attitude changes; the other (Goldstein, 1959) found that the high fear-arousing communication was less effective than the milder versions, as in the Janis and Feshbach experiment. But in both experiments, the indicators of emotional arousal showed no significant differences between the so-called high- and low-fear conditions and hence the data are of dubious relevance for ascertaining the effects of strong versus mild intensities of fear arousal. It should be noted, however, that a nonmonotonic relation clearly emerged when Goldstein compared high versus low predisposed subjects sorted on Mainord's (1956) personality measure of chronic avoidance tendencies. (Goldstein calls the high scorers "avoiders" and the low scorers "copers.") The curve obtained from Goldstein's data, which is shown in Fig. 6, is almost the same as the curve obtained for the Janis and Feshbach (1954) data in Fig. 5. In the case of Goldstein's data, however, the degree of arousal is based on estimated ordinal position of the four subgroups on the arousal continuum and there is no evidence that the "avoiders" were more highly predisposed to become emotionally aroused by threat material on tooth decay and gum disease than the "copers."

Evidence that strong fear arousal might under certain conditions be more effective than mild arousal in modifying attitudes, despite whatever resistances may be evoked, is provided by Niles' (1964) experiment, which compared different versions of a film on smoking and lung cancer. The strong-fear-arousing version, which included a technicolor sequence showing the surgical removal of a young man's cancerous lung, with all the gory details, proved to be more successful in inducing college students to resolve to give up smoking than a milder threat version that included the same case study of a lung cancer patient, leaving out the surgical sequence. But this outcome held only for a particular subgroup who initially reported feeling low vulnerability to the threat and not for the subgroup located at the highest level on the arousal continuum. Niles used two predispositional measures that proved to be significantly correlated. One was the neurotic anxiety scale developed by Janis and Feshbach (1954) for their study of high school students. For the college students in Niles' experiments, this measure did not yield statistically significant results. The second personality scale, however, which was developed by Niles for the purpose of assessing college students' feelings of vulnerability to illness, provided a significant interaction with degree of acceptance, like the interaction effect found by Janis and Feshbach (1954).

Using Niles' data from the feelings of vulnerability scale, we again obtain an inverse U-shaped function, as shown in Fig. 6. Verbal acceptance of the antismoking recommendations presented in both versions of the film shows a gradual but pronounced rise as we move from low to intermediate levels of arousal, followed by a sharp drop for the subgroup highest on the arousal continuum. This evidence, however, is not entirely compelling because the assumed ordinal position of the four subgroups on the fear continuum was only partially borne out by Niles' analysis of variance of arousal scores based on three questionnaire items dealing with feelings of fear; the only significant finding concerning reported feelings of fear was a main effect for the mild versus strong fear appeals. In view of this finding, the corresponding attitude change results showing a main effect for the mild versus strong fear appeal would appear to be a more dependable result than those showing an interaction effect between this stimulus variable and the predispositional variable. If we consider only the main effects, Niles' results imply that a very high level of arousal can have a markedly facilitating effect on attitude change.

Leventhal (1965) has culled a few findings from other experiments that he believes bear out the same tendency (e.g., Leventhal and Niles, 1964; Leventhal and Watts, 1966), but he acknowledges that this additional evidence comes from ambiguous studies, with both positive and negative effects showing up on different indicators of acceptance. The most impressive evidence he cites comes from a study by Leventhal et al. (1965) that shows the facilitating effects of a relatively low degree of fear arousal. In this experiment, a behavioral measure was obtained from the records of a university health center to ascertain the effectiveness of different versions of a warning communication that recommended antitetanus shots. A mild and strong fear-appeal version were found to be about equally effective in inducing students to obtain the shots, as compared with a control communication that gave the same recommendations without any fear-arousing material. Additional results also showed that the fear appeals were more effective when accompanied by specific information as to where, when, and how to get the shots. Those given a great deal of such information, as compared to those given relatively little, were more likely to obtain inoculations, irrespective of whether they had received the strong or mild fear-arousing version. But none of the subjects exposed to the specific information and the recommendation without the fear-arousing material went to the health center for the shots. In this instance, some minimum degree of fear-arousal apparently was necessary, along with the specific instructions, in order to instigate protective action in line with the communicator's recommendation. These findings provide additional empirical support for the first of the three main propositions derived from the analysis of reflective fear (Section II, F).

IV. Theoretical Model for Analyzing Determinants of the Optimal Level of Arousal

A. Examples of High and Low Optimal Levels

Many experimenters are justifiably reluctant to draw any conclusions as to whether emotional arousal has a predominantly facilitating or interfering effect when they find that a strong fear-arousing communication, as compared with a milder version, produces more change on one indicator of acceptance but less change on another equally relevant indicator. Some would undoubtedly feel much happier if all indicators of attitude change in their experiments were to point to a uniformly positive or a uniformly negative effect of high arousal, so as to give a simple answer to the simple question they are trying to answer. But, as was suggested at the outset of this chapter, it seems to me that no uniform answer should be expected because the question is too simple, based on unwarranted assumptions that prevent them from discovering whatever lawful relations may underlie their seemingly inconsistent data. A mixed outcome might prove to be a genuine and repeatable interaction effect, reflecting different optimal levels of arousal for different types of recommendations (such as feasible versus infeasible means for averting the predicted danger). Such differences might be clearly revealed as two distinct nonmonotonic curves with different optimal levels of arousal (such as optimal level A versus B in Fig. 4) if the experiment were properly designed to provide more complete data covering a large range of values on the arousal continuum.

Some suggestive evidence, which might illustrate just such a difference in optimal levels, is reported in a study by Leventhal and Watts (1966). Their experiment yielded opposite outcomes for two specific recommendations contained in an antismoking communication: The strong-fear-arousing version, as compared with the medium-fear and the mild-fear versions, produced less acceptance of the recommendation to obtain a chest X-ray but produced more acceptance of the recommendation to stop smoking. All subjects were visitors at a state fair and were shown one or another version of a movie giving information on the relationship between smoking and lung cancer. In the low-fear condition, the subjects were shown a color film depicting the threat of cancer by means of charts, diagrams, and the narrator's comments. In the moderate-fear condition, the audience was exposed to an additional film sequence telling the story of a small town newspaper editor who discovered that he had lung cancer. In the high-fear condition, the same case study was presented along with a 10-minute color sequence in which the camera focused on the site of the operation, showing close-ups of the opening of the chest and removal of the lung. The overt behavior of large numbers of the viewers (looking away, groaning, crying) gave credibility to the subjects' reports that the surgery sequence was highly disturbing.

A comparison of the conditions showed that the movies were effective in arousing differential amounts of fear. Among smokers eligible for X-rays, the greatest degree of conformity with the recommendation to have an X-ray taken at a nearby mobile unit was found in the group exposed to the mildest-fear version of the movie; significantly less conformity ($p < .01$) occurred in the group exposed to the strong-fear-arousing version, just as was found in the Janis and Feshbach (1953) experiment on acceptance of recommended dental hygiene practices.

In order to follow up on subsequent X-ray taking and changes in smoking habits, a questionnaire was sent to all subjects five months afterward. Only about half the subjects in each condition returned the questionnaire, but the analysis of reports of X-ray taking showed nearly perfect correspondence with the results found immediately following exposure at the fair. When reported success in cutting down on smoking was examined it was found that the greatest success ($p < .07$) occurred in the subjects who had been exposed to the high-fear condition (79%), as compared with those in the moderate-fear (57%) or low-fear (57%) conditions.

Further analyses showed that plans to stop smoking, in all conditions, were positively correlated with the belief that giving up smoking would be an effective deterrent to lung cancer. Thus, the data are compatible with subsidiary analyses reported by Janis and Feshbach (1953), indicating that the subjects in the high-fear condition who failed to accept the communicator's dental hygiene recommendations felt insecure about the protective devices made available to them and expressed a need for additional reassuring information. Similar correlational data suggest that the smokers exposed to the strong-fear-arousing communication tended to doubt the efficacy of taking X-rays for coping with the threat. Leventhal and Watts draw the inference that X-rays were probably regarded as a detective measure that might lead to painful surgery, like that shown in the strong-fear-arousing movie, and at best could merely prevent a serious danger (onset of lung cancer) from becoming worse, whereas decreasing smoking was perceived as a protective measure that could avert the onset of lung cancer and thus be a much more cogent means for coping with the threat.

According to Leventhal and Watt's data, the curve for acceptance of the recommendation to have an X ray taken is a descending function as we go from low to moderate to high fear arousal (53% versus 44% versus 6%); whereas, for the very same levels of arousal, the curve for acceptance of the recommendation to cut down on smoking tends to be an ascending function (57%, 57%, 79%). These curves can be readily interpreted in terms of the model shown in Fig. 4 as an increase in optimal level for a more cogent recommendation. Let us suppose that the low-, moderate-, and high-fear conditions in the Leventhal and Watts experiment produced differential degrees of arousal corresponding to points 6, 7, and 8 on the baseline in Fig. 4. We can see quite graphically, then, the implications of the hypothesis that for the same degree of arousal, the optimal level will tend to be higher (e.g., optimal level D versus C) for a recommendation perceived as being highly efficacious for averting the danger than for a recommendation perceived as being less cogent. As we move from points 6 and 7 to point 8 on the arousal dimension, we would have an ascending curve for the "stop-smoking" recommendation if the optimal level were at D. In contrast, points 6, 7, and 8 would yield a descending curve for the X-ray recommendation if the optimal level for this less cogent recommendation were at C.

In Fig. 4, point 8 on the descending portion of curve C falls below the base level of acceptance that would be induced by the nonthreat material in the communication (e.g., the X-ray recommendation alone, without any fear-arousing material, presented by an authoritative public health source). Leventhal and Watts do not furnish the data on the base level of X-ray taking, but it seems highly probable that it is significantly higher than the 6% found for smokers, especially since 25% was the comparable estimate of the base line for the incidence of X-ray taking in a similar mobile X-ray unit at a similar state fair (Leventhal and Niles, 1964). If this estimate is essentially correct, we would conclude that the low and moderate levels of arousal produced a significant gain in acceptance of the X-ray recommendation (as represented by points 6 and 7 on the curve for optimal level C, both of which are above the base level of acceptance), whereas the high fear condition produced a boomerang effect (as represented by point 8).

From this example, we can see how a number of new research questions can be generated by the use of the theoretical model represented in Fig. 4. One obvious question is whether we would find the curve for X-ray taking to be an ascending rather than a descending function if we were to repeat the Leventhal and Watts experiment using persuasive communications that arouse less fear than the technicolor films they employed. We would predict, according to the first of the three main propositions in Section II, F, that at lower levels of fear arousal (e.g., points 1–6 along the arousal continuum) we would find increased acceptance of the X-ray recommendation with increased fear; diminishing returns would set in only when we exceed the optimal level.

Another research question that arises from the theoretical analysis is whether we would find the expected diminishing returns for the recommendation to stop smoking if the level of arousal were increased beyond that evoked by the high fear condition in the Leventhal and Watts experiment. Suppose we carried out an experiment that included measures of the effectiveness of feature-length films that highlight the horrors of lung cancer in persons of the same age and in circumstances similar to those of most members of the audience, without adding any new information that might affect the base level of acceptance. We might then be able to compare point 8 with points 9 and 10 in order to see if we obtain a descending function, as predicted for a curve that has its optimal level at D. Moreover, if we did find this outcome and if we had reason to believe that point 10 was still well below the level of maximum stress tolerance, we would expect that the diminishing returns at these relatively high levels of arousal would not be attributable primarily to temporary cognitive impairment, but rather would be mediated by essentially the same types of psychological resistances (e.g., defensive denial of personal vulnerability to the danger or aggression toward the communicator) that mediate the diminishing returns found for other types of recommendations that have a lower optimal level (see the second of the three main propositions in Section II, F).

Furthermore, we would be led to pose yet another research question: Are there any content variables that could be introduced into the very strong-fear-arousing communication that would tend to counteract the resistances, so that an even higher optimal level could be achieved, approaching the maximum level of stress tolerance? If the appropriate set of optimizing variables were found, then a communication that arouses fear at points 10 or 11 on the arousal continuum, instead of producing less acceptance than one that arouses fear at level 8, would be expected to be maximally successful. The model indicates that it should be theoretically possible for a persuasive communication containing an extraordinarily powerful fear appeal (such as at point 11 in the diagram) to be more effective than an equivalent communication containing a less powerful appeal. Case studies suggest that this sometimes happens when a physician gives a patient the shattering news that his lung X-ray shows unmistakable signs of a precancerous condition that will become increasingly dangerous if he does not immediately stop smoking. Some preliminary experimental evidence, which will be described later (Section V, D), suggests that this lead might be well worth pursuing.

B. A THREE-DIMENSIONAL REPRESENTATION OF THE MODEL

From the foregoing discussion, it is apparent that we need to focus research on interactions between level of arousal and various other variables, such as those content factors that affect the recipients' appraisal of the efficacy of the means recommended for coping with the threat. Other content variables might affect their willingness to continue acknowledging the seriousness of the threat after being jolted by an emotional appeal. There are also a number of source and situational variables that could make it relatively easy or difficult for the audience to ignore the communicator's warning. Personality variables would also be expected to interact with level of arousal, particularly those that give rise to individual differences in readiness to react with defensive avoidances that enable one to satisfy the need for reassurance by minimizing personal vulnerability to potential dangers.

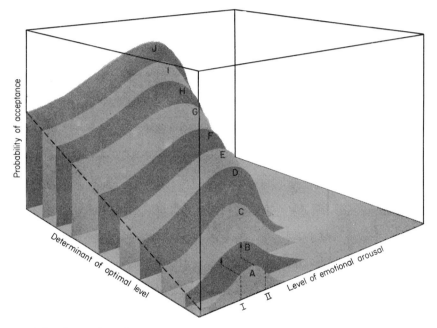

Fig. 7. A three-dimensional model for analyzing effects of emotional appeals (from Janis, 1968).

According to the assumptions introduced earlier in the analysis of reflective emotions, we expect that when a warning stimulates a high level of fear, shame, or guilt, the audience can be expected to scrutinize the communicator's statements more carefully than ever, looking for weak links in his chain of arguments and spotting obvious loopholes that they can seize upon to ignore his disturbing message. In general, any content or situational factor that bolsters the argumentation of a fear-arousing communication, or that seals off the most obvious loopholes, would be expected to have the effect of raising the optimal level if it prevents the recipient from using one or another dominant form of resistance that he otherwise would use to escape from the unpleasant emotional state that momentarily discomforts him as he thinks about the threat. Any interacting variable that influences the optimal level in this way can be conceptualized as a third dimension. Figure 7 shows a three-dimensional model of the effects of emotional appeals in persuasive communications, which is another way of representing the family of curves shown in Fig. 4. Here again, the different optimal levels in the diagram (e.g. A, B, C, and D) are intended to illustrate the assumption that the optimal level of emotional arousal for inducing acceptance of a communicator's recommendations will vary as a function of any content, situational, or predispositional factor that influences the relative balance of interfering and facilitating effects elicited by a given intensity of emotional arousal. A central task of experimental research on the effects of emotional appeals is to discover these interacting determinants and to describe the way they alter the acceptance curve. With the development of new quantitative techniques for assessing attitude change, degree of arousal, and other interacting variables, we can look forward to obtaining the necessary data for plotting a series of curves that will enable us to delineate a three-dimensional surface like the one shown in the figure.

In the diagram, we can see that as we move along the third dimension, which represents any interacting variable, the surface shows a characteristic rise: The peak of acceptance moves toward higher and higher levels of arousal, generating a contour that rises toward the upper right-hand corner of Fig. 7, where the maximum level of stress tolerance would be reached. Although the shift in the optimal level in this example happens to be monotonic, it would not necessarily be so in all instances; the optimal level often might prove to be a nonmonotonic function of the two interacting variables (for example, showing a peak at optimal level D and declining thereafter).

Although we may not be able to make all the quantitative measurements necessary for plotting a surface like the one displayed in Fig. 7, the three-dimensional model helps us to state more precisely the expected outcomes when we are dealing with interacting determinants of the optimal level. Most of the determinants are likely to produce a higher degree of acceptance at all levels of arousal, but the model leads us to predict that they will produce a relatively greater gain at those points on the arousal continuum that approach the new optimal level. To put it another way, the presence of a new optimal level should be manifested by a second-order difference showing a disproportionate amount of gain in acceptance from higher levels of emotional arousal. This rather complicated point can be illustrated by the roman numerals shown in Fig. 7 at two different levels of emotional arousal. Suppose, for example, that the interacting determinant under investigation is the perceived efficacy of the recommendation. This is a variable that can readily be manipulated simply by giving the subjects prior information bearing on the degree of success to be expected from adopting the recommended means for coping with the threat. Low levels of efficacy can be induced by informing the subjects in advance that the recommended means has not yet been tested, is based on purely speculative guess work, is known to have a number of defects, and is regarded by leading authorities as providing only the flimsiest kind of protection against the danger. Higher values of perceived efficacy can be induced by changing these informational inputs and by refuting the most obvious loopholes that members of the audience are likely to think of when this recommendation is presented to them.

Let us suppose we are dealing with a minimally effective recommendation that has an optimal level at A in Fig. 7. If the perceived efficacy of the recommendation were increased, let us say by refuting some of the perceived loopholes, the optimal level might be shifted to B. If we now compare the relative effectiveness of two fear appeals, a mild one represented by point I and a stronger one represented by point II, we can see the emergence of a very large second-order difference. The mild appeal will show a slight increase in effectiveness, reflecting the stronger argumentation of the nonthreat material in the persuasive communication. This base increment is shown by a rise in the floor, which steadily increases with increased levels of the efficacy determinant. In other words, if the same informational inputs are presented without any threat material at all, a determinant such as perceived efficacy of the recommendation can be expected to have a direct effect on the probability of acceptance. This means that when perceived efficacy is relatively high, the degree of acceptance will be higher at zero level of arousal, where the curve starts, than when perceived efficacy is relatively low. This difference in starting point is essentially what is reflected by the small increment in curve B over curve A for the mild appeal, at point I. But when we look at the effect of the stronger appeal, at point II, we can see a disproportionately large increase, which reflects the shift in the optimal level. Point II intersects curve A on its descending portion, where diminishing returns have already rendered the communication only slightly effective; whereas this same point intersects curve B at a place near its maximal level and so there is a marked gain in acceptance. A significant second-order difference of this type indicates that the optimal level has been significantly shifted. (The problem of designing research to test for this type of interaction effect will be discussed in more detail later.)

It follows from what has just been said about this three-dimensional surface that whenever a warning communication that has a relatively low optimal level of arousal is altered in a way that prevents one or another form of resistance from becoming dominant, the motivational gain from strong-fear arousal will no longer be outweighed by interfering motivational effects. The prediction, therefore, is that a greater second-order difference will be found from adding more effective devices that counteract resistances (or from adding arguments that plug the loopholes) in a strong-fear-arousing version of a communication than in a milder threat version. This implication of the model, which has not yet been tested, will require a much more complex type of experiment than has hitherto been carried out.

V. Discussion of the Model

A. IMPLICATIONS FOR THE DESIGN OF ATTITUDE-CHANGE EXPERIMENTS

The foregoing theoretical analysis leads us to ask some new research questions concerning the effects of emotional arousal. The main question that most research workers have been asking is whether emotional arousal increases or decreases acceptance for a given type of persuasive message or for persuasive communications in general. When we conceptualize the consequences of facilitating and interfering effects in terms of a family of curves, like those depicted in Fig. 7, we are led to replace this question with: What are the determinants of the optimal level of emotional arousal for inducing acceptance of a given type of persuasive message, or of persuasive communications in general? Among the variants and subspecies of this new question are the following: For what types of threat content does the optimal level tend to be relatively low and for what types relatively high? What communication factors will raise the optimal level from a low to a moderate level? What are the various constellations of factors that will raise the optimal level to such a high degree that it approaches the upper limit of maximum stress tolerance? If the basic assumptions in the theoretical analysis are valid, the reorientation of research toward working out the parameters of the optimal level, by specifying the conditions under which the optimal dosage of emotional arousal will be raised or lowered, should provide us with much more consistent, replicable, and additive findings than we have hitherto been obtaining from our experiments in this field of research.

When we examine the testable implications of any specific hypothesis concerning interacting determinants of the optimal level of arousal, we soon realize that we must plan for more complicated and more costly experimental research than we are accustomed to. No longer can we continue to use the traditional design, comparing the effectiveness of a series of three or four communications that vary in the amount of fear-arousing material, which would form the basis for plotting only *one* curve of the type represented in the three-dimensional diagram of the family of curves with different optimal levels (Fig. 7). Instead, we must now think in terms of a factorial type of design that will provide data for plotting at least two contrasting curves and in most instances this will require collecting at least twice as many data in each experiment as in the traditional design. Occasionally this can be done without much added expense, as in the Leventhal and Watts (1966) experiment that obtained evidence indicating that the optimal level of arousal for one recommendation ("Cut down on smoking") was significantly higher than for another ("Have your chest X-rayed"). In this experiment the two recommendations were presented in the same antismoking communication and the comparison did not require increasing the number of experimental groups beyond the three needed to compare the effects of a mild-, a moderate-, and a strong-fear appeal. But when other types of determinants are investigated, at least twice as many experimental groups will be required in order to obtain the data for plotting two or more curves.

Three or four times as many groups may be needed in a factorial design to test the interacting effects of certain determinants that are expected to have a nonlinear relationship to the optimal level of arousal. As an example, consider the hypothesis that an intermediate degree of prior familiarity with the threat will make for a higher optimal level than either low familiarity (which makes for defensive avoidance via blanket reassurances) or high familiarity (which increases the probability that the audience will be aware of alternative solutions that can out-compete the one recommended by the communicator). At least nine experimental groups would be required: three conditions of familiarity (induced by varying amounts of prior information) with three levels of fear arousal induced by varying amounts of threat content. In their efforts to plot the curves, experimenters are likely to become discontented with only three levels of fear arousal, but again the effort to obtain more refined experimental data points—ideally, ranging from a very low degree of emotional arousal through a series of intermediate degrees up to as high a level as is ethically warranted—will entail a considerable proliferation of experimental groups. Obviously, research workers will not invest their limited resources in such a huge enterprise unless they can expect a commensurate return.

B. REFORMULATION OF HYPOTHESES ABOUT INTERACTING DETERMINANTS

Although the theoretical model has not yet been tested with an eye to confirmation or disconfirmation, it may offer some immediate payoff by helping to bring order to the relevant research data now at hand and by pointing up the next generation of hypotheses, suggested by prior findings, that bear on the interacting determinants of successful emotional appeals.

A number of investigators, puzzled by the inconsistent findings from experiments on fear-arousing communications, have tried to find a solution by selecting interacting factors that might explain why sometimes a positive effect on acceptance will be obtained from increased emotional arousal and at other times a negative effect. In addition to those already mentioned, a few excellent suggestions have been made concerning potential determinants of arousal effects including various factors that enter into believability of the threat (Rosenblatt, 1962) and the ease of assimilating the recommended precautionary action (Insko *et al.*, 1965). But the investigators have formulated their interaction hypotheses in an unnecessarily restrictive way, in terms of two contrasting monotonic functions (an ascending versus a descending curve). As will be seen shortly, this type of formulation can be extremely misleading and is likely to generate experiments that provide incomplete and inappropriate data for testing the predicted interaction effects. In the discussion that follows, I shall try to show how a reformulation of these hypotheses in terms of the theoretical model represented in Fig. 7 can help us to state more precisely the experimental outcomes that are predicted and integrate seemingly disparate findings that might otherwise be misjudged if we continue to look only for contrasting monotonic relations.

The research consequences of the proposed reformulations can best be seen if we take a specific hypothesis as an example. Let us consider a hypothesis suggested by Insko *et al.* (1965), which is based on the plausible assumption that fear arousal is relatively ineffective when it comes as a punishment for something the person has been doing, but is highly effective when used to induce avoidance of future actions. Their formulation of the hypothesis is in terms of contrasting monotonic functions: When fear arousal increases from a low to a high level, acceptance will decrease if the communicator's recommendation is to change a currently ongoing activity (punishment); but it will increase if the recommendation is to avoid a possible future activity (avoidance). From this compound hypothesis, the investigators predicted that smokers would be less influenced to quit by a strong fear-arousing communication that plays up the detrimental consequences than by a mild one, whereas nonsmokers would be more influenced to avoid starting to smoke by a strong fear-arousing communication than by a mild one. Insko and his collaborators attempted to test only one of these monotonic predictions by a classroom experiment with nonsmoking seventh-grade students, using strong-versus mild-fear-arousing versions of an antismoking communication. They found that immediately after the communication the children exposed to the strong-fear-arousing version were more likely to report that they plan to avoid becoming smokers than those exposed to the mild version. The investigators interpret this finding as confirmatory evidence for one of the two predictions based on the punishment versus avoidance hypothesis.

It will be noted, however, that Insko and his co-workers tested only one part of the compound hypothesis and obtained observations for only two contrasting points on the curve. This decision was evidently based on their assumption that a monotonic ascending curve would be found all along the fear-arousal continuum for the avoidance type of recommendation. On the same basis, they predict that a monotonic descending curve should be found for the punishment type of recommendation. But this formulation of their predictions would require them to accept the evidence from several experiments cited earlier (e.g., Niles, 1964; Leventhal and Watts, 1966) as disconfirming the other part of their compound hypothesis, since the findings showed that a strong-fear-arousing version can be more effective in inducing smokers to change their ongoing smoking activity than milder versions.

If we reformulate the punishment versus avoidance hypothesis in terms of differences in optimal level of arousal, we are led to conclude that none of the experiments carried out so far is relevant. The reformulated hypothesis would be as follows: The optimal level of arousal will generally be lower for persuasive communications containing recommendations to stop performing an ongoing activity than for those containing recommendations to avoid starting some future activity, when all other factors are held constant. This hypothesis appears to be plausible in the light of the theoretical considerations put forth by Insko *et al.* We would expect the amount of resistance mobilized by a threat-reducing recommendation to be much less when people are told to avoid starting a new activity than when they are told to stop performing a customary action, particularly if it has become a well-established habit and is a daily source of pleasure. (One advantage of thinking of the amount of mobilized resistance as a major component of the mediating process is that it alerts us to consider certain limiting conditions with respect to the type of recommendations to which the hypothesis might apply—for example, in this case, the resistances that make for a relatively low optimal level would be expected to operate only for those ongoing activities that are habitual sources of pleasure or that entail high social visibility). The main point is that when we reformulate the hypothesis in terms of the optimal level concept, we can readily specify the type of factorial design needed to obtain the crucial evidence for testing the predicted interaction effect and for investigating the expected limiting conditions. Within the same experiment, the two types of recommendations must be compared (preferably by using more than one example of each) across a series of arousal values, so that we can see how acceptance varies as a conjoint function of type of recommendation and degree of arousal.

The specific prediction to be tested is that we shall find a significant second-order difference showing that for one type of recommendation (avoidance) there is a greater gain in acceptance from increasing the level of fear arousal than for the other type of recommendation (punishment). This formulation allows for a much more liberal test than the original formulation by Insko *et al.* in terms of first-order differences, since the reformulation can take account of the strong possibility that the mild- and strong-fear-arousing communications used in any given experiment may not fall within the portion of the arousal continuum where the two curves being compared show the maximum amount of contrast. If we look at the family of curves in Figs. 4 or 7, we can readily see that when we have two curves with different optimal levels (such as optimal C versus optimal D in Fig. 4) only a limited set of arousal values (such as points 6, 7, and 8) will show that the curve with the higher optimal level ascends while the one with the lower optimal level descends. If certain other arousal values happen to be investigated (for example, points 3, 5, and 7 in Fig. 4) we would find that the curve with the higher optimal level (D) ascends while the one with the lower optimal level (C) also ascends at first and then levels off, which would be contrary to the formulation by Insko *et al.*; nevertheless, the difference in the two ascending slopes would show up as a significant second-order difference, revealing the predicted difference in optimal level. From further inspection of the family of curves in Figs. 4 and 7 it is apparent that two curves with different optimal levels can take on many different configurations, some of which could be completely confusing and misleading if we were to look only at first-order differences.

Instead of accepting only one configuration as confirmatory evidence (an ascending curve for the avoidance type of recommendation and a descending curve for the punishment type of recommendation), the reformulation enables us to discern a confirmatory trend in many different configurations, provided that they yield the predicted second-order difference. Thus, the curve for the punishment type of recommendation may prove to be ascending, as in the Leventhal and Watts (1966) experiment, or descending, as in the Janis and Feshbach (1953) experiment, but these first-order differences tell us nothing about the interactions we are trying to test; the evidence can be confirmatory in either instance if the contrasting curve for the avoidance type of recommendation shows a relatively greater gain in acceptance.

It should also be noted that if the arousal values under investigation cover only a narrow range on the arousal continuum, the experiment may be dealing with a sector of the two curves that are too remote from the optimal level to show any differences at all (for example, if data were collected only for points 1, 2, and 3 in Fig. 4, the experiment would fail to detect any second-order difference between one curve with an optimal level at B and another with an optimal level at C or any higher point). This is one of the main reasons why experimenters should attempt to use a wide range of intensities of emotional stimulation in future research on the effects of emotional appeals and to provide evidence that some gross differences in level of arousal were elicited, corresponding to a fairly broad band along the arousal continuum.

The foregoing comments call attention to the need for developing more precise methods of assessing the absolute level of emotional arousal. Because of the shortcomings of all measures of fear arousal currently in use, it is generally unsafe to make any quantitative comparisons of the results from one experiment with those obtained from another, since we have no dependable way of assessing the level of arousal in relation to any fixed points on the fear continuum. Perhaps a combination of affect measures (including content analyses of the subjects' verbal reports, records of facial expressions, and physiological indicators of autonomic responses during exposure to the communications) can be developed that will enable investigators to find out which sector of the arousal continuum they are investigating, so that ultimately the data from different experiments designed to investigate the same variables can be validly combined into a single significance test.

C.   NEW RESEARCH QUESTIONS GENERATED BY THE MODEL

In preceding sections, several examples have been given to show how the theoretical model of differential optimal levels of arousal, as represented in Figs. 4 and 7, might be used to integrate some of the apparently contradictory evidence from experiments on fear-arousing communications. Such a model would be of little value, however, if it merely enabled us to explain away divergences. This is a serious problem because the present model is formulated in terms of variables and hypothetical concepts that at present can be only crudely defined in relation to observable stimulus events and quantitative measurements of behavior. It is all too easy to misuse the model in a purely speculative way to account for any outcome whatsoever; an armchair psychologist can always find a portion of some curve that will match up with any experimental findings bearing on the relation between acceptance of recommendations and level of emotional arousal. Obviously, the proper use of the model is to generate new hypotheses and to make us aware of alternative ways of interpreting the outcome of experiments already carried out.

Earlier the point was made that the model inclines us to look for a disproportionate gain in the amount of attitude change produced by a fear appeal whenever a communicator adds an effective refutation or takes out a source of irritation that succeeds in overcoming one or another form of audience resistance. The same prediction of a disproportionate amount of gain would apply to any special communication device that is capable of preventing defenses from becoming mobilized, including the use of role playing or of dramatic movies such as the medical case study of a cancer victim presented in the antismoking film used in the Niles (1964) and the Leventhal and Watts (1966) experiments, which may be able to evoke identification with the victim and thereby break through a person's usual defenses against personal involvement in the threat. If we pursue this line of thought one step further, we can see how some of the fresh research ideas generated by the theoretical model might enable us to test specific predictions.

A major assumption discussed in the theoretical analysis of reflective emotions, it will be recalled, is that whenever fear, shame, or guilt is aroused there will be a powerful increase in motivation to acquire a new coping or avoidance response. When the conditions that make for a relatively high optimal level are present, this increased motivation will operate in the direction of increasing acceptance of the communicator's recommendation. But when the conditions that make for a relatively low optimal level are present, the motivational increment reinforces either some form of defensive avoidance that results in ignoring the threat or some alternative means for coping that is not recommended by the communicator. Under these conditions, high arousal will have a predominantly interfering effect and give rise to less acceptance than low arousal. It follows, therefore, that any communication factor that can markedly raise the optimal level will reverse the impact of high arousal, so that instead of inducing relatively less attitude change than low- or moderate-arousal versions of the same communication, the "beefed-up" strong-arousal version will now induce more attitude change than any other version.

Speaking metaphorically, if a strong-fear appeal has an adverse effect on an audience, we should assume it is because the motivational power of high arousal is being captured by one or another form of resistance that is being unintentionally provoked by what is being said about the disturbing threat; but if this motivational gain can be captured away from the resistances, not only will the boomerang effect be eliminated, but the communicator's recommendation will be put into orbit. The theory leads us to expect that whenever a strong-fear-arousing communication is found to be less effective than a milder version, the outcome is always potentially reversible. To accomplish the reversal, however, we must be able to identify the resistances that are being mobilized and find the appropriate contents to insert into (or to take out of) the communication in order to diminish or by-pass them.

Although the formulation is still rather vague, the central idea can be made operational in the form of a set of predictions that, with a certain amount of ingenuity in working out the procedures, probably could be rigorously tested. Elsewhere (Janis, 1968) I have described in detail the required research design, which involves many more steps than the traditional ones used in communication research and, so far as I know, has never been tried out. The following is a summary of the main steps required.

1. A traditional type of communication experiment would be carried out, preferably in a field situation, comparing a series of fear appeals of widely different intensities for the same persuasive message. The first question to be answered pertains to the predicted curvilinear relation between level of arousal and degree of acceptance of the communicator's recommendation about how to avert the threat (such as giving up smoking in order to avoid lung cancer): When acceptance is plotted against arousal, do we obtain an inverted U-shaped curve?

2. If the predicted relation is verified, the next phase of the research would be to ascertain the sources of resistance that contribute to the decrement in the descending portion of the curve. Special interview procedures (including, for example, the type used in the resistance-assessment experiment by Janis and Terwilliger, 1962) would be employed to find out how the resistances manifested by subjects exposed to the strongest fear-arousing versions differ from those manifested by subjects exposed to the milder versions. The results from this part of the investigation should consist of a detailed description of the subjects' suspicions, doubts, and counterarguments, as well as of their ideas about alternative solutions for the threat.

3. The initial experiment would then be repeated with new samples of equivalent experimental groups, but this time some new (carefully pretested) versions of the communication would be used that contained additional materials specifically designed to counteract the dominant forms of resistance. It would be advantageous to use three versions of the basic persuasive message for each level of fear stimulation, in a factorial design: (1) a high-counteraction version, which attempts to refute or alleviate all the dominant sources of resistance; (2) a partial-counteraction version, which attempts to refute or alleviate about half of the dominant resistances while making no attempt to counteract the other half; and (3) a no-counteraction version, which merely presents the same basic communication used in the initial step, with no changes to take account of the observed sources of resistance. Two main predictions, derived from the theoretical model, would then be tested: (a) when degree of acceptance is plotted against arousal, the three resulting curves for high, partial, and no counteraction should again turn out to have an inverted U-shaped form; (b) a significant interaction between degree of counteraction and

degree of arousal should be found such that the optimal level occurs at a lower point on the fear arousal continuum for the no-counteraction version than for the partial-counteraction version, which in turn is at a lower point than the complete-counteraction version.

If none of the foregoing predictions is fully confirmed, the key assumptions entering into the theoretical model will have to be discarded as erroneous. If the last prediction concerning a significant interaction effect is disconfirmed while the other predictions are confirmed, it will be necessary to change the postulates concerning the facilitating effects of increased arousal and perhaps to reconstruct the model using a threshold type of curve (as depicted in the third section of Fig. 3) instead of the ascending type of curve (as shown in Figs. 4 and 7).

Before launching a costly research project along the lines of the schematic outline just presented, a considerable amount of technical tooling-up will be required in order to work out effective ways of discovering dominant forms of resistances and of assessing the experimenter's success in counteracting them. Such work is currently under way in our social psychology laboratory at Yale University, but it may be a long time before we are ready to put any crucial predictions to the test. In the meantime, however, the theoretical model can be useful for suggesting some other new lines of research.

D. HEURISTIC VALUE EXEMPLIFIED BY RECENT EXPERIMENTS ON EMOTIONAL ROLE PLAYING

As an example of the heuristic value of the model, our recent experimental research on emotional role playing can be cited, which began with a series of exploratory studies initiated in order to discover a psychological technique that would enable people to tolerate a relatively high level of fear arousal without becoming so resistant that they would reject the message. This search was based on the expectation, derived from the theoretical model, that strong fear arousal will lead to increased attitude change if we can find some way of counteracting the interfering effects that ordinarily are dominant over the facilitating effects of high emotional arousal. From field observations of behavior changes in green combat troops, disaster rescue workers, and medical personnel following their first "baptism of fire," it seemed quite plausible to presume that attitudes and decisions could be markedly transformed by a single harrowing incident (Janis, 1968). A field study by DeWolfe and Governale (1964) also suggests that positive changes in attitudes and behavior occur among student nurses as a result of being exposed to a high fear condition. After a six-week assignment on the tuberculosis wards of a hospital, where the danger of being infected was constantly present, the nurses showed much more acceptance of the officially recommended precautionary measures than a control group of comparable nurses who were given no direct experience on tuberculosis wards. At first, the nurses exposed to the actual threat of the disease became extremely apprehensive about becoming infected. Later on, they gradually developed some degree of emotional adaptation, but they nevertheless continued to adhere more rigorously than ever before to the safety precautions they had been taught in nursing school.

Such direct confrontation with the threat seems to be extraordinarily effective in breaking through the defensive facade that normally enables a person to maintain an unwarranted but highly cherished attitude of complacency. When verbal warnings given time and again by authorities in the community remain ineffective, direct exposure to hazardous conditions sometimes seems to have a qualitatively different impact, breaking through the person's usual avoidance defenses to such a degree that he ends up replacing blanket reassurances by a new attitude that embodies a healthy respect for the danger. The crucial factor here is probably the perceived probability of being exposed to actual danger, which may be an important determinant of the optimal level of arousal. Once people become convinced of their personal vulnerability to a potential source of danger, their resistance to authoritative recommendations seems to be strikingly diminished. If so, a single direct confrontation with danger might increase the optimal level to a point where it approaches the highest peak on the acceptance curve, where we expect little defensive avoidance and correspondingly high readiness to be converted to a new plan of action by an authoritative communicator.

Are there any psychological devices that a counselor might use to prevent resistances from becoming dominant in order to achieve comparable breakthrough effects? This was the question to which my collaborators and I sought an answer. After obtaining some promising leads from preliminary explorations, we carried out a series of experiments that show the effectiveness of a special type of role-playing device.

In the first experiment (Janis and Mann, 1965), a psychodramatic situation was set up in which the subject played the role of a medical patient beginning to suffer from the harmful consequences of cigarette smoking. Twenty-six young women served as subjects, all of them smokers who had expressed no intention of trying to cut down on their cigarette consumption. In the experimental group, each subject was told that in playing the role of the patient in a doctor's office, she should express her spontaneous personal reactions, just as if it were actually happening to her. The experimenter, in the role of physician, wore a white coat and used various props, such as X-ray photographs of the lungs, in order to make the situation as realistic as possible.

Five different scenes were acted out, including one in which the cancer victim is thinking over the bad news while waiting for the physician to arrange for her hospitalization in the surgical ward, and is soliloquizing (aloud) about her error in not having stopped smoking before it was too late. This role-playing procedure proved to be an extraordinarily disquieting experience for the subjects, and generated many more signs of intense fear arousal than the control condition, which involved exposing an equivalent group of young women to the same information without any active role playing. The control subjects listened to a tape recording of an authentic session that had been conducted with one of the subjects in the experimental group.

The results showed that emotional role playing had a markedly greater effect than the control condition in modifying attitudes about smoking and in changing smoking habits. This technique of emotional role playing seems to provide unusual empathic experiences similar to those that occasionally lead to spectacular "conversions" among physicians, relatives, and friends of cancer victims. There are numerous indications that the high level of fear and vigilance aroused by the realistic quality of this type of role-playing procedure may be an important factor in the subjects' acquisition of antismoking attitudes and in the subsequent changes they reported in their smoking habits.

In a follow-up study, Mann and Janis (1967) found that over an 18 month period, the emotional role players who had participated in the initial experiment continued to report a significantly greater decrease in number of cigarettes consumed than the passive controls. This outcome suggests that a single one-hour session of emotional role playing might have a profound long-term effect upon smokers who initially have no intention to change their cigarette consumption, since the results indicate that for a sizable percentage of the sample the decision to cut down on smoking, once elicited, was still governing the subjects' smoking behavior years later.

In a replication and extension of the earlier research, Mann (1968) compared three equivalent groups of men and women given different types of role-playing procedures: One group went through the same fear-arousing procedure used in the first experiment, which required each subject to enact the role of a cancer victim; a second group was given a cognitive procedure, which required each subject to enact the role of a debater arguing against smoking. The third group was given a shame-arousing procedure, which required each subject to enact the role of a helpless smoking addict. The results showed that the fear-arousing procedure was much more effective than either the cognitive or the shame-arousing procedure. Mann also found that the amount of attitude change produced by the fear-arousing procedure was increased by giving subjects increased opportunity for verbalization while playing the role. The findings from Mann's study, like those from the earlier Janis and Mann experiment, indicate that emotional role playing can function as a device for "repackaging" information that is already available to the person in a way that leads to a change in his or her own self-image of personal vulnerability to health hazards. The same conclusion is partially supported by another experiment by Nowlis and Janis (1967) in which we worked with middle-aged people who came to a "smoking clinic" in order to obtain help in cutting down on their excessive smoking.

The findings from these experiments on emotional role playing seem to be in line with the expectation that increased attitude change can be produced by introducing special psychological procedures to reduce the usual psychological resistances that prevent people from taking full account of available public health information. In terms of the hypothetical curves represented in Figs. 4 and 7, the emotional role-playing procedure evidently has the effect of shifting the optimal level for the average subject from a relatively low level to a much higher one, enabling him to tolerate very strong emotional arousal without becoming predominantly resistant or defensive. Thus, the person would be more likely to change his attitudes under these dramatic role-playing conditions that if he were shown a television program or an illustrated magazine article that passively exposed him to the same fear-arousing information. It should also be noted that some of the evidence cited earlier, from experiments by Leventhal and his co-workers on the effectiveness of a fear-arousing movie sequence (showing a lung cancer victim undergoing surgery), suggests that certain types of empathy-eliciting devices might be found to augment the effectiveness of movies and other mass-media communications. Insofar as the assumptions of the theoretical model can be regarded as plausible, we are encouraged to continue the search for ways and means of breaking through the average individual's defensive facade, so as to transform a long-standing attitude of complacency into one of vigilance and heightened receptivity to precautionary recommendations.

E.   CONCLUSION

Although a number of new substantive hypotheses have been suggested, it seems to me that the most important heuristic value of the theoretical model discussed in this paper is in the sphere of posing new types of questions for systematic research on emotional arousal and attitude change. Of particular importance for those of us who have become increasingly pessimistic about making progress in this research area, as we continue to encounter gross inconsistencies between the outcome of the latest experiment and the one before that, is the reformulation of the central problem. Instead of continuing to ask unproductive questions about how acceptance varies as a function of different intensities of emotional arousal, we can turn to a set of theoretically oriented questions that may be much more productive: What are the determinants of the optimal level of arousal?

ACKNOWLEDGMENTS

The author thanks Professors William McGill and William J. McGuire for their valuable criticisms of the first draft of this chapter, and Professor Leonard Berkowitz for his excellent criticisms and editorial recommendations.

REFERENCES

Beier, E. G. (1951). The effect of induced anxiety on flexibility of intellectual functioning. *Psychol. Monogr.* **65**, No. 9.

Berkowitz, L., and Cottingham, D. R. (1960). The interest value and relevance of fear arousing communications. *J. abnorm. soc. Psychol.* **60**, 37–43.

Berkun, M., Bialek, H., Kern, R., and Yagi, K. (1962). Experimental studies of psychological stress in man. *Psychol. Monogr.* **76**, 1–39.

Brown, J. S. (1961). *The motivation of behavior.* New York: McGraw Hill.

DeWolfe, A., and Governale, Catherine. (1964). Fear and attitude change. *J. abnorm. soc. Psychol.* **69**, 119–123.

Dollard, J., and Miller, N. (1950). *Personality and psychotherapy.* New York: McGraw-Hill.

Duffy, Elizabeth. (1962). *Activation and behavior.* New York: Wiley.

Easterbrook, J. A. (1959). The effect of emotion on cue utilization and the organization of behavior. *Psychol. Rev.* **66**, 183–201.

Freud, S. (1936). *The problem of anxiety.* (Translated by H. A. Bunker.) New York: Norton.

Goldstein, M. (1959). Relationship between coping and avoiding behavior and response to fear-arousing propaganda. *J. abnorm. soc. Psychol.* **58**, 247–252.

Haefner, D. (1956). Some effects of guilt-arousing and fear-arousing persuasive communications on opinion change. Unpublished tech. rep. Aug. 15, 1956, Office of Naval Res., Contract No. N6 ONR 241. (Mimeo. abridgement of unpublished doctoral dissertation, Univ. of Rochester.)

Hall, J. F. (1961). *Psychology of motivation.* Philadelphia: Lippincott.

Hebb, D. O. (1955). Drives and th C. N. S. (conceptual nervous system) *Psychol. Rev.* **62**, 243–254.

Hovland, C. I., Janis, I. L., and Kelley, H. H. (1953). *Communication and persuasion.* New Haven, Connecticut: Yale Univ. Press.

Insko, C. A., Arkoff, A., and Insko, V. M. (1965). Effects of high and low fear-arousing communication upon opinions toward smoking. *J. exp. soc. Psychol.* **1**, 256–266.

Janis, I. L. (1958). *Psychological stress.* New York: Wiley.

Janis, I. L. (1962). Psychological effects of warnings. In C. W. Baker and D. W. Chapman (Eds.), *Man and society in disaster.* New York: Basic Books.

Janis, I. L. (1968). *The contours of fear: Psychological studies of war, disaster, illness, and experimental stress.* New York: Wiley.

Janis, I. L., and Feshbach, S. (1953). Effects of fear-arousing communications. *J. abnorm. soc. Psychol.* **48**, 78–92.

Janis, I. L., and Feshbach, S. (1954). Personality differences associated with responsiveness to fear-arousing communications. *J. Pers.* **23**, 154–166.

Janis, I. L., and Leventhal, H. (1965). Psychological aspects of physical illness and hospital care. In B. Wollman (Ed.), *Handbook of clinical psychology*. New York: McGraw-Hill.

Janis, I. L., and Leventhal, H. (1967). Human reactions to stress. In E. Borgatta and W. Lambert (Eds.), *Handbook of personality theory and research*. Chicago: Rand McNally.

Janis, I. L., and Mann, L. (1965). Effectiveness of emotional role-playing in modifying smoking habits and attitudes. *J. exp. Res. Pers.* **1**, 84–90.

Janis, I. L., and Milholland, W. (1954). The influence of threat appeals on selective learning of the content of a persuasive communication. *J. Psychol.* **37**, 75–80.

Janis, I. L., and Terwilliger, R. (1962). An experimental study of psychological resistances to fear-arousing communications. *J. abnorm. soc. Psychol.* **65**, 403–410.

Kausler, D., and Trapp, E. (1960). Motivation and cue utilization in intentional and incidental learning. *Psychol. Rev.* **67**, 373–379.

Korchin, S. (1965). Some psychological determinants of stress behavior. In Klausner, S. (Ed.) *The Quest for Self-Control*. New York: The Free Press, pp. 247–266.

Lazarus, R. S. (1966). *Psychological stress and the coping process*. New York: McGraw-Hill.

Leventhal, H. (1965). Fear communications in the acceptance of preventive health practices. *Bull. N. Y. Acad. Med.* **41**, 1144–1168.

Leventhal, H., and Niles, Patricia. (1964). A field experiment on fear arousal with data on the validity of questionnaire measures. *J. Pers.* **32**, 459–479.

Leventhal, H., and Niles, Patricia. (1965). Persistence of influence for varying durations of exposure to threat stimuli. *Psychol. Rep.* **16**, 223–233.

Leventhal, H., and Singer, R. P. (1966). Affect arousal and positioning of recommendations in persuasive communications. *J. Pers. soc. Psychol.* **4**, 137–146.

Leventhal, H., and Watts, Jean C. (1966). Sources of resistance to fear-arousing communications on smoking and lung cancer. *J. Pers.* **34**, 155–175.

Leventhal, H., Singer, R. P., and Jones, Susan. (1965). The effects of fear and specificity of recommendation upon attitudes and behavior. *J. Pers. soc. Psychol.* **2**, 20–29.

Ley, P. (1966). What the patient doesn't remember. *Med. Opin. Rev.* **1**, 69–73.

Luchins, A. S., and Luchins, E. H. (1959). *Rigidity of behavior: A variational approach to the effect of Einstellung*. Eugene, Oregon: Univ. of Oregon Books.

McGuire, W. J. (1967). Personality and susceptibility to social influence. In E. Borgatta and W. Lambert (Eds.), *Handbook of personality theory and research*. Chicago: Rand McNally.

Mainord, W. (1956). Experimental repression related to coping and avoidance behavior. Unpublished doctoral dissertation, Univ. of Washington.

Malmo, R. B. (1958). Measurement of drive: an unresolved problem in psychology. In M. Jones (Ed.), *Nebraska symposium on motivation, 1958*. Lincoln, Nebraska: Univ. of Nebraska Press.

Mann, L. (1968). The effects of emotional role playing on smoking attitudes and behavior. *J. exp. soc. Psychol.*

Mann, L., and Janis, I. L. (1967). A follow-up study on the long-term effects of emotional role playing. Mimeo ms. (To be published.)

Moltz, H., and Thistlethwaite, D. L. (1955). Attitude modification and anxiety reduction. *J. abnorm. soc. Psychol.* **50**, 231–237.

Mowrer, O. H. (1950). *Learning theory and personality dynamics*. New York: Ronald Press.

Niles (Kafes), Patricia. (1964). The relationship of susceptibility and anxiety to acceptance of fear-arousing communications. Unpublished doctoral dissertation, Yale Univ.

Nowlis, G., and Janis, I. L. (1967). Factors influencing the effectiveness of emotional role playing in modifying attitudes and actions. Mimeo ms. (To be published.)

Nunnally, J. D., and Bobren, H. M. (1959). Variables governing the willingness to receive communications on mental health. *J. Pers.* **27**, 38–46.

Osler, S. F. (1954). Intellectual performance as a function of two types of psychological stress. *J. Exp. Psychol.* **47**, 115–121.

Robbins, P. R. (1962). Self-reports of reactions to fear-arousing information. *Psychol. Rep* **11**, 761–764.

Rosenblatt, P. C. (1962). Persuasive value of threat and amount of attitude change advocated. Unpublished doctoral dissertation, Northwestern Univ.

Schachter, S. (1964). The interaction of cognitive and physiological determinants of emotional state. *Advanc. exp. soc. Psychol.* **1**, 49–80.

Schlosberg, H. (1954). Three dimensions of emotion. *Psychol. Rev.* **61**, 81–88.

Singer, R. P. (1965). The effects of fear-arousing communications on attitude change and behavior. Unpublished doctoral dissertation, Univ. of Connecticut.

Skinner, B. F. (1938). *The behavior of organisms.* New York: Appleton-Century-Crofts.

Sullivan, H. S. (1953). *The interpersonal theory of psychiatry.* New York: Norton.

Zemach, Mina. (1966). The effects of guilt-arousing communications on acceptance of recommendations. Unpublished doctoral dissertation, Yale Univ.

COMMUNICATION PROCESSES AND THE PROPERTIES OF LANGUAGE[1]

Serge Moscovici

ÉCOLE PRATIQUE DES HAUTES ÉTUDES
UNIVERSITÉ DE PARIS
PARIS, FRANCE

Along with experimental results, this chapter presents certain theories about the establishment of a field devoted to the psychosociological study of language. The importance of the analysis of linguistic phenomena is not yet sufficiently recognized in social psychology; on the other hand, linguists have not paid much attention to the possible contributions of our science. A great many studies of the processes of verbal communication have been made, but until now they have been without a unifying corpus of common problems and concepts. I do not intend to inventory these studies, nor do I propose a synthesis of them here; but I do want to call attention to some aspects of social interaction involving language as a mode of relation and a dimension of human behavior. Only in the long run can we hope to see a true psychosociology of language substituted for the unrelated psychosociological ventures that only occasionally touch on linguistic facts.

[1]The experiments mentioned in this chapter were carried out with the help of Claudine Humbert, Michel Plon, and Jean Székely. Continuous collaboration with Claude Faucheux has had a great impact on the general trend of this research program.

225

The first part of this chapter reviews present trends in the study of linguistic behavior and the second part proposes several hypotheses regarding this behavior and describes attempts to provide experimental verification for the hypotheses.[2] The third part of the paper is a brief discussion of certain questions raised by the notion of a valid social psychology of language.

I. Language as a Field of Social Psychology

A. LANGUAGE WITHOUT COMMUNICATION AND COMMUNICATION WITHOUT LANGUAGE

The last ten years or so have been marked by a growing interest in linguistic phenomena and the phenomena of communication. There has been a fruitful association between the behavioral and natural sciences in this respect (Cherry, 1957; Carrol, 1958). This is worth mentioning, for it lends force to the question, raised by Ferdinand de Saussure (1955, p.21), "What relations exist between linguistics and social psychology?" Truthfully speaking, contact between these two social sciences, on a concrete as well as theoretical level, are, if not nonexistent, at least limited (Miller, 1951). We can understand this limited contact fairly readily if we examine the dominant orientations in each discipline regarding the communicative function, the essential function of language.

When linguists consider this function, the communication process appears as an abstraction. The physical and physiological nature of communication receives privileged treatment. Linguistics textbooks put the greatest emphasis on the speaker's biological capacities. The organs of speech and the anatomy and physiology of the ear are described in minute detail, with their discriminatory aptitudes, as if the listener were distinguished from the speaker, or sender, by the act of hearing or by motor articulation of sounds (Malmberg, 1953). These specialized works show a relative indifference to the social and psychological attributes of the persons concerned. Such phenomena as the anticipating or assuming of the role of the other, or the handling of classifications, exercise an incontrovertible influence on the stylistic devices that order and implement communication (Schatzman and Strauss, 1954), but do not find a place in this framework. The roles of speaker and listener and the varied nature of their interaction intervene in linguistic theory, the explanation of language properties, only secondarily (Slama-Cazacu, 1961). We are led to believe that all that is necessary is to define and clarify the encoding and decoding operations that

[2] I leave out of my field of study all that concerns semantics. A most interesting discussion of the contribution of social psychology to semantics can be found in Rommetweit (1966).

serve to transmit information. Such reasoning posits an essential sameness of encoders and decoders, as if they differ only in their position at one or the other end of the chain of communication. Inquiries about the varied nature of their interaction or about the diversity of their purposes and their relationship are considered irrelevant. Verbal emission is regarded as the product of a single permutable subject who is now a speaker, now a listener; it is not regarded as the joint product of two individuals, each of whom behaves in a definite way, depending on his role. Thus, a sort of soliloquy for several voices is substituted for true dialogue. In that perspective, the fields of study of both communication and language are narrowed simultaneously. Jakobson (1961, p. 250) commented on the risks that this attitude entails: "Attempts to construct a model of language without any relation either to the speaker or to the hearer and thus to hypostasize a code detached from actual communication threaten to make a scholastic fiction from language."

Finally, the classic distinction between *langue*—a stable system of relationships among lexical units—and *parole*—an ensemble of uses of this system by the members of a community—has permitted the severing of linguistic phenomena from their extralinguistic foundations. Consequently, emitters, receivers, and their relations are depicted as ideal, universal types. In wanting to make language an autonomous and purely formal entity, linguistics has forgotten the speaking subject and has created a mirror image, equally formal and autonomous, of communication:

His distinction [de Saussure's] between *la langue* and *la parole* supplied the rationale for treating the systemic features of linguistic events independently of the social behavioral matrix in which they occur. It made it conceptually feasible to prosecute the study of the structural properties of utterances in an objective and rigorous fashion without regard to the overwhelmingly difficult problems associated with the analysis of their functional properties. The substantial successes of structural studies is without doubt largely due to de Saussure's freeing of linguistic analysis from the entanglements of functional concerns. But these successes have prompted a large number of modern linguists, especially those of rigidly operationalist persuasions, to deny any relevance of functional considerations for their own endeavors and, occasionally, to deny also the possibility that such considerations are even susceptible of scientific treatment (Bastian, 1959).

The autonomy of *la langue* was actually established for epistemological reasons in order to determine the subject matter of linguistics. This autonomy was accompanied by a reaction against psychology (Antal, 1964). The psychology aimed at was, however, *individual* psychology. "The linguistic system," Hjemslev wrote (1935, p. 86), "and the values it is composed of, are not psychological facts. Both system and values are independent from the individual." Thus, because the elements of language were not reducible to individual behavior, their psychological character was denied. The arguments that support this separation of linguistic phenomena from one area of psychology are not valid for the whole of psychology, unless one confuses the whole with one of its parts—and that confusion has been made. It would be pointless to pretend on the strength of those arguments that language is equally independent of groups and group norms and interactions. It then follows that linguistic systems and their values are psychological facts, facts that a discipline—social psychology—within psychology as a whole can approach with its own orientation.

The position I have just described is, to tell the truth, increasingly contested. The distinction between *la langue* and *la parole* is not rigidly maintained (Ruwet, 1964). Several writers insist that the differentiation of languages can be understood only as a result of differentiation of communication systems. Zinkin (1962, p. 148) demonstrated that "the differences between languages are defined by their mechanisms of communication." No wonder. The purpose of linguistic signs and rules is to facilitate the various modes of communication. The properties of verbal codes—the rules of their production and operation—should therefore be adapted to the individuals and groups that use them, to the needs and kinds of action that bring these people together. Reality, as well as theory, shows us there is no ideal, universal type of hearer or speaker, no universal encoding or decoding of verbal signs. On the contrary, there are only *classes* of speakers and listeners; their attributes correspond to particular forms of communication, creating speeches adapted to these forms (Benveniste, 1958). The very organization of messages could not be envisaged in a vacuum, apart from the reasons for their formulation, such as, especially, conveying information or exercising influence. "An adequate theory of language," Wiener (1954, p. 93) wrote, "as a game should distinguish between these two varieties of language, one which is intended primarily to convey information and the other primarily to impose a point of view against a willful opposition."

The theoretical and experimental study of classes of speakers and listeners, their intentions and actions, the circulation of information, and the function of persuading, undoubtedly belong to social psychology, at least insofar as the foregoing deal with the combination and selection of linguistic signs and rules. One must recognize, however, that studies of communication have not been used to understand linguistic behavior; they have not even taken serious account of linguistic behavioral qualities and specificity (Miller, 1951; Bresson, 1966). The most superficial glance confirms the existence of this nonlinguistic bias, which prevails generally in social psychology.

Thus, the messages exchanged by subjects in different communication networks (Shaw, 1964; Flament, 1965) are usually composed of letters and syllables. Experiments in this area have been conceived as if the nature and organization of the system of linguistic signs were unrelated to the circumstances of their transmission. Heise and Miller (1951) showed very early, however, the existence of a properly linguistic dimension. These authors gave their subjects—in three experimental situations—material consisting either of monosyllables, or of a number of words from which a sentence was to be constructed, or of a single word that was to be used in making anagrams. The efficiency of the networks changed as a function of the verbal level at which the subjects operated; the noncentralized network was better suited to the handling of monosyllables, and the centralized network to the ordering of the words in a sentence. Other studies have shown relations between sociometric links, verbal capacities, and the needs or tasks to which language responds (Gruen and Bierman, 1960; Dinoff *et al.*, 1962; Knutson, 1960; Rosenthal, 1957; Herman, 1961; Hare, 1952).

We cannot say, however, that this evidence has had an influence on theoretical thought, or that it has given rise to further scientific work. The lexical or syntactic indices are usually assimilated to any kind of indices, and their particularities are overlooked. All that is verbal in social inter-action seems to be of secondary interest and does not raise any specific questions. The situation is not radically different where content analyses (de Sola Pool, 1959; Berelson, 1952) or the experimental study of persuasion processes are concerned. Content analyses applied to the mass media most often consist of a count of themes or of key words (such as democracy or bolshevism); they rarely constitute an examination of the semantic field, of the syntactic organization of the messages. The new rhetoric is, in a sense, not made use of to any great extent. There is no concern with sorting out the imprint left by the persuader's intention or desire to change the other's conduct or attitude. Little attention is given to the linguistic styles peculiar to the various media, or to messages likely to induce trust, to attract others, to induce fear, and so on. The experimental studies touch on such factors as the credibility accorded to the source of emission, the influence of the amount of threat contained in a message, the personality traits (self-esteem, persuadability) of the receiver, the effects of primacy or recency, and the written or oral character of the message (Hovland *et al.*, 1953). Ideally, not only the *content* but also the *style* of messages destined to express credibility, threat (in short, all speeches adapted to the expression of social status, feeling, and so on) should be included in a thorough investigation of the communication processes. More is involved here than the relative omission of these linguistic aspects; even when they have been dealt with, attempts to do so have sometimes created confusion. Thus, there have been several attempts to study the differential impact of a written text and of an orally presented text, but with contradictory results. The implicit intention was to compare an oral communication with a written one, a message emitted on the radio with a message in a newspaper, an informal situation with a formal one (Knower, 1936; Wilke, 1934). The probability of particular effects is described by McGinnies (1965, p. 11) in these terms: "Since attitude change is essentially a learning process, such learning as occurs may be impeded or facilitated by those structural features of a given language that distinguish its oral forms."

Starting with this hypothesis, one could conceive of two versions of an identical text being presented to the subjects; the oral version being more redundant, more colloquial, and containing more adverbs and verbs, the written version being less redundant, containing more nouns and, of course, being grammatically more "correct." In fact, we actually are dealing with the *same* text, which is heard by a portion of the subject—oral presentation—and read by the other subjects —written presentation. Now, it is evident that what characterizes a message is not so much its *mode of emission* as its *mode of composition.* An "oral" speech and a speech *emitted* orally are two totally different things from the linguistic and psychosociological points of view. More than this, the *hearing* and the *reading* of the same message, generally in "written" style, do not necessarily call upon the particular processes of learning that are involved in attitude change, for the structural features of this message in a given language are identical. Every speaking subject recognizes the difference between the case in which "one writes as one speaks" and that in which "one speaks as one writes."

These few examples testify to the widespread tendency to consider communication under its nonverbal aspect, or to overlook its verbal aspect. The constitution of a domain of psychosociological study of language (Faucheux and Moscovici, 1966) implies an interest in verbal communication as a specific field of study that can teach us something about human behavior. Linguistics can contribute valuable information to this field (Olmsted and Moore, 1952). It cannot, however, be considered as a source of solutions; nor can its categories be adapted as they are, as is sometimes done (Ervin-Tripp and Slobin, 1966). The categories of linguistics were conceived, we have seen, without taking into account that which it is essential for us to know, namely, the processes by which individuals and groups interact. Despite these restrictions, however, a rapport between these two disciplines could be established if we were to give up envisaging language without communication and communication without language.

B. LINGUISTIC BEHAVIOR AS AN INDEX AND MEDIUM OF SOCIAL INTERACTION

Language and the behavior associated with it are not systematically examined in social psychology. With rare exceptions (Brown, 1965), the textbooks refer to linguistic behavior only in passing. However, I do not see why this specifically human and social phenomenon would be less rich in scientific implications and less worthy of attention than the cognitive and emotional phenomena to which we dedicate so much care. Let us be content with blaming the difficulties of experimentation with linguistic material, so variable on the one hand and so difficult to handle on the other. Some orientations, nevertheless, do exist in the domain of the psychosociological study of linguistic behavior. I will attempt to define them and to stress their particularities.

Social psychology is especially interested in the production, or the generation, of linguistic signs, rules, and events. The acquisition or learning of the elements of language does not and cannot be one of these preoccupations because, one, the production and the acquisition of language can be separated only in pathological cases; and two, learning processes have little importance in everyday social exchanges. "It is evident," observes Chomsky (1964, p. 8), "that rote recall is a factor of minute importance in ordinary use of language."

In the unfolding of an interaction between individuals or groups, the linguistic sign appears in two forms. First, it is an *index* of the rapport between individuals—or groups—of their position in a social scale, of their desire to obey or to command, and so on. The leader can impose himself by an amount of verbal emission, just as he can distinguish himself by his position in a network or by other outward signs, such as his habits and resources. In this respect, the linguistic sign hardly differs from any other index that reflects the same attitudes or hierarchial differences in a given social structure. Moreover, this use of the elements of language does not imply that their particular qualities have played a role in the emergence of an individual as a leader, to retain our example. Second, the chain of linguistic signs seems to constitute a *medium*, a field of social interaction, to the extent to which their properties—from the point of view of redundance or from the grammatical point of view—are utilized to contribute precisely to a particular effect. For example, to transmit a great deal of information within a limited time it is best to use more nouns and adjectives than usual. Similarly, to establish more formal relations with someone else, a speaker should avoid redundance and should use sentences with simple grammatical patterns. We shall show later that a message intended to bring about an action differs, from the linguistic point of view, from one that is meant to change an attitude. Thus, in these cases, the properly linguistic dimensions—

in addition to the volume of speech—affect the individual and social behavior. We can establish an analogy with clothes-wearing. We wear different garments when attending a ceremony or a funeral from those worn when carrying out our more ordinary roles in everyday life. The color, style, and other characteristics of our garments situate us at once within a defined social field, and contribute to the establishment of a particular mode of relation. In this sense, clothing, like speech, is a medium of inter-action between individuals or groups. But clothing can also appear, apart from this accommodation to certain social rules, as a "badge," an index of an individual's social position by the mere fact that this individual is well dressed or ill dressed. This is demonstrated by a well-known experiment by Lefkowitz *et al.* (1955) in connection with traffic signal violations. A man attired in a pressed suit, shined shoes, white shirt, and tie produced a higher incidence of pedestrian violations in imitation of his behavior than the same transgression performed by the same person dressed in soiled patched trousers, scuffed shoes, and so forth. The garments gave prestige in the case cited; the people who follow a well-dressed person probably think that they are less likely to be punished in the circumstances. It was not the garments per se that induced the imitation, however; the important element was the meaning of garments in the social system of rewards and punishments.

The description of some characteristic research work will permit a better understanding of these two aspects, index and medium, in the study of linguistic behavior and of their accompanying theoretical orientations.

1. Volume of Verbal Emission, Perception of Others, and "Speaking Order"

The existence of a "speaking order" has often been ascertained in small groups. Bass *et al.* (1958) showed that the time spent speaking in an initially leaderless discussion group is correlated with the status of leader. Shaw and Gilchrist (1956), Mann (1961), and Kirscht *et al.* (1959) observed that the individuals who speak or communicate most have a greater likelihood of being selected as leaders. Riecken (1958) and Hoffman and Maier (1964) noted that persons who ranked high in talkativeness succeeded better in imposing their opinions on the group in problem-solving situations. The volume of verbal emission is thus both a means of securing leadership in a group and a sign that orders the individual group members by status levels.

A study by Bales (1951) was the starting point for a series of further studies worth describing. Bales *et al.* (1951) recorded the "linguistic acts" produced in groups ranging in size from three to ten members. They represented the totality of these acts by a matrix, with rows corresponding to initiators and columns to receivers. The acts addressed to the group as a whole were also registered. The following proposition was suggested: the participants ranked by the total number of acts they initiated would also be ranked by the total number of acts that they received and that they addressed to specific other individuals and to the group as a whole. Bales suggested that the frequencies of acts followed a harmonic distribution. But although there was a tendency of leaders to initiate more acts and to participate more, there was little agreement between the data and the theoretical curves. It seemed that a more complex model was necessary to account for the data. Stephan (1952) and Stephan and Mishler (1952) showed, on the contrary, that a simpler model could be applied if one assumed that: (a) there exists a "verbal participation potential" among the members of the group; (b) there is no systematic interference with the free expression of these potentials; and (c) the roles of the group members are not well differentiated. There was a satisfactory correlation of the model with the obtained data. More recently, Horvath (1965) proposed a stochastic model to account for the same results. This model supposed that each individual in the group had the same conditional probability of intervening in a conversation. A hierarchy is constituted in the communication process and from then on there is a certain order in which the individuals, consciously or not, enter into the verbal interaction.

With this body of evidence as a point of departure, Bavelas *et al.* (1965), following Oakes *et al.* (1960), undertook to establish the relationship between a person's status in a group and his capacity to emit a great many opinions concerning a problem common to the members of the group. The authors assembled groups of four people who did not know each other. Each subject occupied a position, determined in advance, around a table. In front of him, and comparatively screened from the sight of the others, the subject found a reflector box on which he saw two small lights, one red and one green, that were controlled by the experimenter. The task consisted of the discussion of three cases. In common with all reinforcement experiments, the discussion of the first case permitted the establishment of a baseline rate of verbal emission for each individual. The second case provided occasion for actual experimental reinforcements, while the degree of extinction of the effects of reinforcement was determined during the discussion of the third case. After each of the three discussions the experimenter administered a sociometric questionnaire. (There were actually five experiments carried out following this general procedure, but all of them do not concern us here.)

In the first experiment, after the first case discussion among the members of the group and the subsequent gathering of the sociometric data, the subjects were ranked according to the hierarchy of the sociometric choices and their degree of talkativeness. The subjects who had spoken least and who had received the fewest sociometric choices, described as "target-people," were singled out. In the course of the second case discussion, during the experimental manipulation, these subjects were reinforced; that is they received encouragement to speak. The other subjects, on the contrary, were inhibited, that is, they were discouraged from participating in the discussion. To do this, before the group approached the analysis of the second case, the experimenter came back into the room and informed the subjects that certain groups would be "provided with feedback information as to how they are doing as the discussion proceeds." This information was to be provided with the help of the two small red and green lights. The group was told that when a subject emitted an opinion that permitted the group as a whole to progress, the green light in front of him would flash. On the other hand, if a subject voiced an opinion that created an obstacle to the solution of the problem, he would be notified by a flash of the red light. The target-people, those who had spoken least and who had received fewest sociometric choices in the first part of the experiment, of course received the greatest number of green signals, whereas the other subjects received the most red signals for the same kind of verbal emissions. The experiment was designed to show that appropriate reinforcements can cause a person to increase his participation in interpersonal exchanges. As expected after discussion of the second case, the target-people spoke more and subsequently received an increased number of sociometric choices.

Other experiments demonstrated that encouraging the target-person without discouraging the others from participating verbally or, for that matter, only discouraging the other members of the group without encouraging the target-person, does not produce a modification in the sociometric choices or the quantities of verbal emission. The lesson of this fascinating, even if not surprising, research is clear: the "speaking order" affects the perception of the individual group members and of their status. On this point the results are incontestable. There was a very strong correlation ($r = .84$) between the quantity of verbal emissions and the sociometric rank.

If I have presented this experiment at length it is to do more than support the importance of the speaking order. The latter phenomenon is probably restricted to groups in which the nature of the activity does not require a differentiation of roles. Together with Faucheux (Faucheux and Moscovici, 1960), I have shown that case discussion is not the only kind of activity that requires groups to develop hierarchic structures of communication. I especially wanted to deal with the system of signs implied by certain mathematical (Coleman, 1960) or psychological models, and by these experimental studies. In the Bavelas *et al.* experiment (1956) there is *simultaneous* positive reinforcement of the chosen subject and negative reinforcement of the other subjects. Of course, one could argue that the sociometric changes occur because the experimenter, by encouraging or discouraging a person, passes an implicit judgment on that person's capacities and provides information regarding his ability to solve the problem submitted to him. In this respect, the chosen leader is selected not because of the volume of his verbal output but because of his ability to achieve the purposes of the group. But let us accept the investigators' hypotheses. The experiments show how communication patterns affect leadership. In communication network studies, it has been demonstrated, the person who has been put in a prominent communication position receives more leadership choices. In effect, these experiments show that, in addition to having the leader emerge by putting him in the center of a star-shaped network, thus suppressing the other members' access to certain channels, the experimenter can control the communication at its source by substituting the privilege of volume for the privilege of ecological position. Whether this volume is a volume of words or a volume of noises or gestures is not, a priori, important. What is important is that there is a system of signs that signals the position and role of the subject in solving the problem given to the group.

But every system of signs does not, strictly speaking, constitute a language; in the same way, any sign, even if it has a meaning, is not a linguistic sign (Martinet, 1965). Red, yellow, and green traffic lights are highly organized systems of signs, just as are the different pitches of sound emitted by a bugle in a barracks; none of these signs constitute a language. Despite the support of words, the verbal behavior has no further proprieties in the cited studies, and the communication is, strictly speaking, a non-linguistic communication. It does not differ fundamentally from the communication found in the various species not possessing true language. Bees, in the observations of von Frisch (1950), signal the orientation or distance of a source of food by the form and rhythm of their dance. In such experiments as those of Bales *et al.* (1955), Oakes *et al.* (1960), Bavelas *et al.* (1956), the amount of verbal emission only marks the social position of the individual and focuses the group on him. For this reason, I say the language involved in these studies is really only an ensemble of *indices*; it intervenes as a system of signs in general, but its specific traits, its particular structures, are not involved in the production of corresponding effects.

2.   The Process of Influence and the Organization of Discourse

To illustrate the second direction, that which relates the lexical and syntactic properties of language to the process of communication, there is a quasi-experimental study by Back (1961). He proposed to relate the exercise of power to the patterns of messages in the channels of communication. More precisely, he hypothesized that messages intended to change an attitude are repetitive in content and varied in form, whereas messages having the purpose of instigating an action are more varied in content and more repetitive in form. The length of sentences and number of subordinate clauses indicate especially formal fluctuations. Nouns and adjectives—content words—provide more of a measure of the quantity of information. One should observe some important formal variations and a relatively low percentage of nouns and adjectives in communications that have as their main intent the change of attitude. Conversely, communication intended to produce an action manifests standardized propositional constructions, together with a relatively higher proportion of nouns or adjectives, or both.

The material used in this study came from a content analysis of the speeches of Franklin Delano Roosevelt, Billy Graham, and Norman Vincent Peale. Back observed that the variance of sentence construction is greater in the case of communications aiming at inducing a change of attitude than in those having the initiation of action as their objective. There is no significant difference between the two forms of communication in the percentage of nouns or adjectives.

As a demonstration of the dependence of the content and form of the message on the structure of groups, Back and Strickland (cited in Back, 1961), conceived the following experiment. They gave the task of writing a pamphlet to groups of three students. Three jobs were defined: the gathering of data; the conception of the plan; and coordination. The students were made to believe that each person had a different task. The task was accomplished individually and, in fact, each student played the role of a designer. Communication between individuals was possible only through written messages. The two experimental conditions were the following: (a) In the "group condition," emphasis was placed on the work in common, on the collective nature of the rewards, and the jobs were presented as interchangeable; (b) in the "organizational" condition, attention was called to efficiency in the work and to the individual nature of the rewards; the assignment of the different functions supposedly was in accord with abilities measured through a test. As expected, in the second condition, with emphasis given to the more formal character of the relationships and to efficiency, the variability of the sentences was less and the percentage of nouns and adjectives higher. Discussion of the results of these experiments is difficult, however, for the published tables do not show the means that were obtained. In addition, lexical redundance is not measured directly, but is inferred from the proportion of nouns and adjectives. Nonetheless, the fact remains that the processes of influence, the modes of communication defined by the researchers, were reflected in a lexical and syntactic structuring of messages. This structuring allows one to see particular modes of interaction and of social communication at work. The nature of the different parts of speech, the construction of the sentences—properly linguistic facts, therefore, that cannot be attributed to any other system of signs—is the medium through which influence is exercised and conduct is instituted.

The two described directions—the first striving to grasp the role of verbal behavior as compared to other indices of social behavior, the second more particularly interested in analysis of the relations between linguistic manifestations and communication processes—delimit the essentials of a domain of the study of language in social psychology. I do not know what their most fertile meeting point will be. I suggest that each direction has, or should have, its own program, scientific problems, and operational techniques. The research studies I have pursued, and which will now be described, fall within the framework of the second orientation. Taking as a starting point the dimensions of social communication as they have been established by social psychology, I wanted to show that they lead to a correlative organization of language, and hence, that they explain certain of its lexical and syntactic aspects.

II. Theoretical and Experimental Observations of Linguistic Behavior

A. Description of the Nature of Dependent and Independent Variables

The theoretical and experimental study of linguistic behavior has, so far, not been carried beyond a fairly general and relatively simple level. Present conditions do not permit more complex analyses. There are as yet no clear rules concerning the value of measures, procedures for the sampling of subjects, or even the description of variables. The comparison of research results is, if not impossible, at least arbitrary (Mahl and Schulze, 1964). Given this situation, it would be of little avail to bring up now the finer points of either the sociopsychological or linguistic aspects of the problem. Rather, it is more important to acquire familiarity with the specific quality of language and to map out the principal aims of the research. Only when, thanks to an increase in the number of converging studies, research units have created their own "culture" in this field, will it be possible to treat more sophisticated hypotheses empirically.

With these limitations in mind, we now present an inventory of the phenomena that need to be related to each other, along with a list of variables to be considered.

1. Systems of Communication and Channels of Communication

Regarding the processes of communication—that is, the production of codes and of messages adjusted to a particular code—a distinction should be made between *systems* and *channels* of communication, a distinction that is directly linked to the situation of the speakers and to the operations they perform. Let us take two subjects (individuals or groups) exchanging messages. In transmitting or receiving these messages they may have either of two purposes: they may want to maintain or to change behavior, or they want to maintain or change their relationship. The object, whether close or distant, accepted or rejected, is always present, since a text or a speech is always a text or a speech about something. The interdependence of these interpersonal relationships and the attitude or position toward the object gives communication the character of a system (Newcomb, 1953). However, depending on such factors as the nature of the transmitter or receiver and the interactions involved, a whole series of communication systems might be established. Thus, transmission of an item of information or the exercise of influence are two distinct goals, involving different interactions; the first is based on reciprocity, the second on power. Each purpose calls forth different roles or categories of transmitters and receivers. I have chosen this example expressly to illustrate the multiplicity of systems of communication. A theory of communication seeks to specify the variables that make it possible to define these systems (Moscovici, 1955, 1961), and according to which, among other things, the corresponding linguistic behavior can be predicted.

Channels of communication are defined primarily by the technical characteristics of their functioning and the physical characteristics of the symbols they convey. These can be clearly distinguished by an independent observer. A list of these characteristics necessarily covers several dimensions, since it must include gestures, the voice, writing, telephone, radio, Bavelas networks, and more. The social and psychological connotations of these characteristics are no less important than their physical and ecological dimensions. Writing is endowed with a certain aura of solemnity in our society, whereas gesticular expressions accompany more informal meetings. Reading books and even newspapers is generally an individual activity; going to the movies or watching television often are activities of a more collective nature. Thus, channels of communication are above all complex psychological areas that call forth a set of stimuli and appropriate responses. It is at least from this angle that channels of communication should be considered in conjunction with linguistic behavior.

Systems of communication embrace a relationship between partners, concretely expressed in a message whose utterance causes a change in the activity of its recipient. Channels of communication are defined by physical, social, and psychological surroundings and by the means available to the speaking subject for conveying his message to a recipient. These elements determine the two functions the partners will adopt and the abilities they will call on to perform each of these functions.

One of these functions is *regulatory*, corresponding to the subject's goal of either conveying information or exercising influence. Essentially, this function involves *encoding* or *decoding* a message in a given context. Different efforts will, obviously, be required to encode, or organize, a speech, according to whether its purpose is to induce fear, to secure agreement, or to have an object recognized by another person. The other function is a *reproductive* one in that the subject must make certain that his message is adapted to the medium he is using for transmission; he must also seek to protect the message against any noise that might cause it to deteriorate or lessen its chances of being heard or understood. The passage from inner speech to external speech, the varying presentations of research results made by the same person in front of students or colleagues, in an article for a learned journal, or in a newspaper with a large circulation, perfectly illustrate the chain of constant *recodings* that we all carry out. Without subjecting these functions to rigid separation or exhaustive analysis, we can state that they require different strategies from, and impose definite restraints on, the speaker. It follows that the study of linguistic behavior must distinguish among statements according to how they relate to systems of communication and to channels of communication, respectively. There is no direct correlation between the two, nor is it possible to make the same predictions applicable to both. It is not enough to say, in order to establish the relationship between communication and language, that the latter fulfills a function of the former; the context of this function is decisive for what has been called the "economics of language" (Marschack, 1965).

2. Hypotheses Concerning the Influence of Communication Processes on Lexical Redundance and Syntactic Organization

As regards language, two kinds of variables may be kept in mind. The first is the degree of use of lexical units, or their repetition rate in a verbal chain; that is, the *redundance* of the speech uttered during verbal interaction. Research has shown (Bresson, 1966) that the frequency of occurrence of words, their rarity or abundance, as well as their availability (Moscovici and Humbert, 1960b), directly influence the processes of learning and observation. We can suppose that in communication these same factors act to increase the precision of the codes used and the distinctness of the different parts of the message.

The second variable is the *syntactic organization*, that is, the association of vocables, taking into account their role as parts of speech, according to certain rules or diagrams. Within this organization, the grammatical categories of verb and noun (present in all languages) represent the opposite ends of a continuum, the entire linguistic structure being built around them (Martinet, 1965; Robins, 1952). Efforts have been made, using statistical compilations, to show that there is a certain connection between redundance and the grammatical function of words. Thus, nouns are included among "rare" words and verbs among "frequent" words. One cannot conclude that this is always the case, however; above all, there are no grounds for stating that in every kind of message, nouns and adjectives convey a greater amount of information. This would be confusing their lexical dimension with their syntactic dimension, as is to some extent the case in the above-mentioned study by Back (1961). As noted, in that study nouns and adjectives are treated not only as parts of speech, but also as indices of variations in information content and vocabulary, which is not warranted as a general rule.

The description of independent and dependent variables—the former being associated with the communication processes, the latter with the linguistic structure—does not have a merely classificatory purpose. This description, together with certain theoretical notions (Brondal, 1933), leads to the formulation of an initial set of hypotheses:

(1) Linguistic variations resulting from changes of and within systems of communication—that is, from interactions between speaking subjects relative to each other and to a referent—are chiefly lexical variations; they refer largely to the redundance of language.

(2) Linguistic variations resulting from the transition from one channel of communication to another—that is, from the necessity of reproducing in or translating into one channel of communication a message elaborated in another— concern predominantly the parts of speech, the *syntactic* aspect of language.

These hypotheses refer to the relations between the communication processes and components of linguistic structure. I have tried to verify them empirically through a set of experimental studies, described later, that make it possible to arrange and simplify the parts of a picture whose general outlines are still blurred.

B.   DIMENSIONS OF COMMUNICATION SYSTEMS AND PATTERNS OF SPEECH

The forces that impel people to communicate also act on the nature of verbal transactions and determine the kinds of codes that are constructed on such occasions. A system of communication includes, I have shown, two speakers who exchange opinions, judgments, orders, about an object. Relations between the individual or social subjects must be distinguished from the relations of each subject to the object of these exchanges. The former define the dimension of *pressure* in the system, whereas the latter define the dimension of *distance*.

1. Inference Pressure

The pressure in a social system can be conceptualized in relation to the action, the hierarchy, or the norms of a group. Festinger (1950) has argued that this pressure influences communication in a group when the group, in order to move toward its goal or to establish a social definition of reality, compels its members to reduce the attitudinal divergences separating the members. Let us simply state that this pressure toward opinion uniformity exists as soon as communication becomes instrumental to the satisfaction of some common need. Often the only function of communication is to establish a relationship between two subjects, or to maintain an existing relationship. At other times, on the other hand, subjects have to communicate in order to exchange items of information or to make a common decision after agreement has been reached.

Pressure obviously does not arise only where divergences of opinion stand in the way of "group locomotion." Pressure can also develop from the exercise of power in a hierarchical social structure (Back, 1961; Ziller, 1955). The holders of power, whether to attain their own ends or to validate their positions (French, 1956), have an interest in imposing their opinions or in reducing the opinion discrepancies between themselves and other group members. Conformity molds the whole behavior pattern (Gerard, 1953; March, 1956; Argyle, 1957); it is also at work when norms are invoked to compel the members of a group to obey given rules (Thibaut and Strickland, 1956), or when these norms possess a mode of communication and a language of their own (Bernstein, 1964). Whatever the manifestations of the pressure, they all combine to establish a common code. In the process that leads to it, whether by selection or by inhibition, one of the subcodes takes a predominant place and imposes itself as a privileged diagram for the elaboration of the messages. The results of such a code are easy to picture. The code reduces uncertainty as to the meaning of the partner's discourse; this entails an increased predictability concerning future emissions and an increased sensitivity of the speaking subjects toward one another.

Such changes with time appear in a study by Palmore et al. (1959) of the interaction between therapist and patient. The authors recorded the verbal emissions in eight psychotherapy cases over a period of eleven months. On the basis of those emissions, they distinguished three categories of discourse: (a) *primary system references*, which concern reciprocal therapist-patient role relations; (b) *evaluative statements*, in which each partner gives or asks for appraisals or statements of value; and (c) *affective statements*, which comprise statements directed toward or expressing emotions. There was an increasing correlation of these categories of discourse in the emissions of the therapist and of the patient, and, in terms of indices of sensitivity, an increasing sensitivity of the therapist and of the patient toward each other's verbalizations. We are here dealing with a temporal effect of continued interaction which—even if it has not been demonstrated unquestionably by other studies, particularly that of Feldstein and Jaffe (1963)— probably exists all the same. Among the most striking results of social interaction are the "private languages" that are instituted among members of a group or in the course of interindividual transactions. The possession of a common code, allowing an anticipation of answers and creating an awareness of the consequences of one's own verbal formulations, facilitates the whole process of encoding and decoding. This common code and accompanying cognitive similarity simplifies the organization of messages, and the efficiency of communications as a whole is increased.

Harms (1961) showed that listeners have a better understanding of speakers of their own social status—that is, possessors of a verbal code similar to their own—than of speakers of another social status. Triandis (1960), on the other hand, explored the relationship between cognitive similarity and communicative similarity. Cognitive similarity is defined as the extent to which individuals use the same attributes to describe certain events in their environment, and is measured by comparing subjects' judgments about twelve triads of pictures of emotional expression. The communicative similarity concerns the communality of dimensions used by individuals in the actual process of communication. In the experiment the subjects, arranged in pairs, were to play six "games." In each game, each subject had two pictures, one of which was common to the partners. These two people were seated at opposite sides of a table in such a way that they could not see each other, and were required to find out which was the identical picture. The pictures came from the same set of pictures used in the measurement of cognitive similarity. The subjects were allowed to send as many messages as they wanted during a period of 12 minutes, and at the end of the twelve-minute period they guessed at the identity of the common picture. Communicative similarity was measured by a content analysis of the messages, each of which consisted of a pair of polar opposites, such as "intelligent-unintelligent," or "good date-poor date," and a number between one and seven signifying the degree to which the first adjective described the picture. There was also, of course, a measure of communication effectiveness.

For our present purposes the essential results were as follows. (a) The greater the attribute similarity, the greater the communication effectiveness in a pair. (b) The greater the communication similarity, the greater the communication effectiveness. (c) In addition—and this is of particular interest—subjects who were cognitively similar, and therefore had a common code, tended to send fewer messages in accomplishing their assigned task. Shibuya (1962) obtained the same results. If a code is shared by the persons in communication they need not state everything explicitly or spend much time eliminating the ambiguities in their communications. A smaller number of elements can therefore be used or combined to produce the same effects.

This is true even at the phonetic level; Haudricourt (1961) showed that where there is one predominant language, the number of phones used by the speakers is smaller than where there is an equalitarian bilingualism.

Finally, all these pressures lead to a cognitive stabilization and coordination of the people in communication. We can speak, in this regard, of *inference pressures*, because simultaneously they require the construction of a common code and compel speakers to adapt their messages to it. Thus, we can distinguish these pressures from other—equally social—pressures (those of the audience and the time, for instance), which do not imply any particular relation between message and code and which we will call *external pressures*.

2. Distance

Distance represents the position of an individual or a group relative to a referent, that is, an object or event, with respect to which one communicates. Its importance for the understanding of interpersonal relations has been emphasized by such writers as Heider (1958) and Fiedler (1953) and, in the field of communications, by Fearing (1953). Some additional explanations are needed here. Imagine the case of a mathematician discussing mathematics with a nonmathematician; the distance from the object—in this case, mathematics—will be small for the mathematician but great for the layman. A more problematic aspect of distance is the number of contexts in which an object, however familiar, exists. For two mathematicians, mathematics is a comparatively circumscribed object, provided that they have the same specialty. If, on the other hand, their discussion is about democracy, they are confronted with an object that can be considered in a variety of contexts—political, historical, moral, religious, and others. In these examples, distance suggests the number of different subcodes that the speakers will have to use in order to communicate about a given object. Because the mathematical repertory is not as accessible to the layman as to the mathematician, the two speakers must communicate in a roundabout way, via repertories that are more accessible to the nonmathematician. In the discussion of democracy the object itself demands the successive use of multiple subcodes. The more numerous the various repertories—different regions, Lewin (1938) would have said—needed to communicate, the greater the distance. Although distance can have physical or social aspects that can determine verbal behavior, as was shown by Wiener and Mehrabian

(1965) and by Mehrabian (1965), on the psychological plane, distance depends on the perceptions and attitudes of the subject.

From the foregoing definitions of the dimensions pressure and distance in a system of communication, the following hypotheses about their effect on the properties of language can be made.

(*a*) Inference pressure, which acts when it is necessary to choose a common code and to fashion the messages according to it, causes increased lexical redundancy.

(*b*) The pressure to reduce divergences of opinion or to prevent the development of these divergences brings about a decrease in the quantity of verbal emission. There is less incentive to communicate in such cases (Festinger, 1950; Schachter, 1951).

(*c*) The greater the subject's distance from a referent, the greater the number of repertories he tends to use; conversely, there is less lexical redundancy when the referent is remote.

(*d*) The greater a subject's distance from a referent, the greater his volume of verbal emission will be, because he must use a greater number of subcodes to communicate effectively.

These hypotheses disclose that pressure and distance have inverse effects on lexical variations in speech. Pressure tends to decrease, whereas distance tends to increase, the volume and diversity of vocabulary.

3. Inference Pressure and External Pressure: Experimental Results

To demonstrate the action of inference pressure on linguistic behavior, we devised three simple experimental situations. In each, five pairs of subjects were asked to discuss the influence of movies on juvenile delinquency.

Subjects in the first condition were simply asked to discuss the proposed theme; no time limit was indicated at the outset, and the discussion was stopped after twenty minutes. This situation provided a comparison for the two other conditions and was designed to create a simple relation between partners.

Subjects in the second situation were asked to reach some conclusion. After fifteen minutes, the experimenters warned the participants, in a neutral tone, that they had only five minutes left, thereby reinforcing the inference pressure. Communication in this case no longer had a simple function of exchange; its aim was the elaboration of a common point of view.

The third experimental situation was designed to isolate the possible effects of a purely external pressure, time. The allotted time (fifteen minutes) was announced at the outset, and every five minutes the subjects were reminded of the amount of time left.

The dialogues were tape-recorded to permit linguistic analysis and assessment of the dependent variables as follows:

(*a*) The mean volume of emission per minute was obtained by counting the total number of words the subjects used in their discussions and dividing this number by the length of the discussion.

(*b*) The degree of repetition of words, or lexical redundance, is difficult to calculate, for despite numerous attempts (Carroll, 1938; Chotlos, 1944; Harnack, 1953; Herdan, 1956, 1960; Becker *et al.*, 1961; Somers, 1961), no satisfactory means of measurement have been worked out yet. I have chosen two indices to describe lexical variation, one—the type/token ratio—because it sometimes allows the establishment of the significance of the obtained differences, and the other—the informational temperature—because it is theoretically more satisfying, although it does not permit significance tests.

The type/token ratio has been widely used; it is calculated by relating the different words used (type) to the total number of words emitted (token). The informational temperature is a method of measurement proposed by Mandelbrot (1954), who took up the study of Zipf's law (Zipf, 1949) concerning the relation between frequency and rank of words in a text and gave it rigorous formulation. He showed that it is possible to evaluate the quantity of information emitted in the course of a verbal interaction. If a word or group of words is repeated n times, the rate of information yielded in an interval of time decreases as the binary logarithm of n number of repetitions. Mandelbrot evaluated the redundance of a message as representing a "cost" to the encoder and a quantity of information for the decoder. The informational temperature, or cost, for the emitter, for example, decreases when the redundance of the verbal transactions increases.

(*c*) The third measure was the input of new words during the exchange between speakers; it is related to lexical redundance since it represents the number of new words the speakers introduce at different moments to attain the purpose of their communication.

What results might be expected from each of the three experimental arrangements just described? The first, or control, group could be expected to display considerable verbal emission, a comparatively varied vocabulary, and an increasing input of new words, since the subjects were invited to express their opinions without being restrained by the necessity of establishing a common code or following a predetermined line of discussion.

In the third situation, where external pressure was imposed, the partners were given the impression of not having enough time. They did not become involved in a real conversation; all their exchanges were modified by their preoccupation with the experimenter's impending order to stop. Each person tried to say something, responding to his partner only in order to cope with the situation. We would, therefore, expect retarded verbal emission and a smaller number of encoded words than in the other groups. On the other hand, since the verbal transactions have no particular goal, the lexical variety should be greater. The input of new words during any portion of the discussion period is not likely to vary either one way or the other (see Table II).

In contrast to both the control and external pressure conditions, the second, or inference pressure, condition necessitated some verbal planning. Subjects who are told to come to a conclusion can be expected to reduce their field of exploration, curtail the possible divergences from their topic, and organize their discussion so as to reach the assigned goal. We can therefore assume that the volume of verbal emission would be less than that in the control condition. There should be less diversity of vocabulary than in the first two situations, and lexical redundance should therefore increase. The input of new words (that is, words not used before) should tend to diminish steadily during the discussion.

TABLE I

LEXICAL VOLUME AND REDUNDANCE OF SPEECH IN DIFFERENT PRESSURE CONDITIONS
(COMPARISON BETWEEN CONDITIONS)

| | | Indices of redundance | |
	Lexical volume	Informational temperature[a]	Ratio[b]
Control	1.060	.80	.0871
Inference pressure	.881	.72	.0566
External pressure (time)	.595	.86	.1151

[a]No significance test is as yet available for the informational temperature index of Mandelbrot.

[b]Ratio of number of specific words to lexical volume. Difference in volume of vocabulary and specific words is significant at $p = .001$.

These predictions have generally been verified. The left-hand column of Table I shows that the mean volume of verbal emission per minute decreases from the control condition to the inference pressure condition to the external pressure condition. Examination of the indices of the redundance of speech in Table I shows that there is an agreement between predictions and data. The rate of repetition of words is highest where inference pressure intervenes and lowest where external pressure acts to create a sort of verbal scatter.

The expected differences in the input of new words during the discussion are also evident (Table II). By dividing the total time that two subjects

TABLE II

FREQUENCY OF SPECIFIC WORDS DURING EACH THIRD OF THE TOTAL CONVERSATION TIME[a]

	1st	2nd	3rd	Total
Control	.0745	.0837	.1011	.0871
Inference pressure	.0663	.0566	.0459	.0566
External pressure	.1194	.1120	.1144	.1151

[a] A specific word appears in only one of the thirds. This index reflects, therefore, the quantity of new words that appear while the subjects speak. As in the case of informational temperature, the greater the index, the smaller the redundance of speech.

All values shown differ significantly at the level of $p = .001$; reading horizontally (intrasituation) except for external pressure: and reading vertically (intersituation) except for the last third when comparing control with external pressure condition.

spent conversing into three equal periods the new words that appeared in each period of the dialogue were isolated. The number of new words increased in the control condition from the first to the third period. No variation is observable in the external pressure condition. On the other hand, in the inference pressure condition, when subjects were impelled to form a common code and to adapt their messages to it in the course of its establishment, the appearance of new words decreased steadily from the first to the third part of the conversation. The speakers tended increasingly to choose words from the stock of words already used.

The tendencies just examined correspond to the processes invoked by Simon (1955) to explain Zipf's law by a stochastic model. Simon affirms that in the genesis of a text two processes are at play: *association*, which consists in drawing words from previously emitted sequences, and *imitation*, characterized by the borrowing of words from sources other than those already explored. As indicated by the data, the first process certainly contributes to making the vocabulary more repetitive, the second to diversifying it. The data show that, where inference pressure is stronger, the words introduced into the discussion by association with previous words are more numerous than those introduced by borrowing from new subcodes.

The results just presented can be compared with those of Bernstein (1962), Lawton (1963), and Robinson (1956), who found that working-class children use a restricted code, a relatively poor, repetitive vocabulary, to express themselves verbally, whereas middle-class children use an elaborate code, more varied and richer in lexical units. These codes exist on a continuum and represent the dominance of a system of communication in a specific social environment, a particular mode of adaptation to that environment. The difference between these two kinds of codes, illustrated by collective linguistic behavior, corresponds to a greater normative pressure in the case of the restricted code than in the case of the elaborate one. This sociological description grasps what the psychosociological analysis of verbal interactions isolates for experimental verification.

4.   The Referent and the Elaboration of the Corresponding Vocabulary

Let us now examine experiments designed to investigate the effects of the second dimension, distance, on the organization of messages. This dimension implies that if a referent—object or event—is "close," it will be evoked with the help of a less extended, more repetitive vocabulary. The more "distant" an object is, the greater the subject's recourse to multiple sources of information and expression in order to concretize it, to communicate about it. When distance increases, vocabulary diversifies, the informational temperature and the volume of verbal emission increase. This phenomenon has its equivalent on the cognitive plane. Sherif (1961) has demonstrated that the number of categories a subject uses in classifying objects increases as his ego involvement decreases.

As was indicated earlier, variation in distance can result from (a) the perceived divergence between subject and referent, or the diverse contexts in which a referent may exist, requiring the use of a corresponding number of linguistic repertories, or both these factors; and (b) the context of the relationship in which a referent is embedded. A subject's impression of his partner contributes to the structure of the referent's framework and to the stressing of one or another of its facets. The same object can be placed at a distance, or imagined in an entirely new manner, or may become another object, depending on the listener. The mathematics of which one mathematician speaks to another probably differs from that which the same mathematician would present to a layman.

The linguistic consequences are the same whatever the cause of variation in the distance. The following observations demonstrate these consequences.

In the first study, five subjects, all professional psychologists, were asked to speak successively on the following themes: the interview; the Algerian war; the P.T.T. (French postal, telegraph, and telephone system). Ten minutes were allotted for each topic. A second study employed three interviews in the course of a survey of the automobile market. Each subject was invited to talk about his car. As in a role-playing situation, the subject was told to imagine first that his interlocutor was a *friend*, then that he was a *specialist*. For the sake of convenience, the subjects played the first role longer than the second, thirty minutes as against eighteen.

What predictions can we make? For professional psychologists the elaboration of a talk on interviewing techniques implies recourse to a comparatively unified language and repertory. The Algerian war, at the time of the study, evoked various languages and repertories—political, moral, religious, and more. The French postal system, known for the variety of its activities and services, exists in the most varied contexts, so that a subject asked to speak about this institution would have to use frames of reference and description that are quite remote from one another. Hence, lexical redundance would be highest for the interview theme and lowest for the P.T.T. theme. Conversely, there should be a regular increase in verbal emission from the first to the third theme. The recourse to new words proper to each theme should follow a parallel development, corresponding to the need for multiple repertories. Using the same variables as in the experiments on pressure, the results (Table III) confirm all these predictions about the effect of distance. Despite a tendency in the expected direction, however, the difference in volume of emission is significant only between the first and the third theme. We did not find any differences between individuals in linguistic behavior. We can add that, in another experiment in which the subjects—following the same scheme—had to give their opinions in writing, analogous results were obtained.

TABLE III

LEXICAL VOLUME AND REDUNDANCE AT THREE LEVELS OF DISTANCE

		Indices of redundance	
Theme[a]	Lexical volume[b] (avg./min.)	Informational temperature	Ratio[c]
1	701	.88	.0877
2	711	.92	.1046
3	777	.98	.1139

[a] The first theme involved the smallest distance, the third the greatest distance.

[b] Differences in volume between the first and third themes are significant at the level of $p = .001$.

[c] Ratio of number of specific words to lexical volume. Differences in specific words between each of the themes are significant at the level of $p = .001$.

The parameters relevant to the second study are obvious. Each individual who spoke to a friend did so in the perspective of an ordinary conversation. When he had to speak to a specialist, however, special effort was needed, in order to describe the car from a more technical angle. In the latter situation, subjects referred to less familiar parts of the automobile, especially those relating to the motor, its construction, and its efficiency. The tendencies manifested ought to be analogous to those noted previously: (a) the degree of redundance should decrease with distance; or to put it another way, when discussing one's car with a specialist, one would use the same lexical terms less often; (b) volume of verbal emission would increase in the same direction; (c) more technical words would be used when addressing

TABLE IV
LEXICAL VOLUME AND REDUNDANCE ACCORDING TO DISTANCE

Listener	Lexical volume	Indices of redundance		
		Informational temperature	No. of technical words	Ratio[a]
Friend	9.229	.91	551	.060
Specialist	5.592	.95	960	.173

[a] Ratio of number of technical words to lexical volume.

a specialist than when addressing a friend. As can be seen in Table IV, the data satisfactorily confirm (a) and (c).

No real increase in verbal emission was noted. This could be due to inhibitions, caused by even an imaginary new situation. All in all, however, the general pattern of results supports the hypotheses presented.

5. More Experimental Evidence Concerning the Effects of Distance and of Pressure to Communicate

The relation between *distance to the object, or referent*, and *inference pressure between speaker and listener* has been studied implicitly by Maclay and Newman (1960), Leavitt and Mueller (1951), and Rosenberg and Cohen (1964). But Krauss and Weinheimer, in a series of three experiments, examined this relation most systematically. The way they defined and gathered their linguistic material differs from that described earlier, but their results parallel those already presented and lend themselves to the same interpretation. In their first experiment, Krauss and Weinheimer (1964) varied the distance to the object or referent. Their subjects had to match pairs of cards, that is, to identify the figures that were similar. There were six ambiguous figures on each card. Three of the six figures (the *discriminating figures*) appeared in permuted position and the other three (*redundant figures*) occupied the same position in each subject's set of cards. In order to match the pairs of cards, the subjects had to communicate, describing the cards to permit their identification. This operation was repeated several times according to the degree of probability of appearance of the figures in a set. The general hypothesis was that the ambiguous figures, which would be mentioned infrequently, required the use of reference phrases with a long mean length. The opposite presumably would be observed for the frequently mentioned figures. Repetition would be expressed in a shortening of the reference phrases. The obtained results are in accord with this reasoning. The figures, or referents, that are most distant from the speaker force him to use a greater number of qualifiers, a more varied vocabulary, in order to accomplish his task, because of the unfamiliar character of the figures on one hand, and the necessity of providing spatial coordinates in view of their permutation on the other. The effect of the repetition discloses another aspect of the same process. A selection operates among the terms that designate the referent as it takes a more and more precise place in the set. From then on, the subject can dispense with mentioning certain qualifiers and can use a smaller number of repertories. From the description that permits the subjects to grasp the referent as a variation of a common object (such as, "a boomerang with a notch in the blade") to the designation that individualizes this referent in a more general class (such as "boomerang"), the recourse to a shortened version of the initial reference phrase is obvious.

Though the predicted trends are verified, this experiment raises a few questions. To be sure, with the repetition of the figures, some sort of familiarization occurs and reference phrases become shorter. Is this, however, only the result of repetition, as the current interpretation has it? Why do reference phrases become shorter? Does the object cease being ambiguous in the subjects' eyes after being seen again and again, or are the subjects placed in a situation in which they have to create a code and, once this code has been created, can they then communicate via shorter messages?

Another experiment by the same authors (1965a) dealt with the interaction of speaker and listener and the role of feedback in facilitating recognition of figures. This recognition depends on the establishment of a common code: a pressure is exerted in that direction. The reduction of the reference phrases result.

Here is the authors' description of their subjects' task:

> The subject, the speaker, was given a single 3 × 5 inch card containing six novel graphic designs. The other subject, the listener, was given six cards containing the same six designs with their positions permuted. On one of the listener's cards the position of the six figures was identical to that of the speaker's single card. The pair's task was to determine which card it was. Each pair of subjects performed the matching task a total of 16 times. The order of presentation was randomized for each pair. Over all, a total of 15 figures were used. Three of the 15 figures appeared in all 16 trials and it is the response to these figures which will be considered . . . .

The authors distinguished two kinds of feedback: (a) concurrent feedback, or the listener's feedback of the speaker's message as the latter is being delivered ("Huh? Okay."); and (b) confirmation feedback, or the listener's reaction, registered after the speaker's message has been completed, which indicates the effectiveness of the message. Subjects communicated either with or without concurrent feedback. After each message, the listener made a selection from among a set of referents. Following the sixteen choices, the subjects received confirmation on all the trials (100% C) or they received confirmation on half the trials and disconfirmation on the other half (50% C). The two variables are thus manipulated in a systematic manner.

The hypotheses were (a) that speakers will use shorter reference phrases when concurrent feedback is admitted; and (b) that speakers will use shorter reference phrases when confirmation is received than when he is told his selection is incorrect. Confirmation in this case reveals the efficacy of the phrases used to facilitate identification. The dependent variable is, of course, the length (in number of words) of the name given the three figures presented in each trial. The results were as expected: subjects used shorter reference phrases when communicating with concurrent feedback and receiving 100% confirmation. Reference phrases grew still shorter after several repetitions of the trials. In general, however, repetition affected each of the four conditions differently; the presence or absence of concurrent feedback, or the degree of confirmation, influenced encoding behavior more than repetition per se. We noted that fluctuations of vocabulary were related to both the remoteness of the referent and the pressure that develops as subjects try to establish, via feedback, a code with which to identify the figures. Contraction of phrases is not necessarily caused by a change in the distance of the pair from the referent. For verbal output to be modified, subjects need only assume (Starkweather, 1956)—as in our experiment, where the subjects addressed a friend—general similarity and be convinced, by the responses during (concurrent feedback) and after (confirmation feedback) emission, of the efficiency of their messages.

In the third experiment by Krauss and Weinheimer (1965b) distance was more specifically a consequence of the many varied contexts in which a referent could be grasped, the number of repertories essential for the transmission of information about it. The point of departure had been provided by a verified observation (Brown and Lenneberg, 1954; Glanzer and Clark, 1964; Lanz and Shtefflre, 1964) that the number of words used to encode an object is an index of its codability. Highly codable reference objects have short names, whereas the names of less codable referents are longer. This variance in length is determined in relation to all the referents from which a given object is to be distinguished. As Brown put it, a zebra in a herd of zebras is less codable than the same zebra in a herd of elephants. To identify the zebra among the elephants, the encoding individual need only have recourse to the classification of animal species. Several criteria must be used, however, to single out one animal from a homogeneous herd of zebras: such as, that it runs faster, is on the left, and so on. Krauss and Weinheimer sought to demonstrate that a referent's position among similar objects (low codability), or in contrasting surroundings (high codability) acted simultaneously with the feedback to determine the length of reference phrases.

They posited that reference phrases are longer when the referent is located among several similar referents and when the speaker and listener do not interact.

Twenty-four Munsell color chips, having the same notation as those used by Brown and Lenneberg (1964), and each mounted on a white card, were used as referents. The twenty-four chips, which represented the referent array, were placed next to one another in a cardboard frame. In the similar (low codability) situation the four referent colors were adjacent in the hue order series. In the dissimilar (high codability) condition, the four colors were six places apart. Each subject or subject-pair saw all twenty-four colors twice, once in a similar array, once in dissimilar array. The subjects were to describe the colors either in a monologue or with a partner. The effects of the two variables were statistically significant. Reference phrases used in describing the similar referent array and in the monologue were generally longer. The interaction of the two series of conditions was also important; there was greater differentiation between similar and dissimilar array when the subject interacted with another than when he had no partner. In fact, when the objective was identification of a color in a dissimilar array by a pair of subjects, it was not so much a question of an interaction of variables as of a summation of the effects of greater pressure and smaller distance compared to all the other situations.

Results of this experiment agree with those of the experiments described earlier and with my theory about the relation of the dimensions of the system of communication to the degree of emission and the diversity of the language produced by partners in a sequence of verbal transactions. By introducing more rigorous instructions and imposing more uniform experimental arrangements, it would probably be possible to sort out more definite tendencies. More adequate means of measuring the dimensions, distance and pressure are also needed.

C. GRAMMATICAL CODES AND SPEAKING SITUATIONS

1. The Distribution of the Parts of Speech

Language redundance depends on pressure and on distance, but these dimensions seem to have no effect on the distribution of parts of speech in verbal discourse. Vocabulary variation, according to the hypothesis we formulated at the outset, has no direct, foreseeable relation to syntactic organization. Experimental findings in this area are conclusive. The experiments described earlier showed that the results we sought showed up regularly in measurements of word volume and redundance. Emission frequency in relation to verbal categories—such as nouns, verbs, and adjectives—remained almost identical under all described conditions

TABLE V

DISTRIBUTION OF PARTS OF SPEECH IN RELATION TO PRESSURE AND DISTANCE

	Nouns	Verbs	Adjectives	Adverbs	Personal pronouns	Functional words *et al.*
Social pressure						
Control condition	15	18	6	12	13	37
Inference pressure	14	17	7	12	14	35
External pressure	14	17	7	14	16	32
Distance						
Interview	14	18	7	13	14	34
Algerian War	14	17	8	12	15	34
P.T.T.	15	18	8	13	12	34
Speaking to a:						
Friend	15	17	8	12	13	35
Specialist	16	18	7	13	12	34

(Table V). The counterproof exists, I believe, in another series of experiments, still in progress and only mentioned here, that concern the relation between cognitive style and linguistic style. In these experiments subjects are shown three pictures and are asked to (*a*) describe the contents of the pictures, (*b*) make up a story using the elements discerned in them, and (*c*) tell the story, using dialogue and indicating action spots. The distribution of parts of speech (Table VI) varies from one "style" to another; lexical redundance remains relatively unchanged. Thus the lexical and syntactic aspects of language seem to be markedly autonomous. The study by Back

TABLE VI

DISTRIBUTION OF PARTS OF SPEECH IN RELATION TO COGNITIVE STYLE

	Nouns (%)	Verbs (%)	Adjectives (%)	Adverbs (%)	Personal pronouns (%)	Functional words (%)	Informational temperature
Description	17	16	8	14	16	29	.96
Story	15	18	7	12	18	30	.96
Novel	11	23	6	13	23	24	.97

(1961) cited earlier provides additional confirmation of this autonomy. The properties of speech that is meant to change an attitude or to instigate an action differ significantly, especially in clause variation, but not in the distribution of grammatical categories. Grammatical modification is noted, however, when subjects are induced to use a channel of communication that is either more, or less formal. In the former case, messages are richer in nominative clauses; in the latter, there are fewer nominative clauses. Thus, the static frequency of occurrence of grammatical categories observed in our experiments is not surprising, since our subjects have always communicated orally, face to face.

2. Specific Effects of Channels of Communication

A message presupposes a code; transmitting it entails problems relating to the channel of communication. Striving to convince, causing to act, and instructing all imply considerable attention to the role a partner plays and to the result of interaction with a partner. Language resumes the characteristics of a raw material when a speaker wants to do more than just convince or instruct; that is, when he adapts his speech to certain technical means, such as writing or the telephone, or to circumstances, like an examination or a legal debate, that involve strict ritual. The system of signals takes on a certain autonomy and demands specific structuring; the use of language is no longer relatively automatic, in particular when it is necessary to recode, translate, or pass from one channel of communication to another. Distribution of parts of speech and syntactic organization are determined by these channels.

3. Four Speaking Situations

In this section I propose to establish certain connections between the grammatical elements of language and the channels of communication. To do this, I have chosen a class of channels of communication that have a quasi-physical aspect. They are inherent in the organization of every society. Hymes (1962, 1964) called attention to the importance of these "speaking situations" for the comprehension of linguistic models to which the members of a community have recourse. People in a specific culture are aware of the significance of a certain setting. In a conference room, in church, at a writing-table, emitters and receivers submit to common conditions and manifest known and expected patterns of verbal, gesticulatory, and written behavior. In each of these cases, spatial order, social relations, and channels of communication are closely linked (Ervin-Tripp, 1964). Conversely, the establishment of defined social relations is always accompanied by a specific spatial orientation; accordingly, space becomes something different from a mere receptacle or territory where several organisms are situated. Some ingenious experiments have confirmed these observations. Steinzor (1950) ascertained that, in a group discussion, the maximal number of emissions are directed to the person opposite. Making use of the analysis of these phenomena. Hearn (1957), Sommer (1959, 1961), and Strodtbeck and Hook (1961) verified that the arrangement of individuals in space, their status, and their communications are unquestionably related, so that individuals seated at the extremities of a rectangular table have a greater chance of being elected leaders, and so on. We will not dwell on these data here.

The preceding findings corroborate the idea that the position of an individual in an environment determines his access to privileged channels of communication, and that all individuals concerned strive to keep them functioning. Psychotherapeutic techniques indicate preferences for specific speaking situations, such as the therapist-patient relation and the monitor-group relation, in order to obtain necessary psychological material. Cultures are attracted or repelled by certain channels—Crozier (1964) described the fear of face-to-face situations in French culture—and social or religious organizations develop certain channels by which they are ultimately identified (for instance, the Roman Catholic Church by the confessional).

We selected a series of speaking situations involving the problem of message transmission that were likely to evoke language closely resembling that which is used in the two basic forms of linguistic behavior in our civilization, writing and oral exchange (Jousse, 1925; Uldall, 1944). We had already determined the qualities of oral and written language in a previous experiment (Moscovici and Humbert, 1960a). Written language is generally more elaborate, less redundant, syntactically better structured, and uses more nominative clauses than common oral speech, which is generally more redundant, less elaborate, less well organized syntactically and employs more verbs. Rate of linguistic emission is smaller when writing. Four explanations of these differences have been offered: (1) More complex neuromuscular processes and greater conscious effort are required for writing than for speaking (Horowitz and Newman, 1964). (2) Verbal messages presuppose the presence of another person, whereas written messages address an absent person (Vigotsky, 1962), so that the entire range of gesticulatory and mimetic signals that can be used in speaking are inapplicable to written communication. Moreover, all such nonlinguistic signals as interjections and exclamations are replaced by the characteristics of formal syntax (Vendryes, 1950). (3) Speaking is a frequent, familiar, quite automatic process and, whereas writing is a rarely exercised mode of expression, it implies conscious, concentrated adaptation to a communication channel that is only occasionally used (Vigotsky, 1962; Fraisse and Breyton, 1959; Horowitz and Newman, 1964). (4) Finally, each instance of both oral and written communication inheres in a specific social situation that largely determines the emitters' and receivers' behavior (Moscovici and Humbert, 1960a). The norms of a particular situation are extended to the speech. When, for example, in certain circumstances, we speak the way we write, we thereby conform to a societal norm that influences verbal emission.

The first of the foregoing explanations can be considered rather unlikely.

Horowitz and Berkowitz (1964) were unable to confirm it. They found the expected differences between written and oral messages, but the principal characteristics of written language differed only slightly whether subjects wrote by hand, or a stenotype machine, or with a typewriter. No correlation could be made between muscular effort and the properties of speech. To test the three remaining explanations and to discover the grammatical variations that characterize both written and spoken language, I experimented with four speaking situations, arranged and evaluated as follows (Moscovici and Plon, 1966).

The subjects, students in the last grades of a Parisian *lycée*, volunteered to take part in the experiments. They were asked to discuss the movies for a survey. We were careful not to choose as partners subjects who were friends. Each discussion between partners lasted 20 minutes, but subjects were not told the allotted time beforehand. The experimental situations differed from one another only with regard to the position of the subjects.

   a. Face-to-face (FF). The two subjects in this, the control group, were seated opposite and facing each other; invited by the experimenter to exchange opinions on the proposed topic, they used this familiar communication channel quite spontaneously. (Four pairs of subjects were used in all.)

   b. Back-to-back (BB). Indicating that the subjects should seat themselves with their backs to each other, the investigator proposed the topic, as he had to the control group. Each subject was prevented, by his position, from observing and reacting to nonlinguistic signals emitted by the other. A whole segment of habitual elements in verbal interaction was eliminated, as Hockett (1961, p. 59) noted: "In the normal face-to-face situation of speech communication, there is a good deal of interchange of information which is not carried by the speech signals at all, but by the continuous train of socially conditioned bodily movements and gestures which both accompanies speech and goes on during silence." The subjects had to rely solely on linguistic means in order to communicate. Furthermore, their unusual and unfamiliar conversational posture required that they establish an entirely new channel of communication. Again, four pairs of subjects were used.

   c. Side-by-side (SS). The two subjects were seated side by side as in their *lycée* classrooms. Before telling them the topic of their discussion, however, the experimenter reminded them that in a classroom a student is not supposed to turn toward his neighbor. As in the first two situations, the subject could use (or perceive) gestures and facial expressions only with difficulty. On the other hand, the situation itself was familiar. The participants were only reminded not to deviate from the face-forward rule that held in the classroom situation. The linguistic tendencies observed in the second (BB) experiment should have been yet more pronounced in these conditions because of the formalized communication suggested by the position of the participants. Five pairs of subjects were used.

d. Screen (Sc). Before the subjects entered the experiment room, a screen was installed. A chair was placed on each side of the screen. The chairs, placed face to face and turned toward each other visibly suggested an arrangement suitable for face-to-face conversations. The students were permitted to choose the side of the screen on which they preferred to sit. When they were seated, the experimenter told them their topic. This fourth arrangement reproduced the first situation, that of the customary face-to-face conversation, except for a modification that made it comparable to the back-to-back condition, the elimination of any possibility of exchanging information by nonlinguistic means. Five pairs of subjects were used.

TABLE VII

PROPORTIONS OF NOUNS, VERBS, AND FUNCTIONAL WORDS IN FOUR SPEAKING SITUATIONS [a]

	Proportions			Comparison with FF Results		
	Functional words	Nouns	Verbs	Functional words	Nouns	Verbs
Face-to-face	.249	.125	.215	—	—	—
Screen	.237	.124	.215	−.012	−.001	.000
Side-by-side	.278	.145	.189	+.029	+.020	−.026
Back-to-back	.286	.137	.201	+.037	+.012	−.016

[a]The observed differences between the FF and SS groups and between the FF and BB groups are significant.

We had hypothesized, concerning these experiments, that: (*a*) the transition from one communication channel to another and the concomitant need to devise a language appropriate to the new channel cause grammatical variations. (*b*) An unfamiliar channel of communication demands on the part of the speakers sustained attention to the organization of the speech, the consistency of their statements, and the checking of the effect of what has been said. In such conditions, spoken language tends to become more like written language. We therefore expected a greater proportion of nouns and connectives and fewer verbs in the back-to-back condition as compared with the face-to-face situation. (*c*) In an unfamiliar or a formalized communication channel, subjects tend to translate their speech into a language that resembles written language. Thus we expected linguistic behavior in back-to-back and side-by-side situations to be similar. (*d*) The elimination of purely gesticulative or mimic elements from a communication channel is not enough to cause modification of syntactic organization. In other words, the grammatical differences between two channels or languages—written and spoken, for instance—*are not due to the conditions of physical stimulation*, but to the relation these channels create between sender and receiver. This relationship determines the field, or structural ensemble, characteristic of each speaking situation, and this characteristic field dictates the choice between linguistic alternatives.

These hypotheses were confirmed by our results (see Table VII). We found the expected syntactic differences between the back-to-back and side-by-side conditions, on the one hand, and the face-to-face arrangement on the other. No difference was observed between the face-to-face arrangement and that where the screen was used. On the whole, verbal output of the back-to-back and side-by-side participants resembled written language, whereas language emitted in the face-to-face and screen discussions was generally like spoken language. The specificity of the two major kinds of linguistic behavior, speaking and writing, results from the emitter's familiarity with the setting in which the message is produced and from the psycho-sociological connotations of that setting (see the third and fourth explanations listed earlier). Purely physical factors that affect the visibility of non-linguistic stimuli are not the only important ones. As a whole, our hypotheses were substantiated.

4. Discussion

These results suggest two questions that warrant consideration. The first concerns the elimination of visual means of communication, as effected in the back-to-back and screen conditions. We find that linguistic behavior manifested by the face-to-face controls was modified in the back-to-back situation but *not* when the screen was used. At first glance this observation seems in accord with the view currently accepted by some, that nonlinguistic signals play a dominant role in communication (Davitz, 1964), acting as substitutes for linguistic signs. At the close of an experiment, Rosenberg and Langer (1965, p. 596) concluded: "They [the findings] permit the conclusion that postural gestures may function as an independent source of communication. Consequently, it reinforces the theoretical notion that such expressions may be used by adults in conjunction with or as a substitute for verbal-linguistic communication." In the screen experiment, however, suppression of nonlinguistic signals had no marked effect; participants conversed as though gestures, body movement, and facial expressions did not normally play a major role in communication or serve as cues for transmitting information. Our own two experiments tended to confirm this view. The subject obliged to talk with someone side-by-side or back-to-back acted as if this positioning implied that something was forbidden: "Of all possible available repertoires, you may not (or cannot) use the nonlinguistic one." Therefore, he neither gesticulates, moves about, nor accompanies his words with facial or tonal variations. All his efforts seem concentrated on producing a "text" or awaiting another, that is, on a meaningful sequence of words and the response they evoke. Imposing a physical obstacle such as a screen on the general setting of a face-to-face conversation does not imply that subjects must avoid, or adopt, a particular linguistic or nonlinguistic repertory, nor does it eliminate the possibility of using gestures or combining spoken language with the vocal and expressive devices of mimicry. Though aware that he cannot be seen, the subject speaks and acts as though this were unimportant because nothing in the situation tells him that he should change languages. Apparently most nonlinguistic signals normally used in conversation function as emphases, props, and accompaniments to verbal discourse, but are not consciously used as communication signals. In short, postural and gesticulative elements are a unit that along with verbal elements, a speaker requires more to facilitate his own encoding activity than to transmit a specific fact to someone else. The importance of this coordination at the level of habits and synkineses is often underestimated.

Miller (1963), among others, gave support to this interpretation. He studied the phenomenon of verbal satiation, that is, the loss of meaning a word undergoes when an individual repeats it rapidly several times in sequence or looks at it fixedly for a long period of time. This phenomenon prompted the question: does the movement associated with a word affect the process of satiation? During a period of pretraining, Miller had his subjects repeat a word in order to determine the level of satiation (that is, the moment at which the word lost meaning for them). In addition, they had to fit an action to the word pronounced by the experimenter, in time with the rhythm of a metronome. The words chosen were "push," "pull," "raise," and "lower"; they had to be accompanied by appropriate action in varying combinations. For "pull" and "push," the movements consisted of pulling and pushing a drawer. For "raise" and "lower," the object was a window. After this preliminary training, subjects had to repeat the word and perform the action simultaneously, very rapidly, not stopping until the word had lost its meaning. Four possibilities were used: (a) concordance: word and action corresponded; (b) discordance: word and action were opposed; (c) difference: word and action were different (such as "push" combined with the action of raising); (d) no action. Words accompanied by an action (the effect was most pronounced for the word "push") retained their meaning longest, regardless of whether the action was concordant, discordant, or different. One may conclude that physical movements help to retain the meaning of a word and reinforce the general activity of the speaker.

Results of the back-to-back and screen experiments are not contradictory. Contrary to certain opinions, and despite their function as indicators of perception, signals that convey emotion or nonverbal meaning have no decisive part in the transmission of information. Their considerable expressive value does not justify our bestowing on them the status of autonomous genuine "languages." The tendency to overrate the affective, the ineffable, and various physical agglomerates that qualify as stimuli has resulted in a downgrading of speech that is structured, clear, and systematically organized to the same level as anything that resembles it or occasionally produces the same results. This explains the equating of verbal and nonverbal communication, and the consideration given the possibility that the latter can be entirely substituted for the former.

The second difficulty stems from the possibility of interpreting our results in another way. One can say that a person is encouraged to use a particular language in a particular situation and that he chooses to do so when the circumstances arise. In a drawing-room, or classroom, on a podium, or when writing, society teaches that a particular type of speech and a certain repertory are appropriate. From this viewpoint our experiments do not demonstrate an essential link between a communication channel and the linguistic behavior produced with reference to it, but rather that associations induced by social conventions force us to resort to certain previously acquired verbal habits. If this is so, our experiments established only a truism, not a relation between the characteristics of a message and the setting in which it is conveyed. In fact, however, the explanation that language is chosen to fit a particular situation applies only to side-by-side conditions where the subjects, though not specifically asked to do so, probably spoke as if they were in school. This explanation cannot be extended to fit back-to-back test conditions, for which no particular previously learned language could be considered most apt; the objective requirements of the act of communicating are therefore necessarily related to the subjects' verbal output in such a situation. The choice of a familiar repertory and the creation of one suitable for a given speaking situation can result in similar linguistic behavior. The genesis of certain types of speech, not merely the capacity to use them once they have been learned was the object of our research.

In general, our experiments confirmed a correlation between channels of communication and the grammatical characteristics of spoken messages. Although relations between individuals were not the same in every case, we found the object of the discussion could be grasped in a more general way in back-to-back and side-by-side conditions than in face-to-face or screen situations. The mental effort of composition and the intervals necessary for preparation and choice of linguistic material (Goldman-Eisler, 1961; Kasl and Mahl, 1965; Maclay and Osgood, 1959) differed in the two (back-to-back and side-by-side versus face-to-face and screen) speaking situations—a fact reflected by the output volume and the lexical redundance.

The amount of verbal repetition and output volume were not as great in back-to-back and side-by-side dialogues as during face-to-face and screen communications, a finding that paralleled the observed tendency to use written language in the former and spoken language in the latter situations (Moscovici and Humbert, 1960a). Further investigation of the theory of communication channels and more sophisticated experimental techniques will permit better isolation of the desired effects.

III. Some Open Questions

The concepts and experiments presented in the preceding sections constitute an attempted psychosociological study of the relations between communication and language. I emphasized earlier that we were not, in the formulation of hypotheses, to go beyond a rather general level, in view of the scarcity of the accumulated knowledge. Any progress in this area raises some inevitable questions about the legitimacy of the undertaking, however; they relate to (1) the definition of the field of psycholinguistics, and (2) the role accorded to verbal conditioning.

1. Psycholinguistics describes itself as "concerned in the broadest sense with relations between messages and the characteristics of human individuals who select and interpret them" (Osgood and Sebeok, 1965, p. 4). In reality, it is a junction of *individual* psychology and certain sectors of linguistics. It focuses on the learning, competence, and performance of an individual when acquiring or using the elements of language. The acquisition and use of language originate in its production by individuals, from childhood, and are refined by learning, applying, and varying the application of the rules, and by playing with words. This continuous creation of speech takes place in the presence of, or in cooperation with, others. Competence, performance, and everything involved in encoding or decoding a message, reflects individual characteristics as well as interindividual ties.

The experiment of Krauss and Weinheimer (1965b) on color codability was significant in this regard. It demonstrated that the interaction of speaker and listener converges with their abilities to encode or decode an item of information coming from the referent. No less dramatically significant was the case studied by Luria and Yudovich (1959) of twins whose linguistic capacities developed only after they were separated and thus obliged to communicate with others. In these circumstances, the competence and performance of each twin disclosed their intersubjective situation more markedly than characteristics generally inherent in individuals.

Equally uncertain, theoretically (Moscovici and Ackermann, 1961), is the nature of the linguistic unit used in most studies. This unit is either a word, syllable, or sign dissociated from the system to which it belongs. Thus isolated, does it retain the specific properties of language? Recently, under the impetus of Chomsky (1964), the syntactic organization of language structure has been given more consideration (Ervin-Tripp and Slobin, 1966). Whether it is a sign or a system of signs, language can be effectively studied only insofar as it exists in a social context, which is also that of its extra-linguistic determinants. Outside this context, the individual who perceives or learns does not perceive or learn what is specific to language. We quote de Saussure (1955, p. 34), not for his authority but mostly for the truth he formulates, a truth that apparently has not yet been assimilated by the students of language: "There is, first of all, the superficial conception of the public at large: it sees only a nomenclature in language. . . . Then there is the point of view of the psychologist, who studies the mechanism of the sign in the individual: it is the easiest method, but it does not lead beyond individual execution, and does not reach the sign, which is social by nature. . . . "

Foregoing the easy method, the concrete activity of individuals generating codes (Brown and Ford, 1961) and representations (Brown, 1958; Miller, 1964) must be not the goal, but the point of departure for a study of the properties of language and of verbal behavior. Extralinguistic circumstances, such as motivations and the accompanying social relationships, cannot be neglected. They help us determine the meaning and the place that we must accord to the usage and to the acquisition of the verbal capacities of each individual. I subscribe, therefore, to Rommetweit's conclusion (1966, p. 15): "Empirical psychological evidence of relevance can hardly be established until social psychologists invade the area of psycholinguistic research." The latter cannot be conceived without a redefinition of the program and attitudes that constitute the foundation of this research.

2. The Skinnerian model of conditioning (Skinner, 1957) inspired a whole series of experiments examining verbal behavior (Verplanck, 1955; Salzinger, 1959) based on a familiar paradigm: if an experimenter said "Hm" every time a subject emitted a plural noun, emission of plural nouns automatically increased. If a physical stimulus was substituted for the verbal one, the effect was the same. Bachrach et al. (1961) and Kanfer et al. (1963) obtained analogous results in studies of interaction involving two or three subjects. A closer look at findings in this area indicates that they are ambiguous: in the circumstances, interpersonal relations or the conditions of communication could have been the causative factors just as easily as conditioning. Thus, Sipolski (1960) hypothesized that the interpersonal relation of experimenter and subject determined verbal learning, so that an experimenter could more thoroughly influence and condition a group that found him attractive than one that did not. He further posited that the effect of influence, or reinforcement, was greater when experimenter and subjects were "compatible" (similar). He devised an everyday situation in which his subjects' verbal behavior was reinforced. One experiment involved

two groups, one more, the other less, attracted by the experimenter. A second experiment centered on an experimenter who was presented to a first group as "more like," and to a second as "less like," themselves. Results corroborated the hypotheses; groups on which the experimenter had a psychological hold were sensitive to verbal reinforcement. Reece and Whitman (1962) also demonstrated the effect of an experimenter's attitude on the number of reinforced plural words emitted by subjects. Cairns and Lewis (1962) showed the importance of personality traits. They demonstrated that psychologically dependent persons placed in a situation where outside approbation seemed important would be conditioned more than less dependent individuals. They thus confirmed that in this case verbal learning is a function of the personality trait dependency, and that verbal response is meant to secure social approval. Farber (1963) demonstrated this interpretation more directly. His subjects had to construct sentences using the pronouns I, you, he, or they, with a different verb in each case. Every time a subject used the pronoun you, the experimenter said "Good"; at other times, he said nothing. One of the important findings was that subjects who *discovered* the relation between using you and the experimenter's approval used you more and more, whereas there was no change in the frequency with which the other subjects used the second-person pronoun. Moreover, "conformist" subjects evinced a markedly increased use of the pronoun you.

Thus, the selective variation of verbal output that is often attributed to conditioning can with equal justification be considered a result of such interpersonal factors as influence, attractiveness, and dependency. It is understandable that Greenspoon (1962, p. 546), the originator of this research trend, recently concluded: "The review of the literature on verbal conditioning leaves many issues in doubt, including the legitimacy of the phenomenon of verbal conditioning." Without using intermediary learning mechanisms, the properties of verbal behavior can be explained by examining interpersonal relations, or social interactions, and the norms that govern them, or the rules observed, by those participating in them.

Social psychologists and sociologists, lacking any deep interest in the psycholinguistic area of reality, have generally given the foregoing questions short shrift (Smith, 1966). We must eventually decide, however, whether to acknowledge the uniqueness of language and then to study it properly, or to disregard it entirely. Since its relevance cannot be denied, we are obliged to undertake the thorough theoretical and experimental exploration of language that its nature and ramifications warrant.

REFERENCES

Antal, L. (1964). *Content, meaning and understanding*. The Hague: Mouton.

Argyle, M. (1957). Social pressure in public and private situations. *J. abnorm. soc. Psychol.* **54**, 172–175.

Bachrach, A. J., Caudland, O. K., and Gibson, J. F. (1961). Group reinforcement of individual response experiments in verbal behavior. In A. Berg and B. Bass (Eds.), *Conformity and deviation*. New York: Harper & Row, pp. 258–285.

Back, K. W. (1961). Power, influence and pattern of communication. In L. Petrullo and B. Bass (Eds.), *Leadership and interpersonal behavior*. New York: Holt, Rinehart & Winston, pp. 137–164.

Bales, R. F. (1951). *Interaction process analysis*. Reading, Massachusetts: Addison-Wesley.

Bales, R. F., Strodtbeck, F. L., Mills, N. T., and Roseborough, M. E. (1951). Channels of communication in small groups. *Amer. Sociol. Rev.* **16**, 461–468.

Bass, B. M., Pryer, M. W., Gaier, E. L., and Flint, A. W. (1958). Interacting effects of control, motivation, group practice and problem difficulty on attempted leadership. *J. abnorm. soc. Psychol.* **56**, 352–358.

Bastian, J. (1959). Review of *Words and things*, by R. Brown. *Word* **15**, 353.

Bavelas, A., Hastorf, A. H., Gross, A. E., and Kite, W. R. (1965). Experiments on the alteration of group structure. *J. exp. soc. Psychol.* **1**, 55–70.

Becker, S. W., Bavelas, A., and Braden, M. (1961). An index to measure contingency of English sentences. *Lang. Speech* **4**, 139–145.

Benveniste, E. (1958). De la subjectivité dans le langage. *J. Psychol. norm. path.* **55**, 257–265.

Benveniste, E. (1966). *Problèmes de linguistique générale*. Paris: Gallimard.

Berelson, B. (1952). *Content analysis in communication research*. New York: Free Press.

Bernstein, B. (1962). Social class, linguistic codes and grammatical elements. *Lang. Speech* **5**, 221–240.

Bernstein, B. (1964). Elaborated and restricted codes: their social origins and some consequences. *Amer. Anthropol.* **66**, 55–69.

Bresson, F. (1966). Langage et communication. In J. Piaget and P. Fraisse (Eds.), *Traité de psychologie expérimentale*. Vol. 8. Paris: Presses Univ. France, pp. 1–92.

Brondal, V. (1933). L'autonomie de la syntaxe. *J. Psychol.* **1–4**, 217–225.

Brown, R. W. (1958). *Words and things*. New York: Free Press.

Brown, R. W. (1965). *Social psychology*. New York: Free Press.

Brown, R. W., and Ford, M. (1961). Address in American English. *J. abnorm. soc. Psychol.* **62**, 375–385.

Brown, R. W., and Lenneberg, E. H. (1954). A study in language and cognition. *J. abnorm. soc. Psychol.* **49**, 454–462.

Cairns, R. B., and Lewis, M. (1962). Dependency and the reinforcement value of a verbal stimulus. *J. consult. Psychol.* **26**, 1–8.

Carroll, J. B. (1938). Diversity of vocabulary and the harmonic series law of word-frequency distribution. *Psychol. Rec.* **2**, 379–386.

Carroll, J. B. (1958). Communication theory, linguistics and psycholinguistics. *Rev. Educ. Res.* **28**, 79–88.

Cherry, C. (1957). *On human communication*. New York: Wiley.

Chomsky, N. (1964). *Current issues in linguistic theory*. The Hague: Mouton.

Chotlos, J. W. (1944). A statistical and comparative analysis of individual written language samples. *Psychol. Monogr.* **56**, 77–111.

Coleman, J. S. (1960). The mathematical study of small groups. In H. Solomon (Ed.), *Mathematical thinking in the measurement of behavior*. New York: Free Press, pp. 1–149.

Crozier, M. (1964). *Le phénomène bureaucratique*. Paris: Seuil.

Davitz, J. R. (Ed.) (1964). *The communication of emotional meaning*. New York: McGraw-Hill.

de Saussure, F. (1955). *Cours de linguistique générale*. Paris: Payot.

de Sola Pool, I. (Ed.) (1959). *Trends in content analysis*. Urbana, Illinois: Univ. Illinois Press.

Dinoff, M., Rickard, H., Kew, J. K., and Timmons, E. D. (1962). The stability of group verbal behavior. *Psychol. Rec.* **12**, 323–325.

Ervin-Tripp, Susan M. (1964). An analysis of the interaction of language, topic and listener. *Amer. Anthrop.* **66** (6), Pt. 2, 86–102.

Ervin-Tripp, Susan M., and Slobin, D. I. (1966). Psycholinguistics. *Annu. Rev. Psychol.* **17**, 435–474.

Farber, J. E. (1963). The things people say to themselves. *Amer. Psychologist* **18**, 185–197.

Faucheux, C., and Moscovici, S. (1960). Etudes sur la créativité des groupes: II. Tâche. structure des communications et réussite. *Bull. C.E.R.P.* **9**, 11–22.

Faucheux, C., and Moscovici, S. (1966). Contribution to a psychosociology of language. Paper read at Sympos. Int. Congr. Psychol., Moscow, August 4–11.

Fearing, F. (1953). Toward a psychological theory of human communication. *J. Pers.* **22**, 71–88.

Feldstein, S., and Jaffe, J.(1963). Language predictability as a function of psychotherapeutic interaction. *J. consult. Psychol.* **27**, 123–126.

Festinger, L. (1950). Informal social communication. *Psychol. Rev.* **57**, 279–292.

Fiedler, F. E. (1953). The psychological distance dimension in interpersonal relations. *J. Pers.* **22**, 142–150.

Flament, C. (1965). Les processus de communication. In J. Piaget and P. Fraisse (Eds.), *Traité de psychologie expérimentale*. Vol. 9. Paris: Presses Univ. France, pp. 171–216.

Fraisse, P., and Breyton, M. (1959). Comparaison entre les langages oral et écrit. *Année psychol.* **59**, 61–71.

French, J. R. P., Jr. (1956). A formal theory of social power. *Psychol. Rev.* **63**, 181–194.

Gerard, H. B. (1953). The effect of different dimensions of disagreement on the communication process in small groups. *Hum. Relat.* **6**, 249–271.

Glanzer, M., and Clark, W. H. (1964). The verbal loop hypothesis: conventional figures. *Amer. J. Psychol.* **77**, 621–626.

Goldman-Eisler, Frieda (1961). The distribution of pause durations in speech. *Lang. Speech* **4**, 232–237.

Greenspoon, J. (1962). Verbal conditioning and clinical psychology. In A. J. Bachrach (Ed.), *Experimental foundations of clinical psychology*. New York: Basic Books, pp. 510–553.

Gruen, W., and Bierman, R. (1960). Determinants for verbal communication among strangers. *Psychol. Rep.* **7**, 463–469.

Hare, A. P. (1952). A study of interaction and consensus in different sized groups. *Amer. sociol. Rev.* **17**, 261–268.

Harms, L. S. (1961). Listener comprehension of speakers of three status groups. *Lang. Speech* **4**, 109–122.

Harnack, R. V. (1953). Problems in measuring discussion process. *J. Communication* **3**, 13–16.

Haudricourt, A. G. (1961). Richesse en phonèmes et richesse en locuteurs. *L'Homme* **1**, 5–10.

Hearn, G. (1957). Leadership and the spatial factor in small groups. *J. abnorm. soc. Psychol.* **54**, 269–273.

Heider, F. (1958). The psychology of interpersonal relations. New York: Wiley.

Heise, G. A., and Miller, G. A. (1951). Problem solving by small groups using various communication nets. *J. abnorm. soc. Psychol.* **46**, 327–335.

Herdan, G. (1956). *Language as choice and chance*. Groningen: P. Noordhoff.

Herdan, G. (1960). *Type/token mathematics*. The Hague: Mouton.

Herman, S. N. (1961). Explorations in the social psychology of language choice. *Hum. Relat.* **14**, 149–164.

Hjemslev, L. (1935). La catégorie des cas : étude de grammaire générale. *Acta Jutlandica* **7**, 1–184.

Hockett, C. F. (1961). The mathematical theory of communication. In S. Saporta and J. R. Bastian (Eds.), *Psycholinguistics*. New York: Holt, Rinehart & Winston, pp. 46–67.

Hoffman, L. R., and Maier, N. R. F. (1964). Valence in the adoption of solutions by problem-solving groups: concept, method and results. *J. abnorm. soc. Psychol.* **69**, 264–271.

Horowitz, M. W., and Berkowitz, L. (1964). Structural advantage of the mechanism of spoken expression as a factor of differences in spoken and written expression. *Percept. mot. Skills* **19**, 619–625.

Horowitz, M. W., and Newman, J. B. (1964). Speech and written expression. An experimental analysis. *J. abnorm. soc. Psychol.* **68**, 640–664.

Horvath, W. (1965). A mathematical model of participation in small group discussion. *Behav. Sci.* **10**, 164–166.

Hovland, C. I., Janis, I. L., and Kelley, H. H. (1953). *Communication and persuasion.* New Haven: Yale Univ. Press.

Hymes, D. (1962). The ethnography of speaking. In T. Gladwin and W. C. Sturtevant (Eds.), *Anthropology and human behavior*. Washington, D. C.: Amer. Anthrop. Soc., pp. 13–54.

Hymes, D. (1964). Toward ethnography of communication. *Amer. Anthrop.* **66**, 1–34.

Jakobson, R. (1961). Linguistics and communication theory. In R. Jakobson (Ed.), *Structure of language and its mathematical aspects*. Amer. Math. Soc., Vol. 12, pp. 245–252.

Joos, M. (1962). *The five clocks.* The Hague: Mouton.

Jousse, M. (1925). Etudes de psychologie linguistique. Le style oral rythmique et mnémotechnique chez les verbo-moteurs. Paris: Alcan.

Kanfer, F. H., Bass, B. M., and Guyett, I. (1963). Dyadic speech patterns, orientation and social reinforcement *J. consult. Psychol.* **27**, 199–205.

Kasl, S. V., and Mahl, G. F. (1965). The relationship of disturbances and hesitations in spontaneous speech to anxiety. *J. Pers. soc. Psychol.* **1**, 425–433.

Kirscht, J. P., Lodahl, T. M., and Haire, M. (1959). Some factors in the selection of leaders by members in small groups. *J. abnorm. soc. Psychol.* **58**, 406–408.

Knower, F. H. (1936). Experimental studies of changes in attitude. II. A study of the effect of printed arguments on changes in attitude. *J. abnorm. soc. Psychol.* **30**, 522–532.

Knutson, A. L. (1960). Quiet and vocal groups. *Sociometry* **23**, 36–49.

Krauss, R. M., and Weinheimer, S. (1965a). Concurrent feedback, confirmation and the encoding of referents in verbal communication. Murray Hill, New Jersey: Bell Telephone Lab.

Krauss, R. M. and Weinheimer, S. (1965b). The effect of referent array and communication mode on verbal encoding. Murray Hill, New Jersey: Bell Telephone Lab.

Krauss, R. M., and Weinheimer, S. (1964). Changes in reference phrases as a function of frequency of usage in social interaction: a preliminary study. *Psychon. Sci.* **1**, 113–114.

Lanz, D. L., and Shtefflre, V. (1964). Language and cognition revisited. *J. abnorm. soc. Psychol.* **69**, 472–481.

Lawton, D. (1963). Social class differences in language development: a study of some samples of written work. *Lang. Speech* **6**, 120–143.

Leavitt, H. J., and Mueller, R. A. H. (1951). Some effects of feedback on communication. *Hum. Relat.* **4**, 401–410.

Lefkowitz, M., Blake, R. R., and Mouton, J. S.(1955). Status factors in pedestrian violation of traffic signals. *J. abnorm. soc. Psychol.* **51**, 704–706.

Lewin, K. (1938). *The conceptual representation and the measurement of psychological forces.* Durham, North Carolina: Duke Univ. Press.

Luria, A. R., and Yudovich, F. Y. (1959). *Speech and the development of mental process in the child.* London: Staples Press.

McGinnies, E. (1965). Written versus oral presentation of a communication. O.N.R. Tech. Rep. No.6.

Maclay, H., and Newman, S. (1960). Two variables affecting the message in communication. In D. K. Wilner (Ed.), *Decisions, values and groups*. New York: Macmillan (Pergamon) pp. 219–229.

Maclay, H., and Osgood, C. (1959). Hesitation phenomena in spontaneous English speech. *Word* **15**, 19–44.

Mahl, G. F., and Schulze, G. (1964). Psychological research in the extralinguistic area. In T. A. Sebeok, A. S. Hayes, and M. C. Bateson (Eds.), *Approaches to Semiotics*. The Hague: Mouton, pp. 51–124.

Malmberg, B. (1953). *Structural linguistics and human communication*. Berlin: Springer.

Mandelbrot, B. (1954) Structure formelle des textes et communication. *Word* **10**, 1–27.

Mann, R. D. (1961). Dimensions of individual performance in small groups under task and social-emotional conditions. *J. abnorm. soc. Psychol.* **62**, 674–682.

March, J. G. (1956). Influence measurement in experimental and semi-experimental groups. *Sociometry* **19**, 260–271.

Marschack, J. (1965). Economics of language. *Behav. Sci.* **10**, 135–140.

Martinet, A. (1965). *La linguistique synchronique*. Paris: Presses Univ. France.

Mehrabian, A. (1965). Communication length as an index of communicator attitude. *Psychol. Rep.* **17**, 519–522.

Miller A. (1963). Verbal satiation and the role of concurrent activity. *J. abnorm. soc. Psychol.* **6**, 206–212.

Miller, G. A. (1951). *Language and communication*. New York: McGraw-Hill.

Miller, G. A. (1964). The psycho-linguists: on the new scientists of language. *Encounter* **23**, 29–37.

Moscovici, S. (1955). Logique et langage dans la propagande. *Bull. Psychol.* **8**, 434–451.

Moscovici, S. (1961). La psychanalyse, son image et son public. Paris: Presses Univ. France.

Moscovici, S., and Ackermann, W. (1961). Processus d'association et dimensions des signes linguistiques. *Bull. Psychol.* **15**, 209–222.

Moscovici, S. and Humbert, C. (1960a). Etude sur le comportement verbal, langage oral et langage écrit. *Psychol. franc.* V(3), 175–186.

Moscovici, S., and Humbert, C. (1960b). Usage et disponibilité comme facteurs déterminant la durée de reconnaissance des stimuli verbaux. *Bull. Psychol.* **13**, 406–412.

Moscovici, S., and Plon, M. (1966). Les situations-colloques; observations théoriques et expérimentales. *Bull. Psychol.* **19**, 702–722.

Newcomb, T. M. (1953). An approach to the study of communicative acts. *Psychol. Rev.* **60**, 393–404.

Oakes, W. F., Droge, A. E., and August, B. (1960). Reinforcement effects on participation in group discussion. *Psychol. Rep.* **7**, 503–514.

Olmsted, D. L., and Moore, O. K. (1952). Language, psychology and linguistics. *Psychol. Rev.* **59**, 416–420.

Osgood, C. E., and Sebeok, T. A. (1965). *Psycholinguistics*. Bloomington, Indiana: Indiana Univ. Press.

Palmore, E., Lennard, H. L., and Hendin, H. (1959). Similarities of the therapist and patient verbal behavior in psychotherapy. *Sociometry* **22**, 12–22.

Reece, M., and Whitman, R. (1962). Expressive movements, warmth and verbal reinforcement. *J. abnorm. soc. Psychol.* **64**, 234–236.

Riecken, H. W. (1958). The effect of talkativeness on ability to influence group solutions to problems. *Sociometry* **21**, 309–321.

Robins, R. H. (1952). Noun and verb in universal grammar. *Language* **28**, 289–298.

Robinson, W. P. (1956). Close procedure as a technique for the investigation of social class differences in language usage. *Lang. Speech.* **8**, 42–55.

Rommetweit, R. (1966). Linguistic and non-linguistic components of communication: Notes on the intersection of spsycholinguistic and social psychological theory. Paper read at the Third European Conf. exp. soc. Psychol., Royaumont, France.

Rosenberg, S., and Cohen, B. O. (1964). Speakers' and listeners' processes in a word communication task. *Science* **145**, 1201–1203.

Rosenberg, B. G., and Langer, J. (1965). A study of postural-gestural communication. *J. pers. soc. Psychol.* **2**, 593–597.

Rosenthal, F. (1957). Some relations between sociometric position and language structure of young children. *J. educ. Psychol.* **48**, 483–497.

Ruwet, N. (1964). La linguistique générale aujourd'hui. *Arch. Europ. Sociol.* **5**, 277–310.

Salzinger, K. (1959). Experimental manipulation of verbal behavior: a review. *J. gen. Psychol.* **61**, 56–94.

Schachter, S. (1951). Deviation, rejection, and communication. *J. abnorm. soc. Psychol.* **46**, 190–207.

Schatzman, L., and Strauss, A. (1954). Social class and modes of communication. *Amer. J. Sociol.* **60**, 329–338.

Sebeok, T. A. (1965). Animal communication. *Science* **147**, 1006–1014.

Shaw, M. E. (1964). Communication networks. *Advan. exp. soc. Psychol.* **1**, 111–147.

Shaw, M. E., and Gilchrist, J. E. (1956). Intra-group communication and leader choice, *J. soc. Psychol.* **43**, 133–138.

Sherif, Carolyn W. (1961). Categorization in social judgment. Norman, Oklahoma: Inst. Group Relations. (Mimeo.)

Shibuya, Y. A. (1962). A study in the relationship between cognitive similarity and communication effectiveness. *Japan. Psychol. Res.* **4**, 173–177.

Simon, H. A. (1955). On a class of skew distribution functions. *Biometrika* **42**, 425–440.

Sipolski, A. (1960). Effect of interpersonal relationships upon verbal conditioning. *J. abnorm. soc. Psychol.* **60**, 241–246.

Skinner, B. F. (1957). *Verbal behavior.* New York: Appleton-Century-Crofts.

Slama-Cazacu, T. (1961). *Langage et contexte.* The Hague: Mouton.

Smith, M. B. (1966). Three textbooks: a special review. *J. exp. soc. Psychol.* **2**, 109–118.

Somers, H. H. (1961). The measurement of grammatical constraints. *Lang. Speech* **4**, 150–156.

Sommer, R. (1959). Studies in personal space. *Sociometry* **22**, 247–260.

Sommer, R. (1961). Leadership and group geography. *Sociometry* **24**, 99–110.

Starkweather, J. A. (1956) Content-free speech as a source of information about the speaker. *J. abnorm. soc. Psychol.* **52**, 394–402.

Steinzor, B. (1950). The spatial factor in face-to-face discussion. *J. abnorm. soc. Psychol.* **45**, 552–555.

Stephan, F. (1952). The relative rate of communication between members in small groups. *Amer. sociol. Rev.* **17**, 482–486.

Stephan, F., and Mishler, E. G. (1952). The distribution of participation in small group: An exponential approximation. *Amer. sociol. Rev.* **17**, 598–608.

Strodtbeck, F. L., and Hook, H. L. (1961). The social dimensions of a twelve-man jury table. *Sociometry* **24**, 397–415.

Thibaut, J. W., and Strickland, L. H. (1956). Psychological set and social conformity. *J. Pers.* **25**, 111–129.

Thorndike, E. L. (1946). The psychology of semantics. *Amer. J. Psychol.* **59** (4), 613–633.

Triandis, H. C. (1960). Cognitive similarity and communication in dyad. *Hum. Relat.* **13**, 175–183.

Uldall, H. J. (1944), Speech and writing. *Acta linguistica* **4**, 11–16.

Vendryes, J. (1950). Langage oral et langage par gestes. *J. Psychol. norm. pathol.* **43**, 1–33.

Verplanck, W. S. (1955). The control of the content of conversation: reinforcement of statements of opinion. *J. abnorm. soc. Psychol.* **51**, 668–676.

Von Frisch, K. (1950). *Bees, their vision, chemical sense and language.* Ithaca, New York: Cornell Univ. Press.

Vigotsky, L. S. (1962). *Thought and language.* Cambridge, Mass.: M.I.T. Press; and New York: Wiley.

Wiener, M., and Mehrabian, A. (1965). *Beyond meaning: A communication channel in verbal behavior.* (Mimeo.)

Wiener, N. (1954). *The human use of human being.* New York: Doubleday.

Wilke, W. H. (1934). An experimental comparison of the speech, the radio and the printed page as propaganda devices. *Arch. Psychol.* **169**.

Ziller, R. C. (1955). Scales of judgment: a determinant of the accuracy of groups decisions, *Hum. Relat.* **8**, 153–164.

Zinkin, N. I. (1962). Four communication systems and four languages. *Word* **18**, 143–172.

Zipf, G. K. (1949). *Human behavior and the principle of least effort.* Reading, Massachusetts: Addison-Wesley.

THE CONGRUITY PRINCIPLE REVISITED: STUDIES IN THE REDUCTION, INDUCTION, AND GENERALIZATION OF PERSUASION[1]

Percy H. Tannenbaum

MASS COMMUNICATIONS RESEARCH CENTER
UNIVERSITY OF WISCONSIN
MADISON, WISCONSIN

[1]The research reported in this chapter was conducted largely under Grant G-23963 from the National Science Foundation, Division of Social Science. Some of the preliminary work was supported by grants from the Graduate Research Committee of the University of Wisconsin from funds supplied by the Wisconsin Alumni Research Foundation. The present chapter was written while the author was a fellow at the Center for Advanced Study in the Behavioral Sciences, Stanford, California. He is grateful for the support of these various institutions, and for the liberal manner in which such support was provided and administered. He also acknowledges the assistance of several graduate students who participated in this research, principally Jacqueline Macaulay, Eleanor Norris, Kjell Nowak, and Stephen Schleifer.

I. Introduction

As is amply testified in previous volumes of this series and other such recent publications, social psychology has made substantial and rapid strides in its development as a bona fide behavioral science. Leading this trend has been the emergence, within the last decade or so, of a number of apparently independently developed but highly related theoretical principles which generally fall under the rubric of *balance* or *consistency* theories. One thinks immediately of the tremendous influence of cognitive dissonance theory (cf. Festinger, 1957, 1964; Brehm and Cohen, 1962). In the realm of interpersonal behavior, there is Heider's (1958) pioneering balance theory, and its elaborations by Newcomb (1953, 1959) and by Cartwright and Harary (1956). While the foregoing formulations also deal extensively with attitudinal phenomena, more specific attitude models are those based on cognitive-affective balance (Abelson and Rosenberg, 1958; Rosenberg, 1960; Rosenberg and Abelson, 1960) and, of particular interest to us here, the principle of congruity (Osgood and Tannenbaum, 1955; Osgood *et al.*, 1957).

There are, to be sure, some important differences among these theoretical schemes—for example, in range of application, degree of elaboration and specification, and for that matter, in the definition of the basic motivational state. More to the point, however, particularly considering their more or less independent development, is their common characteristic: the basic premise of a tendency within the human organism to minimize cognitive inconsistency and to strive toward consistency. Such a basic postulate and its attendant assumptions within the various theories have generated a wide variety of theoretical considerations and research undertakings, as the contemporary literature of social psychology attests. Collectively, these approaches have lead at least one authority to characterize them as representing "the first truly general . . . and compelling theoretical system in social psychology" (Brown, 1962).[2]

[2]It is not our function here to present a complete review of the current status, the similarities and differences, of the cognitive consistency theories. Such reviews have been

One of the main areas of application of these consistency models has been that of the formation and modification of attitudes. Indeed, the congruity principle was initially developed for just this problem (Osgood and Tannenbaum, 1955)—to account for the attitude change resulting from a given communication situation—although it has since been extended to other cognitive areas, such as word mixture studies (cf. Osgood *et al.*, 1957), color and shape connotations (Tannenbaum, 1966a), interpersonal impression formation (e.g., Willis, 1960; Triandis and Fishbein, 1963), and other complex social stimuli (e.g., Podell and Podell, 1963; Manis *et al.*, 1966).

The simple and not atypical communication situation to which the congruity principle was originally applied is one in which an identifiable *source* makes an *assertion* about some *concept* or object. Prior to exposure to such a message, the individual has attitudes toward any number of potential sources or concepts, which he can maintain without any problems. The issue of congruity arises with the assertion of the message; it is only then that the particular source and the particular concept are brought into an evaluational relationship to each other as the source assumes a position favorable or unfavorable to the concept. Under certain conditions—for example, where the preexposure attitudes toward the source and toward the concept are both favorable and the direction of the assertion is also favorable—there is no incongruity, and no pressure toward change is generated. Under other defined circumstances—for example, when one initially favorable source makes a favorable assertion about a decidedly negative concept—incongruity obtains and, according to the theory, pressure is generated to change the attitudes toward the objects of judgment involved in order to achieve congruity.

The principle of congruity can be applied in this manner to account for conditions under which attitudes toward the source, the concept, or both, will be expected to change; the change always depends on the pre-communication attitudes toward both objects and on the nature of the assertion linking them. The theory further predicts the *direction* of attitude change for the source and for the concept: always toward increased congruity. The theoretical postulates also allow the derivation of a set of specific formulas to account for the respective *magnitudes* of change, although there are, as one might expect, a number of qualifying conditions and corrective factors involved in applying such formulas. [See Osgood and Tannenbaum

---

offered in the past by, for example, Zajonc (1960), Osgood (1960), and Brown (1962), and more recently by McGuire (1966b). At the time of this writing, a group (consisting of R. P. Abelson, E. Aronson, W. J. McGuire, T. M. Newcomb, M. J. Rosenberg, and P. H. Tannenbaum) is periodically convening at the Center for Advanced Study in the Behavioral Sciences to explore this general area in more detail.

(1955) for a more detailed account of the underlying assumptions, development of the predictive formulas, and the limiting conditions.] While the original experimental findings (Osgood and Tannenbaum, 1955) show substantial support for the predictive formulas (for example, correlations between predicted and obtained attitude changes on the order of .90 or better), their accuracy and underlying logic have recently been called into question (cf. Triandis and Fishbein, 1963; Fishbein and Hunter, 1964; Rokeach and Rothman, 1965).

Our concern here, however, is not so much with the derived formulas and other such details of the theory as it is with the more general theoretical premise that attitude change, at least in the communication situation we have posed, is a direct consequence of the condition of incongruity. The attitude change occurs in response to the incongruity, and functions to reduce it. This reasoning amounts to an essentially self-regulative, automatic, homeostatic model—perhaps more so than any of the other consistency or balance theories—in which the upsetting of a condition of equilibrium elicits a state of disequilibrium which provides the impetus for its own reduction. Such a homeostatic principle has long been considered a fundamental mechanism for the regulation of a variety of bodily functions (such as the balance of oxygen and carbon dioxide in the blood and internal temperature control). Although not originally derived from such general homeostatic considerations, the various consistency theories, and particularly the congruity principle, have much in common with other homeostatic models. One distinction, however, is that whereas physiological homeostasis usually involves the maintenance of an existing level of equilibrium, the congruity principle allows for balance at a variety of levels, mostly different from the original state of affairs. That is, what is important is not the maintenance or restoration of a predetermined ideal level, but the notion of a tendency toward any consistent or balanced situation.

In the decade or so since its introduction, the congruity principle has not been applied to attitude change issues beyond the kind of problems to which its original formulation referred. Recently, however, we have used the basic model to attempt to deal with several additional theoretical issues that have arisen in the persuasion area. This chapter is a report of current applications of the congruity model.

The main impetus to this recent research was a concern with the opposite side of the attitude change coin. We sought to account not so much for the modification of attitudes but rather for the reduction of such change. Accordingly, we will consider several strategies suggested by the theory to accomplish such reduction of persuasion. We will also report on the results of various combinations of these strategies. Our work in this area closely parallels that derived from another approach to the development of resistance to persuasion (cf. McGuire, 1964). In our studies we have used the experimental procedures developed by McGuire but have hypothesized different mechanisms to account for the results. Thus, we also have several studies to report which were designed to test these alternative hypotheses.

As so often happens, embarking on this program of research led to the consideration of related phenomena. For one thing, it raised anew the question of the relative efficacy of different modes of *inducing*, as well as reducing, attitude change. Because of the close theoretical affinity between promoting and reducing attitude change, this chapter will include several such investigations. Another, possibly serendipitous, consequence of this research was a closer look at the problem of the *generalization* of attitude change, also considered within the framework of congruity theory.

II. Strategies for the Reduction of Persuasion

The advent of the various consistency theories, along with other recent findings in the attitude and opinion change area, has not been without untoward implications. By providing a theoretical base and generating research on specific persuasion strategies, the theories have raised the specter of a public increasingly vulnerable to a variety of persuasive manipulations. Cohen (1960) was led to such a gloomy view in his summary of relevant studies. But he also saw a possible silver lining to this Orwellian cloud: "On the positive side, let us hope that any principles derived . . . are equally applicable for developing resistance to persuasive inducements [and] may provide a basis for inoculation of the individual against manipulation" (Cohen, 1960, p. 318). While Cohen may have been more concerned with the social and political values of such a situation, his comments have an important theoretical relevance in that theories of how attitudes are formed and changed also carry implications for the *reduction* of such change.

In a previous contribution to the *Advances in Experimental Social Psychology*, McGuire (1964) has, in his typically thorough and scholarly manner, provided a comprehensive review of a variety of investigations dealing with this general problem of resistance to persuasion. Several distinctive approaches and many specific studies are described (although many were not necessarily originally conceived of in that context). Additional references, including some of the work reported here, can be found in the 1966 *Annual Review* (McGuire, 1966a). For the most part, the earlier research in this area did not stem from consistency theory. More recent work, including that dealing with the effects of warnings of coming belief attacks (Allyn and Festinger, 1961; Festinger and Maccoby, 1964; Kiesler and Kiesler, 1964) and perceived choice in exposure to the persuasive communication (Freedman and Steinbruner, 1964), has involved dissonance theory applications.

By far the most ambitious and systematic approach to the problem of inducing resistance to persuasion has been McGuire's own *inoculation theory*.[3] While having some roots in the so-called selective exposure postulate of dissonance theory—that people tend to defend their beliefs by avoiding information contrary to their viewpoints—inoculation theory can be treated independently of this generally accepted (cf. Festinger, 1957; Klapper, 1960) but still questionable (Steiner, 1962; Freedman and Sears, 1966) premise. McGuire deliberately focuses on "cultural truisms"— various widely held beliefs about health practices, on the assumption that such unquestioned beliefs are maintained in a noncontroversial, ideological-ly aseptic environment, and hence are highly susceptible to attack since the individual is both unmotivated and unpracticed in defending them. He reasons that prior messages which merely offer support for the initial belief fail to induce resistance to the subsequent attack since they merely "belabor the obvious." If anything, the supporting messages make the individual overconfident but no less vulnerable. McGuire proposes that a prior treatment, such as a refutation of the attack, can serve as a threat to the existing belief by alerting the recipient to the possibility of attack. This threat should stimulate the individual to muster defenses for the opinion and make him less vulnerable to the coming massive attack— a procedure quite analogous to biological immunization, such as that of a person raised in a germ-free environment who is inoculated with a weakened virus.

In a systematic series of experiments, McGuire has marshalled con-siderable support for such a theoretical position. Not only does he find the foregoing prediction regarding the superiority of the refutational over the supportive treatments to hold (McGuire and Papageorgis, 1961); he also finds that the refutation of one set of arguments generalizes to provide immunization against a different set of arguments (Papageorgis and McGuire, 1961). Furthermore, he noted that the supportive treatment gains in efficacy when combined with the refutational (McGuire, 1961b), and that both treatments, more particularly the supportive, confer more resis-tance when preceded by a warning of the impending attack (McGuire and Papageorgis, 1962). These results, along with an assortment of other evidence, are in accord with the threat-provoking, defense-arousing ratio-nale of inoculation theory.

[3]The most comprehensive statement of the theory and the supporting evidence is contained in McGuire's chapter in the first volume of this series McGuire, 1964). Earlier versions may be found in McGuire's earlier writings (e.g., McGuire and Papageorgis, 1961; McGuire, 1961a).

The congruity principle has also recently been applied to the problem of reducing the effect of persuasion. This work has dealt with a basic communication setting in which the main attack on the belief consists of a favorably evaluated source making a strongly negative assertion against a favorably evaluated concept. This is an intrinsically incongruous situation, and the theory predicts, among other things, a resultant negative shift in attitude toward the concept. The problem posed, then, is how to eliminate, or at least significantly reduce, this unfavorable attitude change.

Application of the principle of congruity to such a situation stems from its central postulate that the existence of an incongruity directly generates the pressure toward change, and that such pressure is absent when the situation is a congruous one. Accordingly, any means of reducing the prevailing degree of incongruity should render the situation more congruous and thus serve to reduce the degree of attitude change.

Four such strategies for reducing the degree of persuasion were derived from congruity theory. These strategies were first tested in an original study designed for just that purpose (Tannenbaum *et al.*, 1966). In the present section, we shall describe the results of this initial investigation, along with the findings from replications of the four treatments which were conducted in somewhat different settings as parts of other studies. Since each strategy has its own particular theoretical basis, and since the four were manifested in somewhat different forms, we will consider them individually at this stage. Our immediate purpose is to present the rationale for each treatment and to consider the experimental results in terms of that rationale. We want first to determine if each treatment works as intended before we proceed to other considerations.

A. GENERAL METHODOLOGICAL CONSIDERATIONS

To allow for comparison of our results with McGuire's, the belief issues used in the original and in most of the subsequent studies were similar to those employed by McGuire: various health measures, such as frequent toothbrushing to prevent dental decay, regular medical checkups in the absence of specific illness, and the use of X rays for the detection of tuberculosis. The main attack on such beliefs in the initial study consisted of a message purporting to be an official statement from the United States Public Health Service (USPHS). According to pretesting, this agency was a clearly favorable source for the undergraduate student subjects. In subsequent studies, the source was usually identified by name as a professor of medicine, for reasons that will become clearer later. In either case, the attack message first stated generally, and then argued specifically, four separate and seemingly telling points against the particular health practice.

The various belief-defense messages representing the persuasion-reduction strategies were given to subjects to read either before or after the belief-attack message. The sequence in which a defense message is read *before* an attack message will be referred to as *immunization*. In this situation, the subject's belief is assumed to be at least partially "immunized" against the effects of later attacks. The reverse sequence, where the attack message is read before the defense message, will be termed *restoration*. In the latter situation, the attack message presumably has some initial success and thus the defense message in effect "restores" the belief to something like its initial state. In addition to the main experimental treatments, two control groups were usually included, one that read no messages (that received no treatment) at all, the other that read only the main attack.

Attitudes toward the particular health practice were assessed on a set of 15-point scales similar to those employed by McGuire (1964), sometimes using only one such scale, sometimes using several, which were then averaged to a single score. Both after-only and before-after designs were employed. In the latter, the beliefs measures were administered at the very outset of a testing session (that is, before any message exposure) and after the full experimental treatments (that is, after both defensive and attack messages); on a few occasions, however, intermediary measures were taken after individual message treatments. Because earlier research (cf. Tannenbaum, 1956; Hovland *et al.*, 1957) has shown the degree of attitude change to be related to initial attitudinal position, we have usually employed analysis of covariance, with the dependent variable being either the after-scores or the before-after change scores, adjusting for the before-scores. In general, independent groups of subjects were used in the various testing conditions, with each experimental group receiving both a defense treatment and the main attack in either the immunization or restoration sequence. Where more than one health topic was employed in a single design, we have preferred to expose subjects to messages on only one topic—a preference which is underlined for us by the findings of other studies (see Section VI) indicating a generalization of change from one manipulated topic to another. Thus, different subjects are used in each condition.

B. DENIAL TREATMENT

Basic to the congruity principle is the premise that incongruity arises only when the cognitive elements involved are brought into evaluative relationship to one another via an assertion (Osgood and Tannenbaum, 1955, p. 43). The communication situation we have posed has a negative assertion being made by an initially favorable source about a favorable concept. Thus, if the particular source and concept can be dissociated by severing the negative linkage between them in the main attack message, then the degree of incongruity, and hence the pressure toward change, should accordingly be reduced.

In our main study, this strategy was made manifest in a message purporting to be a press release from the source of the main attack (USPHS) denying any connection with the "recent statements erroneously attributed" to it. The message carefully avoided taking any side on the issue, nor did it comment at all on the major points of argumentation contained in the main attack. This form of the denial treatment was not effective in lessening attitude change, either in the immunization (denial-then-attack [DA] mean = 9.06) or restoration (attack-then-denial [AD] mean = 9.96) conditions; both means being significantly less ($p < .05$) than the mean in the no-treatment control group ($0 = 11.77$) group but not significantly higher than the mean in the attack-only ($A = 8.56$) group. A similar finding was obtained in a subsequent replication, with the denial strategy again not reducing the negative belief change to a significant degree. Both results are in keeping with the journalistic adage that "a denial never catches up with a false story" (cf. Hall, 1965).

In more recent investigations, some variation in the messages operationalizing this treatment have been introduced, with some noteworthy consequences. One particularly critical addition was that the source not only denied making the attributed assertion but also expressed a stand in favor of the specific health practice. In such cases, the denial treatment turned out to be quite effective in reducing the degree of persuasion. In one such study (Macaulay, 1965), both the denial-attack and attack-denial conditions were significantly ($p < .02$ and $p < .01$, respectively) different from the attack-only control group. In another investigation using only the X-ray issue and only the immunization sequence, this new form of the denial strategy resulted in significantly ($p < .05$) less attitude change (-4.79 from initial belief level) than in the attack-only condition (-8.44). However, attitude change in this denial condition was significantly ($p < .02$) greater than in the no-message condition ($+.30$).

The fact that the source in this procedure disclaims responsibility for the main attack on the truism and takes a position contrary to that attributed to him is entirely consistent with the theoretical rationale offered for this treatment. The essence of the denial strategy is to negate the impression that *that* source was against *that* concept. Mere denial may help weaken the linkage, but some doubt may linger and hence some incongruity may remain. To restore an appreciable degree of congruity the favorable source must actively be in favor of the favorable concept. He erases all doubt of his position by asserting an opinion directly contrary to that of the main attack. It is not at all surprising, then, that the initial, relatively naive, versions of the denial treatment failed in producing their intended effect, and that its more recent manifestations, incorporating this critical element of a positive stance toward the concept, succeeded.

C. SOURCE DEROGATION TREATMENT

The communication situation we have posed involves a favorable source making a negative assertion about a favorable concept. A less incongruous situation would prevail in this case if the source were negatively evaluated. Thus, another indicated strategy was to derogate the source of the main attack in a separate message, either before (immunization sequence, SA) or after (restoration sequence, AS) subjects read the belief attack. Hopefully, this message would result in subjects adopting a negative attitude toward the source.

In our main study, this treatment took the form of the USPHS being attacked as "incompetently staffed (and) riddled with political appointees." In this study the strategy was found to be effective only in the immunization sequence; there was significantly ($p < .05$) less attitude change in the SA condition (mean = 10.62) than in the attack-only condition (A mean = 8.30). This SA change was not significantly greater than in the no-message control condition (0 mean = 11.86). The AS mean was 8.54, not appreciably higher than the A mean. When evaluation of the source was examined, it was found that the intended negative shift in attitude toward the USPHS source did not take place in either the SA or AS conditions.

Again, we introduced some variations designed to make this strategy more effective, and more pronounced results were obtained. For one thing, the institutional USPHS was dropped as the main source and was replaced by a single individual who was identified as "Dr. William J. McGuire, Professor of Medicine (or Dentistry) at Columbia University" (the real Dr. McGuire, who of course authored the original materials, was in the department of social psychology at Columbia and kindly consented to allow us the use of his name). The source derogation treatment in these cases consisted of a faculty committee report recommending dismissal of their colleague on grounds of "unethical and unprofessional behavior," including the issuing of "unjustified statements to the public." In one study in which all the messages were delivered orally, the manipulation was very successful in downgrading the source and showed very clearly significant differences in final belief level between the 0 (13.26), SA (10.43), and A (5.19) conditions. In another study, an increase in the relative efficiency of the restoration condition was noted—AS (6.60) was still not significantly higher than A (5.96), but was not significantly lower than SA (7.88).

D. REFUTATION TREATMENT

The change in attitude toward the concept in the communication context we posed can be considered to derive from at least two factors. One is the basic incongruity of a positive source taking a negative position vis-à-vis a positive concept. (It is primarily to reduce this inconsistency that the denial and source derogation treatments were directed.) The second factor involves the assertion itself. It not only serves to link source and concept, but also carries the argumentation and reasoning against a favorable evaluation of the concept. The assertions were particularly important in this series of experiments; they were rather detailed and really quite convincing arguments against the health practice. The fact that our data reflect such pronounced attitude change in the attack-only treatments—roughly, from above 12.00 to lower than 6.00 on the 15-point scale—cannot be attributed simply to the source-concept inconsistency. The force of the assertion itself must also be reckoned with.

In the initial formulation of the congruity theory, Osgood and Tannenbaum (1955) explicitly recognized such a factor, referring to it as the *assertion constant*. This was taken as the impact of the message per se on the concept, and was conceived of as being absorbed totally by the concept rather than the source. The assertion constant was recognized as being separate from the pure source-concept congruity relationships involved. Its value was estimated in the original data (Osgood and Tannenbaum, 1955) by assessing the relative difference between source and concept change within similar conditions. In a subsequent elaboration of the congruity principle, however, it was further speculated that the degree of incongruity, and hence the pressure toward change, was related to the intensity of the assertion—more incongruity with more intense messages (Osgood et al., 1957, p. 213). To our knowledge, however, such hypothesis has not undergone appropriate empirical testing.

In terms of our present concerns, it is clear from the foregoing line of reasoning that an appropriate way to lessen attitude change would be to *weaken* the assertion as such. This could be accomplished if the subject were made to question the validity of the attack arguments. The procedure would be even more effective if such a manipulation were totally to rebut, and perhaps even reverse, the salient points of the attack.

We reasoned that a detailed and explicit refutation of the attack message would best accomplish such an assertion-weakening goal. In our original study, such a refutation was attributed to a special professional (medical or dental, depending on the issue) committee without mentioning USPHS or otherwise specifically identifying the main attack. In each case, the message clearly stated each argument offered against the health practice and then offered a point-by-point rebuttal. The specific materials used here were adapted from McGuire's messages. But while this treatment is given the same "refutation" label and utilized highly similar materials in McGuire's investigations and ours, it should be noted that the fundamental theoretical rationales are quite different—an important point to which we shall return later in this chapter.

The results of this refutation treatment show it to be the most effective strategy for reducing persuasion in both the immunization (RA) and restoration (AR) sequences. In the original study, the refutation mean for the immunization sequence (12.46) was not only significantly ($p < .02$) higher than the attack-only mean (8.82), but it was higher, although not significantly so, than the no-message control mean (11.70). Similarly, the AR (10.45) restoration condition was significantly ($p < .01$) higher than A, but not significantly lower than 0. These general results have held uniformly, in more than a half-dozen assorted replications, usually with the RA condition somewhat if not significantly superior to the AR sequence.

E. Concept Boost Treatment

In developing the predictive implications of the basic postulate of a pressure toward change stemming from an incongruous situation, Osgood and Tannenbaum (1955) argued that this total pressure is not necessarily equal for the source and the concept; the total pressure toward change is distributed between source and concept in inverse proportion to the respective intensities of the original attitudes toward source and concept. In so doing, Osgood and Tannenbaum invoked one of the more widely accepted empirical generalizations in attitude theory: that more intense attitudes are less susceptible to change than weaker ones (cf. Tannenbaum, 1956; Klapper, 1960).

This general rule has direct application to the present situation. That is, if the initial attitude toward the concept can be boosted and made even more intensely favorable, it should be less susceptible to subsequent persuasion attempts in a negative direction.

The strategy is similar to McGuire's so-called supportive treatment, and again the messages used were adapted from his materials. In our versions, these messages were identified as coming from a professional committee (as in the refutation treatments). They merely offered the supportive evidence for the particular health practice without any direct reference to the main attack arguments.

For a variety of reasons, the concept boost treatment was used only in the immunization sequence (BA) in the original and subsequent studies. The BA mean (10.85) proved to be significantly ($p < .05$) higher than the attack-only mean (8.39) and very close to the no-message control group mean (11.22), even though there was no indication that the treatment had created the expected favorable attitude change. In an additional study, however, a significant ($p < .001$) strengthening of the concept belief (from 11.91 to 13.29) was noted. McGuire (1961b), too, found a significant strengthening of belief after exposure to the supportive manipulation. Contrary to our findings above, however, he claims that this strengthening is not effective in conferring a significant degree of resistance to the belief attack (McGuire, 1964, pp. 206–207).

III. Combinations of Congruity Strategies

We have seen that when the conditions were right each of the four strategies derived from congruity theory considerations was successful in accomplishing a reduction in attitude change, at least in the immunization sequence. It would also appear that there are differences in relative efficacy between treatments. While it is tempting to accept such differences at face value and attribute them to the differences in respective theoretical mechanisms, there are other factors present that might also be important. For example, in order to make the various strategies operational in their own ways, there were differences in length of the treatment messages; the refutation generally was longer than the others. Similarly, it is difficult to estimate the comparative effects of such factors as reality of the presentation or acceptability to subjects—all quite apart from the relative effects of the strategies as such.

Nevertheless, it is possible to study such relative effects by investigating various pairings of the individual treatments. This approach stems from the fundamental theoretical consideration that if two treatments are independent of one another in the manner in which they achieve their effect, they should be nonredundant in their combined effect. More specifically, independence of the effects of two treatments, each of which produces some degree of reduction of attitude change, implies that the two in combination should be superior to either of the component treatments alone.

Such comparisons have another theoretical implication. When two treatments are independent, their combination should yield an *additive* effect: Two significant and mutually exclusive treatments in union should be equal to the simple summation of their independent effects. If, however, such an additivity model does not hold—that is, if the combination is significantly greater or less than the addition of the component effects—then some kind of *interactive* model is indicated. If the combination is greater than additivity, a *facilitative* model, in which the strategies enhance each other's effects, is suggested. If the combination is significantly less than that expected from pure additivity, then a *redundant* model, whereby the effects overlap somewhat, is suggested.

We can thus examine the various pairings in terms of independence and nonindependence of the component strategies. Examination of the six possible pairings resulting from the four main strategies suggests that the components of four of the combinations appear to be independent. For these we expect the combination to be superior to either of the components and for additivity to obtain. Although we were able to test the first hypothesis for each, the assessment of the additivity model was not possible to accomplish in precise terms. The two remaining combinations are theoretically nonindependent and some degree of redundancy of effect is indicated such that the effect of combination should not equal the summed effects of the components. In addition, for one of the independent combinations we were able to ascertain whether an additional variation—having both treatments emanate from the same or different sources—produced an expected facilitative effect.

A. COMBINATIONS OF INDEPENDENT TREATMENTS

1. Source-Refutation Combination

Clearly, among the more successful single treatments uncovered in the original set of studies were the source derogation and refutation strategies. Clearly, too, the mode of operation of each as a persuasion reducer, at least in terms of the congruity model, suggests that these strategies are quite independent in their effect. The source attack involves a simple congruity mechanism. It is directed at the particular cognitive relationship involved in the given communication situation, and has little if anything to do with the nature of the argument against the health practice involved. The refutation treatment, on the other hand, is specifically directed at this argument attacking the concept. It is concerned with invalidating the attacking assertion itself. Although this may possibly lead to a less incongruous situation, its main focus is on reducing the weight of argumentation rather than on the particular source-concept relationship.

Because of such obvious nonredundancy in their respective mechanisms, these two treatments were selected in a test of some of the predictions made earlier involving a variety of combinations of the two strategies (Tannenbaum and Norris, 1965). Four single treatments were employed: the source derogation in both the immunization (SA) and the restoration (AS) sequence, and the refutation treatment in the same sequences (AR and RA). There also were four combined treatments: two "massed" versions with both strategies either before (SRA) or after (ASR) the main attack; and two "distributed" versions, one with the source treatment preceding the attack and the refutation following (SAR), and the other in the reverse sequence (RAS). In this manner, each combination could be compared with its respective components: for example, SRA with SA and RA; RAS with RA and AS; and so on. Only the X-ray issue was employed in this study, and belief toward the topic was assessed on a single 15-point scale used in the earlier research.

a. Single versus combined treatments. Table I presents the results of the comparisons between each combination and its respective components. (The higher the score, the greater the resistance is to the persuasion attempt.) A significant superiority for the combined treatment is indicated in each of the comparisons involved, in perfect keeping with the theoretical predictions. Each strategy is enhanced by the addition of the other, suggesting that the two do indeed function in separate and independent ways. In terms of relative enhancement, we find the refutation to contribute significantly ($p < .05$) more when added to the source derogation treatment than vice versa, suggesting that the refutation is indeed the superior of the two as a persuasion reducer.

TABLE I

RESISTANCE TO PERSUASION COMPARISON OF COMBINED WITH COMPONENT
TREATMENTS FOR THE SOURCE DEROGATION AND REFUTATION CONDITION[a]

Combination		Components		diff.	p[b]
SRA	(13.20)	SA	(8.00)	6.78	.001
		RA	(10.60)	3.39	.002
ASR	(11.30)	AS	(7.30)	5.22	.001
		AR	(9.40)	2.48	.02
SAR	(11.50)	SA	(8.00)	4.56	.001
		AR	(9.40)	2.74	.01
RAS	(12.10)	RA	(10.60)	1.97	.05
		AS	(7.30)	5.61	.001

[a] Data from Tannenbaum and Norris (1965).

[b] Based on the within-group error term from a one-way analysis of variance across all ten test groups. The higher the score, the greater the resistance to the attack-persuasion attempt.

Comparisons among the four combined treatments themselves indicate that SRA was significantly ($p < .05$) more effective in lessening persuasion than the other three, with no differences among the latter. Further detailed examination of the data revealed this SRA superiority was not due to a general massed versus distributed superiority. The two massed conditions taken together (SRA + ASR, mean = 12.25) were not significantly more effective than the two distributed conditions taken together (SAR + RAS, mean = 11.80). Rather, the SRA superiority arises from the fact that both component treatments appeared in their maximized form as immunizers. That is, both the source derogation and refutation strategies by themselves were more effective in the immunization than in the restoration sequence. Hence, when both are combined in the immunization version, as in the SRA treatment, their joint effect is greater.

b. *Additivity assessment.* Our data do not allow for a totally adequate test of the additivity model implied by the independence of the two component treatments. It was possible, however, to evaluate the obtained results in terms of those expected purely on the basis of additivity (see footnote 16, Tannenbaum and Norris, 1965, p. 154, for the method of calculating the expected values). Even though only four such instances are available, we found the relationship between obtained and expected values to be just short of the 5% level $[r = .951; Nr^2(X^2) = 3.62; .05 < p < .06 (1 df)]$—not enough to suggest any real departure from the additivity assumption.

Another implication of additivity is that the interaction between the two treatments is not significant. Appropriately, no such significant interaction was found in four specific analyses of variance conducted for this purpose (see Table VI, Tannenbaum and Norris, 1965, p. 155). Although the additivity hypothesis is a null hypothesis and so cannot be disproved, these results do provide a basis for rejecting the alternative facilitative or redundancy models—both of which imply a significant interaction effect—thus leaving additivity as the best available explanation for the obtained findings.

2. Refutation-Denial Combination

It can also be reasoned from our earlier discussion that the refutation and denial treatments should also be independent in their locus of effect. Again, the refutation is presumed to operate on the assertion itself, weakening its impact on the concept. As with the source derogation, the denial treatment is essentially aimed at reducing the incongruity in the source-concept relationship. It seeks to break the linkage between the source and concept by having the source strongly deny authorship of the main attack. In so doing, he may invalidate the specific relationship between source and concept, but he does not invalidate the force of the assertion itself, which the subject may now ascribe to some other unnamed source.

a. *Single versus combined treatments.* As part of another investigation in this program of research, Macaulay (1965) was able to compare combinations of the denial and refutation strategies with each by itself, again under both immunization and restoration conditions. Because of other purposes in the study, certain special conditions obtained. As we have noted before (see Section II, B), the denial treatment here had the source both disclaiming any connection with the attack statement and taking a firm position in favor of the health practice (X-ray diagnosis for TB detection). Furthermore, in the combined condition the denial and refutation were more directly associated than in the previous source refutation study. Here, the two treatments were issued in a single message and were, moreover, identified as emanating from the same source: that is, from the very source to which the attack was attributed. The source, then, not only denied making the attack statements but also attacked the attack, as it were, by issuing the specific point-by-point refutation of the arguments against the X-ray issue. This, it should be noted, is not an implausible situation; for instance, it is not uncommon for public officials both to deny and refute rumors attributed to them in the public media. We expected that such a situation would enhance the efficacy of the combined treatments, possibly producing a facilitative effect beyond pure additivity.

Eight independent groups of subjects were employed: the denial and refutation singly in immunization and restoration sequences (DA, AD, RA, AR), and the combinations in immunization (DRA) and restoration (ADR) sequences as well, along with the usual A and 0 control groups. This particular study (Macaulay, 1965) employed a wider variety of measures than before—largely aimed at providing a more direct assessment of the refutation mechanisms (see Section IV)—including four of the 15-point belief items similar to those used in the previous work with the X-ray issue.

The main findings relevant to our present interests are shown in Table II. Earlier analysis had indicated that each of the single treatments induced a significant amount of resistance to change (as compared with the A control group), and it is apparent that each of the combinations is significantly superior to its respective components taken singly, as predicted. That is, the addition of either the refutation or the denial treatment does contribute significantly to the presence of the other. The relative contribution of the refutation to the denial is significantly (by roughly a 2:1 ratio, $p < .02$) more than the denial adds to the refutation, again indicating refutation is the best single resistance-creating treatment.

In checking for departure from additivity, it was found that the obtained ADR mean (10.61) was somewhat higher than that expected from pure additivity (9.86), suggestive of a facilitative effect. In the immunization sequence, however, DRA (10.65) was somewhat less than expected (11.16). Moreover, when evaluated by the interaction test, these departures from additivity were considerably short of significance, so that we are again left with the additivity model as being the most parsimonious to account for the obtained data.

b. *Same versus different sources.* In the preceding study, the cards were stacked, as it were, in favor of a strong combined effect since the

TABLE II

RESISTANCE TO PERSUASION MEANS FOR INDIVIDUAL AND
COMBINED DENIAL AND REFUTATION TREATMENT[a,b]

Sequence	Treatments					
	Refutation		Denial		Combined	
Immunization	(RA)	9.60_b	(DA)	8.17_{cd}	(DRA)	10.65_a
Restoration	(AR)	8.96_{bc}	(AD)	7.51_d	(ADR)	10.61_a

[a] Means showing the same subscript are not significantly different at the .05 level by Duncan range test.
[b] Data from Macaulay (1965).

refutation and denial both came from the same source. What would happen if we had different sources for each of the defense treatments? It was possible to examine the effect of this differentiation in a separate study in which the two critical conditions (both in the immunization sequence only) were: (1) where the source of the attack issued the denial but another source offered the refutation ($R_y D_x A_x$), and (2) where the source of all three was the same ($R_x D_x A_x$). Indexed in terms of the before-after change score, the same-sources $R_x D_x A_x$ condition actually yielded a net increase in the concept belief score (adjusted mean $= +.33$ on a 15-point scale), whereas the $R_y D_x A_x$ condition showed a net negative change (-1.82). The difference between the two conditions is significant at the .05 level. Thus, there was a significant increment in immunization when the source who denies the statements attributed to him actually contradicts those statements. One possible explanation here—and one supported by some incidental findings in still another separate investigation—is that by issuing the refutation the alleged source of the attack removes any possible semblance of a source-concept incongruity that might otherwise still linger, even with the denial condition present. There is not only a repealing of the assertion itself and a lessening of the incongruity, but also as complete a repudiation of the attack and its attendant implications of incongruity as can be provided.

3. Source-Boost Combination

Similar to the earlier lines of reasoning, another apparently independent combination is provided by the pairing of the source derogation and the concept boost strategies. As before, the former is aimed at reducing the inherent source-concept incongruity and is focused on the source element. On the other hand, the boost strategy is not directly concerned with the incongruous relationship as such, being directed only at strengthening and intensifying belief in the concept itself.

These two strategies were examined in their separate and combined states in the immunizing sequence as part of an investigation trying various pairs of treatments on the X-ray issue. The results clearly showed the SBA combination (11.05) to be significantly superior ($p < .05$ and $p < .02$, respectively) to the SA (8.95) and BA (7.75) treatments in conferring resistance to persuasion. Both treatments apparently add significantly to the presence of the other. There is also an indication that the source attack adds somewhat more to the boost than vice versa. With only single cases available, the interaction test is even more limited, but again no real departure from additivity is obtained.

4. Denial-Boost Combination

The same study included conditions to allow for an assessment of still another presumably independent combination: the denial, which deals with the incongruous relationship, and the boost, focused on strengthening the concept. These too were studied on the X-ray issue and only in the immunization sequence.

The results again support the general prediction of the DBA combination (9.95) being superior to either the DA (8.05) or BA (7.75) components. There is a suggestion in the data that the addition of the denial strategy helps the boost treatment somewhat more than the reversed situation, though the difference is not quite significant ($p = .15$ approximately). This is not totally unexpected, since it can be argued that the denial treatment by itself already contains some aspects of the boost; the source, in this situation, not only dissociates himself from the attack but actually expresses strong support in favor of the X-ray procedure. Even though actual arguments for such support are not offered directly, it is conceivable that this would in itself help intensify the concept attitude (a possibility which was, unfortunately, not specifically assessed in the study).

B. COMBINATIONS OF NONINDEPENDENT TREATMENTS

1. Refutation-Boost Combination

The foregoing discussion of the denial and boost strategies suggests that the concept boost may overlap with other treatments. This is not readily expected in the combination between boost and source attack, since the latter would not be at all expected to affect the concept attitude itself, and our earlier results (see Section III, A,3) tend to support this. In the case of the refutation and boost treatments, however, we might well expect a quite substantial degree of overlap or redundancy. As we shall see subsequently (Section III), a number of somewhat differing mechanisms might conceivably account for the immunizing effect of the refutation. Our previous reasoning has suggested that the main function of the refutation is to weaken the force of the assertion. As this strategy has been manifested in the actual messages, however, the very act of refuting the attack arguments also involves making both general and specific assertions in favor of the concept, much as does the boost treatment. Indeed, the messages representing these two strategies were deliberately prepared to be quite similar—the boost uses much the same statements as the refutation but it does not define the specific arguments against the health practice, and thus does not engage in any explicit counterargumentation.

McGuire (1962) studied combinations of similar versions of the refutation and supportive treatments. He found that while the refutation considerably abetted the efficacy of the concept-supporting boost, the latter did little to raise the resistance offered by the refutation alone. Although his interpretation of such a finding is in terms of the inoculation theory of resistance to persuasion, the result is to be expected from the present reasoning as well. To McGuire, the boost is insufficient because it does not contain the alerting and defense-provoking threat to a person's belief, but can achieve this added critical factor when the refutation is added. In the terminology of the present theoretical framework, on the other hand, the two treatments are nonindependent, and hence should be nonadditive in their effect. Furthermore, since the refutation contains most of the boost and then some, we would expect it to gain less from the addition of the somewhat redundant boost than the latter would gain from the somewhat novel refutation.

This was investigated as part of the above-mentioned study of different strategy pairings, again dealing only with the X-ray issue in the immunization condition. In general agreement with McGuire's earlier findings and with the present predictions, the combined RBA treatment (11.20) was significantly ($p < .01$) superior to the BA (7.75) in creating resistance to the attack, but not significantly different from the refutation-only RA (10.80) group. Such a finding also suggests a significant departure from additivity in the direction of a lower or somewhat redundant combined effect, a suggestion that is supported by a significant interaction effect ($F = 4.64$; $1/76$ df; $p < .05$).

Although the boost strategy gains significantly from the addition of the refutation, there is no reciprocation in the reverse direction. Whether this finding results from the processes emphasized in McGuire's inoculation theory or from those specified by the somewhat different reasoning provided here—or, for that matter, from some third set of factors—is something we cannot determine at present. Furthermore, since the theories are not logically incompatible, it is even possible that both theoretical positions are correct.

2. Denial-Source Derogation Combination

Having two treatments that are partly or completely redundant is one way of achieving nonadditivity of combined effect. What about the situation where the presence of one treatment appears to violate or operate contrary to the functioning of another? In such instances, one would expect to find that the combination of the two is *less* effective than one or the other component alone.

Such a possibility could occur in the remaining one of the six possible combinations, that of the source derogation and denial treatments. Both of these treatments are intended to reduce the inconsistency of a favorable source taking a position against a favorable concept, but they do so by somewhat different means. In the source derogation, the intent is to discredit the source, to make him negative and of low credibility. The denial does not seek to alter the source attitude in any way, but rather to sever the alleged relationship. The success of this treatment depends on the source's being regarded as trustworthy and favorable, for otherwise the source would not be trusted and his denial would not be taken seriously. But this is just the sort of negative reaction the source attack procedure is designed to elicit. Accordingly, the two treatments, while seemingly appropriate each on its own, become incompatible when brought together.

In order to explore the consequences of such a situation, the separate and combined versions of the denial and source attack strategies were compared (again, on the X-ray issue in the immunization sequence). The combined strategies (SDA mean = 7.60) provided significantly ($p < .05$) *less* resistance to the persuasion attempt than the source attack (SA mean = 8.95) and also less, but not significantly, than the denial (DA mean = 8.05). The SDA mean was, however, still significantly ($p < .05$) higher than the attack-only control mean (5.60). That the denial does not gain (in fact, it loses somewhat) in effectiveness when the source attack is added is to be expected since its operation depends on the source's remaining in a favorable light, which the source manipulation clearly contradicts. Similarly, the significant decrement in the source attack treatment when the denial is added is also to be expected. The denial presumably works by creating an accepted, more congruous situation from the incongruous one established by having a negative source making an unfavorable assertion about a positive concept; the denial treatment essentially contends that the incongruous relationship does not really exist.

IV. Mechanisms of the Refutation Treatment

One of the more consistent findings emerging from the foregoing data is the clear superiority of the refutation treatment as a persuasion reducer. In none of our studies has it failed to produce a significant lessening of attitude change, whether in the immunization or restoration sequences. Further, it has generally produced more resistance to persuasion than any of the other single treatments under more or less similar circumstances, a relative efficacy that is further attested to in the combined treatment studies.

These findings tend to corroborate those of McGuire in pointing to the power of the refutation manipulation, although it must again be recognized that while McGuire's and our messages representing this strategy are quite similar, they are not identical. Indeed, the refutation treatment lies at the very heart of McGuire's inoculation theory, which maintains that the individual is both unmotivated and unpracticed in defending his belief in the kind of "cultural truisms" being dealt with. Accordingly, the indicated strategy is to provide the motivation and material for defense "by making him aware of the vulnerability of the truism ... [and by giving] careful guidance in developing defensive material" (McGuire, 1964, pp. 201–202). The refutation treatment is designed to perform both these functions. By first raising the arguments to be encountered in the attack, it presumably is a threat that alerts the individual to muster his defenses. Then, by providing a specific rebuttal of the attack, it theoretically supplies the useful information with which to construct those defenses.

The position we have adopted emphasizes the assertion-weakening attributes of the refutation treatment. This, in fact, is what use of the term *refutation* implies—a point-by-point explicit countering of the attack arguments, rendering the attack invalid. Although this hypothesized mechanism is derived from general congruity principle considerations, the conjecture is surely not unique to our theoretical position. Indeed, McGuire himself apparently recognized this probable process when he referred to the refutation defense as serving to "weaken the plausibility of the [attack arguments]" (McGuire, 1961b, pp. 193–194).

As we noted in our consideration of the combination of the refutation and concept boost treatments (Section III, B, 1), there is an additional resistance-inducing mechanism that may be attributed to the refutation strategy: Both explicitly (by actually stating so outright) and implicitly (in the act of providing counterarguments to those raised in the attack), the refutation may serve to strengthen and intensify the belief, much in the manner suggested for the boost strategy itself. Such opinion intensification (or similar effects on other possible components of the attitude; cf. Guttman, 1954) may then help blunt the impact of the subsequent attack.

Thus, four principal mechanisms by which the refutation treatment may accomplish reduction of persuasion are indicated: the threatening, defense-alerting and defense-providing aspects emphasized in inoculation theory, and the attack-weakening and concept-boosting attributes we have tended to accentuate. The evidence in favor of inoculation theory is quite formidable, but it is also rather circumstantial (cf. Macaulay, 1965). This position is, to be sure, not unique in social psychology, largely because we lack *direct* measures of many of the postulated theoretical mechanisms, but it does raise the issue of alternative explanations. In most of the experiments cited by McGuire, the assertion-weakening characteristic of the refutation could account for the obtained data just as readily as does the threat-providing aspect underlined by inoculation theory. Similarly, it is possible to explain the results of the studies reported in this chapter employing inoculation theory considerations.

Within the context of our over-all research program we have conducted a number of investigations over the past few years which relate directly to the mechanisms posited for the refutation treatment. Some of these have already been described. Several additional analyses will be reported in this section. In so doing, we will consider both the inoculation and congruity approaches to the refutation treatment.

A. ALERTING DEVICES

McGuire's earlier versions of inoculation theory tended to emphasize the critical role of the refutation in alerting the individual to the possibility of attack, with less attention being given to the actual content of the refutation message. Thus, the relative superiority of the refutation over the supportive condition (McGuire, 1961a; McGuire and Papageorgis, 1961) was attributed to the former's having the crucial threat component. The increase in efficiency of the supportive defense when the refutation was added to it (McGuire, 1961b) is similarly explained by postulating the addition of a threat-arousing motivation created by the refutation. It was also found that although the supportive treatment did more to strengthen belief prior to the attack than did the refutation, it elicited even less resistance to persuasion (McGuire and Papageorgis, 1961), tending to rule out the concept-strengthening mechanism as an important immunizing consideration. More impressive evidence for the defense-alerting character of the refutation came from the demonstration that the refutation of one set of arguments apparently generalized to confer resistance to another set of arguments (Papageorgis and McGuire, 1961). Not least, an independent threat, in the form of a warning of the impending attack, was shown to enhance the effectiveness of both refutation and supportive defenses, but particularly of the latter, which presumably did not have the necessary threat component to begin with (McGuire and Papageorgis, 1962; McGuire, 1964).

In one of our earlier studies, conducted some time before McGuire's later work became available, several alerting devices were studied to determine whether they alone would provoke resistance to the subsequent attack. There were five different levels of alert, varying from a general alert, which merely indicated that various health practices, including toothbrushing (the key single issue in this study), were worthy of periodic evaluation and discussion, to one that specifically singled out toothbrushing and explicitly presented the four main points against the practice to be encountered in the attack. The intermediate steps varied in terms of explicitness of the details of the arguments to be raised against toothbrushing. An additional condition included a warning of a "severely critical" attack. The purpose of these variations on the alerting theme was to attempt a more specific location of the source of the alerting mechanism—if, indeed, such a mechanism were to be found.

The results indicated that none of the alerting conditions produced a final belief score that was significantly different from the attack-only group. Indeed, only one condition, which merely mentioned the toothbrushing issue as specifically deserving of reevaluation and discussion, had a score higher than the control condition, all others scoring even below the attack mean. If anything, then, there is some evidence that presumable alerting or threatening conditions facilitate the attack (although the differences fall far short of significance), but no evidence for any alert-created resistance.

It is obvious from this and other studies that alerting the subject that his belief is not all that secure, or even directly threatening his belief, is insufficient for producing resistance to persuasion. For one thing, if it were true, the attack itself could be considered such a threat, but it obviously fails to stimulate defense on the belief. More to the point, as the foregoing results showed, McGuire and Papageorgis (1962) also found a warning to be inadequate by itself.

But, although it emphasizes the threat component, inoculation theory does not maintain it is sufficient. The individual must also have the material from which to construct defenses. The refutation treatment apparently contains both these necessary elements. Additional highly convincing support for the theory is that when both elements are presented separately, by providing a threatening warning along with the supportive message, the resistance was greater than in the supportive condition and not less than that noted for the refutation condition (McGuire and Papageorgis, 1962). (However, when our versions of these two conditions, that is, a warning with the boost treatment, were attempted in a recent study, we found the combination to be less effective than the refutation.) In any case, while the data supporting inoculation theory are indeed impressive, it is still not clear how the refutation works. The lack of a difference between refutation and supportive-plus-warning does not necessarily prove that the two conditions work by the same means. Barring an independent message of threat as such, it is just as reasonable to assume that a warning weakens the attack rather than threatens or motivates the individual. Similarly, the results of another study in which the threat factor was manipulated by varying the number of arguments against the belief (McGuire, 1964) can be accounted for in terms of relative weakness of the attack.

B. EFFECTS OF DIFFERENT MESSAGE SOURCES

1. Varying Source of Refutation

Another of our earlier studies was undertaken to determine whether the influence of the refutation treatment was constant or whether it would vary as a function of the kind of source with which it was identified. In terms of congruity theory, we would expect attitude toward the source to influence the acceptability of a message. Thus, if the refutation were identified as coming from a favorable source, its impact should be more pronounced and hence the resistance it may confer should be enhanced. On the other hand, if the refutation were issued by an unfavorably regarded source, the subject should tend to discount it, and its influence in reducing the attack's impact would be lessened.

A study was undertaken in which the same refutational message for the X-ray issue was assigned to both a favorable (a fictitious Dr. John A. Schmidt, Professor of Clinical Medicine at Johns Hopkins Medical School) and an unfavorable (a fictitious *Truth and Health* magazine, distributed through health food stores) source. A third group read an irrelevant story dealing with food for astronauts. All three groups were subsequently exposed to the main attack message, in all cases identified as coming from our generally favorable Dr. William J. McGuire.

The results were clear-cut, showing that although both refutation treatments conferred significant degrees of resistance to subsequent persuasion, the one with the negative source conferred significantly less ($p < .01$). (Means: refutation–positive source, 11.33; refutation–negative source, 8.37; attack-only, 6.38.)

Just what inoculation theory would predict in such a situation is difficult to ascertain, largely because it does not address itself to such variables as message sources and the like. One could argue that, regardless of the source of the refutation, the two ingredients specified by inoculation theory as necessary and sufficient for the induction of immunization—the motivating threat and the defensive information—are present in both the favorable and unfavorable source conditions, and thus equal degrees of resistance should be induced.

It can also be argued, however, that a refutation emanating from a negative source provokes less threat than one from a positive source, and that there is therefore less motivation to utilize the defensive information.

By the same token, it cannot be said that the results demonstrate that the refutation operates as an assertion-weakening device. Although the findings are clearly in accord with congruity theory predictions, they do not prove anything about the refutation mechanism per se. They do indicate that the refutation effect is not uniform, but is itself subject to other influences.

2. Varying Attack Source

In a subsequent study, some variations on the design just described were introduced. In this case, there were two versions of the attack treatment: one with a favorable (Schmidt), the other with an unfavorable (the health fad magazine), source. The only source of the refutation was favorable (McGuire). The two main attacks appeared either as attack-only conditions, or with each preceded by the refutation, subjects being randomly assigned to the four experimental conditions.

The findings are summarized in Table III, which presents the mean before-after change scores resulting from the attack adjusted by convariance for variations in initial (preexposure) attitudinal position. We find that when the two attacks are presented by themselves, the attack from the negative source leads to significantly ($p < .02$) less opinion change, a finding similar to those of many earlier studies on differential source effects and in perfect keeping with the usual congruity theory predictions. When the refutation is

TABLE III
MEAN CHANGES FOR DIFFERENT ATTACK SOURCES
WITH AND WITHOUT REFUTATION TREATMENT[a]

	Refutation treatment			
Attack source	None		Positive source	
Positive	(A +)	− 6.00	(R + A +)	− 1.48
Negative	(A −)	− 3.76	(R + A −)	+ .92

[a]All means are significantly ($p < .05$) different from one another by Duncan range test. Negative scores signify changes in accord with the attack.

presented prior to the positive-source attack, there is a marked ($p < .01$) diminution in the effect of the attack, as we have found repeatedly in several earlier studies. When the refutation from the favorable source is combined with the subsequent attack from a negative source, there is an actual increase in favorability of attitude toward the concept. Such a strengthening of belief is also in keeping with congruity principle predictions. Both a negative attack source and a positive refutation source would bring about such a favorable opinion change, in this case apparently enough to overcome a fairly strong negative assertion. Thus, we find a significant effect due to the attack source, and a significant influence of the refutation treatment, with the interaction between the two being nonsignificant.

A key comparison here, and the main reason the study was conducted, is between the refutation-plus-positive-attack $(R+A+)$ and the negative-source, attack-only $(A-)$ conditions. The former condition represents the usual application of the refutation treatment, the effect of which we have ascribed to its weakening the impact of the attack. It was reasoned that the $A-$ treatment also represents a way of weakening the assertion's impact. Thus, if the two conditions produced the same reduction of persuasion, this finding would constitute support (but not confirmation) of the hypothesis of an assertion-weakening mechanism. In fact, as shown in Table III, there is a differential reduction of persuasion, with the $R+A+$ condition producing significantly $(p < .05)$ more resistance than $A-$. Again, there is no way of guaranteeing that the two conjectured means of weakening the assertion indeed function that way. But even assuming that they do, the relatively greater efficacy of the $R+A+$ condition implies that the refutation does something that a negative attack source does not do, something beyond their common weakening of the attack. It is quite possible that this additional element is made up of the threat- and defense-arousing characteristics inoculation theory attributes to the refutation treatment.

C. IMMUNIZATION VERSUS RESTORATION

One of the less successful predictions derived from inoculation theory has concerned possible order of effects in the presentation of various defense treatments. In particular, McGuire has argued that, with the refutation treatment, the restoration sequence should preserve the belief better than the immunization sequence. The assumption here is that the attack itself serves as a stronger motivating threat than the refutation. Thus, in the restoration sequence, subjects should make more appropriate use of the defense materials provided by the refutation since they will be highly motivated in this direction by the preceding attack—more so, at least, than in the reverse sequence.

No such difference showed up, however, in McGuire's (1961a) study bearing on this point. McGuire felt at the time that this could be explained by an insufficient time lag between attack and defense, and that a longer period might result in a superior restoration sequence effect. This reasoning paralleled his belief that a longer time period was necessary for the refutation to make its effect manifest as an immunizer (McGuire, 1962). It happened that in one of our studies (Tannenbaum et al., 1966), a full week was allowed between messages. There was indeed a difference between sequences, but it was significantly $(p < .05)$ in favor of the immunization condition.

As a matter of fact, in a number of additional comparisons of the two sequences, with the refutation strategy appearing both by itself and in combination with other treatments, the results have consistently favored immunization over restoration, though not always to a statistically significant degree. The same results obtain in the case of the source derogation treatment and, to a somewhat lesser degree, with the denial strategy. (We never did employ the concept boost manipulation as a restorative condition.)

There are a variety of possibilities to account for this greater effectiveness of the immunization sequence. For example, one can derive a prediction from inoculation theory opposite to that of McGuire's prediction. In the immunization sequence, the refutation is viewed as threatening but not overwhelming the belief, thus stimulating defense for the coming attack, much in the manner that inoculation with a weakened virus can stimulate the production of defensive antibodies. Continuing the biological analogy, introducing the inoculation after the strong attack is futile since the unalerted defenses have already—as in the case of the barn door that is closed after the horse has been stolen—been overcome. In the same manner, the rather powerful nature of the main attack may have already subdued the defenses provided by the refutation in restoration conditions. While this reasoning, if extended far enough, could lead us to predict no reductive effect for the restoration sequence, which is clearly not the case, it does allow for a superior immunization influence.

Alternatively, one can just as readily attribute the differential effect to a more pronounced weakening of the attack, in keeping with our theoretical emphasis. The attack, according to our rationale, is directly weakened by the refutation. The attack may also be indirectly weakened by other strategies: derogation of the attack source (as we have argued earlier) and denial. If such attack weakening takes place, it should be more effective if done before the attack has had a chance to take maximum effect, that is, in the immunization sequence.

Some empirical support for this position is contained in the study by Macaulay (1965), to be described in more detail later. This study involved the refutation and denial treatments, and included a judgment of the quality of the attack message as a separate (from the belief measures as such) dependent variable. Subjects in the immunization condition rated the attack (6.73 on a 15-point scale) as being less fair and believable than did those in the restoration sequence (8.30), the difference being sufficient at beyond the .02 level.

Such an interpretation, it should be noted, has some of the earmarks of the general hypothesis of the superiority of primacy over recency in persuasion, a problem that is still not fully resolved (e.g., Insko, 1964; Anderson and Barrios, 1965; Lana, 1964). Another possibility is that, in the restoration sequence, the attack produces a change in attitude such that the subsequent defense treatment is then dissonant (Keisler and Keisler, 1964) or incongruous (Tannenbaum and Norris, 1965) with the new belief. The defense therefore loses some of its effectiveness. As with the other possible explanations, this is purely speculative at present. In the absence of more direct measures of the possible mechanisms involved, we must allow for alternative explanations, although Macaulay's above-mentioned findings provide some more direct support for the attack-weakening process.

D. GENERALIZATION VERSUS SPECIFICITY OF DEFENSE

A rather telling point in favor of inoculation theory has been the demonstration that the refutation of one set of arguments against a belief generalizes to induce immunity to an attack composed of a somewhat different set of agruments (Papageorgis and McGuire, 1961; McGuire, 1961a). Such a finding is in perfect accord with the position that the refutation, by threatening the belief, stimulates the building of defenses which should then reduce the impact of any subsequent attack. The finding also runs counter to the analysis of the refutation as essentially an attack-weakener, since the latter position argues that the refutation contradicts the specific attack arguments, and hence should be effective only against such an attack. It is also possible, however, that the refutation of one set of arguments implies that the originally favorable position was indeed the proper one and that refutation thus serves to diminish the influence of *all* subsequent attacks. Further, while the demonstration of any degree of generalized resistance is impressive in itself, the results do indicate more resistance when the attack arguments are the same as those refuted rather than novel ones (Papageorgis and McGuire, 1961; McGuire, 1961b). Moreover, in one case (McGuire, 1961b), the refutation failed to produce any significant degree of generalization.

A separate investigation of our own focused directly on this issue of generality versus specificity of the refutation mechanism by utilizing a design in which all subjects were exposed to two related but separately focused attacks on the belief, with variations in the degree of relevance to these different attacks of an intervening refutational condition. The particular belief concerned the benefits of regular toothbrushing. The general attack on this practice used by both McGuire and ourselves in earlier research was divided into two separate attack messages. One (A_a) argued that toothbrushing does not really do any good in promoting dental hygiene, that it is an unnecessary practice as far as health is concerned. The second attack (A_b) argued that toothbrushing was not only futile but that it was positively dangerous in that it could induce damaging effects to dental and general health. Four experimental groups were employed, each receiving both the A_a and A_b attacks, in that order, but receiving different treatments between the two attacks. One group received only a refutation of the first attack (R_a); another group received only a refutation of the second attack arguments (R_b); a third group received refutations of both attacks (R_{ab}), while the fourth group, serving as a control condition, received no intervening treatment at all (R_o). Ratings were obtained on a set of three 15-point scales, each administered at three points in the procedure: a base-line measure prior to any exposure at all (T_1); after the first A_a attack and the particular refutation treatment (T_2); and the last after the second A_b attack (T_3).

This design allowed assessment of several effects of interest in determining the mechanism of the refutation strategy. Of direct concern is whether there is a differential effectiveness of the various refutation treatments, as the notion of specificity of effect would maintain, or if they all are more or less equally effective, as inoculation theory would hold. The various refutation treatments have three different loci of effect: in terms of reducing the impact of attack A_a, of attack A_b, or of both attacks combined.

Table IV summarizes the various findings. The first column presents the T_2-T_1 change scores, and thus reflects the impact of attack A_a along with the refutation treatments, which of course serve as restoration conditions in this respect. Here we find rather marked evidence for specificity of effect: Where the refutation treatments contain specific counterarguments relative to the A_a attack arguments (that is, in conditions R_a and R_{ab}), there is a significant and equal reduction of persuasion. In the case of R_b, however, where the refutation counterarguments are not directly relevant, there is more negative attitude change, not significantly less than that in the attack-only control.

TABLE IV

MEAN BELIEF CHANGE ACCORDING TO TYPE OF REFUTATION TREATMENT
AND LOCUS OF EFFECT[a]

| Refutation treatment | Effect | | |
	First attack (A_a) (T_2-T_1 change)	Second attack (A_b) (T_3-T_2)	Total (T_3-T_1)
R_a	-0.21_a	-4.98_d	-5.19_y
R_b	-5.45_b	-1.98_c	-7.43_y
R_{ab}	-0.21_a	-1.02_c	-1.24_x
R_o	-8.02_b	-7.86_e	-15.88_z

[a] *Within the same column only*, means with the same alphabetical subscript do not differ from each other at the .05 level by Duncan multiple range test. The greater the negative score the more effective was the attack.

The data on T_3–T_2 change reflect the impact of the A_b attack. In this case, the different refutation treatments act as immunizers. Again, there is evidence for specificity in that the more relevant conditions—R_b and R_{ab}, both containing rebuttals of the specific A_b arguments—confer the most resistance, with the difference between them being nonsignificant. However, here we also find some evidence for generalization, since R_a treatment, where the refutation materials are not directly relevant, does show less T_3–T_2 change than the attack-only control group. It is to be noted, however, that this reduction of change is significantly less than when the information is directly appropriate, as in the R_b and R_{ab} conditions.

The last column reflects the over-all change accruing from both attacks. As expected, the condition where the arguments from both attacks are refuted, R_{ab}, shows the most resistance. The groups that get only partial refutation, R_a and R_b, each change more, but still significantly less than the attack-only control. The R_a condition exhibits somewhat less change than R_b but the difference falls short of significance ($p = .15$).

Thus, the findings offer strong support for the specificity hypothesis implied by the congruity principle notion of an assertion-weakening mechanism. There is also some evidence for a generalization effect, however, particularly in terms of the significant degree of resistance provided by the R_a treatment to the A_b attack. As we pointed out at the beginning of this section, though, this can be interpreted in terms other than the arousal of defense from the R_a treatment.

Further support for the specificity model is obtained when the data are analyzed separately for each of the belief items, instead of across all three at once. The three items were prepared so that one reflected the main focus of the A_a attack, another of the A_b attack, and the third was a general evaluative statement not particularly linked to either attack. The detailed analysis indicates that these items are indeed sensitive to the respective treatments. There was a substantial degree of specificity rather than generalization in the refutation treatments. Thus, the R_a and R_{ab} groups show substantial change at T_2 on the relevant A_a attack item, with relatively little effect on the nonrelevant item reflecting attack A_b. Conversely, groups R_b and R_{ab} show more change on the second item than the first at T_3. For the most part, the general item changes along with the directly relevant one in each case.

E. DIRECT ASSESSMENT OF MECHANISMS

Mention has already been made of the study of Macaulay (1965), especially in reference to the combination of the refutation and denial treatments (Section III, A, 2) and in terms of the immunization versus restoration comparisons (Section IV, C). In addition to such aims, a major purpose of this study was to attempt a more direct assessment of the various mechanisms suggested for the refutation treatment through the use of specific question-naire items. Although there are some recognized weaknesses in employing these items, the data are of some use since the main dependent variable in this and other studies, the actual belief measures, were inadequate for the purpose of discriminating among the several possible mechanisms.

In this study, it will be recalled, there were four single treatments—denial and refutation in both immunization and restoration sequence (DA, AD, RA, AR)—and two combined DRA and ADR conditions, along with the usual A and 0 control groups. In addition to the regular belief items, subjects were asked to express their reactions to various aspects of the messages on a set of 9-point scales; all, including the belief items, were administered on an after-only basis. Analysis on such items is focused on the various refutation groups in comparison with those receiving either the denial or no defense treatment at all.

1. Defense Arousal

A number of items were included to get at factors presumed to underlie the stimulation of defense mechanisms by the refutation strategy. One concerned the subjects' interest in receiving more information on the X-ray topic; inoculation theory implies that the refutation subjects would be more interested in having such information. In general, a relatively high degree of interest (6.73 on the 9-point scale) in this information was found across all groups, with no differences to speak of between groups.

A similar prediction was made for expressed certainty of belief in the X-ray practice; the notion was that those people feeling threatened would feel less certain, and those stimulated to develop defenses would feel more confident. Again, however, there were no differences between groups; all conditions, including the no-message control, showed only moderate certainty (mean = 5.50 on 9-point scale). This measure relates somewhat to one employed by Papageorgis and McGuire (1961) where their subjects were asked to record as many individual arguments as they could in support of the various truisms employed. Although there was a slight tendency for the refutation subjects to list more supportive statements than those in the no-defense treatment, the difference also failed to reach significance.

Macaulay also included an item assessing the perceived position of the attack message, in order to test the hypothesis advanced by Manis and Blake (1963) that the belief threat would lead those subjects who had not been immunized to assimilate the message to their own position. Again, however, there was no support in the data, with subjects in all conditions generally judging the attack message to be equally strong against the practice.

2. Belief Strengthening

As we have noted, another mechanism suggested for refutation to function is that it strengthens and intensifies the belief. McGuire and Papageorgis (1961), however, reported that while there was such a slight strengthening effect for the refutation, it was less than for the supportive treatment, although the refutation then turned out to be by far the more effective immunizer. McGuire has further elaborated upon such an apparent "paper tiger" phenomenon, pointing to "the peril of assuming the immunizing effectiveness of a defense to be a direct function of its apparent strengthening effect" (McGuire, 1964, pp. 207–208).

Macaulay included two statements concerning supportive points for the main belief in her inventory of belief measures, and found the refutation-only treatment led to stronger endorsement of these items (8.66) than the denial-only (6.99) group, although the difference falls just short of statistical significance ($p = .06$). In addition, there is a significant difference for these items between the combined DRA and ADR groups (10.10) and the no-message control group (8.45), indicating some strengthening of belief. Macaulay concluded, from these and other correlational data, that "observed differences tend to support the prediction that refutation works at least in part by belief strengthening, but these differences are not all statistically significant . . . the hypothesis has not been strongly confirmed but has received enough support not to be dismissed" (Macaulay, 1965, p. 53).

3. Assertion Weakening

Reference has already been made to judgments of the fairness and believability of the attack message in connection with the earlier discussion of immunization and restoration sequences. Such an index is of obvious interest here since it relates directly to the mechanism suggested by congruity theory as being most responsible for the effectiveness of the refutation.

The findings across all conditions were unequivocal. There was a significant ($p < .01$) difference in attack rating between conditions where the refutation treatment was present (6.83) and when it was absent (9.20). This difference existed under both immunization and restoration conditions, more so in the former, as we noted earlier.

In this connection, it should also be mentioned that Papageorgis and McGuire (1961) included such an index in their attempt to identify the mechanism for the refutation condition. They used a set of ten semantic differential-type scales designed to measure the judged quality of the attack arguments. Their results also pointed to a weakening in the credibility of the attack when it was preceded by a refutation defense. And, in connection with our earlier comment of what it may be that generalizes from a refutation of one set of arguments conferring immunity against a different set, it was also found that such a weakening of the attack was equally apparent in the refutation-same and refutation-different conditions.

It is clear that the refutation condition, whatever else it might do, substantially alters the force of the assertion. Given the fact that we are generally dealing with fairly strong assertions to begin with, such assertion weakening is clearly one factor that must be considered in determining how the refutation treatment effects resistance to persuasion. There is evidence from a number of studies reported here that this is indeed the case, and that such a mechanism provides a quite parsimonious accounting of the various findings. But there is evidence, too, that the mechanisms suggested by McGuire's inoculation theory are also at work.

As we have indicated before, these two major approaches are not natural enemies. The main difference between them is one of emphasis rather than contradiction. It is more than possible that both theoretical positions are valid and that both may be operative in a given application of the refutation strategy. As McGuire has noted in a somewhat different context, inoculation theory does "not rule out the possibility that other components of the refutational defense also would contribute to resistance to persuasion, any more than Boyle's law implies the invalidity of Charles' law" (McGuire, 1964, p. 215). Macaulay (1965) has taken a similar stance, offering an "additive multifactor model" representing contributions from both congruity and inoculation theory, and we here advocate a corresponding position.

V. Persuasion via Congruity and Information Processes

It is apparent that underlying much of our work in developing resistance to persuasion are two general and quite different processes by which persuasion, and hence its reduction, may be accomplished. On the one hand, we have relied heavily on rather straightforward congruity principle procedures whereby the elements involved in a cognitive relationship are in a congruous or balanced state, or where the existence of incongruity generates pressures toward attitude change. This type of reasoning is best exemplified by the rationale for the source derogation treatment as a means of inducing immunization, and this rationale, in turn, stems directly from the earlier work on the congruity principle in situations involving the induction, rather than reduction, of attitude change. Mechanisms of this type generally belong in the realm of "psycho-logic", to use Abelson and Rosenberg's (1958) most apt term.

On the other hand, there is the position that much attitude change, or lack of it, stems from the inherent informational content of a message. Katz, for example, speaks of attitude change occurring when, among other things, an individual "finds his old attitudes in conflict with new information and new experiences, and proceeds to modify his beliefs" (Katz, 1960, p. 190). Similarly, Brehm and Cohen (1962) refer to the "information processing" that goes on upon exposure to a message, with the incoming information being weighed and considered against existing cognitions, and there are numerous other such conceptualizations. In the present context, such an approach would attribute much of belief change in the various attack conditions of our research to the novel (for the subject, at least) information being presented against the particular health practice. By the same reasoning, the refutational defense confers resistance to persuasion largely because it provides direct information that refutes or contradicts the arguments in the attack.

The basic dichotomy referred to here can take many different forms, and both can be present in different or even the same situations (cf. Kelman and Eagly, 1965). In some ways, the contrast is reminiscent of earlier research in the field of persuasion comparing between so-called rational versus emotional appeals. The accumulated evidence on this issue is rather spotty and divided, with some studies purporting to demonstrate superiority for the emotional appeal (e.g., Hartmann, 1936; Menefee and Granneberg, 1940; Lewan and Stotland, 1961), others claiming more or less equal effectiveness (e.g., Knower, 1935; Weiss and Lieberman, 1959) and at least one (Weiss, 1960) indicating a stronger rational effect. Other factors, however, were rarely equivalent between the critical experimental conditions, and it is more than likely that the relative effectiveness of the two approaches interacts highly with personality (cf. Hovland et al., 1949) and situational characteristics.

Although most of out attention in this chapter has been directed to the problems of reduction of persuasion, such concerns led us to a reexamination of the relative efficacy of the congruity and informational approaches as inducers of attitude change. Two studies on this theme were conducted, and these in turn led to an additional study on the reduction of attitude change.

A. VARYING SOURCES OR INFORMATION INPUTS

The basic method we adopted, one calculated to reduce the possible contamination of factors other than the theoretical mechanisms, was to use the double-attack paradigm similar to that employed in the study of the specificity of refutation (Section IV.D). The belief area selected was the use of X rays for the detection of TB. As with the toothbrushing issue used earlier, it was possible to divide the arguments of the attack into two separate messages, one supporting the contention that X rays are unnecessary (A_a) and a second featuring information that X rays are positively damaging to a person's health (A_b). Similarly, two different sources, both judged as highly favorable on pretests, were employed; one was a professor of radiology (S_x), the other the Surgeon General's Office (S_y).

Four basic groups of subjects were used, each group receiving two message exposures. All groups were first exposed to the A_a attack from either S_x or S_y, the four groups varying in terms of the redundancy of the second message relative to the first. For Group I, the situation was totally redundant, that is, the same source issued essentially the same statement in the second message as in the first. For Group II, the second message was also identified as coming from the same source, but contained new information in the form of A_b attack. For Group III, a different source issued the same A_a attack. Group IV had both sources and information nonredundant, with a different source issuing a different attack. Belief measures were assessed on three of the usual 15-point scales prior to the first message and after the second, the analysis being conducted on the change scores, covarying for initial belief score.

Table V presents the relevant data. The covariance analysis revealed a significant ($p < .01$) difference between the two source treatments, and somewhat less but still significant ($p < .05$) between the two attack treatments, with the interaction effect being negligible ($F < 1$). This testifies that both mechanisms are effective in their own right, but more so for the congruity strategy. This is seen more clearly in the comparison between the

TABLE V

ADJUSTED MEAN CHANGE SCORES ACCORDING TO SOURCE AND
ATTACK CONDITIONS[a]

	Same sources	Different sources	Marginals
Same attacks	-3.21_a	-5.68_c	-4.45
Different attacks	-4.45_b	-6.55_c	-5.50
Marginals	-3.83	-6.12	

[a] Means with different subscripts are significantly different from one another at the .05 level.

individual cell means. Both theories predict that the least total change would occur in the totally redundant (Group I) condition and the largest change in the totally nonredundant (Group IV) condition, which is plainly the case. The new information, redundant source condition (Group II) is superior to the Group I mean, as expected from the information-processing approach. However, the main congruity strategy reflected in Group III (redundant information, different sources) produces significantly more change than the corresponding Group II mean, and is, moreover, not significantly less than the maximum Group IV mean. Thus, although there is evidence that both treatments—varying the information content, or varying the identified sources—produce significant increments of persuasion, the latter procedure is relatively more effective.

B. CONGRUITY VERSUS INFORMATIONAL CONSISTENCY

A similar means of investigating the differences between the two persuasion processes was utilized in another study involving the two-message paradigm. In this case, the topic was a relatively neutral concept, teaching machines, and two messages were prepared, one with information favorable to the concept (I +), the other with unfavorable information (I −). Similarly, two different sources were employed, one favorable (S +), the other unfavorable (S −). Four groups were employed, each one getting two messages from the two different sources, but in different combinations.

Group I received the S + I − and the S − 1 + messages, while Group II received the S + I + and the S − I − messages. In both cases, the pair of messages are consistent with one another in the congruity principle sense but are inconsistent in terms of only the informational content. Thus, in Group I, a favorable source being against the concept is perfectly congruous with an unfavorable source being for the concept, both conditions creating pressure toward a negative shift in attitude toward the concept. From a purely informational standpoint, however, the message contents are contradictory and, assuming that the I + and I − effects are roughly equal, they should cancel one another. Similarly, in the Group II situation, congruity theory would predict a substantial positive attitude change toward the concept, both messages being consistent in that direction, while the inconsistent information would again predict a minimal change in one direction or the other.

The two remaining conditions present the opposite prediction situation. In Group III, the S + I + and S − 1 + messages were used. In terms of the informational approach, these messages are consistent in a favorable direction, and a substantial positive change is indicated. From a congruity position, however, the messages are inconsistent. But the congruity principle does recognize an assertion constant and would thus allow for some positive attitude change, but less than in the Group II situation. Similarly, Group IV had the S + I − and S − I − messages, again representing informational consistency but congruity inconsistency. The former position would here predict a strong negative shift, whereas congruity, again mindful of some assertion effect, would allow for only a slight change in a negative direction.

Within each group, the order of presentation of the two messages was alternated across subjects to control for any possible order effects. In this study, judgments of the concept were obtained on a set of semantic differential scales, with ratings across four scales, which had high loadings on the evaluative factor, constituting the attitudinal measure. These scales were administered before and after the two-message exposure, the covariance analysis being conducted on the change scores.

The results, presented in Table VI, completely confirm the congruity theory predictions. In the two instances where the theory predicts favorable changes, such changes occur, but significantly ($p < .02$) more so for Group II than for Group III, also as predicted. Groups I and IV also exhibit the anticipated unfavorable changes, the former significantly ($p < .05$) more than the latter. There is almost a complete washout of the informational effect as such, with the congruity theory providing by far the most parsimonious accounting for the obtained results.

TABLE VI

ADJUSTED MEAN CHANGE FOR VARIOUS CONDITIONS OF
CONGRUITY AND INFORMATIONAL CONSISTENCY

Condition	Messages		Group	Mean change
Congruity consistency, informational inconsistency	S+I−	S−I+	I	−4.16
	S+I+	S−I−	II	+5.36
Congruity inconsistency, informational consistency	S+I+	S−I+	III	+2.30
	S+I−	S−I−	IV	−2.42

A recent study by David Sears at UCLA (personal communication) yielded somewhat similar findings. A political situation in the state of California during a recent gubernatorial election campaign was utilized. In one condition, partisan Democrats were told that both their own candidate and the Republican candidate agreed on an issue (as in Groups III or IV in the experiment just described) while another such group was told only the position of the Democratic candidate. Contrary to what might be expected in such a situation, but consistent with congruity theory, there was actually less change in the advocated direction in the condition where both candidates agreed. However, subjects in that condition apparently felt more confident in their belief, an added variable that we unfortunately did not include in our own study.

C. APPROPRIATENESS OF DEFENSE TO ATTACK

Given two basic and somewhat different processes to account for the induction of attitude change, there are also two corresponding processes for eliciting resistance to persuasion. An interesting question for research is thus presented when we contrast the two defensive with the two attacking strategies. In keeping with the general theoretical position we have adopted earlier, we would predict that the more appropriate and directly relevant a given defensive treatment is to the attacking strategy, the more effective that defense should be.

To examine this proposition, an experiment was conducted in which two main attacks on the X-ray belief were administered. One attack merely consisted of a statement by a respected source (an alleged dean of medicine at a well-known university and chairman of the "National Medical Research Board") condemning the practice as "useless and even dangerous... almost criminal to use for the detection of TB considering the presence of much safer, more advanced techniques." This attack (A_s) merely established that the source was strongly against the practice but did not give any information as such regarding the specific points of contention. The second attack (A_I) was not identified as coming from any particular source, but featured in detail the four arguments against the practice, much as in earlier versions of the main attack.

Within each attack condition, there were three variations of pre-attack defensive treatment. One consisted of a derogation of the source (D_s) of the A_s attack. This was considered to be a defense more appropriate to the A_s than to the A_I attack. The second defense was a detailed refutation of the A_I attack arguments, without any mention of the source as such (R). This was considered to be a more appropriate defense for the A_I attack than for the A_s attack. To provide a baseline control, subgroups within each attack version did not get any defensive pretreatment at all. Pretreatment and posttreatment belief measures were obtained, the analysis being conducted on the change scores covarying for initial position.

Table VII contains the adjusted mean change scores for each experimental condition. Both attack versions produced substantial degrees of persuasion, significantly more for A_I than for A_s. When the A_I attack was preceded by the directly relevant refutation defense (R), a very significant ($p < .001$) reduction of change was noted. When the inappropriate source derogation defense was used with A_I, however, no such diminution in impact of the attack resulted.

For the A_s attack, the more relevant D_s defense induced a significant degree of resistance, although not nearly as marked as the D_R defense for the A_I attack. It is also apparent, however, that the refutation does confer some degree of immunity of the attack. Although the difference between the A_s attack by itself and the less appropriate refutational defense is not quite significant ($.15 > p > .10$), the D_R change is not significantly more than that for the D_s defense.

TABLE VII

ADJUSTED MEAN CHANGES FOR DIFFERENT DEFENSE AND ATTACK TREATMENTS[a]

Attack treatment	Defensive treatment		
	None (D_0)	Source derogation (D_S)	Refutation (D_R)
Source statement (A_S)	-4.60_b	-3.14_{cd}	-3.72_{bc}
Informational (A_I)	-6.43_a	-6.06_a	-1.98_d

[a] Means with the same subscript are not different from one another at the .05 level.

Thus, while we generally find that the defense that is directly relevant to the attack's mechanism is most effective in reducing the persuasive impact of that attack, the D_R treatment demonstrates some generalization in its influence—certainly more than the D_S defense. A similar phenomenon was noted earlier (Section IV, D) when it was found that although the refutation was more effective when it coped with the same arguments as the attack, it also showed some ability to immunize against novel arguments. Again, the present data do not allow us to determine the instrumentality of such apparent generalization; it may be because the refutation stimulates defense building, or because it causes one to be suspicious of any forthcoming attack, or because of both. For that matter, it may be the result of some quite different factor.

VI. Generalization of Attitude Change

It sometimes happens that in the course of pursuing one line of research other areas of equal or even more theoretical interest present themselves. Such a case occurred in our program of research, where work on the reduction of persuasion uncovered some findings involving the generalization of attitude change from one concept, toward which attitude had been manipulated, to others where no specific manipulation had taken place. This, in turn, led to some more deliberate efforts to apply the congruity principle to the area of persuasion research.

A. AFFECTIVE SIMILARITY

Our original interest in this phenomenon was stimulated by a more or less chance set of consequences in our original investigation of the various congruity theory strategies for resistance to persuasion (see Section II). In that study, three separate belief issues were employed (X rays for the detection of TB; regular toothbrushing; and regular medical checkups) in a before-after testing design. Independent groups were used, such that subjects in any one group were experimentally manipulated on only one of the belief issues. To facilitate administration of the testing, however, both pre- and posttreatment belief measures were obtained from all subjects on all three issues; that is, for any given group or subject, there was one manipulated concept (MC) and two nonmanipulated "filler" concepts (NMCs). Although our main concern in the study was the change on the manipulated concepts, change scores were also available for the filler items.

There was little basis to expect any substantial change within each group on the nonmanipulated concepts. There was no mention of the filler issues in any of the experimental messages and no information at all about them was conveyed. However, examination of the data revealed slight, generally negative shifts in the change scores, and it was decided to subject these data to somewhat closer scrutiny.

The particular focus selected was to examine the change scores for a particular pair of NMCs in terms of their respective similarity to the particular MC for that subject. For each of the three concepts, the pre-exposure attitude scores on a 15-point scale were available, and it was thus possible to divide the two NMCs, in a given case, in terms of their proximity in these initial ratings vis-à-vis the MC in that case. The rationale for such a focus stems from the repeated demonstration in learning theory research (cf. Mostofsky, 1965) of the generalization of some conditioned response as a function of similarity of the unconditioned stimuli. It was similarly reasoned here that if there were any spread of persuasion from the manipulated to the nonmanipulated concepts it would be systematically related to the similarity in initial (preexposure) attitude—the more similar the initial ratings between MC and NMC, the greater the degree of generalization.

In the first analysis the two NMCs for a given subject (these, of course, varied across the three concepts, since the MCs also varied) were cast into two categories of relative closeness in preexposure attitude scores to the MC. Such allocation was made regardless of direction or magnitude of the differences involved: the NMC closer to the MC in either direction was put in the "closer" category, the other NMC into the "further" category. In the event of a tie, the data for that subject were discarded.

The results supported the similarity model. Most changes were in a negative direction, in accord with the generally negative shifts for the MC in the various experimental conditions, but significantly ($p < .02$, Wilcoxon paired replicates test) more so for the more similar preexposure attitudes (mean change $= -2.24$) than the less similar attitudes ($+0.36$). Moreover, when the data were subsequently analyzed in terms of the magnitude of the MC-NMC differences, the usual negatively decelerating generalization gradient was obtained—the greatest negative change found where the NMCs were minimally different from the MC, this change becoming increasingly less as the difference became greater.

These findings, along with highly similar ones in another study, which involved both positive and negative attitude changes, are consistent with the view that attitudes are learned responses (cf. Doob, 1947; Hovland et al., 1953) and, as such, may be acquired and altered through indirect as well as direct means. Earlier studies have demonstrated that the affective components of highly evaluated words and concepts could be transferred on other verbal stimuli through classical conditioning procedures (e.g., Staats and Staats, 1958; Staats et al., 1959; Das and Nanda, 1963), and we now find a similar phenomenon for the transfer of attitude change. The findings are also consistent with the view that attitudinal objects tend to be structured and clustered on the basis of perceived attributes or relationships, and that change in one element of a related structure tends to precipitate changes in the other elements. McGuire (1960) demonstrated such a transference between logically related elements of a syllogism, and the present data tend to support a similar position in terms of pure attitudinal similarity (cf. Osgood and Tannenbaum, 1955).

B.   GENERALIZATION FROM CONCEPT TO SOURCE

The foregoing findings, obtained mainly as by-products to an experiment directed along quite different lines, led to a reconsideration of the earlier work on the congruity principle in terms of a generalization paradigm. In the initial studies (Osgood and Tannenbaum, 1955; Tannenbaum, 1956), communication messages were used in which an identifiable source made an assertion for or against a given concept, but with the bulk of the argumentation directed at the concept. In addition to the expected change in attitude toward the concept, the results supported the prediction of appropriate change in attitude toward the source. Since the source was merely mentioned in the message and not specifically manipulated, this situation can also be viewed as an instance of generalization of change in the concept to the source. In this case, however, the relationship between manipulated and nonmanipulated elements is in terms of a directed evaluative association and not, as in the foregoing, of mere affective similarity.

In terms of the generalization paradigm, there are two main cognitive operations involved: the establishment of the directed relationship between source and concept, and the manipulation of the attitude toward the concept. In the original experiments, these two operations were accomplished in the same message and thus it was impossible to have the two operations in contrast to one another; for instance, the source could not be against the concept and yet have the concept supported.

These two steps were independently manipulated in a recent study (Tannenbaum and Gengel, 1966), thus allowing for a more complete test of the congruity theory predictions. The source-concept linkage was established first, then the concept attitude was altered without any reference to the source, the main dependent variable being the change in attitude toward the source. On the basis of pretesting, three psychologists, two fictitious and one actual, were selected as being essentially neutral sources. Each was subsequently linked with a neutral concept (teaching machines), one source being in favor of the concept (S+), another adopting an unfavorable position (S−), and the third being in a neutral relationship (S_0). A separate message was subsequently administered, half the subjects getting information designed to create a favorable attitude toward teaching machines, the other half getting negative information. Attitude measures were obtained on four semantic differential scales before and after the messages.

Predictions for change in attitude toward the sources can be readily derived from congruity theory. Where the concept changes favorably, we would expect S+ to change in a favorable direction too, and we would expect S− to change negatively. Conversely, when the concept changes unfavorably, S+ should change unfavorably, but S− favorably. In both cases, S_0 should not change appreciably one way or the other.

TABLE VIII

MEAN ATTITUDE CHANGE TOWARD SOURCES
ACCORDING TO TYPE OF CONCEPT MANIPULATION [a,b]

Concept manipulation	Source linkage		
	Favorable (S+)	Neutral (S_0)	Unfavorable (S−)
Positive ($n = 57$)	$+4.75_a$	$+4.08_a$	$+1.87_{bc}$
Negative ($n = 67$)	$+1.44_b$	$+3.59_a$	$+3.61_{ac}$

[a] Means with the same subscript are not significantly different from one another at the .05 level (by one-tailed Dunn Test). The comparisons apply only within a given row or column, but not across both simultaneously.

[b] Data from Tannenbaum and Gengel (1966).

The fit of the experimental data to the theoretical predictions may be seen in Table VIII. One immediate discrepancy is readily apparent: all changes are in a favorable direction. Further, S_0 shows substantial positive change under both concept manipulation conditions. A plausible explanation is that a general halo effect accrued to all sources as a function of the setting of the various messages. In order to make the situation appear realistic, subjects were informed in the first message that the three psychologists appeared at a symposium on the topic of teaching machines at a meeting of the American Psychological Association. It is possible that for our subjects (undergraduate students) any psychologist appearing at such a symposium must be an authoritative and favorably regarded person. Further, S_0 was identified as the chairman of the symposium, but was referred to as a "principal authority on learning theory," and this statement may have contributed to the favorable impression of him.

In any case, even if all differences are in a positive direction, the relative changes may still be examined, and here there is general support for the congruity theory predictions. Within the positive manipulation condition, $S+$ shows significantly ($p < .01$) more favorable shift than $S-$, as predicted. Also as predicted, $S-$ shows significantly more favorable shift than $S+$ when the concept is negatively manipulated. Looking at a specific source across the two manipulations, we found the predicted greater favorable change on $S+$ in the positive rather than the negative manipulation; no difference on S_0; but, contrary to the prediction, lack of a significant difference for $S-$. On this last comparison, however, a t test, which is also appropriate here, was significant ($t = 1.98$; 122 df; $p < .05$).

Thus, although the findings were not entirely as predicted, the results generally conform to congruity theory expectations. As Tannenbaum and Gengel (1966) point out in their fuller report on this study, the predicted differences are sharpened when the analysis is conducted with control for actual change in attitude toward the manipulated concept, rather than in terms of expected change, with all differences at $p < .01$.

Further evidence on such concept-to-source generalization of persuasion was obtained as part of the study reported in the following section, this time using a single source differentially associated (for different groups) with the same concept and omitting the neutral linkage condition. In this case, with somewhat "cleaner" experimental conditions obtaining, the results more clearly support the theoretical predictions. All changes in source attitude were in the predicted directions, including anticipated negative shifts, and all predicted differences were highly significant (see Table 2 in Tannenbaum, 1966b).

C. MEDIATED GENERALIZATION

A further extension of the congruity principle as a model for the generalization of attitude change is readily apparent. A source may be evaluatively linked to more than one concept, each such linkage constituting a specific cognitive relationship. Change in attitude toward one concept influences that particular source-concept relationship, and may result, as we have seen, in change in attitude toward the source in order to put that relationship on a congruous basis. But this modification in the source introduces an incongruity in its relationship with a second concept (even though the latter concept is not specifically manipulated) and attitude toward the second concept should change in order to resolve that new incongruity. Thus, generalization of persuasion from one concept to another may be effected in the absence of any direct linkage between the two conepts and mediated through their association with a common source.

Materials similar to those used in the preceding experiment were employed in a new study designed to examine this phenomenon (Tannenbaum, 1966b). Pretesting allowed for the selection of two neutral concepts—teaching machines (TM) and "Spence learning theory" (LT)—and a single neutral source. All subjects were first exposed to a message in which the source's position on both concepts was established. Four such conditions being used were: one in which the source stated positive positions on both concepts (*pp* condition); another with the source favoring TM but negative to LT (*pn* condition); a third with the source against TM but in favor of LT (*np* condition), and the fourth with the source being against both concepts (*nn* condition). After a half-hour interval of irrelevant activity, all subjects were exposed to a message designed to manipulate the attitude toward only the TM concept, without any mention at all of either the source or the LT concept. Half the subjects in each linkage condition received a message favorable to TM (*P* treatment), the other half an attack against TM (*N* treatment). Attitudes were again assessed (with semantic differential evaluative factor scales) before and after the exposures, the analysis being conducted on the appropriate change scores.

By tracing the expected patterns, from the manipulated TM change to corresponding change in the source attitude and hence to LT change, one could test the congruity theory predictions. For example, in the *Pnp* condition, the experimental manipulation should lead to a favorable TM attitude. Since here the source was originally against what is now a positive object, the source attitude should change negatively. As this newly negative source is favorable to the LT concept, according to the theory, the subjects' attitude toward LT should shift in an unfavorable direction. Similarly, the congruity principle predicts favorable LT changes in the *Ppp*, *Nnp*, *Npn*, and *Pnn* conditions, and unfavorable LT changes in the *Ppn*, *Nnn*, *Npp*, and *Pnp* conditions.

Table IX presents the appropriate data, and indicates that all observed changes are in the predicted direction, without exception. The four cells in which a positive LT change is predicted all change in that direction, with the differences among them being nonsignificant. Similarly, the four predicted negative changes all obtain, again without differences between them. However, the differences between matched pairs of positive and negative changes (that is, within each linkage column) are all significant.

These data provide impressive support for the congruity principle

TABLE IX

MEAN ATTITUDE CHANGE ON NONMANIPULATED (LT) CONCEPT[a,b]

TM concept manipulation	Source-concept linkages			
	pp	*pn*	*np*	*nn*
Positive (*P*)	$+2.84_a$	-1.92_c	$-.76_{bc}$	$+1.56_a$
Negative (*N*)	-2.72_c	$+.60_{ab}$	$+2.12_a$	-2.52_c

[a] Means with the same subscript are not significantly different at the .05 level by Newman-Keuls test.

[b] Data from Tannenbaum (1966b).

formulations. In this connection, it is important to note what conditions would differentiate between predictions based on the mediated generalization model suggested by congruity theory and predictions based on the assumption of direct transfer of persuasion from concept to concept, without the mediating source. One theoretical basis for such differentiation is suggested by our earlier findings on direct generalization (Section VI, A), as well as by demonstrations of attitude generalizations by mediated conditioning procedures (Staats *et al.*, 1959; Das and Nanda, 1963). However, we would then expect LT changes to generally follow the direction of TM changes, but this is clearly not the case: the *Ppn* and *Pnp* conditions show negative rather than positive change, and the *Npn* and *Nnp* conditions show positive rather than negative change. In all four critical cases the results confirm the congruity predictions, but are contrary to what would be expected from the direct transfer notion.

VII. Concluding Remarks

Our central concern in this chapter was with a recent program of research involving theoretical considerations based on the principle of congruity in persuasion. In general, the findings to date offer fairly strong support for the congruity principle as a model for attitude change, and hence for the reduction of the generalization of attitude change. Strategies suggested by the theory for diminishing the impact of messages fared quite well singly and in combination, and the theory was found to supplement McGuire's inoculation theory by suggesting an additional, if not necessarily alternative, set of mechanisms to induce resistance to persuasive inducements. Similarly, congruity theory held up most favorably in contrast to a rather straightforward integration-of-information approach in producing appropriate attitude change. It also proved to be a powerful predictive model to account for generalization of persuasion in given communication situations.

While the research reported here stemmed from congruity principle considerations, it is likely that many of the findings could be quite readily explained by one or another of the other consistency models. In part, this is due to a basic similarity between these various models, at least in their central premise of a tendency toward cognitive consistency. It may also be partly due to the generally vague nature of some of the basic mechanisms involved in the several theories, which tends to inhibit clear-cut comparisons between them.

Perhaps one point of distinction between congruity and the other consistency models is its lack of specification of an intervening stress or discomfort variable to mediate between the existence of inconsistency as such and behavior for its resolution. It is in this sense that congruity theory assumes more the characteristics of a semiautonomous, self-regulating process for the maintenance of psychological harmony. One of our current research interests lies in questions concerning stress states: Does stress indeed accompany the presence of inconsistency? Are there different modes for the reduction of the stress state? Does the reduction of the discomfort as such also effect the inconsistency? And so on. There are some major methodological problems involved in such undertakings, but the theoretical significance of the problem warrants continuing efforts. Space limitations prohibit a complete presentation of such efforts here.

The fundamental homeostatic mechanism attributed to congruity theory is perhaps most apparent in the generalization studies where changes in evaluation of an object of judgment occur without any direct manipulation of that object. It is more than likely that many of our "real-life" attitudes are formed and modified along just such lines. Political attitudes constitute a prime example. Most of us rarely have any direct contact or experience with a political personality, but we often develop quite intense attitudes for or against him as a result of the stands he assumes on a number of issues toward which we already have some well-defined attitudes. Once formed, such attitudes toward this politician become factors around which other opinions are developed as he continues to take positions pro or con a number of novel political issues. To be sure, such opinion formation does not always take place in a complete vacuum of factual information, but quite often such information considerations occupy a secondary role.

In this connection, it is possible to suppose that individuals differ in terms of relative susceptibility to persuasion via pure congruity manipulations, involving the use of more distinctively "psycho-logical" inducements as against more "logical" information, or reasoning, or both. This represents another area of research that has begun to occupy our attention, but we are prevented from reporting it in detail in this chapter, not only by limitations of space but also by the preliminary nature of some of the findings. However preliminary, the evidence to date suggests a range of individual differences in this regard. Moreover, there appears to be a relationship between a person's relative vulnerability to a particular type of inducement to change and his susceptibility to the same type of resistance-to-change manipulation. On the assumption that these are acquired predespositions, we are probing for possible antecedent learning conditions that make for such differential susceptibility. In addition, we are exploring situational factors that may influence susceptibility to one or another mode of persuasion within the same individual.

REFERENCES

Abelson, R.P., and Rosenberg, M.J. (1958). Symbolic psycho-logic: a model of attitudinal cognition. *Behav. Sci.* **3**, 1–13.

Allyn, Jane, and Festinger, L. (1961). The effectiveness of unanticipated persuasive communication. *J. abnorm. soc. Psychol.* **62**, 35–40.

Anderson, N.H., and Barrios, A.A. (1965). Primary effects in personality impression formation. *J. abnorm. soc. Psychol.* **63**, 346–350.

Brehm, J.W., and Cohen, A.R. (1962). *Explorations in cognitive dissonance.* New York: Wiley.

Brown, R.W. (1962). Models of attitude change. In R.W. Brown, E. Galanter, E.H. Hess, and G. Maudler (Eds.) *New directions in psychology.* New York: Holt, Rinehart & Winston, pp. 3–85.

Cartwright, D., and Harary, F. (1956). Structural balance: a generalization of Heider's theory. *Psychol. Rev.* **63**, 277–293.

Cohen, A.R. (1960). Attitudinal consequences of induced discrepancies between cognition and behavior. *Publ. Opin. Quart.* **24**, 297–318.

Das, J.P., and Nanda, P.C. (1963). Mediated transfer of attitudes. *J. abnorm. soc. Psychol.* **66**, 12–16.

Doob, L.W. (1947). The behavior of attitudes. *Psychol. Rev.* **54**, 135–156.

Festinger, L. (1957). *A theory of cognitive dissonance.* New York: Harper & Row.

Festinger, L. (Ed.) (1964). *Conflict, decision, and dissonance.* Stanford, California: Stanford Univ. Press.

Festinger, L., and Maccoby, N. (1964). On resistance to persuasive communications. *J. abnorm. soc. Psychol.* **68**, 367–380.

Fishbein, M., and Hunter, Ronda (1964). Summation versus balance in attitude organization and change. *J. abnorm. soc. Psychol.* **69**, 505–510.

Freedman, J. L., and Sears, D. O. (1966). Selective exposure. *Advance. Exp. Soc. Psychol.* **2**, 58–97.

Freedman, J. L., and Steinbruner, J. D. (1964). Perceived choice and resistance to persuasion. *J. abnorm. soc. Psychol.* **68**, 678–681.

Guttman, L. (1954). The principal components of scalable attitudes. In P. Lazersfeld (Ed.) *Mathematical thinking in the social sciences.* New York: Free Press.

Hall, M. (1965). The great cabbage hoax. *J. pers. soc. Psychol.* **2**, 563–569.

Hartmann, G. W. (1936). A field experiment on the comparative effectiveness of "emotional" and "rational" political leaflets in determining election results. *J. abnorm. soc. Psychol.* **31**, 99–114.

Heider, F. (1958). *The psychology of interpersonal relations.* New York: Wiley.

Hovland, C. I., Lumsdaine, A. A., and Sheffield, F. (1949). *Experiments on mass communication.* Princeton, New Jersey: Princeton Univ. Press.

Hovland, C. I., Janis, I. L., and Kelley, H. H. (1953). *Communication and persuasion.* New Haven, Connecticut: Yale Univ. Press.

Hovland, C. I., Harvey, O. J., and Sherif, M. (1957). Assimilation and contrast effects in reactions to communication and attitude change. *J. abnorm. soc. Psychol.* **55**, 244–252.

Insko, C. A. (1964). Primacy versus recency in persuasion as a function of the timing of arguments and measures. *J. abnorm. soc. Psychol.* **69**, 381–391.

Katz, D. (1960). The functional approach to the study of attitudes. *Publ. Opin. Quart.* **24**, 163–205.

Kelman, H. C., and Eagly, Alice H. (1965). Attitude toward the communicator, perception of communication content, and attitude change. *J. abnorm. soc. Psychol.* **1**, 63–78.

Kiesler, C. A., and Kiesler, Sara B. (1964). Role of forewarning in persuasive communication. *J. abnorm. soc. Psychol.* **68**, 547–549.

Klapper, J. (1960). *The effects of mass communication.* New York: Free Press.

Knower, F. H. (1935). A study of the effect of oral argument on changes of attitude. *J. soc. Psychol.* **6**, 315–344.

Lana, R. E. (1964). Three theoretical interpretations of order effects in persuasive communications. *Psychol. Bull.* **61**, 314–320.

Lewan, P. C., and Stotland, E. (1961). The effects of prior information on susceptibility to an emotional appeal. *J. abnorm. soc. Psychol.* **62**, 450–453.

Macaulay, Jacqueline R. (1965). A study of independent and additive modes of producing resistance to persuasion derived from congruity and inoculation models. Unpublished doctoral dissertation, Univ. of Wisconsin.

Manis, M., and Blake, J. R. (1963). Interpretation of persuasive messages as a function of prior immunization. *J. abnorm. soc. Psychol.* **66**, 225–230.

Manis, M., Gleason, T. C., and Dawes, R. M. (1966). The evaluation of complex social stimuli. *J. pers. soc. Psychol.* **3**, 404–419.

McGuire, W. J. (1960). A syllogistic analysis of cognitive relationships. In C. I. Hovland and M. J. Rosenberg (Eds.), *Attitude organization and change.* New Haven, Connecticut: Yale Univ. Press, pp. 65–111.

McGuire, W. J. (1961a). Resistance to persuasion conferred by active and passive prior refutation of the same and alternative counterarguments. *J. abnorm. soc. Psychol.* **63**, 326–332.

McGuire, W. J. (1961b). The effectiveness of supportive and refutational defenses in immunizing against persuasion. *Sociometry* **24**, 184–197.

McGuire, W. J. (1962). Persistence of the resistance to persuasion induced by various types of prior belief defenses. *J. abnorm. soc. Psychol.* **64**, 241–248.

McGuire, W. J. (1964). Inducing resistance to persuasion: some contemporary approaches. *Advanc. exp. soc. Psychol.* **1**, 191–229.

McGuire, W. J. (1966a). Attitudes and opinions. *Annu. Rev. Psychol.* **17**, 475–514.

McGuire, W. J. (1966b). The current status of cognitive consistency theories. In S. Feldman (Ed.), *The consistency motive.*

McGuire, W. J., and Papageorgis, D. (1961). The relative efficacy of various types of prior belief-defense in producing immunity against persuasion. *J. abnorm. soc. Psychol.* **62**, 327–337.

McGuire, W. J., and Papageorgis, D. (1962). Effectiveness of forewarning in developing resistance to persuasion. *Publ. Opin. Quart.* **26**, 24–34.

Menefee, S. C., and Granneberg, A. G. (1940). Propaganda and opinions on foreign policy. *J. soc. Psychol.* **11**, 393–404.

Mostofsky, D. I. (Ed.) (1965). *Stimulus generalization.* Stanford, California: Stanford Univ. Press.

Newcomb, T. M. (1953). An approach to the study of communicative acts. *Psychol. Rev.* **60**, 393–404.

Newcomb, T. M. (1959). Individual systems of orientation. In *Psychology: a study of a science*. Vol. 3. New York: McGraw-Hill.

Osgood, C. E. (1960). Cognitive dynamics in human affairs. *Publ. Opin. Quart.* **24**, 341–365.

Osgood, C. E., and Tannenbaum, P. H. (1955). The principle of congruity in the prediction of attitude change. *Psychol. Rev.* **62**, 42–55.

Osgood, C. E., Suci, G. J., and Tannenbaum, P. H. (1957). *The measurement of meaning*. Urbana, Illinois: Univ. of Illinois Press.

Papageorgis, D., and McGuire, W. J. (1961). The generality of immunity to persuasion produced by pre-exposure to weakened counterarguments. *J. abnorm. soc. Psychol.* **62**, 475–481.

Podell, Harriet A., and Podell, J. E. (1963). Quantitative connotation of a concept. *J. abnorm. soc. Psychol.* **67**, 509–513.

Rokeach, M., and Rothman, G. (1965). The principle of belief congruence and the congruity principle as models of cognitive interaction. *Psychol. Rev.* **72**, 128–142.

Rosenberg, M. J. (1960). An analysis of affective-cognitive consistency. In C. I. Hovland and M. J. Rosenberg (Eds.), *Attitude organization and change*. New Haven, Connecticut: Yale Univ. Press, pp. 15–64.

Rosenberg, M. J., and Abelson, R. P. (1960). An analysis of cognitive balancing. In C. I. Hovland and M. J. Rosenberg (Eds.), *Attitude organization and change*. New Haven, Connecticut: Yale Univ. Press, pp. 112–163.

Staats, A. W., and Staats, Carolyn K. (1958). Attitudes established by classical conditioning. *J. abnorm. soc. Psychol.* **57**, 37–40.

Staats, A. W., Staats, Carolyn K., and Heard, W. G. (1959). Language conditioning of meaning using a semantic generalization paradigm. *J. exp. Psychol.* **57**, 187–192.

Steiner, I. D. (1962). Receptivity to supportive versus nonsupportive communications. *J. abnorm. soc. Psychol.* **65**, 266–267.

Tannenbaum, P. H. (1956). Initial attitude toward source and concept as factors in attitude change through communication. *Publ. Opin. Quart.* **20**, 413–425.

Tannenbaum, P. H. (1966a). Colour as a code for connotative communication. In H. Spencer (Ed.), *The Penrose annual*. London: Lund, Humphries, pp. 115–121.

Tannenbaum, P. H. (1966b). Mediated generalization of attitude change via the principle of congruity. *J. pers. soc. Psychol.* **3**, 493–499.

Tannenbaum, P. H., and Gengel, R. W. (1966). Generalization of attitude change through congruity principle relationships. *J. pers. soc. Psychol.* **3**, 299–304.

Tannenbaum, P. H., and Norris, Eleanor L. (1965). Effects of combining congruity principle strategies for the reduction of persuasion. *Sociometry* **28**, 145–157.

Tannenbaum, P. H., Macaulay, Jacqueline R., and Norris, Eleanor L. (1966). The principle of congruity and reduction of persuasion. *J. pers. soc. Psychol.* **3**, 233–238.

Triandis, H. C., and Fishbein, M. (1963). Cognitive interaction in person perception. *J. abnorm. soc. Psychol.* **67**, 446–453.

Weiss, W. (1960). Emotional arousal and attitude change. *Psychol. Rep.* **6**, 267–280.

Weiss, W., and Lieberman, B. (1959). The effects of "emotional" language on the induction of change of opinions. *J. soc. Psychol.* **50**, 129–141.

Willis, R. H. (1960). Stimulus pooling and social perception. *J. abnorm. soc. Psychol.* **60**, 365–373.

Zajonc, R. B. (1960). Balance, congruity, and dissonance. *Publ. Opin. Quart.* **24**, 280–297.

AUTHOR INDEX

Numbers in italics refer to pages on which the complete references are listed.

SUBJECT INDEX